HOSEA, JOEL, AMOS, OBADIAH

HOSEA

by
John M Riddle

JOHN RITCHIE LTD
CHRISTIAN PUBLICATIONS

40 Beansburn, Kilmarnock, Scotland

ISBN-13: 978 1 910513 78 1

Copyright © 2017 by John Ritchie Ltd.
40 Beansburn, Kilmarnock, Scotland

www.ritchiechristianmedia.co.uk

All rights reserved. No part of this publication may be reproduced, stored in a retrievable system, or transmitted in any form or by any other means – electronic, mechanical, photocopy, recording or otherwise – without prior permission of the copyright owner.

Typeset by John Ritchie Ltd., Kilmarnock
Printed by Bell & Bain Ltd., Glasgow

Contents

Preface	7
Hosea Introduction	9
Chapter 1	16
Chapter 2	24
Chapter 2A	30
Chapter 3	36
Chapter 4	42
Chapter 5	52
Chapter 6	62
Chapter 7	72
Chapter 8	82
Chapter 9	92
Chapter 10	102
Chapter 11	110
Chapter 12	118
Chapter 13	128
Chapter 14	138
Joel Introduction	150
Chapter 1	156
Chapter 2	166
Chapter 2A	176

Chapter 2B	186
Chapter 3	194
Amos Introduction	204
Chapter 1	210
Chapter 2	220
Chapter 3	228
Chapter 4	238
Chapter 5	248
Chapter 5A	258
Chapter 6	266
Chapter 7	276
Chapter 8	286
Chapter 9	296
Obadiah Introduction	308
Chapter 1	314
Chapter 1A	322

Preface

This book represents the substance of Bible Class discussions on Friday evenings at Mill Lane Chapel, Cheshunt, between September 2012 and March 2013 in the case of Hosea, between September and November 2009 in the case of Joel, between November 2009 and March 2010 in the case of Amos, and in December 2002 in the case of Obadiah. If nothing else, the dates above, which are far from consecutive, mean that in intervening months and years studies proceeded in other parts of God's word. In other words, attempts have been made to achieve a 'balanced diet' in the Friday evening Bible studies.

As with previous publications in the series, the original notes were written without the slightest thought of their eventual appearance in the public domain, and the current volume, like its predecessors, does not purport to be a commentary in the usual sense of the word. No attempt was made at the time to be exhaustive.

According to his obituary in *The Times* (September 27th 2016), J Alec Motyer, was asked near the end of his life for the secret of good Bible scholarship, and replied simply: "Reading, reading, and reading over and over again". That's good advice for us all. Like Timothy, we must all "Strive diligently" to present ourselves "approved to God, a workman that has not to be ashamed, cutting in a straight line the word of truth" (2 Tim. 2:15, JND).

We are also told in the same obituary that J. Alec Motyer "fought off theories" that the book of Isaiah had three authors. Expounding his view that the prophet was inspired by God to write the whole book, he once amused students at the Christian Union in Cambridge by saying, "When I get to heaven and I'm beaten up by three people called Isaiah, I'll know I'm wrong!" Perhaps, therefore, when some preachers get to heaven, they will also be in danger of being 'beaten up', this time by twelve men, including Hosea, Joel, Amos and Obadiah, who took umbrage at being called 'Minor

Prophets'! Full marks to those preachers who say, 'Yes, we call them 'Minor Prophets', but they were 'Major Men of God'.

Peter tells us that the Old Testament prophets were "holy men of God" who "spake under the power of {the} Holy Ghost" (2 Pet 1:21, JND). The Lord's prophet (as opposed to false prophets), was a man who "stood in the counsel of the LORD, and hath perceived and heard his word" (Jer 23:18). Jeremiah himself spoke from "the mouth of the LORD" (2 Chron 36:12). Since "whatsoever things were written aforetime were written for our learning" (Rom 15:4), we can therefore expect to profit from every part of God's word, including what has been called 'the twelve-jewelled crown of the Old Testament'. A word of warning: while all members of 'the book of the twelve' certainly warm our hearts, they also had sharp teeth!

As before, the Bible Class at Cheshunt remains indebted to John Ritchie Ltd for their willingness to publish its notes, something first mooted by Mr John Grant, and to Mr Fraser Munro and the John Ritchie 'team' for their invaluable help in formatting and editing the material submitted to them. The Bible Class also continues to be grateful to Miss Lesley Prentice for having checked and corrected the original manuscripts, something she continues to do, and to Mr Eric Browning for his considerable help in sending copies of current studies by Email to an ever-widening readership.

John Riddle
Cheshunt, Hertfordshire
March 2017

HOSEA

INTRODUCTION

Read the whole book

The prophecy of Hosea is, of course, "the first of those books which are commonly called 'The Twelve Prophets'. Early Rabbis referred to them simply as 'The Twelve', and others called them 'The Twelve-Prophet Book', or 'The Book of the Twelve'. Sometimes they are called 'The Minor Prophets'…but only because they are smaller in size than the great prophecies of Isaiah, Jeremiah, Ezekiel and Daniel" (J. M. Flanigan, *What the Bible Teaches - Hosea*). The Jewish Talmud states that "our fathers made them one book that they might not perish on account of their littleness".

Before addressing the prophecy of Hosea in detail, we must make some general observations about the book. J. Sidlow Baxter (*Explore the Book, Volume 4*) calls Hosea "the prophet of Israel's zero hour" and continues, "The nation had sunk to a point of such corruption that a major stroke of divine judgment could no longer be staved off". The Assyrian invasion was imminent. The nation is described, amongst other things, as "a silly dove without heart: they call to Egypt, they go to Assyria" (7:11), and in consequence, they would not "dwell in the LORD'S land; but…return to Egypt, and…eat unclean things in Assyria" (9:3). Notwithstanding, in His love for them, the Lord would ultimately intervene in recovery and blessing: "O Israel, thou hast destroyed thyself; but in me is thine help. I will be thy king: where is any other that may save thee in all thy cities?…I will ransom them from the power of the grave; I will redeem them from death: O death, I will be thy plagues; O grave, I will be thy destruction; repentance shall be hid from mine eyes" (13:9-10, 14).

The quotation above serves to remind us that the New Testament refers to the book of Hosea on several occasions. It should be noted in this connection that Hosea is called *Osee* in Romans 9:25. This is the Greek form of the

Hebrew name Hosea. The references are found in Matthew 2:15; 9:13; 12:7; Romans 9:25-26; 1 Corinthians 15:55; 1 Peter 2:10.

1) THE POSITION OF THE BOOK

Hosea was an eighth century prophet, and as we usually say when introducing our studies in the so-called 'Minor Prophets', it would be interesting to commence at the exodus from Egypt, and construct a complete table of the prophets sent by God. It would begin with Moses (Deut 18:15; 34:10) and Aaron (Exodus 7:1) and include a great number of men (and some women), some named and some unnamed. The 'writing prophets' alone cover five centuries, viz:

Fifth/sixth century prophets:	Haggai/ Zechariah/ Malachi/ Ezekiel/ Daniel:
Seventh century prophets:	Nahum/ Habakkuk/ Zephaniah/ Obadiah/ Jeremiah:
Eighth century prophets:	Hosea/ Amos/ Micah/ Isaiah:
Ninth century prophets:	Jonah, and as we shall see, in all probability, Joel.

The ninth century (900 - 801 BC) brings us to the era of Elijah and Elisha. The tenth century included the unnamed prophet who cried against Jeroboam's altar, and the "old prophet in Bethel" (1 Kings 13:11). David was a prophet: see Acts 2:30. These examples prove that God was not exaggerating when He said, "Since the day that your fathers came forth out of the land of Egypt unto this day, I have even sent unto you all my servants the prophets, *daily* rising up early, and sending them" (Jer. 7:25). Whilst the oft-quoted words in Acts 14:17 do not refer to the prophets, we can *apply* them in that way, and say that God "left not himself without a witness" so far as the prophetic testimony was concerned. This should encourage us today: He will continue to maintain testimony to "all the counsel of God" (Acts 20:27), and even when Jerusalem becomes the darkest moral blot on earth, He will give power to His "two witnesses... these two prophets" (Rev. 11:3-12). When the Lord Jesus was here, people in the city of Nain "glorified God, saying, That a great prophet is risen up among us" (Luke 7:16), but He had to say, "a prophet hath no honour in his own country" (John 4:44).

2) THE PERIOD OF THE PROPHECY

Hosea lived in turbulent times. The prophecy commences with reference to the relevant kings of Judah, and to Jeroboam, king of Israel, the northern kingdom. "The word of the LORD that came to Hosea, the son of Beeri, in the days of Uzziah, Jotham, Ahaz, and Hezekiah, kings of Judah (they reigned between 810 BC and 698 BC) and Jeroboam the son of Joash, king of Israel (who reigned between 825 BC and 784 BC)". Significantly, there is no mention of Jeroboam's successors, although Hosea's ministry covered their reigns as well. A general reference is made to Zachariah, Shallum, Menahem, Pekahiah, Pekah, and Hoshea: "They have set up kings, but not by me" (8:4), but their names are not mentioned. The period of the so-called 'mushroom monarchs' was marked by anarchy, murder and usurpation, and is dismissed altogether in Hosea 1:1. It almost seems as if God had no wish whatever to even recognise their existence: the grace extended to Jeroboam II (2 Kings 14:26-27) had been exhausted.

The events described in the opening section of the prophecy, Chapters 1-3, evidently took place in the reign of Jeroboam II. The "blood of Jezreel" (referring to events in 2 Kings 10:19-21) had not yet been avenged (1:4-5), and this actually took place in the reign of Jeroboam's son, Zachariah. See 2 Kings 10:30; 15:12.

3) THE PROPHET HIMSELF

Apart from his father's name (Beeri, meaning, it is said, 'man of the well'), we know nothing about Hosea's early life. In fact, we know nothing at all about him, apart from his marriage. Some suggest that he was a baker (see 7:4-7), but this seems speculative, to put it mildly! We know nothing of the prophet's death and place of burial. According to one unproven Jewish tradition, he died in Babylon, and his body was brought back to Israel where it was buried at Safed, north-west of the sea of Galilee. A second tradition says that he was a native of Gilead, and was buried there.

Hosea's name means 'saviour' or 'deliverer' (some say, 'salvation'). There is a correspondence between the names Hosea and Joshua. Joshua is also known as Oshea (Num. 13:8, 16) and Hoshea (Deut. 32:44). Hosea, Oshea and Hoshea are identical in Hebrew, and akin to *Yeshua*, the Hebrew form of 'Jesus'.

4) THE PROPHECY OUTLINED

Hosea was contemporary with Amos, Micah and Isaiah. Hosea and Amos both addressed the Northern Kingdom, but were quite different in approach. In Amos, sin is an outrage of divine **law**, and God **commands** return. In Hosea, sin is an outrage of divine **love**, and God **pleads** for return. It has been nicely said that "Hosea's ministry was one of **love**, whilst Amos' ministry was one of **light.** Amos is not known for his sympathy or warmth, but for his sense of justice and right. Not a sob is to be found in his book for the nation of wicked apostates, and there is only a sigh for the poor". This variation in the preaching of Hosea and Amos illustrates the fact that servants of God can have differing emphases in their ministry, but labour in the same sphere without collision or confusion.

The outstanding feature of this prophecy is the emphasis placed on God's love for His people. It has been aptly said that "the heart of God lies on the surface of Hosea's ministry". Although Israel had failed to reciprocate God's love, and incurred divine displeasure by their infidelity to Him, He still exclaimed, "How shall I give thee up, Ephraim? how shall I deliver thee, Israel? how shall I make thee as Admah? how shall I set thee as Zeboim? mine heart is turned within me, my repentings ('compassions' RV) are kindled together" (11:8) Ultimately, God will say, "I will love them freely" (14:4).

Hosea was no mere orator. He preached out of deep conviction, and was able to do so out of his own experiences in the school of God. This is made very clear by the two main divisions of the book: *(a)* chapters 1-3, Hosea's love for his unfaithful wife; *(b)* chapters 4-14, God's love for His unfaithful people.

a) Hosea's love for his unfaithful wife
As J. Sidlow Baxter points out, Chapters 1-3 are distinct "from all those that follow. They are **narrative**, whereas all the remainder are **addresses**". He continues, "But besides this, these first three chapters are symbolical narrative. The prophet's wife, Gomer, and the three children, Jezreel, Lo-ruhamah, and Lo-ammi, and the tragedy of the prophet's married life, of which these chapters speak, are all symbolical of the relationship between Jehovah and Israel". The command to Hosea, "Go yet, love a woman beloved of her friend, yet an adulteress", reflected God's love "toward the children of Israel, who look to other gods, and love flagons of wine (or 'raisin-cakes', JND)" (3:1). The vicissitudes of Hosea's own marriage relationship enabled him to understand and convey God's deep love for His erring people.

The connection between Chapters 1-3 and 4-14 has been nicely sketched by Jack. R. Riggs (*Hosea's Heartbreak*): "The book of Hosea is the book of the prophet with a broken heart. His heart was broken over the tragic circumstances of his own marriage. His wife spurned his love and faithfulness to her to become the lover of others who had no concern for her, but to use her. Around his own personal family crisis was the historical situation involving his countrymen. Israel had become a prodigal people just as Hosea's wife had become a prodigal wife. Israel had left her husband of many years, the Lord Himself, and joined herself to other lovers, the gods of man's creation. Hosea's own experiences mirrored the historic relationship between the Lord and Israel. Ultimately there was reconciliation between the prophet and his wife, even as there will be a future restoration of Israel by her loving and gracious Lord. In the meantime, however, there was the terrible reality of an adulterous wife and an adulterous people".

b) God's love for His unfaithful people

While, as noted above, Chapters 4-14 are addresses, as opposed to narrative, they can be broadly subdivided, although detailed and logical analysis is far from easy. The section commences with the words, "Hear the word of the LORD, ye children of Israel: for the LORD hath a controversy with the inhabitants of the land, because there is no truth, nor mercy, nor knowledge of God in the land" (4:1). The word "controversy" has a legal connotation, and could be rendered 'lawsuit'. But this is not the uninterrupted message of these chapters (see, for example 6:1-3; 10:12; 11:8-11; 12:6; 13:9-14), and it is certainly not the note on which the prophecy concludes. As noted, the Lord will say, "I will heal their backsliding, I will love them freely" (14:4). We can therefore broadly divide these chapters as follows: *(i)* the Lord's controversy (chs.4-13); *(ii)* the Lord's compassion (ch.14).

i) The Lord's controversy, chapters 4-13. We have already noted the charge against Israel: "there is no truth, nor mercy, nor knowledge of God in the land" (4:1). Derek Kidner sums it all up as follows:

- *in religion*, with other gods, another cult. In the oft-quoted words, "Ephraim is joined to idols: let him alone" (4:17).

- *in politics*, with shabby intrigues and dubious patrons. As already noted, "they call to Egypt, they go to Assyria" (7:11). See also 5:13, "When Ephraim saw his sickness, and Judah saw his wound, then went Ephraim to the Assyrian, and sent to king Jareb: yet could he not heal you, nor cure you of your wound".

- *in morals*, with unbridled violence and moral depravity of every kind, including murder and bloodshed (4:2; 5:2; 6:8); gang-robbery (6:9; 7:1); wide-prevailing adultery (4:2, 11, 14; 7:4); drunkenness (4:11; 7:14).

ii) The Lord's compassion, chapter 14. As we will see in the detailed study, this chapter is both a *bona fide* appeal to Israel at the time, and a description of ultimate national blessing following repentance. Like other prophetical books in the Old Testament, the book of Hosea concludes with national restoration. Sin will not have the last word in Israel's history. "Ephraim shall say, What have I to do any more with idols?" To which the LORD will reply, "I have heard him and observed him" (14:8).

5) THE PRACTICAL IMPLICATIONS
Since "whatsoever things were written aforetime were written for our learning, that we through patience and comfort of the scriptures might have hope" (Rom. 15:4), we must endeavour to ascertain the message of Hosea for ourselves. There is certainly a message for preachers, but with equal certainty, there is a message for every child of God. In fact, the book ends with an undated message to us all: "Who is wise, and he shall understand these things? prudent, and he shall know them? for the ways of the LORD are right, and the just shall walk in them: but the transgressors shall fall therein" (14:9).

a) The message to preachers
Hosea preached with deep feeling. He faithfully stated God's "controversy (lawsuit) with the inhabitants of the land" (4:1). But his faithfulness in exposing the guilt of Israel was accompanied by tender appeal. Preachers are all too prone to say the right thing, but to say it in entirely the wrong way. There is admirable balance in the words, "Speaking the truth in love" (Eph. 4:15).

b) The message to every believer
The principal charge against Israel was infidelity. In Jeremiah's words, they "committed adultery with stones and with stocks" (Jer. 3:9). In the Old Testament, idolatry is frequently presented as adultery, and the New Testament follows suit. See James 4:4. Note 1 John 5:20-21. When love for God diminishes, things go wrong everywhere. The Lord Jesus said, "I have somewhat against thee, because thou hast left thy first love. Remember therefore from whence thou art fallen, and repent, and do the first works" (Rev. 2:4-5).

READ CHAPTER 1:1-2:1

"Take unto thee a wife of whoredoms"

As noted in our introductory study, the prophecy of Hosea falls into two major divisions: *(i)* Hosea's love for his unfaithful wife (chapters 1-3); *(ii)* God's love for His unfaithful people (chapters 4-14).

We also noted, in the words of J. Sidlow Baxter (who has outstanding analytical ability) that Chapters 1-3 are "symbolical narrative. The prophet's wife, Gomer, and the three children, Jezreel, Lo-ruhamah, and Lo-ammi, and the tragedy of the prophet's married life, of which these chapters speak, are all symbolical of the relationship between Jehovah and Israel". In our own words, "The vicissitudes of Hosea's own marriage relationship enabled him to understand and convey God's deep love for His erring people".

As J. Sidlow Baxter rightly observes in connection with these opening chapters, the "story is told consecutively, and at each point the symbolism is explained and applied. Gomer (Hosea's wife, 1:3) is the nation of Israel. The children (Jezreel, Lo-ruhamah, and Lo-ammi, vv.4, 6, 9) are the people of that nation. Hosea's sorrow, patience, compassion, and his final act of redeeming, chastening, and restoring Gomer depict the sorrow, patience, compassion, and love of God towards sinning Israel. The whole tragic story of Israel lies in these first three chapters together with the ultimate triumph of that day yet to be, when God shall say, "I will betroth thee unto me for ever; yea, I will betroth thee unto me in righteousness, and in judgment, and in lovingkindness, and in mercies" (2:19); "I will say to them which were not my people, Thou art my people; and they shall say, Thou art my God' (2:23)". J. Sidlow Baxter summarises Chapters 1-3 most succinctly: "It will be...clear that Chapter 2 is the application of Chapter 1" and "that Chapter 3 looks right to the end of the present age, for its last words are, "Afterward shall the children of Israel return, and seek the LORD their God, and David their king: and shall fear the LORD and his goodness in the latter days" (3:5). He concludes, "the whole story of Israel, past, present, and future, is here, in this symbolic prologue". Chapters 1-3 each repeat this major lesson. All three chapters commence with the unfaithfulness of the nation, and conclude with national restoration by God.

Bearing this in mind, we should notice the following: *(1)* the background (1:1); *(2)* the marriage (1:2-3); *(3)* the children, (1:3-9); *(4)* the restoration (1:10 - 2:1). Although some say that the first verse of Chapter 2 is actually the last verse of Chapter 1, we are told that in the Hebrew text, Chapter 1:10-11 are regarded as the opening verses of Chapter 2. See J. M. Flanigan. Chapter and verse divisions are most helpful (we would have considerable difficulties without them), but they are not inspired!

1) THE BACKGROUND, v.1

"The word of the LORD that came unto Hosea (as it did to John the Baptist, Luke 3:2), the son of Beeri, in the days of Uzziah, Jotham, Ahaz, and Hezekiah, kings of Judah, and in the days of Jeroboam the son of Joash, king of Israel".

Although Hosea's ministry concerned Israel, the northern of the two kingdoms into which God's people were divided after the death of Solomon, it is striking that reference is made to four Judaean kings. "While Hosea warned Judah against sinning with Israel (4:15), and announced that she was plunging headlong into the same ruin as Israel (5:5, 10; 6:4, 11), Uzziah, Jotham, Ahaz, and Hezekiah are probably mentioned to emphasise that the Davidic dynasty alone was the legitimate line" (Jack R. Riggs). So far as Israel is concerned, only Jeroboam is mentioned, and this may be because he belonged to the house of Jehu, who "had been called to the throne by the prophet Elijah at the command of God, for the purpose of rooting out the worship of Baal from Israel, in return for which Jehu had received the promise that his sons should sit upon the throne to the fourth generation (2 Kings 10:30), and Jeroboam, the great-grandson of Jehu, was the last king through whom the Lord sent any help to the ten tribes (2 Kings 14:27)" (C. F. Keil). God always honours His promises.

Hosea lived in turbulent times. According to J. N. Darby's table, the kings of Judah named here - Uzziah, Jotham, Ahaz, and Hezekiah - reigned between 810BC and 698BC. Jeroboam (that is, Jeroboam II) ruled Israel from 825BC to 784BC, but there is no mention of his successors, although Hosea's ministry covered their reigns as well. Israel, the northern kingdom was annexed by Assyria in 721 BC. A general reference is made to

Zachariah, Shallum, Menahem, Pekahiah, Pekah, and Hoshea: "They have set up kings, but not by me" (8:4). But their names are not mentioned. The period of the so-called 'mushroom monarchs' was disastrous: Zachariah was assassinated by Shallum after reigning for six months. Shallum was murdered by Menahem after only one month on the throne in Samaria. Menahem was a dreadful king. He "did that which was evil in the sight of the Lord" including sacking the city of Tirzah which "opened not to him…and all the women therein that were with child he ripped up". He was succeeded by his son Pekahiah who reigned for two years before being assassinated by Pekah, who reigned for twenty years until his death at the hands of Hoshea who reigned for nine years. Hoshea was Israel's final king. His dalliance with Egypt earned him the wrath of Shalmaneser, king of Assyria, who imprisoned him, and deported Israel to Assyria 'lock, stock and barrel'. The whole dreadful story is found in 2 Kings 15:8-31; 17:1-41, but there is no mention of any of these kings in Hosea 1:1. It almost seems as if God had no wish whatever to even recognise their existence: the grace extended to Jeroboam II (2 Kings 14:26-27) had been exhausted.

In turbulent times, then and at other periods, men, like Hosea, "spake as they were moved by the Holy Ghost" (2 Pet. 1:21). Paul urged Timothy to "Preach the word; be instant in season, out of season" (2 Tim. 4:2) and while, in context, the apostle was evidently referring here to the work of the Bible teacher, its relevance to Gospel preaching cannot be ignored.

Evidently, the opening section of the prophecy, Chapters 1-3, was delivered to Hosea in the reign of Jeroboam II. The blood of Jezreel had not yet been avenged (1:4-5), and this actually took place in the reign of his son, Zachariah. See 2 Kings 10:30; 15:10-12.

2) THE MARRIAGE, vv.2-3
"The beginning of the word of the LORD by Hosea. (Compare, "The beginning of the gospel of Jesus Christ", Mark 1:1). And the LORD said to Hosea, Go, take unto thee a wife of whoredoms, and children of whoredoms: for the land hath committed great whoredom departing from the LORD. So he went (note his obedience to "the word of the LORD") and took Gomer (meaning 'completeness' or 'ripeness') the daughter of Diblaim (meaning 'cakes', or 'layers of figs'): which conceived, and bare him a son".

Before Hosea commenced his ministry, he was instructed by God to marry what can only be described as a highly undesirable woman, and in his relationship with Gomer, he would be made acutely aware of God's feelings and love for His equally undesirable people Israel. The marriage was therefore both literal and symbolic. Hosea conveyed the word of God with deep feeling. He knew only too well from personal experience how God felt about His people. There is all the difference in the world between cold, clinical preaching, and preaching that flows from deep feelings and a tender heart. Hosea cannot be accused of 'trafficking in unfelt truth'.

The fact that Hosea was to "take...a wife of whoredoms and children of whoredoms" indicates, it is suggested, **what Gomer would become.** If we understand that Gomer was a harlot at the time of the marriage, we must also understand that Hosea inherited a ready-made family! Patently, this was not the case. The expression, "children of whoredoms" will be explained later. M. F. Unger comments pertinently: "It is highly doubtful that the Lord would have commanded a holy prophet to do what was expressly forbidden to the priests, and frowned upon for Israel as a whole". Hosea was warned, and therefore knew in advance, what his wife would become, just as Jehovah Himself knew in advance what His people would become. They would "play the harlot" (4:15). However, it must be said that respected commentators suggest that this explanation is in conflict with the plain statement, "Go, take unto thee a wife of whoredoms".

There is, we are glad to learn, a third suggestion. We are indebted to J. M. Flanigan for pointing out that "Gomer is not personally called a harlot or a whoremonger, but the land where she dwelt was a land that had 'committed great whoredom departing from the LORD', and there was much immorality in that society. It was from that land of whoredoms that Hosea was commanded to take a wife. She would indeed then be 'a wife of whoredoms' and her children would share in the indictment". Having quoted another authority - "if he took an Israelite, he must necessarily have taken an idolatress: one who worshipped the calves of Jeroboam at Dan or Bethel" - J. M. Flanigan continues, "Sadly, it will be seen that Gomer did, after her marriage to Hosea, lapse into the ways of the land and prove to be unfaithful, actually becoming the slave of one of her lovers". Which is almost another way of saying that the words, "take...a wife of whoredoms", indicate what Gomer would become! There we must leave it. This brings us to:

3) THE CHILDREN, vv.3-9
Three children were born, and their names are invested with prophetical significance. Three stages of judgment are indicated in the names given

to the children: *(a)* Jezreel (vv.3-5); *(b)* Lo-ruhamah (vv.6-7); *(c)* Lo-ammi (vv.8-9). The three stages are each introduced by "I will": "I will break the bow of Israel" (v.5); "I will no more have mercy upon the house of Israel" (v.6); "I will not be your God" (v.9).

a) Jezreeel, vv.3-5
"So he went and took Gomer the daughter of Diblaim; which conceived, and bare him a son. And the LORD said unto him, Call his name Jezreel" (vv.3-4). We are specifically told that "Gomer...conceived, and **bare him** a son". The parentage of Jezreel is undisputed. But that could not be said for the two succeeding children: she "bare a daughter"; she "bare a son" (vv.6, 8), not 'bare **him** a daughter...bare **him** a son'. The change of expression may well be significant, and that Lo-ruhamah and Lo-ammi were "children of whoredoms".

Jezreel means, 'God scatters' and 'God sows', and this chapter elaborates both meanings. However, his name has a double significance in v.4: it anticipated two future events;

i) The destruction of the house of Jehu. "Call his name Jezreel; for yet a little while, and I will avenge the blood of Jezreel upon the house of Jehu" (v.4). Historically, Jezreel was the place where Jehu finally destroyed the remaining representatives of the house of Ahab (2 Kings 10:11). Whilst he purged idolatry to a great degree, he allowed the original images established by Jeroboam I to remain. See 2 Kings 10:29-31. For what he *did* accomplish, he was promised four generations by God, i.e. Jehoahaz, Joash (Jehoash), Jeroboam II, and Zachariah. The last of these was assassinated by Shallum. God's word, as ever, was exact. But why did God "avenge the blood of Jezreel upon the house of Jehu", when he had been anointed for that purpose? (See 2 Kings 9:1-10). The answer lies not in what Jehu did, but the way in which he did it. As Derek Kidner observes: "The events of 2 Kings 10 are a welter of trickery, butchery and hypocrisy...self-interest and bloodlust were his dominant springs of conduct, and it was this that made 'the blood of Jezreel' an accusing stain". Compare Isaiah 10:5-19. We should remember that all too frequently, the right thing is done in the wrong way, with disastrous results for individuals and assemblies.

ii) The destruction of the northern kingdom. "I...will cause to cease the kingdom of the house of Israel. And it shall come to pass at that day, that

I will break the bow of Israel in the valley of Jezreel" (vv4, 5). The "valley of Jezreel" was "the great battle field of Palestine" (M. F. Unger). See, for example, Judges 6:33 and 1 Samuel 29:1. The Valley of Jezreel is the plain of Esdraelon, a large plain lying between Gilboa on the east and the Carmel range of mountains on the west, and stretching some twenty miles from north to south. Esdraelon is also known as the valley or plain of Megiddo. "It is a fertile well-watered stretch of land, and here the last great battle will be fought, usually referred to as Armageddon (Rev. 16:14-16)" (J. M. Flanigan). Now, the same Plain of Esdraelon, where Jehu "slew all that remained of the house of Ahab", would witness, not now the end of Jehu's dynasty, but the defeat of the Northern Kingdom. In other passages, "the bow" of Israel's enemies is broken (see Hosea 2:18 and Psalm 46:9): but here it is "the bow of Israel" itself. The Assyrian did this in the reign of Pekah (2 Kings 15:27-29). In subsequent years, until the final captivity, Israel merely lingered: it was a broken nation.

b) Lo-Ruhamah, vv.6-7
"And she conceived again, and bare a daughter. And God said unto him, Call her name Lo-ruhamah: for I will no more have mercy upon the house of Israel; but I will utterly take them away" (v.6).

Lo-ruhamah means "unpitied", and she represents the second stage of divine judgment: "I will no more have mercy on the house of Israel; but I will utterly take them away" (v.6). This prophecy became history in 721BC, when the Northern Kingdom was taken into complete captivity, transported to Assyria, and its cities repopulated by colonists from the east. See 2 Kings 17:23, "The LORD removed Israel out of his sight, *as he had said by all his servants the prophets*". Including Hosea.

Judah is exempted from judgment at this time: "But I will have mercy upon the house of Judah, and will save them by the LORD their God, and will not save them by bow, nor by sword, nor by battle, by horses, nor by horsemen" (v.7), reminding us of 2 Corinthians 10:4-5. The Assyrians sent threatening emissaries to Jerusalem (2 Kings 18:17-37), but God was true to His word. He saved them, but not "by bow, nor by sword, nor by battle, by horses, nor by horsemen". Judah was saved by divine intervention. The Assyrian army was depleted by 185,000 men (2 Kings 19:35). If one angel caused so much havoc, what would "more than twelve legions of angels" have done had the Lord Jesus called for them? But He said, "But how then shall the scriptures be fulfilled, that thus it must be?" (Matt. 26:53-54).

c) Lo-Ammi, vv.8-9

"Now when she had weaned Lo-ruhamah, she conceived, and bare a son. Then said God, Call his name Lo-ammi: for ye are not my people, and I will not be your God".

Lo-ammi means, "not my people", and he represents the third stage of judgment: "Ye are not my people, and I will not be your God" (v.9). God had said, "If ye will obey my voice indeed, and keep my covenant, then ye shall be a peculiar treasure unto me above all people" (Exodus 19:5-6). The absence of the name "Israel" here, together with the obvious reference to the covenant relationship in Exodus ch.19, may well suggest that this statement refers to the entire nation, Israel and Judah. Judah had been faithful in measure, but was warned, "Though thou Israel play the harlot, let not Judah offend" (4:15). But, alas, Judah ultimately succumbed to idolatry as well: "Therefore shall Israel and Ephraim fall in their iniquity; Judah shall also fall with them" (5:5); "O Ephraim, what shall I do unto thee? O Judah, what shall I do unto thee? For your goodness is as a morning cloud, and as the early dew it goeth away" (6:4).

4) THE RESTORATION, 1:10-2:1

The prophecy now leaps forward, and anticipates Israel's ultimate future in the Millennial Kingdom. Derek Kidner puts it nicely: "The ominous names are not God's last word. At once, as though He cannot bear to leave the matter there, He points to the far future, when everything that these names have stood for will be reversed". These verses bring before us the nation's final blessing, when Israel and Judah will be reunited under "one head" (v.11) - Christ Himself. Compare Hosea 3:5. Bearing in mind the reference to the promise to Abraham (Gen. 22:17). "Yet the number of the children of Israel shall be as the sand of the sea, which cannot be measured nor numbered" (v.10), God is evidently referring here to the twelve tribes in their entirety. See Jeremiah 3:18.

The words, "and it shall come to pass, that in the place where it was said unto them, Ye are not my people, there it shall be said unto them, ye are the sons of the living God" (v.10), reversing v.9, are quoted in Romans 9:26. (Hosea 2:23 is cited in Romans 9:25). Paul quotes the passage in support of the statement: "And that he might make known the riches of his glory on the vessels of mercy, which he had afore prepared unto glory. Even us, whom he hath called, not of the Jews only, but *also of the Gentiles*". But why appeal to a passage which refers clearly to Israel, when describing blessing for Jew and Gentile? The answer is clear: the nation had lapsed into idolatry, and God had severed connection with them: they were no longer "my people", and therefore in the same position as the Gentiles. What God will do for Israel when the nation is restored, He has already done in grace for Jews and Gentiles through the gospel.

As Jack R. Riggs points out, "Paul was using the Old Testament at that point as a matter of application and not of interpretation. He was in no way regarding the prophecy of Hosea fulfilled in the church, and thereby annulled for Israel". Peter also refers to Hosea 1:10 in saying, "but ye are a chosen generation...which in time past were not a people, but are now the people of God: which had not obtained mercy, but now have obtained mercy" (1 Pet. 2:10).

The name, "Jezreel" (v.11), now bears its other meaning. The nation, once '*scattered*' among the Gentile nations, will return from the land of their captivity (see Jeremiah 3:14) to be '*sown*' in her own land. This is expanded in chapter 2:14-23. The statement, "For great shall be the day of Jezreel" (v.11), is fully supported by Old Testament prophecy.

The conditions signified by the names of *all* three children will be reversed. "Say ye unto your brethren, Ammi; and to your sisters, Ruhamah" (2:1). (So, the restored nation will call one another brothers and sisters!) The nation will be acknowledged by God ("Ammi" means 'my people'), and will enjoy His mercy ("Ruhamah" means 'having obtained mercy'). Having worshipped lifeless gods, they will then be called, "Sons of the *living* God" (v.10). Like the believers at Thessalonica, they will turn "to God from idols to serve the living and true God" (1 Thess. 1:9).

READ CHAPTER 2:2-13

"Plead with your mother"

As we have seen, at the commencement of the book, Hosea was instructed to "take a wife of whoredoms", and the reason immediately follows: "For the land hath committed great whoredom, departing from the LORD" (1:2). Hosea Chapter 2 describes this "great whoredom" in more detail. Chapter 1 also describes the future blessing of Israel (see vv.10-11), and Chapter 2 continues by enlarging on the coming restoration of the nation. Chapter 2 is therefore similar in structure to Chapter 1. There is, however, a difference in approach. In Chapter 1, the immediate and ultimate future of the nation is spelt out in terms of the children, whilst here it is spelt out in terms of the mother. Chapter 2 commences with the abrogation of the marriage relationship: "She is not my wife, neither am I her husband" (v.2). Bearing in mind that God will not go back on the marriage vows, this statement can be taken to mean, 'She is no longer a wife to me'. But this changes: "And it shall be at that day, saith the LORD, that thou shalt call me Ishi (husband)" (v.16). The repeated expression, "at that day" or "in that day" (vv.16, 18, 21), indicates that this happy period belongs to the end-time.

The Chapter therefore divides into two main sections: *(1)* Israel's rejection by God (vv.2-13); *(2)* Israel's restoration by God (vv.14-23). Reasons are given in both cases. In the first case, Israel's love had failed. In the second case, God's love will triumph.

1) ISRAEL'S REJECTION, vv.2-13

The section commences, not with a command, but with a plea: "Plead with your mother, plead" (v.2). We have already seen that Hosea could appeal to his people in this way out of deep personal experience. Israel is addressed nationally as "your mother", and the people are addressed individually as "her children". The reason for Israel's rejection is her "whoredoms" and her "adulteries" (v.2). The nation had been unfaithful to God, so much so that He would no longer acknowledge her while she persisted in sin. He therefore

Chapter 2

pleads, through Hosea, "Let her therefore put away her whoredoms out of her sight, and her adulteries from between her breasts; lest I strip her naked, and set her as in the day that she was born, and make her as a wilderness, and set her like a dry land, and slay her with thirst. And I will not have mercy upon her children: for they be the children of whoredoms" (vv.2-4). That is, God would strip her of nationhood, and return her to original conditions of slavery.

The root cause is unfaithfulness to God, and at this point we listen to the New Testament: "Ye adulterers and adulteresses, know ye not that the friendship of the world is enmity with God? Whosoever therefore will be the friend of the world is the enemy of God" (James: 4:4), or "Adulteresses, know ye not that friendship with the world is enmity with God? Whosoever therefore is minded to be the friend of the world is constituted enemy of God" (JND). See also 1 John 2:15. It is significant that the ruin described by Jeremiah was caused for exactly the same reasons: "She weepeth sore in the night, and her tears are on her cheeks: among all her lovers she hath none to comfort her: all her friends have dealt treacherously with her, they are become her enemies" (Lam. 1:2).

We should note that the charge against the nation is elaborated in vv.4-13 with emphasis on the word "lovers" (vv.5,7,10,12,13). Her "lovers" in this particular passage are evidently the Canaanite idols; they are called "Baalim" (plural) in v.13. "The gods of Canaan were largely patrons of fertility" (D. Kidner). Israel had turned to them for help in agriculture, and had become embroiled in all the debased rituals connected with Baal-worship, reminding us that obedience and devotion to God, are our bulwark against spiritual and moral corruption. We should notice:

a) Her determination to follow her lovers, v.5
"And I will not have mercy upon her children; for they be the children of whoredoms. For their mother hath played the harlot: she that conceived them hath done shamefully: for she said, I will go after *my lovers*, that give me my bread and my water, my wool and my flax, mine oil and my drink". It was more than a silly mistake: it was a determined policy: "I will go after my lovers". More than that, it was a deliberate refusal to acknowledge the goodness and blessing of God. His provision was credited to idols. This should promote serious thought:

i) We must never forget that, "Every good gift and every perfect gift is *from above*, and cometh down *from the Father of lights,* with whom is no variableness, neither shadow of turning" (James 1:17).

ii) We must never forget that all that we are and have, belongs to God. He flatly contradicts their statement, "*my* bread...water...wool...flax...oil...drink" (v.5), saying "Therefore will I return, and take away *my* corn in the time thereof, and *my* wine in the season thereof, and will recover *my* wool and *my* flax given to cover her nakedness" (v.9). More than that, Israel had dedicated God's provision to Baal (v.8), in the same way that they used the gold which they brought out of Egypt (Exodus 12:35-36) to make the gold calf (Exodus 32:2-4, 24). "The LORD gave the people favour in the sight of the Egyptians, so that they lent ('gave', margin) unto them such things as they required".

Peter reminds us that we are to be "good stewards of the manifold *grace of God*" (1 Pet. 4:10). All spiritual ability is a divine bestowal, and we are to act as stewards in connection with everything that God gives us:

> Naught that I have my own I call,
> I hold it for the Giver:
> My heart, my strength, my life, my all,
> Are His, and His for ever.

iii) We must never attribute what God has given us to the gods of our own intellect or ability, or to the gods of business and commerce. We should never forget that any ability to serve God is a divine bestowal: "what hast thou that thou didst not receive? Now if thou didst receive it, why dost thou glory, as if thou hadst not received it" (1 Cor. 4:7). We should never forget either that success in business and commerce is equally a divine bestowal: "Thou shalt remember the LORD thy God: for it is *he* that giveth thee power to get wealth" (Deut. 8:17-18). In the words of David in connection with the vast provision for building the temple, "But who am I, and what is my people, that we should be able to offer so willingly of this sort? For all things come of thee, and of thine own have we given thee" (1 Chron. 29:14).

b) Her disillusion with her lovers, vv.6-9
Idolatry never brings satisfaction. Having said, "I will go after my lovers" (v.5), God replies: "Therefore, behold, I will hedge up thy way with thorns, and make a wall, that she shall not find her paths. And she shall follow after *her lovers*, but she shall not overtake them; and she shall seek them, but shall not find them" (vv.6-7). Jeremiah describes idolatry as "broken cisterns, that

can hold no water" (Jer. 2:13). Israel would find no lasting satisfaction in her idolatrous practices. It is all very much akin to the two daughters of the horseleach who cry, "Give, give", but give nothing in return (Prov. 30:15).

The words, "she shall seek them, but shall not find them" (v.7) remind us of Azariah's declaration to Asa: "The LORD is with you, while ye be with him; and if ye seek him, he will be found of you; but if ye forsake him, he will forsake you" (2 Chron. 15:2). And that is exactly what Asa and all Judah did. "And they entered into a covenant *to seek* the Lord God of their fathers with *all* their heart and with *all* their soul...All...Judah **sought him** with their whole desire; and he was **found** of them" (2 Chron. 15:12, 15). The Gospel preacher can rightly say: "Seek ye the LORD while he may be found, call ye upon him while he is near: let the wicked forsake his way, and the unrighteous man his thoughts: and let him return unto the LORD, and he will have mercy upon him: and to our God, for he will abundantly pardon" (Isaiah 55: 6-7). David said, "your heart shall live that seek God" (Psalm 69:32). An idol is nothing else than "a god that cannot save" (Isaiah 45:20).

While Haggai was not referring to idolatry *per se*, it remains that in his day God's people made idols out of their material possessions, and in particular their "ceiled houses". In consequence God 'hedged up their way with thorns, and made a wall, that they should not find their paths'. This is how He puts it: "Ye looked for much, and, lo, it came to little; and when ye brought it home, I did blow upon it. Why? saith the LORD of hosts. Because of mine house that is waste, and ye run every man unto his own house" (Hag. 1:9). Read the whole section, Haggai 1:3-11. Their materialism proved to be "broken cisterns, that can hold no water". Solomon said, "He that loveth silver shall not be satisfied with silver; nor he that loveth abundance with increase: this also is vanity" (Eccl. 5:10).

The New Testament goes further: "they that will be rich fall into temptation and a snare, and into many foolish and hurtful lusts, which drown men in destruction and perdition. For the love of money is the root ('a root', margin) of all evil ('every evil', margin): which while some coveted after, they have erred from the faith, and pierced themselves through with many sorrows" (1 Tim. 6:9-10). The hymn-writer puts it like this:

> *Now the frail vessel Thou hast made,*
> *No hand but Thine can fill -*
> *The waters of the earth have failed,*
> *And I am thirsty still.*

There is something terribly casual about the statement, "I will go and return to my first husband; for then it was better with me than now" (v.7). It is almost as if she is treating God like a safety-net. He is reduced to an option. There is no trace of regret for the pain she had caused, and no sorrow for the way in which she had affronted His love. She thinks she can just pick up the threads of the relationship without further ado. The Lord Jesus made it very clear that something far more thorough was required: "Remember therefore from whence thou art fallen, and **repent,** and do the first works" (Rev. 2:5).

Israel's words, "I will go and return to my first husband; for **then it was better** with me than now", are explained in the verses that follow: "For she did not know (a case of culpable ignorance: see 4:6) that **I** gave her corn, and wine, and oil, and multiplied her silver and gold". It was indeed 'better' for her in the past, but having offered God's gifts to Baal (v.8), they had received nothing in return, and would lose the very gifts they were devoting to idolatry: "Therefore will I return, and take away **my** corn in the time thereof, and **my** wine in the season thereof, and will recover **my** wool and **my** flax given to cover her nakedness" (v.9).

c) Her degradation before her lovers, v.10

"And now I will discover her lewdness ('villainy' or 'folly', JND margin) in the sight of **her lovers**". Israel would be exposed before them as defiled and degraded. Compare Lamentations 1:8, "Jerusalem hath grievously sinned; therefore she is removed: all that honoured her despise her, because they have seen her nakedness; yea, she sigheth, and turneth backward", or "Jerusalem hath grievously sinned; therefore is she removed as an impurity" (JND). Her desolation had earned her, not pity, but loss of respect by the nations that once held her in high esteem. Jerusalem was painfully aware of her disgrace: "yea, she sigheth, and turneth backward".

The Lord Jesus warned His disciples that loss of distinctiveness would endanger their testimony: "Ye are the salt of the earth: but if the salt have lost his savour, wherewith shall it be salted? it is thenceforth good for nothing, but to be cast out, and to be trodden under foot of men" (Matt. 5:13). The world has little time for people who profess one thing, and deny it in practice.

d) Her desolation because of her lovers, vv.11-12

"I will also cause all her mirth to cease, her feast days, her new moons, and her sabbaths, and all her solemn feasts. And I will destroy her vines and her fig trees whereof she hath said, These are my rewards that **my lovers** have given me: and I will make them a forest, and the beasts of the earth shall eat them". Compromise and infidelity destroys joy, and creates barrenness: there is no fruit. The literality of this cannot be doubted. Compare Isaiah 7:23-25, which refers to the desolation of Judah by the Assyrians: "And it shall come to pass in that day, that in every place shall be, where there were a thousand vines at a thousand silverlings (an old English word for a silver coin, probably standing here for a shekel) it shall even be for briers and thorns". The spiritual lesson is clear. We have only to listen to the Lord Jesus: "Ye have not chosen me, but I have chosen you, and ordained you, that ye should go and bring forth fruit, and that your fruit should remain" (John 15:16). No wonder John wrote, "Little children, keep yourselves from idols" (1 John 5:21). Anything in our lives which displaces the Lord Jesus can only be ruinous.

e) *Her decoration for her lovers, v13*
"I will visit upon her the days of Baalim, wherein she burned incense to them, and she decked herself with her earrings and her jewels, and she went after **her lovers**, and forgat me, saith the LORD". God's people evidently "dressed up" when they participated in idolatrous festivals, but had no thought whatsoever of being attractive to God. The New Testament has a great deal to say about this. See, for example, 1 Peter 3:3-4 which although addressed to married sisters, is applicable in principle to men as well: "Whose adorning let it not be that outward adorning of plaiting the hair, and wearing of gold, or of putting on of apparel; but let it be the hidden man of the heart, in that which is not corruptible, even the ornament of a meek and quiet spirit, which is in the sight of God of great price". Paul puts it like this: "Wherefore also we make it our aim, whether at home or absent, to be well-pleasing **to Him**" (2 Cor.5:9, RV).

2) *ISRAEL'S RESTORATION, vv.14-23*
We will consider Israel's restoration by God in our next study.

READ CHAPTER 2:14-23

"I will betroth thee unto Me for ever"

As we have noted, this chapter is similar in structure to Chapter 1. It describes Israel's "great whoredom" (1:2) in more detail, and enlarges on the statement "Then shall the children of Judah and the children of Israel be gathered together, and appoint themselves one head, and they shall come up out of the land (the land of their captivity): for great shall be the day of Jezreel" (1:11).

The Chapter therefore divides into two main sections: *(1)* Israel's rejection by God (vv.2-13); *(2)* Israel's restoration by God (vv.14-23). Reasons are given in both cases. In the first case, Israel's love had failed. In the second case, God's love will triumph.

1) ISRAEL'S REJECTION, vv.2-13

We have already considered the cause of Israel's rejection by God. The charge against the nation is given in vv.4-13 with emphasis on the word "lovers" (vv.5,7,10,12,13). Her "lovers" in this particular passage are evidently the Canaanite idols; they are called "Baalim" (plural) in v.13. We noted the following: *(a)* Israel's determination to follow her lovers (v.5); *(b)* Israel's disillusion with her lovers (vv.6-9); *(c)* Israel's degradation before her lovers (v.10); *(d)* Israel's desolation because of her lovers (vv.11-12); *(e)* Israel's decoration for her lovers (v.13).

It is sad to remember the nation's propensity for idolatry. Joshua was very conscious of this: "Now therefore fear the LORD, and serve him with sincerity and in truth: and put away the gods which your fathers served on the other side of the flood, and in Egypt; and serve ye the LORD. And if it seem evil unto you to serve the LORD, choose you this day whom ye will serve; whether the gods which your fathers served that were on the other side of the flood, or the gods of the Amorites, in whose land ye dwell: but as for me and my house, we will serve the LORD" (Joshua 24:14-15). Centuries later,

Ezekiel described the way in which the nation espoused the gods of Egypt, Assyria and Chaldea (Ezek. 23:1-35). The lesson is clear. "Little children, keep yourselves from idols" (1 John 5:21). Idolatry can take many forms and unless we are on our guard, it can engulf us so easily. This brings us to:

2) ISRAEL'S RESTORATION, vv.14-23

The atmosphere of the chapter now changes completely. Divine sorrow gives place to joy. However, the change is not attributable to reformation on the part of Israel, but rather to divine initiative. "Therefore, behold, *I will* allure her...and speak comfortably unto her (speak tenderly to her heart)" (v.14). Compare Isaiah 40:2: "Speak ye comfortably to Jerusalem ('speak to the heart of Jerusalem', JND)". The word "allure" has the meaning of 'entice...woo...persuade'. God's love for His people is clear from the following:

a) He will give them refuge, v.14

"I will...bring her into the wilderness". This could allude to the wilderness journey of Israel after their deliverance from Egypt, in which case the meaning is that "In tenderness, God would avow His love for her as He did in that wilderness so long ago after the exodus from Egypt" (J. M. Flanigan). In the Lord's own words: "I remember thee, the kindness of thy youth, the love of thine espousals, **when thou wentest after me in the wilderness**" (Jer. 2:2). But it can be better understood with reference to events at the end-time: "And to the woman were given two wings of a great eagle, that she might fly into **the wilderness**, into her place, where she is nourished for a time, and times, and half a time, from the face of the serpent" (Rev. 12:14). National restoration will follow the dark days of the coming Tribulation period (see Dan. 12:1; Jer. 30:7).

b) He will give them hope, v.15

"I will give her her vineyards from thence, and the valley of Achor for a door of hope". The valley of Achor was the place where Israel's sin was purged, and possession of the land followed: "And Joshua, and all Israel with him, took Achan the son of Zerah...And all Israel stoned him with stones...And they raised over him a great heap of stones unto this day. So the LORD turned from the fierceness of his anger. Wherefore the name of that place was called, The valley of Achor, unto this day" (Joshua 7:24-26). But 'the valley of trouble' (Achor) became "a door of hope". Israel went on to conquer Ai (Joshua ch.8), and to subdue the land of Canaan. At the end-time, national sin will again be purged, and the land will be possessed and enjoyed. "And

Sharon shall be a fold of flocks, and the valley of Achor a place for herds to lie down in, for my people that have sought me" (Isaiah 65:10).

c) He will give them joy, v.15
"And she shall sing there, as in the days of her youth, and as in the day when she came up out of the land of Egypt". This clearly refers to Exodus 15:1-19. The song begins with the words, "I will sing unto the LORD, for he hath triumphed gloriously: the horse and his rider hath he thrown into the sea. The LORD is my strength and song, and he is become my salvation" (Exodus 15:1-2). God's people will see every enemy defeated. There was no singing when God visited His people in judgment (Hosea 2:11), but the restored nation will be told "Sing, O daughter of Zion; shout, O Israel; be glad and rejoice with all the heart, O daughter of Jerusalem. The LORD hath taken away thy judgments, he hath cast out thine enemy: the king of Israel, even the LORD, is in the midst of thee; thou shalt not see evil any more" (Zeph. 3:14-15).

d) He will give them affection, vv.16-17
Israel had not long entered Canaan, before idolatry reared its ugly head, and the nation became unfaithful to God. But not now: "and it shall be at that day, saith the LORD, that thou shalt call me Ishi ('my husband': the word suggests an intimate and personal relationship rather than a legal commitment); and shalt call *me* no more Baali ('my lord'). For I will take away the names of Baalim out of her mouth, and they shall **no more be remembered by their name**". The words, "and shalt call *me* no more Baali", are most significant. They represent an ancient version of the current idea that 'really all world religions are the same; we all worship the same God - some do it one way, and others do it another way - and it doesn't really matter what you call Him'. This is abhorrent to God. J. M. Flanigan points out that "Baal had become common in the names of many places, as Baal-hazor (2 Sam. 13:23), Baal-meon (Num. 32:38), Baal-peor (Num. 25:3,5), and in the names of persons too, as Meribaal (1 Chron. 8:34), Jerubbaal (Judges 6:32), Ethbaal (1 Kings 16:31). In the restored Israel all trace of the Baalim would be removed".

e) He will give them security, v.18
i) The words, "And in that day will I make a covenant for them (for their benefit) with the beasts of the field, and with the fowls of heaven, and with the creeping things of the ground", are amplified in Isaiah 11:6-9, "The wolf also shall dwell with the lamb, and the leopard shall lie down with the kid;

and the calf and the young lion and the fatling together; and a little child shall lead them...And the sucking child shall play on the hole of the asp ('adder', JND), and the weaned child shall put his hand on the cockatrice ('viper', JND) den. They shall not hurt nor destroy in all my holy mountain".

ii) The words, "I will break the bow and the sword and the battle out of the earth, and will make them to lie down safely", are amplified in Isaiah 2:4, "And he shall judge among the nations, and shall rebuke many people: and they shall beat their swords into plowshares, and their spears into pruninghooks: nation shall not lift up sword against nation, neither shall they learn war any more".

f) He will give them permanence, vv.19-20
The expression "I will betroth thee unto me", referring to the new covenant (Jer. 31:31-34), occurs three times in these verses.

i) In the first case, it stresses *permanence*: "*I will* betroth thee unto me for ever" (v.19). H. L. Ellison explains this helpfully: "There follows a new betrothal, not a marriage, presumably because the old one had never been finally dissolved, one in which Israel is for the first time fully to know what it means to have God as husband". A new marriage would be a violation of Deuteronomy 24:3-4. The permanence of the relationship is clearly expressed in Isaiah 66:22, "For as the new heavens and the new earth, which I will make, shall remain before me, saith the LORD, so shall your seed and your name remain". It is put beautifully in Jeremiah 31:35-37: "Thus saith the LORD, which giveth the sun for a light by day, and the ordinances of the moon and of the stars for a light by night, which divideth the sea when the waves thereof roar; the LORD of hosts is his name: if those ordinances depart from before me, saith the LORD, then the seed of Israel also shall cease from being a nation before me for ever. Thus saith the LORD; if heaven above can be measured, and the foundations of the earth searched out beneath, I will also cast off all the seed of Israel for all that they have done, saith the LORD". The continuity of the nation, which seemed impossible at the time of writing, is assured. A similar passage is found in Jeremiah 33:19-26.

ii) In the second case, it stresses *righteousness*: "*I will* betroth thee unto me in righteousness, and in judgment, and in lovingkindness, and in mercies" (v.19). The covenant has a righteous basis: the lovingkindness and mercy of divine forgiveness are based on the sacrifice of Christ (Rom. 3:21-26).

Theodore Laetsch (*The Minor Prophets*) puts it helpfully: "It is a betrothal based on righteousness and judgment. Righteousness was also the basis of the Old Testament covenant, a righteousness expressed in God's holy law as given on Sinai...This was, alas, a righteousness to which no man could attain, which called every man into judgment, the inevitable outcome of which would be eternal damnation. Therefore already in the Old Testament the Lord revealed a different righteousness, acknowledged by Him as perfect righteousness, the righteousness of faith in the promised Redeemer, the righteousness of forgiveness of sins, symbolised and foreshadowed in the Old Testament by the shedding and sprinkling of sacrificial blood (Exodus 24:5-8; Lev. 16:14-19). This righteousness was procured in the New Testament by the Son of God, the Lord our Righteousness (Jer. 23:5-6). As man's substitute (Isaiah 53) He satisfied every demand of God's mandatory and punitive righteousness (Rom. 3:21-26; Heb. 9:11-28; 1 John 1:7; 2:2)".

iii) In the third case, it stresses **faithfulness**: "*I will* even betroth thee unto me in faithfulness" (v.20). While this could refer to the faithfulness which the Lord "will implant and cultivate within His partner" (Derek Kidner), it more likely refers to the unalterable faithfulness of the Lord. "God is not a man, that he should lie; neither the son of man, that he should repent: hath he not said, and shall he not do it? Or hath he spoken, and shall he not make it good?" (Num. 23:19).

The result for Israel follows: "and thou shalt know the LORD" (v.20). Compare Jeremiah 31:33-34, "I will put my law in their inward parts, and write it in their hearts...And they shall teach no more every man his neighbour, and every man his brother, saying, Know the LORD: for they shall all know me".

g) He will give them resources, vv.21-22
Notice the supply route. It starts with **God** Himself. He will answer the cry of the **heavens** for the ability to answer the cry of the **earth**, which in its turn will then be able to answer the cry of the **crops**, which will in their turn be able to answer the cry of God's **people** "sown in the earth" and simply called "Jezreel". Put the other way round, "It is all a delightful personification of earth and the fruits of the earth, where Jezreel calls to the corn, and new wine and the oil. These in turn call upon the land to produce harvest and vintage, while the earth calls upon the heavens for rain, and the heavens call upon Jehovah who is the source of all blessing. Jehovah hears and answers the heavens by sending rain" (J. M. Flanigan). He opens His hand

and "satisfieth the desire of every living thing" (Psalm 145:16). Finally, to sum it all up:

h) He will reverse her estrangement, v.23

i) God says, "*I will* sow her *unto me* in the earth". "Jezreel", meaning, in the first place, 'God scatters', now means 'God sows'. The two meanings are found in 1:4; and 1:11.

ii) God says, "*I will* have mercy upon her that had not obtained mercy". "Lo-ruhamah" (1:6) becomes "Ruhama" (2:1)

iii) God says, "*I will* say to them which were not my people, Thou art my people". "Lo-ammi" (1:9) becomes "Ammi".(2:1). In that day, the regenerate nation will respond by saying, "Thou art my God". Never again will she say, "I will go after my lovers" (v.5). It is noteworthy that, in His sovereignty, the Lord takes the initiative. Not 'they shall say, Thou art my God, and He will reply, Thou art my people', but "I will say unto them which were not my people, Thou art my people; and they shall say, thou art my God".

Paul cites this verse when dealing with God's blessing for Jew and Gentile: "that he might make known the riches of his glory on the vessels of mercy... even us, whom he hath called, not of the Jews only, but also of the Gentiles... As he saith also in Osee, I will call them my people, which were not my people; and her beloved, which was not beloved" (Rom. 9:23-25). As we have already noted, Hosea 1:10 is cited in Romans 9:26. What God will do for Israel when the nation is restored, He is already doing in grace for Jews and Gentiles through the gospel. This verse is also cited by Peter: "But ye are a chosen generation, a royal priesthood, an holy nation, a peculiar people; that ye should shew forth the praises of him who hath called you out of darkness into his marvellous light: which in time past were not a people, but are now the people of God: which had not obtained mercy, but now have obtained mercy" (1 Pet. 2:9-10).

READ CHAPTER 3:1-5

"Thou shalt not play the harlot"

Hosea chapters 1 and 2 describe the immediate (at the time) and ultimate future of Israel. See 1:2-9 with 2:1-13, and 1:10-11 with 2:14-23, respectively. Chapter 3 does the same (vv.1-2 with v.5) but also describes the intervening period, and demonstrates very clearly that there is no discontinuance in God's love for His people. The day has not yet dawned when God will say, "I will betroth thee unto me for ever" (2:19), and "I will love them freely" (14:4), but God loved His people with an "everlasting love" (Jer. 31:3).

The chapter therefore commences, "Then said the Lord unto me, Go yet ('Go again', JND: that is, 'again' after 1:2, "Go, take unto thee a wife of whoredoms"), love a woman beloved of her friend, yet an adulteress, according to ***the love of the Lord toward the children of Israel***" (v.1). We should notice that it is God's love for Israel that rekindles Hosea's love for Gomer. He was to love her "***according to***" God's love for Israel. In the words of E. B. Pusey (*The Minor Prophets*), "The prophet is directed to frame his life, so as to depict at once the ingratitude of Israel, or the sinful soul, and the abiding, persevering, love of God". The chapter can be summarised as follows: *(1)* Israel in the past (vv.1-2); *(2)* Israel in the present (vv.3-4); *(3)* Israel in the future (v.5).

1) ISRAEL IN THE PAST, vv.1-2
"Then said the LORD unto me, Go yet, love a woman beloved of her friend, yet an adulteress, according to the love of the LORD toward the children of Israel, who look to other gods, and love flagons of wine. So I bought her to me for fifteen pieces of silver, and for an homer of barley, and an half homer of barley". These verses fall into two clear paragraphs: *(a)* the price Gomer paid for her sin (v.1); *(b)* the price Hosea paid for Gomer's redemption (v.2)

a) The price Gomer paid for her sin, v.1
Gomer's unfaithfulness led her ultimately to slavery, possibly to the slave market: she is "sold under sin" (Rom. 7:14). Hosea sets out, side by side, the

literal relationship between Hosea and Gomer, and the spiritual relationship between Jehovah and Israel. Hosea's experience reflected Jehovah's experience:

"Go yet, love a woman beloved of her friend, yet an **adulteress**".

"According to the love of the Lord toward the children of Israel, who **look to other gods** and love flagons of wine".

The complete incongruity of the situation is unmistakable. The Lord loved them, but **they** loved "flagons of wine", or 'raisin-cakes' (JND), which were evidently delicacies associated with religious feasts. See 2 Samuel 6:19, 1 Chronicles 16:3 and Song of Solomon 2:5. In each case 'flagons of wine' (AV) is translated elsewhere as 'raisin-cakes' or 'cakes of raisins' (JND/RV). These were evidently sweetmeats made of pressed grapes, a delicacy, offered to Baal at the autumn vintage festivals, "for the people mistakenly thought that the good things of the fertile land were gifts from him (Hosea 2:5, 8)" (Jack R. Riggs)

It is worth pausing to ask ourselves to what extent this could be true of ourselves. Does the "love of Christ" constrain **us**? (2 Cor. 5:14). Or have we ignored the command, "Love not the world, neither the things that are in the world. If any man love the world, the love of the Father is not in him?" (1 John 2:15).

The wording of God's command is most significant: "Go yet, love a woman beloved of her friend".

- "Go yet, love a **woman**". Not, 'Go yet, love your wife'. Gomer is described as "an adulteress". He was to love her without resuming the marriage relationship.

- "Beloved of her **friend**". Some commentators take "friend" to mean 'paramour', but it seems more in keeping with the context and object of the passage to see the reference here to Hosea himself. He is not called, 'her husband', just as she is not called, 'your wife'. He is called, "her friend" (*rea*: it can be translated 'companion'), just as she is called, "a woman". Compare Jeremiah 3:20, where the word "husband" (*rea*) is elsewhere translated 'friend' (JND margin). The detail of God's command must have deeply pierced Hosea. Gomer was most unwholesome - "an adulteress" - but he is to love her. If ever a man understood the depth of God's feelings towards His sinful people, that man must be Hosea!

b) The price Hosea paid for her redemption, v.2
Gomer was purchased for "fifteen pieces of silver". That is, at half the price of a gored slave, whether a "manservant" or "a maidservant". See Exodus 21:32. The value of the nine or ten bushels of barley has also been estimated (C. F. Keil) as fifteen shekels of silver.

The Lord Jesus was sold for "thirty pieces of silver" (Zech. 11:12), but He paid an infinite price for Israel's deliverance. One day the nation will say, or sing: "He was wounded for our transgressions, he was bruised for our iniquities: the chastisement of our peace was upon him; and with his stripes we are healed. All we like sheep have gone astray; we have turned every one to his own way; and the LORD hath laid on him the iniquity of us all" (Isaiah 53:5-6). That same infinite price was paid for *our* deliverance as well: "Christ also loved the church, and gave himself for it; that he might sanctify and cleanse it with the washing of water by the word, that he might present it to himself a glorious church, not having spot, or wrinkle, or any such thing; but that it should be holy and without blemish" (Eph. 5:25-27); "Forasmuch as ye know that ye were not redeemed with corruptible things, as silver and gold...but with the precious blood of Christ, as of a lamb without blemish and without spot" (1 Pet. 1:18-19).

2) ISRAEL IN THE PRESENT, vv.3-4
But it was not only the price that is different. Gomer was purchased, and kept at a distance, as Israel is today, for "many days". The Lord 'nourishes' and 'cherishes' His church *now.* The prophetic significance of the story outstrips the story itself, for whilst no specific mention is made of resumed marital relations after the "many days", the full blessing of *Israel* after "many days" is described in v.5. The church is by no means disadvantaged in this respect: the Lord Jesus will "present it (the church) to himself a glorious church, not having spot, or wrinkle, or any such thing; but that it should be holy and without blemish".

The present position of Israel is set out in vv.3-4. For the second time, Hosea sets out, side by side, the literal relationship between Hosea and Gomer, and the spiritual relationship between Jehovah and Israel. Hosea's experience would reflect Jehovah's experience:

"And I said unto her, Thou shalt abide for me **many days**; thou shalt not play the harlot, and thou shalt not be for another man: so will I also be for thee" (v.3).

"For the children of Israel shall abide **many days** without a king, and without a prince, and without a sacrifice, and without an image, and without an ephod, and without teraphim" (v.4).

Having paid the price for her ("I bought her to **me**", v.2), Hosea "said unto her, Thou shalt abide for me many days". The words, "Thou shalt not play the harlot, and thou shalt not be for (omit 'another') man: so will I also be for thee", mean that Gomer would not enter into a relationship with any man - including Hosea - and that Hosea would not enter into a relationship with Gomer. She would be neither adulterous, nor in the enjoyment of conjugal rights.

This is precisely the position of Israel. While she is not in communion with God, she is divinely preserved. Her national identity remains, although, **politically**, she is "without a king, and without a prince", and **religiously**, she is "without a sacrifice, and without an image, and without an ephod, and without teraphim". Two things are clear:

i) The nation would not "play the harlot". So there is no "image", and no "teraphim". The former refers to upright pillars or upright standing stones (*matstsebah*) associated with idolatry. See, for example, 1 Kings 14:23, and 2 Kings 3:2. The latter were household gods. See Genesis 31:19, 34, 35 where the same word is rendered "images". So Israel would be purged of idolatry. But, on the other hand:

ii) The nation would not be in relation to Jehovah. So there is no "sacrifice", and no "ephod". That is, no approach to God, and no revelation by God. This situation would exist, without particular definition, for "**many days**". H. A. Ironside states the situation as follows: "Ever since the destruction of Jerusalem by the Romans they have answered to the description here given...they are left without a sacrifice, for their temple is destroyed and their altar profaned...not only are they without a sacrifice, but without a priest also - "without an ephod" - for all records have long been lost: and though many survive who are in the direct line of priesthood (as shall be manifested in the day of their restoration), yet they cannot now trace their genealogy; and if they could, there is no temple in which to officiate". It is worth saying that during this period, the Lord Jesus is building His church

(Matt. 16:18). But God has not abandoned His earthly people. We come now to "***the latter days***" (v.5).

3) ISRAEL IN THE FUTURE, v.5

"Afterward shall the children of Israel return, and seek the LORD their God, and David their king; and shall fear the LORD and his goodness in the latter days", or "turn with fear toward Jehovah and toward his goodness, at the end of the days" (JND).

We know how this will take place: "the valley of Achor" will become "a door of hope" (2:15). As we have already noted, the valley of Achor was the place where Israel's sin was purged, and possession of the land followed. Israel went on to conquer Ai, and to subdue the land of Canaan. At the end-time, national sin will again be purged, and the land will be possessed and enjoyed. This detail is omitted here, because chapter 3 emphasises the ***reason*** for her return, that is, God's love for His people. Suffice to notice that particular reference is made to "David their king". That is, the rebellious ten tribes will again recognise the throne of David, from which they had seceded. The nation will be re-united. We know that Christ will sit "upon the throne of David, and upon his kingdom, to order, and to establish it with judgment and with justice from henceforth even for ever" (Isaiah 9:7).

The reference to David here must be read in conjunction with Jeremiah 30:9 ("But they shall serve the LORD their God, and David their king, whom I will raise up unto them"), and Ezekiel 34:22-24 ("Therefore will I save my flock, and they shall no more be a prey; and I will judge between cattle and cattle. And I will set up one shepherd over them, and he shall feed them, even my servant David; he shall feed them, and he shall be their shepherd. And I the LORD will be their God, and my servant David a prince among them; I the LORD have spoken it"). It is difficult to escape the conclusion, particularly from the Ezekiel passage, that it will be David himself, raised from the dead, who will act as vice-regent over Israel in the Millennial Kingdom.

READ CHAPTER 4:1-19

"Destroyed for lack of knowledge"

In introducing the prophecy of Hosea, we noted that Chapters 1-3 present the message of the book in **narrative** form, whereas Chapters 4-14 comprise a series of **addresses.** As J. Sidlow Baxter points out, the first three chapters are more than just narrative, they are "symbolical narrative". He continues: "The prophet's wife, Gomer, and the three children, Jezreel, Lo-ruhamah, and Lo-ammi, and the tragedy of the prophet's married life, of which these chapters speak, are all symbolical of the relationship between Jehovah and Israel". The command to Hosea, "Go yet, love a woman beloved of her friend, yet an adulteress", reflected God's love "toward the children of Israel, who look to other gods, and love flagons of wine (or 'raisin-cakes', JND)" (3:1). The vicissitudes of Hosea's own marriage relationship enabled him to understand and convey God's deep love for His erring people.

Jack. R. Riggs (*Hosea's Heartbreak*) points out that "in the second division of the book (Chapters 4-14) there is no direct reference to the tragic marital circumstances of Hosea's life as mentioned in the first part (chapters 1-3). There is, however, the same basic emphasis on the love of the Lord for Israel, and Israel's unfaithfulness to the Lord. These two thoughts constitute the very woof and warp of the second division. The prophet steps from the moral ruin of his own home into the environment of the degenerate people of Israel. His heart is burdened and filled with bitter indignation at the sins of his kinsmen. He exposes and censures the sins of those of all walks of life. The source of their sinful behaviour is traced to their spirit of unfaithfulness toward the Lord. It is a very dark and dreadful picture that is painted of Israelite history. Hosea repeatedly warns of the inevitable judgment which such conduct will bring upon the entire nation".

In summary, the prophecy of Hosea falls into two major parts: *(i)* Hosea's love for his unfaithful wife, Chapters 1-3; *(ii)* God's love for His unfaithful people, Chapters 4-14. If Chapters 1-3 illustrate Israel's unfaithfulness and restoration from a 'real-life' situation, then Chapters 4-14 describe her unfaithfulness in detail, together with her judgment and restoration.

Chapter 4 introduces the Lord's "controversy (*rib*, meaning 'lawsuit') with the inhabitants of the land" (v.1). As Derek Kidner observes, "We are suddenly in a court of law, and God is prosecuting. He has no lack of charges to bring". Israel is not alone in the court-room. The same word (*rib*) is found in the following: "The LORD hath also a controversy with Judah" (12:2). See also Jeremiah 25:31 ("the LORD hath a controversy with the nations"); Micah 6:2 ("Hear ye, O mountains, the LORD'S controversy… for the LORD hath a controversy with his people").

The chapter may be divided as follows: *(1)* God's controversy with Israel (vv.1-5); *(2)* God's condemnation of Israel (vv.6-11); *(3)* God's censure of idolatry (vv.12-14); *(4)* God's counsel to Judah (vv.15-19).

1) GOD'S CONTROVERSY WITH ISRAEL, vv.1-5
We should notice: *(a)* the charge (vv.1-2); *(b)* the sentence (v.3); *(c)* the blame (vv.4-5).

a) The charge, vv.1-2
"There is no truth, nor mercy, nor knowledge of God in the land. By swearing, and lying, and killing, and stealing, and committing adultery, they break out, and blood toucheth blood". We must notice *(i)* the absence of righteousness" (v.1); *(ii)* the presence of unrighteousness (v.2)

i) The absence of righteousness, v.1. "There is no truth, nor mercy, nor knowledge of God in the land". We should bear Titus 2:12 in mind in considering this statement:

- As to the people personally: "no truth". There was an absence of faithfulness in the sense of honesty and reliability. People were not trustworthy.

- As to others: no "mercy". This is the word often rendered "lovingkindness" *(chesed)*. We have already met it in 2:19: "I will betroth thee unto me in righteousness, and in judgment, and in **lovingkindness** *(chesed),* and in mercies", and we will meet it again in 6:6: "For I desired **mercy** *(chesed),* and not sacrifice; and the knowledge of God more than burnt-offerings"). It is an attribute that God loves to exhibit: "he delighteth in mercy (*chesed*)" (Micah 7:18).

- *As to God:* no "knowledge of God in the land". Sin in personal life and sin in social life, is traced to sin in spiritual life. We cannot expect to be right ourselves, and right with others, if we are not right with God. The Scriptures urge us to recognise the implications of "having put on the new man, which according to God is created in truthful righteousness and holiness" (Eph. 4:24, JND). Bearing this in mind, Paul continues, "Wherefore putting away lying, speak every man truth with his neighbour... Let him that stole steal no more... and be ye kind one to another, tenderhearted, forgiving one another, even as God for Christ's sake hath forgiven you" (Eph. 4:25-32). Here is the "truth" and "mercy" that were so conspicuously absent in Hosea's day.

"The knowledge of God" is not only mental acknowledgement of His will, but the **practice** of His will. This can be illustrated from the life of Ezra: "For Ezra had prepared his heart **to seek** the law of the LORD, **and to do it**, and to teach in Israel statutes and judgments" (Ezra 7:10). In commissioning His disciples the Lord Jesus did not say, 'teaching them all things', but "teaching them to **observe** all things whatsoever I have commanded you" (Matt. 28:20). The true "knowledge of God" does not subsist in information about God, but life in harmony with Him. It is said of Josiah that he did "judgment and justice" and "judged the cause of the poor and the needy... was not this to know me? saith the LORD" (Jer. 22:15-16). John 17:3 is now compulsory reading!

ii) The presence of unrighteousness, v.2. Absence of the "knowledge of God in the land" accounts for the fearful list that follows. "By swearing, and lying ('no truth', v.1), and killing ('no mercy', v.1), and stealing, and committing adultery, they break out, and blood toucheth blood".

The New Testament makes the same point: "And even as they did not like to retain God in their knowledge, God gave them over to a reprobate mind, to do those things which are not convenient; being filled with all unrighteousness, fornication, wickedness, covetousness, maliciousness; full of envy, murder, debate, deceit, malignity; whisperers, backbiters, haters of God, despiteful, proud boasters, inventors of evil things, disobedient to parents, without understanding, covenant-breakers, without natural affection, implacable, unmerciful" (Romans 1:28-32). A right relationship with God is our bulwark against moral degeneracy. Remove that, and sins erupt: "they break out", meaning that they flourish unchecked. All restraint is cast aside. The expression, "blood toucheth blood", is no understatement when we remember the violence and bloodshed of Israel's last days. Read 2 Kings 15:8-18. This leads to:

b) The sentence, v.3
"Therefore shall the land mourn, and every one that dwelleth therein shall languish, with the beasts of the field, and with the fowls of heaven; yea, the fishes of the sea also shall be taken away". As Jack R. Riggs points out, "The mourning of the people in the land and the wasting away of the animals are the natural result of the want of rain and the great drought that would ensue". Deuteronomy 11:11-17 gives due warning of the famine and drought that would follow apostasy. It is a graphic picture of the spiritual barrenness that follows disobedience to the word of God.

c) The blame, v.4-5
The people were evidently attempting to blame each other for the situation. "Yet let no man strive, nor reprove another: for thy people are as they that strive with the priest". We now enter disputed territory! Newer versions of the Bible (including the RSV and the Amplified Version) render the verse as follows: "Yet let no one contend, and let none accuse, for with you is my contention, O priest". While this appears to introduce the verses which follow, and therefore seems to fit comfortably into the context, it assumes that the Massoretic Text (the standard Hebrew text) "has suffered slightly in transmission" (Derek Kidner). This particular rendering therefore calls for caution!

It must be said that the text as it stands in the AV, RV, and even in the NIV, is perfectly explainable. If a matter was too difficult for local solution, the contending parties were not to wrangle over the matter but were to bring the matter to "the priests the Levites, and unto the judge that shall be in those days, and enquire: and they shall shew thee the sentence of judgment...And the man that will do presumptuously, and will not hearken unto the priest that standeth to minister there before the LORD thy God, or unto the judge, even that man shall die: and thou shalt put away the evil from Israel" (Deut. 17:8-13). Israel had a strong tendency to rebel against God's judgments just as some would be inclined to rebel against priestly decisions. To do this was a capital offence: "that man shall die". To "strive with the priest" meant death. Israel, by rejecting God, would therefore suffer divine retribution.

When divine judgment fell, the people would have no cause to blame one another since, in their entirety, they were "as they that strive with the priest". Judgment would be all-embracing: "Therefore shalt thou (the people) fall in the day, and the prophet shall also fall with thee in the night, and I will destroy thy mother" (v.5). As we have already noted (see 2:2), "thy mother" is the term that describes Israel nationally. The prophet is later called "the snare of a fowler in all his ways" (9:8). The fact that the prophet (false prophet) falls in the night could be significant. They were, after all, subject to "the rulers of the darkness of this world" (Eph. 6:12). There was "no light in them" (Isaiah 8:20)

2) GOD'S CONDEMNATION OF ISRAEL, vv.6-11
The passage can be summed up in the words "I will also reject thee...I will also forget thy children...therefore will I change their glory into shame...I will punish them for their ways" (vv.6, 7, 9)

a) "I will also reject thee", v.6
"**My people** (note this) are destroyed for lack of knowledge: because thou hast rejected knowledge, I will also reject thee, that thou shalt be no priest to me, seeing thou hast forgotten the law of thy God, I will also forget thy children".

Very clearly, this was a culpable "lack of knowledge". They had "rejected knowledge" and "forgotten the law of thy God". God had supremely blessed His people: they were "Israelites...to whom pertaineth the adoption, and the glory, and the covenants, and the giving of the law, and the service of God, and the promises" (Rom. 9:4). In answering his own question, "What advantage then hath the Jew? or what profit is there in circumcision?", Paul replied, "Much every way: chiefly, because that unto them were committed the oracles of God (Rom. 3:1-2). God had given them "right judgments, and true laws, good statutes and commandments" (Neh. 9:13). The Psalmist put it beautifully, "He shewed his word unto Jacob, his statutes and his judgments unto Israel. He hath not dealt so with any nation: and as for his judgments, they have not known them. Praise ye the LORD" (Psalm 147:19-20).

It was to this people that God said, "If ye will obey my voice indeed and keep my covenant, then ye shall be a peculiar treasure unto me above all people: for all the earth is mine: and ye shall be unto me a kingdom of priests...." (Exodus 19:5-6). But God's people (notice that He calls them "My people") had "rejected knowledge" and "forgotten the law of thy God". In consequence the nation would be "stripped of her priestly rank which would have fitted her to stand before God and the Gentile nations as His truth bearer (Exodus 19:5-6). Now that privileged position would be taken away due to her willful rejection of God's special revelation which had been delivered to her" (Jack R. Riggs). But not for ever: "But ye shall be named the Priests of the LORD: men shall call you the Ministers of our God: ye shall eat the riches of the Gentiles, and in their glory shall ye boast yourselves" (Isaiah 61:6).

The spiritual lessons for believers today are clear. For example, we must "grow in grace, and in the knowledge of our Lord and Saviour Jesus Christ" (2 Pet. 3:18) and we are to "abound yet more and more in knowledge and in all judgment" (Phil. 1:9). By increasing "in the knowledge of God" (Col. 1:10) we will become more effective in serving the best interests of our fellow men and women. See 1 Peter 2:9. By rejecting God's word, Israel lost that ability, and it is to be feared that, in general, the so-called 'Christian church' has followed suit, particularly in the western world. It is so important to "Preach the word; be instant in season, out of season: reprove, rebuke, exhort with all longsuffering and doctrine" (2 Tim. 4:2). But it is equally important for us to "receive with meekness the engrafted ('implanted' or 'rooted') word, which is able to save your souls (that is, from backsliding)" (James 1:21). This means that we are to be "doers of the word, and not hearers only, deceiving your own selves" (James 1:22).

b) "I will also forget thy children", v.6
While some commentators favour the idea that these verses (vv.5-11) refer particularly to the priesthood, and therefore the "children" here are the priests' children, it does seem clear that in using the expressions "your mother" and "her children" (see, or example 2:2, 4) Hosea is referring to Israel nationally and the people individually. However, the context here could point to succeeding generations of Israelites, in which case the very solemn lesson emerges that the spiritual malaise of one generation endangers the next. It is a far cry from the instructions given to Timothy: "the things that thou hast heard of me among many witnesses, the same commit thou to faithful men, who shall be able to teach others also" (2 Tim. 2:2).

c) I will "change their glory into shame", v.7
"As they increased, so they sinned against me: therefore will I change their glory into shame". This is rather different from an earlier statement in the Old Testament, "my people have changed their glory for that which doth not profit" (Jer. 2:11). There, the expression "their glory" refers to the Lord

Himself: "They made a calf in Horeb, and worshipped the molten image. Thus they changed their glory into the similitude of an ox that eateth grass" (Psalm 106:19-20). But here, "their glory", refers either to her wealth and numbers, or, more likely, to her idolatrous worship. Compare, for example, Isaiah 1:29. See also Hosea 10:6. Some men "glory...in their shame". See Philippians 3:19.

d) "I will punish them for their ways", vv.8-11

"They eat up the sin of my people, and they set their heart on their iniquity. And there shall be, like people, like priest: and I will punish them for their ways, and reward them their doings" (vv.8-9). Compare Isaiah 24:1-3. The words "they eat up the sin of my people" imply that instead of condemning sin, they delighted in it. M. F. Unger suggests, however, that this could be understood quite literally: they (the priests) desired "an increase in the people's sins in order that they might enjoy a good supply of choice meat". M. F. Unger, usually a most reliable expositor, rests his suggestion on the word translated "sin" (*chattah*) which, he suggests, refers to the sin-offering, but it has to be said that Young's Concordance certainly gives no support to the suggestion. It is "sin", full-stop! Nevertheless the words, "They eat up the sin of my people" **could** refer to the priests and the people respectively. We have already noticed that the people and the prophet will alike suffer divine judgment (v.5). Now the people and the priest are associated in the same way. Judgment was inevitable. The words, "And there shall be, like people, like priest", indicate that the priests would not escape coming judgment because of their special position. In this connection we should remember that the priests here were not the sons of Aaron, but the successors of the idolatrous priests appointed by Jeroboam, the son of Nebat (1 Kings 12:31-32).

The sinful practices of priest and people would bring total disillusion and dissatisfaction: "for they shall eat, and not have enough: they shall commit whoredom, and shall not increase: because they have left off to take heed to the LORD" (v.10). Contrast the disappointments if we leave "off to take heed to the Lord" (v.10), with the blessings if we "follow on to know the Lord" (6:3). We should notice the connection between harlotry and drunkenness, and the result: "Whoredom and wine and new wine take away the heart" (v.11).

3) GOD'S CENSURE OF IDOLATRY, vv.12-14

We should notice that these verses refer *(a)* to religious evil (vv.12-13a), and *(b)* to moral evil (vv.13b-14).

a) Religious evil, vv.12-13a
"*My people* (note this) ask counsel at their stocks (wooden idols), and their staff (diviner's wand) declareth unto them: for the spirit of whoredom hath caused them to err, and they have gone a whoring from under their God. They sacrifice upon the tops of the mountains, and burn incense upon the hills, under oaks and poplars and elms, because the shadow thereof is good (compare 14:7)". The words, "the *spirit* of whoredom hath caused them to err" (v.12), strongly suggest demonic power. See 1 Cor. 10:20.

b) Moral evil, vv.13b-14
Religious evil and moral evil are inextricably linked. Compare Revelation 2:14 and Exodus 32:4-6. But there is an even graver lesson. Since the men were involved in the immorality associated with idolatry ("for themselves are separated with whores...", v.14), their own families would follow suit. "*Therefore* your daughters shall commit whoredom, and your spouses (JND, 'daughters in law': margin 'brides') shall commit adultery" (v.13). God would not single the women out for punishment (v.14), since the menfolk were no better. How necessary to be "an example of the believers, in word, in conversation, in charity, in spirit, in faith, in *purity*..." (1 Tim. 4:12). All this had a tragic result: "therefore the people that doth not understand shall fall" (v.14). They might have understood had they chosen to do so. But light refused becomes gross darkness.

4) GOD'S COUNSEL TO JUDAH, vv.15-19
Judah is warned against *(a)* hypocrisy (v.15), *(b)* against rebellion (v.16) and *(c)* against compromise (vv.17-19).

a) They were warned against hypocrisy, v.15
"Though thou, Israel, play the harlot, yet *let not Judah* offend; and come not ye unto Gilgal, neither go ye up to Beth-aven, nor swear, The LORD liveth". Compare Amos 4:4, and 5:5. The expression, "The LORD liveth", was pure cant: if they had been true to their convictions, they would have said 'Baal liveth'. But it gave an air of respectability to the place. Notice the change of name: *Beth-el,* the house of God, had become *Beth-aven*, the house of vanity. Gilgal and Bethel had been places of great blessing, and immense spiritual value. *Bethel* recalls outstanding events in the life of Jacob. See Genesis 28 & 35. *Gilgal* was the place of first encampment in the land, with all that was connected with entry to Canaan. See Joshua 4 & 5. Joshua's headquarters were there. *Gilgal* stood for the possession of

the land. But dreadful changes had taken place. See, for example, 1 Kings 12:33. The same story can be told of many assemblies.

b) They were warned against rebellion, v.16

"*For* Israel slideth back as a backsliding heifer" or "Israel is refractory as an untractable heifer" (JND). The RSV reads, "Like a stubborn heifer, Israel is stubborn". That is, like a heifer that "throws off her yoke, and turns backward instead of going forward" (M. F. Unger). The words which follow, "now the LORD will feed them as a lamb in a large place", could be construed as a question: 'Can the Lord now feed them like a lamb in a broad pasture?' But they are more likely an ironic statement predicting Israel's imminent scattering in exile by the Assyrians. The nation, once secure in its land, would now be in "a large place", that is, scattered worldwide, and vulnerable.

c) They were warned against compromise, vv.17-19

"Ephraim is joined to idols: let him alone" (v.17). This is the first of many references to "Ephraim". It was the most influential of the ten tribes. Samaria was located there. It therefore represents the whole nation. The force of "joined" is 'mated'. "Let him alone": that is, 'leave him to himself'. He is beyond correction. Don't get involved, lest you also become involved with idolatry. The New Testament is equally clear: "Be ye not unequally yoked together with unbelievers..." (2 Cor. 6:14-17).

The depth of their sinful involvement is spelt out clearly; the drunken orgy ends, harlotry begins (note, again the connection: see v.11), and the rulers love the shameful proceedings: "Their drink is sour: they have committed whoredom continually: the rulers with shame do love, Give ye" (v.18), or "their drink is sour; they give themselves up to whoredoms; her great men ('shields' margin) passionately love [their] shame" (JND). In the words of M. F. Unger, "their drunken carousing over, they turned to the sin of harlotry. Their rulers (literally, shields', who should have been their protectors) dearly love shame". But judgment, as irresistible as the wind, will sweep them away (v.19). Compare 8:7.

READ CHAPTER 5:1 - 6:3

"He hath withdrawn himself from them"

The previous chapter ends with the prediction of divine judgment on the nation: "Ephraim is joined to idols: let him alone. Their drink is sour: they have committed whoredom continually: her rulers with shame do love, Give ye (or 'her great men passionately love [their] shame', JND). The wind hath bound her up in her wings, and they shall be ashamed because of their sacrifices" (4:17-19). Hosea likens the Assyrian to the wind "binding up the apostate people in its wings and sweeping them away (M. F. Unger).

Our current passage (5:1 - 6:3) describes the *cause* of the coming judgment (5:1-7), together with its *certainty* (5:8-11), *course* (5:12-14), *containment* (5:15), and *conclusion* (6:1-3). Quite clearly, the passage extends to 6:3, and completes the section commencing with 4:1. The structure of the section (4:1 - 6:3) follows the general pattern in Chapters 1, 2 and 3, and ends, as they all end, with divine blessing after divine chastening.

1) THE CAUSE OF THE JUDGMENT, vv.1-7a
We should notice that these verses commence with the people involved (v.1a) and continue with the sin involved (vv.1b-7).

a) The people involved, v.1a
Since infidelity to God is rampant throughout the entire nation, all sections of society are addressed: "Hear ye this, O priests; and hearken, ye house of Israel; and give ye ear, O house of the king; for judgment is toward you". Judgment is pronounced on the religious leadership ("Hear ye this, O priests"), on the nation generally ("Hearken, ye house of Israel"), and on the political leadership ("Give ye ear, O house of the king"). The inclusion of the nation at large is explained later: they "**willingly** walked after the commandment (to worship idols)" (v.11). The order in which the categories are named is important. The priests are put first. They were particularly culpable. They stood, allegedly, between the people and God. The people they influenced

follow, not only the nation generally, but the royal house particularly, reminding us that elders are to be "ensamples to the flock" (1 Pet. 5:3).

Wrong spiritual leadership is censured here, and so are the people that follow it, both small and great. In New Testament days, the assemblies in Galatia were invaded by men who "would pervert the gospel of Christ" (Gal. 1:7), and while Paul censured these false teachers, he also reprimanded those **who followed them**: "I marvel that ye are so soon removed from him that called you into the grace of Christ unto another gospel" (Gal. 1:6). It should be said that the best way to resist error is to preach and practise the truth.

b) The sin involved, vv.1b-7
The charge is laid in v.1: "Ye have been a snare on Mizpah, and a net spread upon Tabor". This evidently refers to the leadership, particularly the "house of the king". The royal house is particularly censured in 7:1-7.

Hosea employs the figure of a trapper hunting game, hence the references to "snare" and "net". We are not told why he refers to Mizpah and Tabor particularly, although according to Jewish tradition, these were places where people *en route* to the temple in Jerusalem were apprehended and murdered. (M. F. Unger). It has been suggested that these two locations are named "as representatives of the places where the religious apostasy of the northern kingdom received official support" (Jack. R. Riggs). Mizpah was located in Gilead to the east of the River Jordan (Judges 10:17; 11:11, 29), while Tabor is the conical-shaped mountain which rises abruptly from the floor of the Valley of Esdraelon located to the west of the Jordan. Since locations from both sides of the River Jordan are cited, the significance may be to illustrate the corruption of the entire nation. As in the case of Gilgal and Bethel (4:15), both Mizpah and Tabor had sacred memories and associations. Mizpah was the place where Jacob and Laban made a covenant (Gen. 31:48-49), and Tabor was the place from which Barak launched his attack on Sisera (Judges 4:12-15).

There are still people waiting for us with snares and nets. Paul puts it like this: "Now I beseech you, brethren, mark them which cause divisions and offences contrary to the doctrine which ye have learned; and avoid them. For they that are such serve not our Lord Jesus Christ, but their own belly; and by good words and fair speeches deceive the hearts of the simple" (Rom. 16:17-18). Absalom is a classic example of someone with "good words and fair speeches". See 2 Samuel 15:1-6. We should now notice the following:

*i) **The depth of their sin**.* "And the revolters are profound to make slaughter" (v.2), or "And the revolters are gone deep in making slaughter (or 'in corruption', margin)" (RV). The word "revolters" (*setim*) means those that have 'turned aside', leading to the rendering, "And they have plunged themselves in the corruption of apostasy" (JND), with the marginal note, 'or, with sacrifices do they go far, or deeply, in revolt'. J. M. Flanigan quotes Jamieson Fausset and Brown here: "He does not say 'to sacrifice', for their so-called sacrifices were butcheries ('slaughter') rather than sacrifices; there was nothing sacred about them, being to idols instead of the holy God".

*ii) **The judgment of their sin**.* "And the revolters are profound to make slaughter, though I have been a rebuker of them all" (v.2) or "but I will be a chastiser of them all" (JND). Their sin would not go unpunished.

*iii) **The knowledge of their sin**.* "I know Ephraim, and Israel is not hid from me" (v.3). This may be an allusion to Mizpah and Tabor, bearing in mind that the former means 'a look out' or 'watch tower' (see Genesis 31:49-50), and the latter means 'height'. Nothing is hid from God. Compare Amos 5:12, "For I know your manifold transgressions and your mighty sins". Hosea mentions at least three things that God knew:

- There was no ***fidelity***, v.3. "Thou commitest whoredom, and Israel is defiled". The "first and great commandment" had been abrogated: "Thou shalt love the LORD thy God with all thine heart, and with all thy soul, and with all thy might" (Deut. 6: 5). Israel had "committed adultery with stones and with stocks" (Jer. 3:9). People still worship 'stocks': they are listed in the 'Financial Times' every day! We must not forget James 4:4, "Ye adulterers and adulteresses, know ye not that the friendship of the world is enmity with God? Whosoever will be the friend of the world is the enemy of God".

- There was no ***liberty***, v.4. "They will not frame their doings to turn unto their God" or "Their doings do not allow them to return unto their God" (JND). Their sins held them with a vice-like grip. Sin robs men of strength of will to obey God. We have already noticed the words, "the spirit of whoredoms" (see 4:12), and suggested that this is best explained by 1 Corinthians 10:20: "But I say, that the things which the Gentiles sacrifice, they sacrifice to devils (demons), and not to God". This is very much in agreement with the words here: "the spirit of whoredoms is in the midst of them, and they have not known the LORD". Many people today are dominated by the occult.

- There was no **humility**, v.5. "The pride of Israel doth testify to his face". See also 7:10. J. M. Flanigan defines this as "the arrogance and insolence with which they practised their idolatry". Peter reminds us that "God resisteth the proud, and giveth grace to the humble" (1 Pet. 5:5). Pride is displayed in self will, rather than submission to God. Judah is also condemned here. This is the first of five dual references in the chapter to Ephraim and Judah: see also vv.9-10, 12, 13, 14. Judah's position had evidently deteriorated. Compare 1:7, 4:15. Ezekiel 23 is an eloquent commentary on the situation.

iv) **The results of their sin**. These are outlined in vv.6-7: "They shall go with their flocks and with their herds to seek the LORD; but they shall not find him; he hath withdrawn himself from them. They have dealt treacherously against the LORD; for they have begotten strange children". Compare Amos 8:11-12.

- **They had lost the presence of God**. He had "withdrawn himself from them" (v.6). They followed in the footsteps of Samson who "wist not that the LORD had departed from him" (Judges 16:20). Through Isaiah, the Lord urged Israel to "Seek...the LORD, while he may be found" (Isaiah 55:6), but here it is too late: God would not be found. The statement "They shall go with their flocks and with their herds to seek the LORD" (compare Isaiah 1:11) echo the earlier words, "I will go and return to my first husband" (2:7). Jack R. Riggs suggests that this refers to "seeking the Lord in the time of national crisis which was to come". But there was no true repentance. See also 7:14-16, "And have not cried unto me with their heart, when they howled upon their beds...They return, but not to the most High: they are like a deceitful bow". Compare Isaiah 1:15, "And when ye spread forth your hands, I will hide mine eyes from you: yea, when ye make many prayers, I will not hear: your hands are full of blood"; and Proverbs 1:28-29, "Then shall they call upon me, but I will not answer; they shall seek me early, but they shall not find me: for that they hated knowledge, and did not choose the fear of the LORD". The Lord Jesus said of the religious fraternity in His day. "Ye hypocrites! Well did Esaias prophesy of you saying, This people draweth nigh unto me with their mouth, and honoureth me with their lips: but their heart is far from me" (Matt. 15:7-8). Could this be said of *us*?

- **They had totally altered the character of the nation**: "They have dealt treacherously (the word is used of marital infidelity: Jer. 3:20; Mal. 2:14) against the Lord: for they have begotten **strange** children". That is, children without the knowledge of God. It was certainly a case of "Lo-ammi" - not my people' - in every sense of the term. There is a strong allusion here to 1:2; "a wife of whoredoms, and children of whoredoms". As we have already noticed, this was far removed from the instructions in Deuteronomy 6:6-7, "And these words, which I command thee this day, shall be in thine heart: and thou shalt teach them diligently unto thy children". Compare Nehemiah 13:24.

The consequences of compromise with the religious world, in this case the idolatrous world, are frightening. Judgment was inevitable, and it would be swift: "Now shall a month devour them with their portions" or "Now shall the new moon devour them with their allotted possessions ('fields', RV.)" (JND). The most likely meaning is that it would take only one month to totally destroy the northern kingdom. This brings us to:

2) THE CERTAINTY OF THE JUDGMENT, vv.8-11
"Blow ye the cornet (*shophar*: a ram's horn) in Gibeah (Saul's home town, 1 Sam. 10:26), and the trumpet (*chatsotserah,* a metallic instrument) in Ramah: cry aloud at Beth-aven (Deborah "dwelt between Ramah and Bethel in mount Ephraim", Judges 4:5), after thee, O Benjamin. Ephraim shall be desolate in the day of rebuke: among the tribes of Israel have I made known that which shall surely be" (vv.8-9). We must note the absolute certainty of God's word: "that which **shall surely be**".

The significance of Gibeah, Ramah and Beth-aven (Bethel) lies in their close proximity to the border between Israel in the north and Judah in the south. The invader would penetrate to the southernmost part of Israel. Gibeah and Ramah were actually in Judah, whilst Bethel was in the north (1 Kings 12:29). Hence the alarm bells in Gibeah and Ramah, and the cry, "Behind thee, O Benjamin!" (JND). Well might Judah tremble: they were little better than their northern neighbours: "The princes of Judah were like them that remove the bound: therefore I will pour out my wrath upon them like water" (v.10). There was sin on both sides of the border. In the south, the "princes of Judah were like them that remove the bound (or 'landmark', the line between the Lord and the false gods of Canaan)", and in the north, "Ephraim is oppressed and broken in judgment, because he **willingly** ('was content', RV) walked after the commandment (of Jeroboam to worship idols, 1 Kings 12:25-33)" (v.11). They became idolaters, with everything associated with it, without protest.

3) THE COURSE OF THE JUDGMENT, vv.12-14
Divine judgment was executed on both houses in two ways: *(a)* by internal decay (vv.12-13); *(b)* by external destruction (v.14).

a) By internal decay, vv.12-13
"Therefore will I be unto Ephraim as *a moth*, and to the house of Judah *as rottenness* ('like dry rot', Amplified Version)". That is, it was gradual and unseen: slow and silent. Faced with growing weakness, both houses ignored the root cause of their malaise, and turned to the Assyrian for help. "When Ephraim saw his sickness, and Judah saw his wound, then *went* Ephraim to the Assyrian, and *sent* to king Jareb: yet could he not heal you, nor cure you of your wound". "King Jareb" is an adjectival expression, meaning, 'a contentious king' (JND footnote). George Adam Smith calls him, 'King Pick-Quarrel!'. Judah went this way in the reign of Ahaz: see 2 Kings 16:7. Israel did the same in the reigns of Menahem and Hoshea: see 2 Kings 15:19-20; 17:3. Hosea later refers to this again: "Ephraim also is like a silly dove without heart: they call to Egypt, they go to Assyria" (7:11), and spells out the consequences: "They shall not dwell in the LORD'S land; but Ephraim shall return to Egypt, and they shall eat unclean things in Assyria" (9:3). Ezra's policy was refreshingly different: "Then I proclaimed a fast there...that we might afflict ourselves before our God to seek *of him* a right way for us.... For I was ashamed to require of the king a band of soldiers and horsemen to help us against the enemy in the way; because we had spoken unto the king, saying, The hand of our God is upon all them for good that seek him..." It worked - of course it worked! "So we fasted and besought our God for this: and he was intreated of us" (Ezra 8:21-23). Psalm 118:8-9 was practised!

b) By external destruction, v.14
Recourse to the Assyrians would bring divine fury: "For I will be unto Ephraim as a *lion (shachal,* a roaring lion), and as a *young lion* (*kephir*, a whelp) to the house of Judah". Judgment would be sudden and visible. There would be no escape then: "*I, even I*, will tear and go away; *I will* take away, and none shall rescue him". Both Assyrians and Babylonians were but instruments in God's hand.

4) THE CONTAINMENT OF THE JUDGMENT, 5:15
The nation will not be permanently under judgment. God will not eliminate His people. See Jeremiah 30:11. The object of discipline is restoration: "I will go and return to my place, till they acknowledge their offence, and seek my face: in their affliction they will seek me early" (5:15).

The words "I will go and return to my place" set out the present position. God no longer pleads with His people: He ceases to act as a husband toward them, which is precisely the position described in Chapter 3. But the purpose of divine discipline will be achieved. This follows: God withdraws His care for Israel, but only "*Till* they acknowledge their offence, and seek my face; in their affliction they *will* seek me early". Compare 3:5: "**Afterward** shall the children of Israel return, and seek the LORD their God, and David their king; and shall fear the LORD and his goodness in the latter days", or, "turn with fear toward Jehovah and toward his goodness, at the end of the days" (JND). This follows:

5) THE CONCLUSION OF THE JUDGMENT, 6:1-3
In these verses we have a tender appeal: "Come, and let us return unto the LORD". It is made by Hosea, and was, undoubtedly, a *boda fide* appeal to the nation at the time. Compare Acts 3:19-20. The sad fact remains that it was disregarded then, but it clearly anticipates the future when it will not be disregarded.

The words, "in their affliction they will seek me early" (5:15), refer to the ultimate affliction of the nation, described as "the time of Jacob's trouble" (Jer. 30:7). God will say, "Why criest thou for thine affliction? Thy sorrow is incurable for the multitude of thine iniquity: because thy sins were increased, I have done these things unto thee". But He will hear their cry: "I will restore health unto thee, and I will heal thee of thy wounds, saith the LORD" (Jer. 30:15-17). In this connection, we must notice: *(a)* the recognition of divine chastening (6:1); *(b)* the restoration of national life (6:2); *(c)* the return of the Lord (6:3).

a) The recognition of divine chastening, 6:1
Previously, Israel had looked elsewhere: but the Assyrians could not "*heal... nor cure*" (5:13). At the end-time they will say, "Come, and let us return unto the LORD (not "king Jareb"): for *he* hath torn, and *he* will *heal us*; *he* hath smitten, and *he will bind us up*". "Instead of arguing with God, or resenting His correction, Hosea leads Israel in humble prayer. This is a prayer that trusts the love of God, and sees His loving hand even in correction. Often rebellious children will complain that their parents do not love them. Of course, the parents do love the child, but in their rebellion and lack of submission they cannot receive or respond to that love. Hosea prays with a different heart. All this leads *us* to ask ourselves if we recognise divine chastening in *our* own lives: 'if ye endure chastening, God dealeth with you as sons' (Heb. 12:7)" (supplied by Justin Waldron).

b) The restoration of national life, 6:2

"After two days will he **revive us**: in the third day he will **raise us up**, and we **shall live** in his sight". This is expressed in terms of resurrection: "he will raise us up". The Lord Jesus "rose again the third day according to the scriptures" (1 Cor. 15:4). The reference to "two days" and to "the third day" is significant. Peter refers to Psalm 90:4 in saying that "one day is with the Lord as a thousand years, and a thousand years as one day" (2 Pet. 3:8). Whilst, undoubtedly, Psalm 90 emphasises the timelessness of God, it does appear that the passage cited by Peter has additional significance, and applies to the words of Hosea here. Israel, the ten tribes, went into captivity in 721 BC: Judah followed in 606 BC, and a remnant returned seventy years later. National life was finally destroyed by the Romans, and for approaching two thousand years - two prophetic days, the "many days" of Hosea 3:4 - the "whole house of Israel" has been 'dry bones' (Ezekiel 37:1-2). But the third prophetic day will come, and the nation will "live in his sight". The millennial day will dawn, and it will be said, "This is **the day** which the LORD hath made; we will rejoice and be glad in it" (Psalm 118:24).

c) The return of the Lord, 6:3

"Then shall we know, *if* (note the italics here) we follow on to know the LORD: his going forth is prepared as the morning; and he shall come unto us as the rain, as the latter and former rain unto the earth", or, "And we shall know - we shall follow on to know Jehovah; his going forth is assured as the morning dawn; and he will come unto us as the rain, as the latter rain that watereth the earth" (JND). The "latter rain" fell in the autumn and prepared the ground for seed: the "former rain" fell in the spring, and prepared the crops for harvest. How important it is to "follow on to know the LORD". See John 10:4, 27.

This verse is beautifully amplified in Malachi 4:2, "But unto you that fear my name shall the Sun of righteousness arise with healing in his wings", and Psalm 72:6, "He shall come down like rain upon the mown grass: as showers that water the earth". His coming is certain: "his going forth **is assured** as the morning dawn; and he **will come** unto us as the rain, as the latter rain that watereth the earth" (JND). The nation will then "know the LORD". See Jeremiah 31:34: "And they shall teach no more every man his neighbour, and every man his brother, saying, Know the LORD: for they shall all know me, from the least of them unto the greatest of them, saith the LORD".

It is worth pointing out that the words, "if we follow on to know the LORD", have been rendered "Let us pursue the knowledge of the LORD" (NKJV). Justin Waldron points out that this "must be more than superficial: it must be a pursuit...Our ambition, with Paul, should be 'that I might know him' (Phil. 3:10). Let us remember in this pursuit that 'he is a rewarder of them that diligently seek him' (Heb. 11:6)".

READ CHAPTER 6:4-11

"Your goodness is as a morning cloud"

While the previous section of the prophecy (5:1 - 6:3) emphasises the certainty of divine judgment upon Israel ("among the tribes of Israel have I made known that which shall surely be", 5:9), it also anticipates divine blessing following national repentance: "After two days will he revive us: in the third day he will raise us up, and we shall live in his sight. Then shall we know, if (or when) we follow on to know the LORD: his going forth is prepared as the morning; and he shall come unto us as the rain, as the latter and former rain unto the earth" (6:2-3), or, "his going forth *is assured* as the morning dawn; and he *will come* unto us as the rain, as the latter rain that watereth the earth" (JND). There is no doubt about His coming. The voices of the "scoffers" will be silenced (2 Pet. 3:3-4).

We noted that these beautiful pictures of the Lord's return to bless His earthly people are amplified elsewhere in the Old Testament:

- *"his going forth is prepared as the morning"* reminds us that "the Sun of righteousness" will "arise with healing in his wings" (Mal. 4:2). This in turn reminds us that the sun is described as "a bridegroom coming out of his chamber, and rejoiceth as a strong man to run a race. His *going forth* is from the end of the heaven, and his circuit unto the ends of it" (Psalm 19:4-6). God's purposes are like sunrise: they are certain.

- *"he shall come unto us as the rain, as the latter and former rain unto the earth"* reminds us that "He shall come down like rain upon the mown grass: as showers that water the earth" (Psalm 72:6). If the Lord had promised to give His people "the rain of your land in his due season, the first rain and the latter rain", always provided that they remained faithful to Him (Deut. 11:14-17), then there can be no doubt about His blessing in this way when they "follow on to know the Lord" in the coming millennial kingdom.

The section of the prophecy now before us commences on an entirely different note. The contrast could hardly be greater: "your goodness is as a morning cloud, and as the early dew it goeth away" (v.4). The passage may be divided as follows: *(1)* unfulfilled promise (v.4); *(2)* uncompromising preaching (vv.5-6); *(3)* unrepentant people (vv.7-11). Notice, therefore, first of all,

1) UNFULFILLED PROMISE, v.4

Both northern and southern kingdoms are addressed with evident pathos: "O Ephraim, what shall I do unto thee? O Judah, what shall I do unto thee?" This is best understood with reference to the Lord's lament over His vineyard, "What could have been done more to my vineyard, that I have not done in it?" (Isaiah 5:4). He had done everything possible to secure the blessing of His people, but while His "going forth is prepared as the *morning*", their "goodness is as the *morning cloud*", and while His coming is described as "the rain, as *the latter and former rain* unto the earth", their goodness is described as "the *early dew*". It is all summed up in the words, "*it goeth away*". After early promise, their goodness proved impermanent and transitory. It all started so well: "I remember thee, the kindness of thy youth, the love of thine espousals, when thou wentest after me in the wilderness, in a land that was not sown" but, alas, early promise soon disappeared: "What iniquity have your fathers found in me, that they are gone so far from me, and have walked after vanity, and are become vain?" (Jer. 2:2-5). In the words of Jack R. Riggs, "Any loyalty which might be observed in Israel was short-lived. It vanished like the morning cloud and the dew. The morning cloud is deceptive since it is a dense mass of vapour which the westerly winds bring from the Mediterranean, but which dissipates when the sun appears. Similarly the dew flees before the warmth of the sun's rays".

The word "goodness" (*chesed*) is translated "lovingkindness" in 2:19, and "mercy" in the current chapter (see v.6). It is used by Jeremiah in describing, as here, the transitory nature of Israel's devotion to God: "I remember thee, the *kindness* of thy youth, the love of thine espousals". See above. But that first love had vanished "as a morning cloud, and as the early dew". They had not continued to reciprocate God's love for them. To the contrary, they had "transgressed the covenant" and "dealt treacherously" (v.7), or, to use earlier language, "the land hath committed great whoredom, departing from the LORD" (1:2).

Centuries later, Paul had to say, "Ye did run well; who did hinder you that ye should not obey the truth?" (Gal. 5:7), and the Lord Jesus had to say to the church at Ephesus, "I have somewhat against thee, because thou hast left thy **first love**" (Rev. 2:4). Can **we** still sing:

> Lord Jesus, I love Thee, I know Thou art mine,
> My rock and my fortress, my Surety divine;
> My gracious Redeemer, my song shall be now –
> 'Tis Thou who art worthy, LORD JESUS, 'tis Thou!

But God had not allowed the matter to rest. He had endeavoured to bring them to repentance. We must therefore notice next:

2) UNCOMPROMISING PREACHING, vv.5-6

"Therefore have I hewed them by the prophets; I have slain them by the words of my mouth: and thy judgments are as the light that goeth forth. For I desired mercy (*chesed*, as noted); and the knowledge of God more than burnt-offerings". We should notice here: *(a)* the strength of the preaching (v.5); *(b)* the clarity of the preaching (v.5); *(c)* the purpose of the preaching (v.6).

a) The strength of the preaching, v.5

God did not employ platitudes. The preaching was incisive, and intended to touch the conscience. "Therefore have I hewed them by the prophets; I have slain them by the words of my mouth". He had faithfully exposed their sin. Alfred Barnes is helpful here: "Since they despised God's gentler warnings and measures, He used severer means. He 'hewed them'... as men hew stones out of the quarry, and with hard blows and sharp instruments overcome the hardness of the stone which they have to work". According to Gesenius, the word "hewed" (*chatseb*) means 'to cut, to hew out, especially stones'. Although the picture is slightly different, this reminds us that the Lord's word is "like a hammer that breaketh the rock in pieces" (Jer. 23:29). As C. L. Feinberg observes, "His message does not lull men in their sins: it crushes the heart to bring it to repentance. The true word convicts and converts, it neither amuses nor entertains".

Moreover, it has the effect of 'slaying' men and women by setting before them the unspeakable consequences of persisting in rebellion against God. This caused Jeremiah to cry, "Why will ye die, thou and thy people, by the sword, by the famine, and by the pestilence" (Jer. 27:13). Ezekiel pleaded with God's people in the same way (Ezek. 18:31; 33:11). At the return of the Lord to earth, men will be **slain** with the sword of him that sat upon the horse, which sword *proceeded out his* mouth" (Rev. 19:21). The Lord Jesus said, "He that believeth not is condemned already, because he hath not believed in the name of the only begotten Son of God" (John 3:18). The Gospel is "the savour of death unto death" to those who are perishing (2 Cor. 2:15-16).

This reminds us that while it is our business to declare the love of God (John 3: 16), it is also our business to follow Paul in reasoning with men and women "of righteousness, temperance, and judgment to come" (Acts 24: 25).

b) The clarity of the preaching, v.5
"Thy judgments are as the light that goeth forth". While this could refer to coming judgment on the nation ('my judgment goeth forth as the light', JND), it does seem that Hosea is referring here to the way in which the prophets had declared God's word. They had done so unmistakably and without ambiguity. It also suggests that they had declared the equity and purity of His judgments. Compare Psalm 37:5-6, where the words "he shall bring forth thy righteousness as the night, and the judgment as the noonday" evidently refer to the clarity of divine approval.

The believers at Thessalonica followed suit: "From you **sounded out** the word of the Lord" (1 Thess. 1:8). The words, 'sounded out', mean 'to sound forth as a trumpet or thunder' (W. E. Vine). The English word 'echo' is derived from the Greek word here *(execheo)*. W. E. Vine observes that the expression 'commonly refers to the sounding of a herald's trumpet.' A similar word *(echos)* occurs in Acts 2:2 ("And suddenly there came a **sound** from heaven"), and Hebrews 12:19 ("the **sound** of a trumpet").

This emphasises the need for clarity and simplicity. Ezra and the Levites "read in the book, in the law of God, distinctly, and gave the sense, and caused them to understand the reading" (Neh. 8:8). Gospel preachers should never forget that their business is to make people understand their need to be saved, and how they can be saved. They must make it clear. A trumpet emits a clear note! It is important to speak up! Preachers should "put a sufficient gap between their upper and lower dentures!" (E. W. Rogers).

c) The purpose of the preaching, v.6
The fact that God's "judgments are as the light that goeth forth" is now explained. He had made his requirements clearly known: "For I desired mercy, and not sacrifice; and the knowledge of God more than burnt offerings". This requirement is frequently stated in the Old Testament. See,

for example, Psalm 51:16-17; Isaiah 1:11-17; Jeremiah 7:4-6. The preaching was intended to promote practical godliness. God's people were 'going through the motions' of obedience to His word by offering sacrifices and burnt offerings, but it was a sham. He looked for "mercy" (*chesed*), that is, for lovingkindness and goodness amongst His people. The "knowledge of God" is nicely defined in the accolade bestowed upon Josiah: "He judged the cause of the poor and needy; then it was well with him: was not this to **know me**? saith the Lord" (Jer. 22:15-16).

Hosea 6:6 is twice cited by the Lord Jesus in this way: "But when Jesus heard that ('Why eateth your Master with publicans and sinners?'), he said unto them, They that be whole need not a physician, but they that are sick. But go ye and learn what that meaneth, **I will have mercy, and not sacrifice**: for I am not come to call the righteous (with all their religious observances), but sinners to repentance" (Matt. 9:12-13); "But if ye had known what this meaneth, **I will have mercy, and not sacrifice**, ye would not have condemned the guiltless" (Matt. 12:7). On both occasions, the Pharisees were reproved: they insisted on ceremonial niceties, and utterly failed to practise "the weightier matters of the law, judgment, mercy, and faith" (Matt. 23:23). "Sacrifice" and "burnt offerings" are only meaningful when they express true devotion. Else they are meaningless. Worse than that, they are offensive to God. We too must beware. There is nothing worse than people, and assemblies, who glory in their orthodox position, but apparently forget the need to "be...kind one to another, tenderhearted, forgiving one another, even as God for Christ's sake hath forgiven you" (Eph. 4:32). Empty ritual is no substitute for true piety. Further passages on this subject are found in 1 Samuel 15:22, Amos 5:21-24, and Micah 6:6-8.

But, alas, the preaching was to no avail, and this, sadly, is made clear in the final paragraph:

3) UNREPENTANT PEOPLE, vv.7-11
"But they like men have transgressed the covenant: there have they dealt treacherously against me" (v.7), or, "But they like Adam have transgressed the covenant" (RV/JND). Some argue for Adam as a place (see Joshua 3:16) but this requires an emendation to the text, altering 'like Adam' to 'at Adam'. In any case, it seems highly unlikely that Hosea would make his point by referring to a location of which nothing is known!

However, while the word "men" (AV) is certainly *adam* in the Hebrew text, it seems unlikely that this refers to the first man Adam. The word *adam* occurs in the Old Testament, after a 'rough and ready' count, on about 450 occasions. It usually means 'man' in the sense of 'a man' or 'mankind'. For the latter see, for example Psalm 8:4: "what is man (*enosh*), that thou art mindful of him? and the son of man (*adam*), that thou visitest him?"; Haggai 1:11, "upon men (*adam*), and upon cattle". Bearing this in mind, the words, "But they like men have transgressed the covenant", simply mean that God's people, like men in general, have broken God's law. "There (referring to the land or, possibly, to Gilead, v.8) have they dealt treacherously against me". We have already noted (see 5:7) that the word "treacherously" is used of marital infidelity: "Surely as a wife treacherously departeth from her husband, so have ye dealt treacherously with me, O house of Israel, saith the LORD" (Jer. 3: 20); "the LORD hath been witness between thee and the wife of thy youth, against whom thou hast dealt treacherously" (Mal. 2:14).

When presented with the covenant at Sinai, the people "answered together, and said, All that the LORD hath spoken we will do" (Ex. 19:5-8). The first two clauses of the covenant said, "Thou shalt have no other gods before me. Thou shalt not make unto thee any graven image....for I the LORD thy God am a jealous God" (Exodus 20:3-5). He is jealous of the affections of His people. Hosea Chapters 1-3 present this covenant in terms of the marriage relationship, and display Israel's failure to remain faithful to God. Like all men, they had failed. Paul uses the same figure in saying, "I am jealous over you with a godly jealousy: for I have espoused you to one husband, that I may present you as a chaste virgin to Christ. But I fear, lest by any means, as the serpent beguiled Eve through his subtilty, so your minds should be corrupted from the simplicity ('wholeheartedness, singleness of devotion, freedom of duplicity') that is in (or 'towards') Christ" (2 Cor. 11:2-3).

As an aside, it is interesting to listen to Job's reference to Adam (in this case, it is to our forefather): "If I covered my transgressions as Adam, by hiding mine iniquity in my bosom....Let thistles grow instead of wheat, and cockle instead of barley" (Job 31:33, 40).

Failure in their covenant relationship with God brought fearful results both locally (vv.8-9), and nationally vv.10-11).

a) Locally, vv.8-9
"Gilead is a city of them that work iniquity, and is polluted with blood. And as troops of robbers wait for a man, so the company of priests murder in the way

by consent (Hebrew '*shekem*', meaning shoulder: see also Zephaniah 3:9): for they commit lewdness". Quite possibly, two locations are named here:

- **Gilead, v.8.** Gilead, as such, was the mountainous region east of Jordan. It was inhabited by Reuben, Gad and the half tribe of Manasseh. While some commentators argue that Hosea refers here to the entire region, and that the word "city" expresses "the thought that the whole land was full of evil-doers as a city is of men" (Delitzsch), it could well refer to the city of Ramoth-Gilead. This was one of the cities of refuge (Joshua 20:8) and if this is the place to which Hosea refers then it certainly did not live up to its purpose. Far from it. The words "polluted with blood" or "tracked with blood" (JND) with a marginal note, 'full of bloodmarks', made it anything but a city of refuge.

- **Shechem, v.9.** The words "by consent" could certainly mean what they say: that the priests were acting together, as one 'shoulder', but since, as noted above, the word "consent" translates *shekem*, it is distinctly possible that the passage refers to Shechem, another 'city of refuge' (Joshua 20:7). Hence the translation: "And as troops of robbers lie in wait for a man, so the company of priests murder in the way of Shechem" (JND), or "toward Shechem (RV). This has the merit of placing two cities of refuge together, one to the east of Jordan (Ramoth Gilead) and the other (Shechem) to the west. Shechem, now known as Nablus, "lay in the narrow valley between the Mounts Ebal and Gerizim so that an ambush was relatively easy. Since Shechem was on the way to Jerusalem it is thought by many expositors that these priests lay in wait for those who were refusing the idolatrous worship of the golden calves at Dan and Bethel, and were making their journey to Jerusalem to worship there, perhaps at one of the feasts" (J. M. Flanigan). The priests were, of course, the successors of the apostate priests commissioned by Jeroboam (1 Kings 12:31). It has been pointed out (T. Miller) that the places to which men could run to avoid bloodshed were the very places where people were waiting to shed blood.

The crimes of robbery and murder amongst God's people have their counterpart in 'biting' and 'devouring': "For all the law is fulfilled in one word, even in this; Thou shalt love thy neighbour as thyself. But if ye bite and devour one another, take heed that ye be not consumed one of another" (Gal. 5:15). As in the case of Mizpah and Tabor (5:1), God knew precisely what was happening in Gilead and at Shechem, reminding us that the Lord Jesus is perfectly aware of the conduct of His people, for good or evil, in each local assembly: "I know thy works" (Rev. 2:2, 9, 13, 19; 3:1, 8, 15).

We should notice that the crime of "lewdness" (*zimmah*) is added: "they commit lewdness ('yea, they commit lewdness')", and it appears that this "most probably refers to an unnatural crime, as in Leviticus 18:17; 19:29" (Delitzsch). The word *zimmah* (translated "wickedness") is used in these passages. See also Leviticus 20:14.

b) Nationally, vv.10-11

It could be said that "a little leaven (locally, vv.8-9) leaveneth the whole lump (nationally, vv.10-11)" (1 Cor. 5:6). The overall situation is summed up in v.10: "I have seen an horrible (*shaaruri,* meaning 'vile') thing in the house of Israel: there is the whoredom of Ephraim, Israel is defiled" (v.10). We should notice the words, "*I have seen*". Whether locally or nationally, "all things are naked and opened unto the eyes of him with whom we have to do" (Heb. 4:13). As Jack R. Riggs points out, Hosea "again uses the figure of adultery common to the book. The northern kingdom had given itself over to spiritual unfaithfulness. All that is painful, detestable and repulsive about physical adultery, is painful, detestable and repulsive about spiritual infidelity".

In context, the final verse of the chapter (v.11) must mean that Judah had not escaped infection: "Also, O Judah, he hath set a harvest for thee" (v.11). This seems plain enough. The law of sowing and reaping is everywhere in Scripture. See Galatians 6:7-8. We could say that Judah had "run with them (Israel) to the same sink of corruption" (1 Pet. 4:4, JND), and proved the accuracy of 1 Corinthians 15:33, that "evil company doth corrupt good manners" (RV). Judah had certainly followed Israel in this way. See Hosea 5:5, 8-14.

However, at first glance, the continuation of the verse appears to take us in a different direction: "Also, O Judah, he hath set a harvest for thee, **when I returned the captivity of my people**" or "Also, for thee, Judah, is a harvest appointed, **when I shall turn again the captivity of my people**" (JND). This poses an apparent problem. Having spoken of a "harvest" for Judah, which, in context suggests that they would reap the results of their sinful ways, it now seems, instead, that blessing (a harvest of blessing) lies ahead. In the long term it certainly *does* lie ahead, but that does not appear to fit the present passage.

The answer to the problem lies in the meaning of the words, "when I shall turn again the captivity of my people" (JND). This does not necessarily mean restoration from captivity in a foreign country, but rather the reversal of misfortune or disaster. See, for example, Job 42:10: "And the LORD *turned again the captivity of Job*". See also Psalm 126:1, "When the LORD *turned again the captivity of Zion*, we were like them that dream". As C. H. Spurgeon observes, "Indeed, the passage is not applicable to captives in Babylon, for it is Zion itself which is in captivity, and not a part of her citizens".

After the northern kingdom (Israel) had been conquered by Assyria, and its population deported (2 Kings 17:6), the Assyrians then invaded Judah (2 Kings 18:13; 2 Chron. 32:1), but were stopped in their tracks when, in answer to Hezekiah and Isaiah's prayers (2 Chron. 32:20), 185,000 Assyrian soldiers were slain in one night (2 Kings 19:35). It was then that "the LORD turned again the captivity of Zion" (Psalm 126:1) and fulfilled the prediction here, "I shall turn again the captivity of my people" (JND). We have already noticed that Hosea 1:7 refers to the repulse of the Assyrian invader in this way.

But what happened next? Hezekiah, above all people, gave envoys from Babylon a conducted tour of his wealth, only to be told that it would all be "carried to Babylon" (Isaiah 39:1-8). And it happened. The sinfulness of Hezekiah's successors, apart from Josiah, brought the Babylonian armies to Judah and Jerusalem, and God's people reaped a bitter harvest. The words, "Also, O Judah, he hath set a harvest for thee" (v.11) mean exactly what they say in the usual biblical sense of "a harvest".

There are other explanations, including an alteration in the chapter division by which part of the verse (v.11) belongs to chapter 6 and part to chapter 7. Those who espouse this explanation read from 6:11 to 7:1 as follows: "When I would return the fortunes of my people, when I would heal Israel, the corruption of Ephraim is revealed, and the wicked deeds of Samaria..." (RSV). The NEB follows suit. However, one problem with both versions is their tendency to confound translation with explanation. But we must leave it there.

READ CHAPTER 7:1-16

"They consider not...that I remember"

Hosea has given us a fairly comprehensive tour of Israel's country districts: Gilgal and Bethaven (4:15), Mizpah and Tabor (5:1), Gilead and Shechem (6:8-9). In fact, we have travelled from south to north, and then from east to west. It has been said that Hosea 6:7-10 "is a sort of miniature guidebook to the geography of sin in Israel: going from one place to another, it catalogues the famous crimes of various localities as an indictment of the whole nation" (J. L. Mays).

We come now to the capital city, to the heart of the nation, and then to the king himself. The chapter commences by embracing the nation at large, then Ephraim, most prominent of the ten tribes, and finally, Samaria, the royal city. Sin lies at the heart of the nation: "When I would have healed *Israel*, then the iniquity of *Ephraim* was discovered, and the wickedness of *Samaria...*" (v.1).

The chapter may be divided as follows: *(1)* the discernment of evil (vv.1-2); *(2)* the depravity at court (vv.3-7); *(3)* the decline in the nation (vv.8-16).

1) THE DISCERNMENT OF EVIL, vv.1-2
These introductory verses centre on *(a)* their sinful actions (v.1); *(b)* God's complete awareness (v.2).

a) Their sinful actions, v.1
"When I would have healed Israel, then the iniquity of Ephraim was discovered, and the wickedness of Samaria: for they commit falsehood; and the thief cometh in, and a troop of robbers spoileth without". While the Lord always has in mind the restoration of His people, their persistent sin precludes divine blessing. In this case, society was permeated by deception and lies. Moreover, people were insecure both at home and in the streets. This has a familiar ring. Society has not changed since Hosea's day. While,

as F. A. Tatford points out, "the words were doubtless intended to be taken literally, there may have been a typical significance in them as well. These people had no protection against evil; having dispensed with moral standards themselves, they were easily influenced by any attack upon the mind and heart. Any thief could rob them of faith and honesty and integrity, as well as of material possessions".

Believers are to behave in exactly the opposite way to Israel here: "Wherefore putting away lying, speak every man truth with his neighbour... Let him that stole steal no more: but rather let him labour, working with his hands the thing which is good, that he may have to give to him that needeth" (Eph. 4:25-28). How glad we are that in the millennial age God's earthly people will enjoy complete freedom from insecurity: "Jerusalem shall be called a city of truth; and the mountain of the LORD of hosts the holy mountain... There shall yet old men and old women dwell in the streets of Jerusalem, and every man with his staff in his hand for very age. And the streets of the city shall be full of boys and girls playing in the streets thereof" (Zech. 8:3-5). No longer will God's people "commit falsehood", and no longer will "robbers" have a free hand. Mugging and child abduction will then be a thing of the past.

b) God's complete awareness, v.2
"And they consider not in their hearts that I remember all their wickedness: now their own doings have beset them about; they are before my face". God has always been thoroughly aware of human wickedness: "And God saw that the wickedness of man was great in the earth, and that every imagination of the thoughts of his heart was only evil continually" (Gen. 6:5). Men and women fail to remember that "The eyes of the LORD are in every place, beholding the evil and the good" (Prov. 15:3) and that "the eyes of the LORD run to and fro throughout the whole earth" (2 Chron. 16:9). As Jack R. Riggs observes, Israel's wicked ways "were very apparent to the Lord, and He stores up knowledge (Psalms 14:2-4; 50:21; 90:8; Hos. 8:13)". He saw their sins all around them "like so many witnesses to testify against them" (M. F. Unger)

This should be a salutary lesson to us all. In New Testament language: "Neither is there any creature that is not manifest in his sight: but all things are naked and opened unto the eyes of him with whom we have to do" (Heb. 4:13). We should notice the references to the heart in the chapter: "they consider not in their hearts" (v.2); "they have made ready their heart" (v.6); "they have not cried unto me with their heart" (v.14). Compare Ezekiel 36:26. See also Hebrews 8:10; 10:16; 10:22.

Corrupt society did not have far to look for its lead; just as far as the palace. King and court were utterly debased. This brings us to:

2) THE DEPRAVITY AT COURT, vv.3-7
There are three references to king and court in this passage, which can be summarised as follows: *(a)* immorality at court (vv.3-4); *(b)* intoxication at court (v.5); *(c)* intrigue at court (vv.6-7). The figure of a baker's oven occurs three times in these verses (vv.4, 6, 7).

a) Immorality at court, vv.3-4
"They make the king glad with their wickedness, and the princes with their lies" (v.3). Centuries later, Paul painted a similar picture. See Romans 1:24-32. Having described human wickedness, with particular reference to sodomy (vv.24-27), he concludes: "who knowing the judgment of God, that they which commit such things are worthy of death, not only do the same, but have pleasure in them that do them" (v.32). Current ecclesiastical and political legislators are following suit. The same delight in evil is evidently found today in the Palace of Lambeth and in the Palace of Westminster.

Hosea charts the progress and process of evil, and we now come to the first of the three references to the baker's oven. "They are all adulterers, as an oven heated by the baker, who ceaseth from raising after he hath kneaded the dough, until it be leavened" (v.4). This describes an oven whose fire is banked up, and needs no immediate attention after fermentation begins. The process proceeds in gentle heat. Moral leaven works in the same way: evil is quietly imagined and anticipated. The picture gallery of the mind must be clean, else we will become corrupted by what Derek Kidner aptly calls "self-propagating passion".

We should notice the words, "until it be leavened". The Lord Jesus used similar language in the parable of the leaven: "The kingdom of heaven is like unto leaven, which a woman took, and hid in three measures of meal, till the whole was leavened" (Matt. 13:33). Paul refers to moral and doctrinal leaven. See 1 Corinthians 5:6-8 and Galatians 5:9 respectively. Leaven does its work silently and invisibly, but its effectiveness is soon apparent. The leaven of immorality began its work when David failed to avert his eyes during a stroll on the roof of his house after an afternoon siesta, and we must carefully note the three stages that led to disaster in his life: he "saw"; he "enquired"; he "took her" (2 Sam. 11:2-4). The debauchery in the court at Samaria was accompanied by drunkenness, which brings us to:

b) Intoxication at court, v.5
"In the day of our king the princes have made him sick with bottles of wine; he stretched out his hand with scorners", or, "In the day of our king, the princes made themselves sick with the heat of wine: he stretched out his hand to scorners" (JND). It takes little imagination to visualise the scene. It is generally thought that "the day of our king" refers either to his birthday or to the anniversary of his enthronement. "The *day*" is spent in drunkenness and ribaldry, and as we shall see, worse follows at *night* (vv.6-7). In fact, the intoxication of the princes (JND) was all part of a plan to get rid of the king. The princes, or court officials, were so drunk that they left "the sovereign entirely defenceless" (F. A. Tatford).

Strong drink impairs a person's judgment and leaves them vulnerable. Solomon had some scathing things to say about the subject. For example, "Wine is a mocker, strong drink is raging: and whosoever is deceived thereby is not wise" (Prov. 20:1). He deals with the subject more extensively as follows: "Who hath woe? who hath sorrow? who hath contentions? who hath babbling? who hath wounds without cause? who hath redness of eyes? They that tarry long at the wine; they that go to seek mixed wine. Look not thou upon the wine when it is red, when it giveth his colour in the cup, when it moveth itself aright. At the last, it biteth like a serpent, and stingeth like an adder. Thine eyes shall behold strange women, and thine heart shall utter perverse things. Yea, thou shalt be as he that lieth down in the midst of the sea, or as he that lieth upon the top of a mast. They have stricken me, shalt thou say, and I was not sick; they have beaten me, and I felt it not: when shall I awake? I will seek it yet again" (Prov. 23:29-35). This is a very accurate description of someone 'under the affluence of incohol'. (No, that wasn't a typing error). This leads to:

c) Intrigue at court, vv.6-7
Plying the princes with drink (v.5) was part of a plot to assassinate the king. If the day was spent "at the wine", then the night was given to plotting and intrigue. Now we have the second reference to the baker's oven: "For they have made ready their heart like an oven, whiles they lie in wait: their baker sleepeth all the night; in the morning it burneth as a flaming fire" (v.6). Having made their plans, the conspirators 'sleep on it' and spring into

action in the morning. F. A. Tatford puts it like this, basing his interpretation on the translation "all night their anger smoulders" (see RV margin): "Still describing the conspiracy against the king, the prophecy declared that the conspirators were inwardly like an oven. The hot passion consumed them like an oven fire while they lay in wait. Their preparations had been made, but their hatred was almost uncontrollable and smoked all night. They slept fitfully, nursing their murderous schemes until the morning When the new day dawned, their anger burst out against their destined victim". All of which reminds us of the New Testament injunction: "Be ye angry, and sin not: let not the sun go down upon your wrath" (Eph. 4:26).

This incorporates the third reference to the baker's oven. Hosea left it smouldering "*all the night*": now, "*in the morning* it burneth as a flaming fire". The explanation is given: "They are all hot as an oven, and have devoured their judges; all their kings are fallen: there is none among them that calleth unto me".

This aptly describes the mayhem of the period. As F. A. Tatford observes: "They devoured or destroyed their rulers...All their kings had fallen. Shallum's murder of Zachariah was followed by Menahem's murder of Shallum (2 Kings 15:14). Four regicides occurred in four decades. Indeed, of Israel's seventeen kings, only eight died a natural death, the other nine being dethroned and murdered by their successors. It was no wonder that the kingdom sank into chaos and anarchy. Yet in such conditions, no one called upon Jehovah. It was a sad commentary on the irreligious state of the nation".

If the court was so fearfully evil, it is hardly surprising that the nation followed suit. We now come to:

3) THE DECLINE IN THE NATION, vv.8-16
This is described under four graphic figures of speech: *(a)* "a cake not turned" (v.8); *(b)* a man with "gray hairs" (vv.9-10); *(c)* "a silly dove without heart" (vv.11-15); *(d)* "a deceitful bow" (v.16).

a) "A cake not turned", v.8
"Ephraim, he hath mixed himself among the people ('peoples', JND); Ephraim is a cake not turned". J. M. Flanigan explains the figure of "a cake not turned": "The people of the East baked these cakes on embers or hot stones on the floor, and they had to be turned regularly during the baking. A cake not turned would be burnt on one side and remain only dough on the other side, not fit for

eating". George Adam Smith is regularly quoted here: "How better describe half-fed people, a half-cultured society, a half-lived religion, a half-hearted policy, than by a half-baked scone". In other words, Ephraim was 'neither one thing or another'. It trafficked with Assyria (see 2 Kings 15:19-20, Isaiah 7:2) and Egypt (2 Kings 17:4), whilst retaining some kind of nominal allegiance to Jehovah (see v.14). The New Testament warns us against following suit: "ye cannot serve God and mammon" (Matt.6:24); "ye cannot drink the cup of the Lord, and the cup of devils (demons): ye cannot be partakers of the Lord's table and of the table of devils (demons)" (1 Cor.10:21).

It had always been God's purpose that Israel should be separated from the nations of the world. She was to dwell alone. See Numbers 23:9; Deuteronomy 33:28. As F. A. Tatford states, Israel "belonged to Jehovah and He was her sufficiency. There was no need to seek the help of pagan powers in her supposed extremity. He was capable of protecting His own people and His own possessions. Their mixing with the other nations was an expression of lack of confidence in Him".

The figure of "a cake not turned" should be compared with the Lord's reference to His people as "the salt of the earth". The figure is different, but the lesson is similar: "Ye are the salt of the earth: but if the salt hath lost his savour, wherewith shall it be salted? It is thenceforth good for nothing, but to be cast out, and to be trodden under foot of men" (Matt. 5:13). See also Revelation 3:15-16: "I know thy works, that thou art neither cold nor hot: I would thou wert cold or hot. So then because thou art lukewarm, and neither cold nor hot, I will spue thee out of my mouth". We ignore the lesson in all three passages to our spiritual peril.

b) "Gray hairs...here and there upon him", vv.9-10
"Strangers have devoured his strength, and he knoweth it not: yea, gray hairs are here and there upon him, yet he knoweth not" (v.9). Whilst the nation thought itself to be in the prime of life, it was unconsciously degenerating. Hence the repetition of "he knoweth...not". Compromise with the world ("he hath mixed himself among the people") brought spiritual weakness and decline. Their alliances might have seemed beneficial at the time, but they resulted in decline. The sad case of Samson stresses the lesson: "I will go out as at other times before, and shake myself. And he wist not that the LORD was departed from him" (Judges 16:20). Compare Rev. 3:17, "thou...knowest not that thou art wretched, and miserable, and poor, and blind, and naked"

The very fact that they were proud of themselves (see also 5:5), proclaimed their decline: "the pride of Israel testifieth to his face: and they do not return to the LORD their God, nor seek him for all this" (v.10). The lesson is clear: "Wherefore let him that thinketh he standeth, take heed lest he fall" (1 Cor. 10:12). Spiritual strength lies in our acknowledged weakness, leading Paul to say, "when I am weak, then am I strong" (2 Cor. 12:10). Ephraim had no sense of need. They were bent on "finding their own solution to their problems and were, therefore, quite unmindful of the Lord" (F. A. Tatford).

c) "A silly dove without heart", vv.11-15
"Ephraim also is like a silly (open to deception) dove without heart (senseless): they call to Egypt, they go to Assyria". Theodore Laetsch (*The Minor Prophets*) describes Israel as "fluttering back and forth undecidedly between Egypt and Assyria...cooing once toward the one and then to the other or to both at the same time, pursuing a weak and vacillating policy of near sighted opportunism instead of relying with their whole heart and soul on God". Ephraim is described in this way for the following reasons:

i) Their behaviour was senseless because it was useless, vv.11-12.
"They call to Egypt, they go to Assyria". Their 'shuttle diplomacy' is illustrated in 2 Kings 17:1-4. They attempted to avert a crisis by making an alliance elsewhere, only to find that the very God they had ignored and forgotten was waiting with His net: "I will spread my net upon them: I will bring them down as the fowls of the heaven; I will chastise them as their congregation hath heard". They looked south-west, and north-east, but they forgot to look up. Such conduct was intolerable to God, and His "net" is in all probability a symbol of the pending captivity. The words, "I will chastise them, as their congregation hath heard", "presumably refer to the admonitions and warnings so often given to the nation by the prophets. As Jehovah had warned and the prophets had so clearly predicted, God's chastening hand would fall upon them" (F. A. Tatford).

ii) Their behaviour was senseless because it was lawless, vv.13-14.
"Woe unto them! For they have fled ('wandered', JND) from me: destruction unto them! because they have transgressed against me: though I have redeemed them ('though I would redeem them', RV; 'And I would redeem them', JND), yet they have spoken lies against me. And they have not cried unto me with their heart, when they howled upon their beds: they assemble themselves ("cut themselves", RV margin, as in Baal worship, 1 Kings 18:28) for corn and wine, and they rebel against me". Notice the

repeated words "against me". They had "wandered" from the Lord, "spoken lies" against Him, and "transgressed" or rebelled against Him. No wonder He said "Woe unto them!... destruction unto them!"

Their bitter regret over the dire straits into which they had fallen was anything but evidence of repentance. It was just that - pure regret: "they have not cried unto me with their heart, when they howled upon their beds". As Derek Kidner observes, "we get a glimpse in verse 14 of their kind of praying - Never mind about 'Thy kingdom come' – 'where's our daily bread?' It was all self-pity". The words, "they assemble themselves for corn and wine, **and they rebel against me"** are almost unbelievable. It's a far cry, to put it mildly, from 1 John 3:22, "And whatsoever we ask, we receive of him, because we keep his commandments, and do those things which are pleasing in his sight".

iii) Their behaviour was senseless because it was thankless, v.15. It was an insult to God's love and care for them in the past. "Though I have bound and strengthened their arms ('I have indeed trained, I have strengthened their arms', JND), yet do they imagine mischief against me". More is said about this later in the prophecy: "I taught Ephraim also to go, taking them by their arms; but they knew not that I healed them. I drew them with cords of a man, with bands of love: and I was to them as they that take off the yoke on their jaws, and I laid meat unto them" (11:3-4). Compare Isaiah 1:2, "I have nourished and brought up children, and they have rebelled against me".

All this reminds us that we should never forget the New Testament injunction, "In everything give thanks; for this is the will of God in Christ Jesus concerning you" (1 Thess. 5:18).

d) "A deceitful bow", v.16
"They return, but not to the most High". Compare 2:7. The name of Israel's national airline - El Al (meaning 'to the height') - comes from "the most High" here. Note: it is not *El Elyon* here, "the most high God, the possessor of heaven and earth" (Gen. 14:22).

But the outward appearance was an illusion. "they turned...but they did not turn upward" (F. A. Tatford). They "are like a deceitful bow". That is, there was nothing dependable about them. The Psalmist puts it like this: "they tempted and provoked the most high God, and kept not his testimonies: but turned back, and dealt unfaithfully like their fathers: they were turned aside (they turned, twisted) like a deceitful bow. For they provoked him to anger with their high places, and moved him to jealousy with their graven images" (Psalm 78:56-58). According to F. A. Tatford, "a deceitful bow" was "one which shot its arrows in the wrong direction...If such a weapon failed the archer in the time of battle, it might be disastrous. It was a forceful image of Israel's dangerous unreliability. They could not be trusted".

The "deceitful bow" would, indeed, prove disastrous. Defeat and captivity loomed: "their princes shall fall by the sword for the rage (*zaam*, 'indignation, insolence') of their tongue: this shall be their derision in the land of Egypt". We have already noticed something of their "rage" ('angry insolence'): "Woe unto them! For they have wandered from me; destruction unto them! for they have transgressed against me. And I would redeem them; but they speak lies against me" (v.13, JND). Compare Jude v.14-15, "Behold, the Lord cometh with ten thousands of his saints, to execute judgment upon all, and to convince all that are ungodly among them of all their ungodly deeds which they have ungodly committed, and of all ***their hard speeches which ungodly sinners have spoken against him***".

Justin Waldron nicely points out that there was no deceit (*dolos*, 'guile', AV) found in the mouth of the Lord Jesus (1 Pet. 2:22), and that the Lord's people are to "lay aside all guile (*dolos*, deceit)" (1 Pet. 2:1). Paul's preaching at Thessalonica was "not of deceit (*plane*, whence 'planet'), nor of uncleanness, nor in guile (*dolos*)" (1 Thess. 2:3), and, with his colleagues, he had "renounced the hidden things of dishonesty, not walking in craftiness, not handling the word of God deceitfully (*doloo*)" (2 Cor. 4:2).

The very powers to which they looked for deliverance would be their downfall. They "call to Egypt, they go to Assyria" (v.11). Very well, "Ephraim shall return to Egypt, and they shall eat unclean things in Assyria" (9:3). Ephraim had insulted the Lord by appealing to the world-powers of the day, and the world-powers of the day would make a successful take-over bid for them. They would be defeated by Assyria and derided in Egypt. Their conduct would give "occasion to the adversary to speak reproachfully" (1 Tim. 5:14). Compare Titus 2:5, 8.

That day was not far off: invasion was imminent: "Set the trumpet to thy mouth, He shall come as an eagle against the house of the LORD, because they have transgressed my covenant, and trespassed against my law" (8:1).

READ CHAPTER 8:1-14

"They have sown the wind, and they shall reap the whirlwind"

As we noticed, the previous chapter ends with a warning of coming judgment: "They return, but not to the most High: they are like a deceitful bow: their princes shall fall by the sword for the rage of their tongue: this shall be their derision in the land of Egypt" (7:16). Now judgment is imminent: "Set the trumpet to thy mouth, he shall come as an eagle against the house of the LORD, because they have transgressed my covenant, and trespassed against my law" (8:1).

In his book, *Hosea, the heart and holiness of God,* G. Campbell Morgan points out (backed by the AV italics) that "In the Hebrew text there is an abruptness about it. Two clarion cries sharply follow: the first, 'the trumpet to thy mouth' (omitting 'set'); the second, 'as an eagle against the house of Jehovah' (omitting 'he shall come'). Campbell Morgan continues: "The method of the Hebrew suggests two sudden trumpet blasts. The message of the prophet was intended to be one of arousal..." This speaks for itself.

The enemy that "shall come as an eagle against the house of the LORD" is Assyria. The Assyrians invaded Israel on several occasions, with the final invasion, under Shalmaneser, culminating in the removal of the king (Hoshea) and the deportation of its people. See 2 Kings 17:1-6. Previous Assyrian invasions, under Pul and Tiglath-pileser, took place during the reigns of Menahem and Pekah. See 2 Kings 15:19-20; 29. F. A. Tatford suggests that Hosea refers to the latter of these two invasions here. We should notice the following:

i) The warning of invasion: "Set the trumpet to thy mouth". The "trumpet" (*shophar*) was a ram's horn. Hosea was therefore told to act as a watchman, whose duties, when "he seeth the sword come upon the land" was "to blow the trumpet (*shophar*), and warn the people" (Ezek. 33:3). The watchman would be exonerated from all blame even if the city fell, provided that he had given due warning. In this case, Hosea, "as a faithful prophet...must warn God's people even though the destruction predicted was merited by by them" (Jack. R. Riggs).

Paul, as a true watchman, was "pure from the blood of all men", and his explanation follows: "For I have not shunned to declare unto you all the counsel of God" (Acts 20:26-27). He made it clear to the Ephesian elders that part of their work was to act as watchmen: "For I know this, that after my departing shall grievous wolves enter in among you, not sparing the flock. Also of your own selves shall men arise, speaking perverse things, to draw away disciples after them. Therefore **watch**, and remember..." (Acts 20:29-31). Elders are men that "watch (*agrupneo*: to be sleepless) for your souls, as they that must give account" (Heb .13:17).

*ii) **The description of the invader**:* "he shall come as an eagle". God was about to fulfil His word: see Deuteronomy 28:49. In the Old Testament, the word *nesher* is always translated "eagle", although some commentators, including F. A. Tatford opt for "the carrion-eating griffon vulture". It has been pointed out that the word is used "as a metaphor for swiftness (Jer. 4:13; 2 Sam. 1:23); dangerous voracity (Hab. 1:8; Prov. 30:17) and majestic superiority (Ezek. 17:3. Exod. 19:4)" (Roy L. Honeycut, *Hosea and His Message*).

*iii) **The prize before the invader**:* "the house of the LORD". Quite obviously, "the house of the LORD" here refers to the northern kingdom, Israel, rather than the temple in Jerusalem. "At the time of the Assyrian crisis in the north, the temple in Jerusalem was not threatened" (Jack. R. Riggs). Even so, the Assyrians did later march further south, and threatened Jerusalem (2 Kings 18:1 - 19:37). Perhaps the acquisition of Israel in the north was preparation for the conquest of Judah in the south, with the rich prize of the temple. However, the expression, "the house of the Lord", can be understood as 'the household of the Lord'. See Numbers 12:7, where the Lord describes Moses as "faithful in all mine house".

*iv) **The reason for the invasion**:* "because they have transgressed my covenant, and trespassed against my law".

- ***"They have transgressed my covenant".*** The word "covenant" describes their basic relationship with God. In Hosea, it is "as binding and intimate as a marriage" (D. Kidner). See comments on 6:7.

- ***"They have...trespassed against my law".*** The word "law" describes the principles which made that relationship harmonious and effective.

F. A. Tatford says it all: "Israel had transgressed God's covenant ordinance and had rebelled against His law. The people had been given every opportunity for repentance, but they had persisted in their course. They had dishonoured Jehovah and apostasised from Him, they had substituted the vile ceremonies of the fertility cult for the specific requirements of the divinely-given religion, they had ignored the divine demands for sanctification and holy living, and in every conceivable way had done despite to God. Punishment could no longer be averted, and they were to learn in exile the lesson they refused to learn in their own land". Frederick Tatford might well have been describing the U.K. today.

Very clearly, this introductory statement (v.1) illustrates the words, "They have sown the wind, and they shall reap the whirlwind" (v.7). This lies at the heart of the chapter, and dictates its character. There are six references to sowing and reaping: *(1)* they would reap the consequences of false profession (vv.2-3); *(2)* they would reap the consequences of false leadership (v.4); *(3)* they would reap the consequences of false gods (vv.4-7); *(4)* they would reap the consequences of false allies (vv.8-10); *(5)* they would reap the consequences of false religion (vv.11-13); *(6)* they would reap the consequences of false security (v.14).

1) THEY WOULD REAP THE CONSEQUENCES OF FALSE PROFESSION, vv.2-3

"Isarel shall cry unto me, My God, we know thee. Israel hath cast off the thing that is good: the enemy shall pursue him". A good commentary on these verses is found in Titus 1:16: "They profess that they know God; but in works they deny him". The profession in Hosea's day sounded very grand indeed: "Israel shall cry unto me, My God, we know thee" (v.2) or, emphasising the strength of their claim: "My God, *we Israel* know thee" (RV). See also JND. They traded on their relationship with God, "You only have I known of all the families of the earth" (Amos 3:2). The balance of this verse stresses the responsibility attaching to that relationship, "therefore I will punish you for all your iniquities". Privilege determines responsibility.

The emptiness of their claim has already been demonstrated (v.1). Now Hosea goes further: "Israel hath cast off the thing that is good: the enemy shall pursue him" (v.3). The word "good" describes the benefits arising from

God's "covenant" and God's "law". If they had been maintained, their quality of life would have been "good" in every sense - spiritually, morally and physically. Compare 1 Timothy 6:6. Sadly, they had rejected the "covenant", the "law", and the "good" that flowed from them. They did not know God at all: "Israel (who said, 'we know thee') hath cast off the thing that is good". Their actions belied their words. As Justin Waldron points out, Jonah said, "I fear the LORD" (Jon. 1:9), but he acted in disobedience to His will.

The Jews in the New Testament were little different. They too claimed a special relationship: "Abraham is our father...we have one Father, even God" (John 8:39, 41). In both cases, the Lord Jesus invalidated their claim: "If ye were Abraham's children, ye would do the works of Abraham...If God were your Father, ye would love me" (vv.39, 42). Matthew 7:21-23 now becomes compulsory reading. Those who will say "Lord, Lord" are nothing but people who "work iniquity". But the New Testament will not allow *us* to distance ourselves too far from Hosea 8 or John 9. "He that saith, *I know him,* and keepeth not his commandments, is a liar, and the truth is not in him" (1 John 2:4). True believers should be characterised by "good works" (Titus 2:14).

They would certainly "reap the whirlwind": "He shall come as an eagle against the house of the LORD...the enemy shall pursue him" (vv.1, 3).

2) THEY WOULD REAP THE CONSEQUENCES OF FALSE LEADERSHIP, v.4

"They have set up kings, but not by me: they have made princes, and I knew it not". This refers, not only to the last kings of Israel, but to the history of the Northern Kingdom generally. Jehu was an exception: see 2 Kings 9:1-3. The throne of David had been rejected (1 Kings 12:16-19). Samaria rivalled Jerusalem. But not for ever: "Afterward shall the children of Israel return, and seek the Lord their God, and *David* their king" (Hos. 3:5).

God Himself had established the throne of David (see, for example, 2 Samuel 7:16), just as He chose the princes of the tribes (Num. 2:3, 5, 7ff; 7:12, 18, 24 ff). New Testament appointments are no different. See Acts 20:28: "The flock, over (in) the which *the Holy Ghost* hath made you overseers". Woe to Israel with its self-appointed leaders, and woe to the assembly that substitutes its choice for God's choice. "Except the Lord build the house, they labour in vain that build it" (Psalm 127:1).

The results of self-appointed kings and princes follow, as they do whenever "the voice of the people (our vaunted democracy) drowns the voice of God; where we set up leaders and regimes supposedly answerable only to ourselves; where we treat even the moral law as subject to the vote or to the climate of opinion" (Derek Kidner).

3) THEY WOULD REAP THE CONSEQUENCES OF FALSE GODS, vv.4-7
Bad leadership results in evil practices: the connection is clear: "They have set up kings, but not by me: they have made princes, and I knew it not. Of their silver and their gold have they made them idols, that they may be cut off" (v.4). Idolatry rears its head. It was so at the very beginning of Israel's history. Jeroboam "made two calves of gold", saying, "Behold thy gods, O Israel, which brought thee up out of the land of Egypt" (1 Kings 12: 28). He had a precedent for this. See Exodus 32:4. Over five hundred years separated the two events. How careful we all have to be! The idolatry at the foot of mount Sinai influenced a man five hundred years later! But idols and idolatry do not have the last word. The idolater will "be cut off". It was about to happen.

The description that follows emphasises *(i)* the helplessness; *(ii)* the hopelessness, *(iii)* the seriousness, and *(iv)* the thoughtlessness of idolatry.

i)   The helplessness of their idolatry, v.5. "Thy calf, O Samaria, hath cast thee off". This stresses its complete inability to help or assist. Compare 1 Kings 18:26, "O Baal, hear us. But there was no voice, nor any that answered". Isaiah paints the picture of Babylons's idols, Bel and Nebo, in transit after the fall of the city. They had to be carried: "Bel boweth down, Nebo stoopeth, their idols were upon the beasts, and upon cattle...They stoop, they bow down together; they could not deliver the burden, but themselves are gone into captivity" (Is. 46:1-2). It should be said that the RV gives a different rendering here: "He hath cast off thy calf. O Samaria".

ii)   The hopelessness of their idolatry, v.5. "How long will it be ere they attain to innocency? ('purity', JND)". We cannot fail to see God's longsuffering here. As already noted He had "hewed them by the prophets; I have slain them by the words of my mouth" (Hos. 6:5). He had faithfully exposed their sin. But to no avail: "Mine anger is kindled against them: **how long will it be** ere they attain to innocency". In the words of F. A. Tatford, "Would they ever be capable of attaining a state of purity again, or was the evil too deep-rooted?" We can add that there was therefore no alternative but sweeping judgment.

*iii) **The seriousness of their idolatry, v.6.*** "For from Israel was it also..." This is a terrible indictment: the calf had not been imposed on them by a foreign power: it emanated from Israel itself. See, again, 1 Kings 12:27-29.

*iv) **The thoughtlessness of their idolatry, v.6.*** It was utterly stupid: "The **workman** made it; therefore it is not God". Hosea draws attention to this later: "And now they sin more and more, and have made them molten images of their silver, and idols according to their own understanding, all of it the work of the craftsmen; they say of them, Let the men that sacrifice kiss the calves" (Hos. 13:2). Compare, for example, Isaiah 40:18-20, 44:9, 20. Notice the way in which Galatians 4:8 refers to idolatry: "Howbeit then, when ye knew not God, ye did service unto them which by nature are no gods". The expression "no gods" is an Old Testament term for idols. See, for example, Jer. 5:7; 2 Chron. 13:9.

In consequence, having "sown the wind", which denotes "devoting effort to vanity" (M. F. Unger): they would "reap the whirlwind" (v.7), that is, they would reap far more than they had sown. But, in another sense, they would reap nothing. Their trusted calf would be "broken to pieces" (v.6), but more - their crops would fail, and anything that was produced would be stripped by the invader: "it hath no stalk (there would be no standing corn): the bud shall yield no meal: if so be it yield, the strangers shall swallow it up" (v.7). Compare Hosea 2:3. The teaching of Galatians 6:7-8 cannot be ignored.

4) THEY WOULD REAP THE CONSEQUENCES OF FALSE ALLIES, vv.8-10

"Israel is swallowed up: now shall they be among the Gentiles as a vessel wherein is no pleasure" (v.8). This has been rendered, "A crock that no one wants" (Jerusalem Bible). H. A. Ironside comments as follows: "This describes in one verse their history over two thousand years. Driven out of their land, scattered among all nations, they have been as a vessel in which God could take no delight". To which we add, 'a vessel in which **nobody** took delight'.

The reason follows, "**For** they are gone up to Assyria, a wild ass alone by himself: Ephraim hath hired lovers" (v.9). Compare 7:11. Read James 4:4. The untameable and obstinate "wild ass" is an apt description of Israel. Interestingly, Ishmael is described as "a wild-ass of a man" (Gen. 16:12 JND). But their alliances would prove disastrous: "Yea, though they have hired among the nations, now will I gather them (God would 'gather them up so that they could not escape' F. A. Tatford), and they shall sorrow a little for the burden of the king of princes" (v.10). This has been rendered, "They will begin to waste away under the oppression of the mighty king (a king of princes)". According to Derek Kidner, this translation (NIV) retains the Massoretic Text. The Assyrian began to dominate in the reign of Menahem, see 2 Kings 15:19-20, and his domination became absolute in the reign of Hoshea, see 2 Kings 17. The "burden of the king of princes" is, in all probability, the burden of taxation and tribute imposed upon them. Compare Isaiah 10: 5-11, where the Assyrian refers to "spoil" and "prey" (v.6), and says, "Are not my princes altogether kings?" (v.8)

The lesson is clear: if we sow alliance with the world, we will reap the whirlwind of domination by the world. Derek Kidner is well worth quoting here: "false religion pays disastrous dividends. But guile and duplicity in any field, political, commercial or personal, are equally perilous tactics to adopt. Dabbling in evil, we may be amateurs; but we are playing with professionals who will make short work of us, as we are warned, not only in the well-known saying of Ephesians 6:12 ('For we wrestle not against flesh and blood, but against...the rulers of the darkness of this world, against spiritual wickedness in high places'), but in the detailed admonitions that lead up to it from Ephesians 4:24 onwards".

5) THEY WOULD REAP THE CONSEQUENCES OF FALSE RELIGION, vv.11-13

The contrast between false religion (v.11) and true religion (v.12) cannot be missed. Israel had espoused the former and rejected the latter.

i) *False religion, v.11.* "Because Ephraim hath made many altars to sin, altars shall be unto him to sin" (v.11). So religion proliferated, but it was totally unacceptable to God. Their altars were "altars to sin" in at least two ways:

- *The multiplicity of the altars was sinful.* Israel had a multiplicity of altars as opposed to the one place of sacrifice designated in the law: "But unto the place which the LORD your God shall choose out of all your tribes to put his name there, even unto his habitation shall ye seek, and thither shalt thou come: and thither shall ye bring your burnt-offerings, and your sacrifices... Take heed to thyself that thou offer not thy burnt-offerings in every place that thou seest: but in the place which the LORD shall choose in any one of thy tribes, there thou shalt offer thy burnt-offerings, and there thou shalt do all that I command thee" (Deut. 12:5; 13-14).

- ***The purpose of the altars was sinful***. While it is tempting to say that the altars in question were devoted to Baal, this is not specifically stated. Israel was given at this time to what M. F. Unger calls "religious syncretism", that is, a religion incorporating orthodox practices and paganism. There can be little doubt that they saw their altars as places where they could atone for their sins and obtain divine favour. In this sense they regarded their altars as "altars to sin", or altars to deal with sin. But the Lord regarded them as "altars to sin" in another sense: they were utterly sinful. There was no reality in their sacrifices as the next verses (vv.12-13) make clear. Derek Kidner suggests that without tampering with the text, but pronouncing the consonants differently (the Hebrew reader was required to supply the vowels), the text could be read 'altars for sin offerings…have become altars for sinning'.

As noted above Israel had dispensed with true religion, and this follows (v.12), but having dealt with this, Hosea returns to their false religion: "They sacrifice **flesh**, for the sacrifices of mine offerings, and **eat it**; but the LORD accepteth them not" (v.13). J. M. Flanigan helpfully suggests that "implication of the indictment….appears to be that, although they did slay animals whose sacrifice should have been for Jehovah, they were more interested in eating the flesh…This would have been in keeping with the heathen around them". M. F. Unger puts it a little more directly: "but the Lord took no delight in those offerings, because Israel did not seek God's glory when giving them: rather, they sought the mere carnal gratification of a full stomach. So their sacrifices were regarded as mere 'flesh', not a genuine offering to God; their religious activity reflected a facet of their religious perversion". Their religion was really self-indulgence. Their sacrifices were just "flesh": not offerings to God.

ii) True religion, v.12. "I have written unto him the great things ('manifold things', JND) of my law, but they were counted as a strange thing". While, in the immediate context, this could well refer to God's instructions for offering and sacrifice, we should also consider the wider application. Although God's people had His **written** word, let alone the spoken word through His servants, they had become deaf to all appeal and all correction. But it is more than that: the words, "a strange thing", mean something alien or foreign to them: "like something coming from an outsider that did not concern them" (M. F. Unger). An appropriate New Testament comment is found in 1 Corinthians 2:14, "the natural man receiveth not the things of the Spirit of God; for they are foolishness unto him: neither can he know them, because they are spiritually discerned".

At approximately the same time, Isaiah censured Judah in the same way: he describes the "great things" of God's law as follows: "Learn to do well, seek judgment, relieve the oppressed, judge the fatherless, plead for the widow" (Isaiah 1:11-17). Compare Micah 6:6-8. The Lord Jesus called the "great things" of God's law, "the weightier matters of the law", and defined them as "judgment, mercy, and faith" (Matt. 23:23). We too must be careful not to have "a form of godliness, but denying the power thereof" (2 Tim. 3:5).

The whirlwind follows: "Now will he remember their iniquity, and visit their sins: they shall return to Egypt" (v.13). See also Hosea 9:3. Although, unlike Judah, Scripture does not record any return to Egypt on the part of Israel, there seems little reason to interpret the statement other than literally. Some suggest that returning to Egypt is simply a metaphor for returning to captivity without necessarily meaning Egypt, but this is hardly sound exegesis! **Nationally**, Israel would **not** return to Egypt (see Hos. 11:5), but **refugees** from the Assyrian onslaught would certainly make their way there (Hos. 9:6).

6) THEY WOULD REAP THE CONSEQUENCES OF FALSE SECURITY, v.14

"For Israel hath forgotten his Maker, and buildeth temples (*hekal*, which evidently refers to either palaces - royal residences - or temples); and Judah hath multiplied fenced cities". In the north, they looked for security through religion (we'll stay with 'temples'): in the south, they trusted in tangible defences. But in both cases, God was ignored.

The whirlwind follows: "But I will send a fire upon his cities, and it shall devour the palaces (*armon*) thereof". The fire which descended and consumed the sacrifices (see, for example, 2 Chron. 7:1) would fall on the cities and palaces of God's people. The Assyrians overran Israel (2 Kings 18:9-12), and captured all Judah's fortified cities except Jerusalem (2 Kings 18:13). The Assyrian invasion of Judah was routed by God Himself (see our comments at Hosea 1:7), but the Assyrians were eventually followed by the Babylonians, and then it was a different story.

In the words of G. Campbell Morgan, "To forsake God is to ensure ruin", but the final comment must be this: "Wherefore we receiving a kingdom which cannot be moved (unlike Israel), let us have grace, whereby we may serve God acceptably with reverence and godly fear (unlike Israel): for our God is a consuming fire" (Heb. 12:28-29).

READ CHAPTER 9:1-17

"Woe also to them when I depart from them!"

The final verse of this chapter sums up its message: "My God will cast them away, because they did not hearken unto him: and they shall be wanderers among the nations" (v.17). Israel's failure to "hearken unto him" is described in three ways in the chapter: *(1)* they had rejected the love of God (vv.1-6); *(2)* they had reviled the servants of God (vv.7-9); *(3)* they had reversed the pleasure of God (vv.10-17).

1) THEY HAD REJECTED THE LOVE OF GOD, vv.1-6
"Rejoice not, O Israel, for joy, as other people: for thou hast gone *a whoring from thy God"* (v.1). It must have been most painful for Hosea to write this. Every word must have pierced his heart. It was akin to his own distressing experience: "Go, take unto thee a wife of whoredoms" (1:2), and that is exactly what she became (3:1).

It is well worth remembering here that their God (v.1) was *Elohim*, the plural form of *Eloah* (singular) which, according to Thomas Newberry, derives from the Hebrew word *ahlah,* meaning to worship or adore. The name "presents God as the one supreme object of worship, the Adorable One".

Israel's infidelity ("thou hast gone a whoring from thy God") was accompanied with great joy. Sin can be pleasurable – for a time. The New Testament refers to "the pleasures of sin for a season" (Heb. 11:25). It was evidently harvest time in this chapter. The fields had been reaped (hence "the cornfloor"), the grapes had been gathered (hence the "new wine"), and the people were given to "joy in harvest" (Isaiah 9:3), but it was *not* 'joy in the Lord'. They attributed their blessings, not to Jehovah, but to Baal, and had become just like the idol-worshipping nations around them. For this reason they are told, "Rejoice not, O Israel, for joy, *as other people* ('as the peoples', JND: that is, as the Gentile nations). The nation had become unfaithful to God, who loved them (11:1, 4) and provided for them, reminding us of the New

Testament warning, "Love not the world, neither the things that are in the world. If any man love the world, the love of (love for) the Father is not in him" (1 John 2:15).

The way in which Israel had "gone a whoring from thy God" is spelt out as follows: "Thou hast loved a reward (referring to the hire of a harlot: in this case it is spiritual harlotry) upon every cornfloor" (*goren dagan*: the word *goren* is usually translated 'threshing floor': *dagan* means 'corn'). This should be read in conjunction with Israel's words, "I will go after my lovers, that give me my bread and my water, my wool and my flax, mine oil and my drink" (2:5). Israel considered that her devotion to Baal secured her food (from the "floor") and drink (from the "winepress"), failing to remember that the Lord "gave her corn, and wine, and oil, and multiplied her silver and gold" (2: 8). But just as the Lord would "return" and, in His own words, "**take away my** corn...and *my* wine" (2:9), so here: "the floor and the winepress shall not feed them, and the new wine shall fail in her" (v.2). Their "joy in harvest", which was nothing else but 'joy in Baal' would be short-lived.

The consequences of their infidelity are now spelt out in terms of lost strength and lost joy. These verses stress their loss of strength and joy in the land (vv.1-2), together with their loss of strength and joy in captivity (vv.3-6).

a) *Their loss in the land, vv.1-2*
i) *God would take away their strength*: "The floor...shall not feed them" (v.2). See Psalm 104:15, "bread which strengtheneth man's heart". Infidelity on our part will rob us of the strength of God's word, for "man doth not live by bread only, but by every word that proceedeth out of the mouth of the LORD doth man live" (Deut. 8:3). If the word of God has lost its appeal to us and become 'as dry as dust', we should ask ourselves if we have 'left our first love' (Rev. 2:4).

ii) *God would take away their joy*: "the new wine shall fail in her" (v.2). See, again, Psalm 104:15, "wine that maketh glad the heart of man" (Psalm 104:15). Compare Isaiah 24:11, "There is a crying for wine in the streets; all joy is darkened, the mirth of the land is gone". See also Jeremiah 48:33. Infidelity on our part will rob us of "the joy of the LORD" (Neh. 8:10).

The Lord Jesus taught that true joy is connected with obedience: "As the Father hath loved me, so have I loved you: continue ye in my love. If ye keep my commandments, ye shall abide in my love; even as I have kept my Father's commandments, and abide in his love. These things have I spoken unto you, that my joy might remain in you, and that your joy might be full" (John 15:9-11).

b) Their loss in captivity, vv.3-6
Israel's sin would bring exile and captivity. "They shall not dwell in the LORD'S land; but Ephraim shall return to Egypt, and they shall eat unclean things in Assyria" (v.3). Israel (called Ephraim) had looked to Egypt and Assyria for help (they "call to Egypt, they go to Assyria", 7:11), and in consequence the very powers to which they looked for deliverance would be their downfall. Ephraim had insulted the Lord by appealing to the world-powers of the day, and the world-powers of the day would make a successful take-over bid for them. The lesson for us is clear: if *we* court the favour of the world, the world will make a takeover bid for *us* as well.

Hosea now emphasises the enormity of their loss in captivity. Their infidelity and resultant exile would incur at least four things:

i) Loss of inheritance in "the LORD'S land", v.3. "They shall not dwell in the LORD'S land". There is a certain emphasis on "The **LORD'S** land": they had treated it as 'Baal's land'. The very nations whose favour they courted (7:11; 8:9) would become their captors. Disobedience has robbed many a child of God of enjoyment of their spiritual inheritance, and made them eat "unclean things". Not all people away from home are like Daniel who "purposed in his heart that he would not defile himself with the portion of the king's meat, nor with the wine that he drank" (Dan. 1:8).

ii) Loss of joy and worship in "offerings to the LORD", v.4. "They shall not offer wine offerings to the LORD, neither shall they be pleasing unto him: their sacrifices shall be unto them as the bread of mourners; all that eat thereof shall be polluted: for their bread for their soul shall not come into the house of the LORD" or "for their bread shall be for themselves ('for their appetite', margin); it shall not come into the house of the Jehovah" (JND). For "wine offerings" see Numbers 15:1-10. They would not be in a position to offer to the Lord. First of all, because they were not in the right place, and therefore sacrifices would not "be pleasing unto him", and secondly, because such sacrifices would be "as the bread of mourners". This is explained by Deuteronomy 26:12-14, where people, ceremonially unclean by their association with death, were excluded from offering to God. Israel, surrounded by the defilement of heathen Assyria, would be in the same position. While there are other explanations, the words, "for their bread for their soul shall not come into the house of the LORD" extend the reference to "the bread of mourners". Sin will rob us of the joy of 'ministering to the Lord' (Acts 13:2).

iii) Loss of fellowship at the "feast of the LORD", v.5. "What will ye do in the solemn day, and in the day of the feast of the LORD?" Compare Hosea 2:11, "I will also cause all her mirth to cease, her feast days, her new moons, and her sabbaths, and all her solemn feasts". These were occasions of fellowship with God, and with one another. See Exodus 23:17, "Three times in the year all thy males shall appear before the Lord GOD". See also Deut 16:11. Hence David's words, "Jerusalem is builded as a city that is compact together: **whither the tribes go up**, the tribes of the LORD, to give thanks unto the name of the LORD" (Psalm 122:3-4). We know, of course, that Jereboam took steps to change this so far as the northern kingdom was concerned: see 1 Kings 12:26. We should remember that "the Lord values our fellowship" (J. Waldron). See Luke 22:15, "With desire I have desired to eat this passover with you before I suffer".

The solemn lessons for ourselves in these verses are clearly expressed by H. A. Ironside: "The very recollections of past joys, of hours and days when the soul delighted in God and found precious food in His word, but make all the more cheerless the restless, unhappy experiences of the backslider in heart as he becomes filled with his own devices".

The section ends on a note of terrible finality: "For, lo, they are gone because of destruction: Egypt shall gather them up, Memphis shall bury them: the pleasant places for their silver, nettles shall possess them: thorns shall be in their tabernacles" (v.6). This evidently refers, not to national deportation to Egypt, but to survivors fleeing from the Assyrian invasion ("they are gone because of destruction"). It seems possible that these refugees sought refuge in Egypt under the aegis of Hoshea's alliance with "So king of Egypt" (2 Kings 17:4). However, Deuteronomy 28:68 refers to prisoners being taken to Egypt and sold there. But whatever the actual event visualised here, there would be no escape from divine judgment. They would die in Egypt. "Memphis was at that time the residence of ancient kings and was notorious as a necropolis, a burial place, and such it would be for those Jews who had fled to Egypt for help. It was situated near to the present Cairo and the great pyramids" (J. M. Flanigan). The lesson for ourselves is clear: compromise with the world will mean that we will be ultimately buried by the world. We will lose our spiritual identity. Compare 8:8, "Israel is swallowed up". The words, "the pleasant places for their silver, nettles shall possess them: thorns shall be in their tabernacles", remind us that we are to "lay up...treasures in heaven, where neither moth not rust doth corrupt, and where thieves do not break through nor steal" (Matt. 6:19-21). It has been aptly said that "there are no pockets in shrouds!" (J. Hay).

2) THEY HAD REVILED THE SERVANTS OF GOD, vv.7-9

The second reason for Israel's misery is introduced by the statement, "The days of visitation are come, the days of recompense are come" (v.7). Divine judgment is expressed impersonally, whereas later it is expressed personally: "He will visit their sins" (v.9). They would only realise the relevance and reality of God's word when it was too late: "The days of visitation are come, the days of recompense are come: *Israel shall know it*". Zechariah makes the same point: "But my words and my statutes, which I commanded my servants the prophets, did they not take hold of (overtake) your fathers? And they returned and said, Like as the LORD of hosts thought to do unto us, according to our ways, and according to our doings, so hath he dealt with us" (Zech. 1:6).

The reasons for "visitation" and "recompence" follow. It should be said that commentators are not all of one mind on the identity of the prophets and spiritual men. It does seem, however, that Hosea is referring here to servants of God, rather than, as some suggest, false prophets. With this in mind, we should notice:

i) What Hosea called God's servants. He refers to the Lord's servants as prophets, spiritual men and watchmen: "The *prophet* is a fool, the *spiritual man* ('the man that hath the spirit', RV) is mad...The *watchman* of Ephraim was with my God" (vv.7-8). While we do not have prophets today (like the apostles, the New Testament prophets were connected with the foundation of the church: see Ephesians 2:20), we certainly have, and need, 'spiritual men' and 'watchmen'. See for example, 1 Cor. 2:14-15 ("he that is spiritual"); Acts 20:31 (to the Ephesian elders: "watch").

ii) What Israel called His servants. "The prophet is a *fool*, the spiritual man is *mad*". (Quite possibly, the "prophet" and the "spiritual man" are one and the same person). It has been pointed out that "the prophets were not especially revered and respected in Israel" (Jack. R. Riggs). See, for example, the description of the young prophet sent to Jehu by Elisha: "one said unto him (Jehu), Is all well? Wherefore came this **mad fellow** to thee?" (2 Kings 9:11). Shemaiah, a false prophet, was of the same opinion about Jeremiah. He had written, evidently more than once, to "all the people... at Jerusalem" and in particular to Zephaniah and his fellow-priests in Jerusalem accusing them of dereliction of duty: "Jehovah hath made thee priest in the stead of Jehoiada the priest, that there should be officers [in] the house of Jehovah, over every **madman and self-made prophet**, that thou shouldest put him in the stocks and in the shackles. And now, why hast thou not reproved Jeremiah of Anathoth, who maketh himself a prophet to you?" (Jer. 29:26-27, JND). See also Amos 5: 10. Paul did not fare any better: see Acts 26:24; 2 Corinthians 10:10. We expect to be called "fools for Christ's sake" (1 Cor.4:10).

The derision of the people for the prophet ("the prophet is a fool") and the spiritual man ("the spiritual man is made"), was engendered by their sinfulness: it was because of "the multitude of thine iniquity, and the great hatred" (v.7). It has been said that "because of the character of their own lives, people cannot bear exposure and condemnation. When truth becomes relevant to one's sin, self-defence dictates that the prophet be discredited as a fool and madman" (Roy L. Honeycutt). But that was not all.

The third reference to God's servants describes them as watchmen: "The watchman of Ephraim was with my God: but the prophet is a snare of the fowler in all his ways, and hatred in the house of God" (v.8). The close association of "watchmen" and "prophet" here strongly suggests that they are one and the same, and this, presumably, may have led to the rendering, "The prophet is the watchman of Ephraim, and people of my God, yet a fowler's snare is on all his ways, and hatred in the house of his God" (RSV). However, the AV rendering is well supported, and makes perfectly good sense as it stands. Ezekiel, was both prophet and watchman, and his role as a watchman is clearly defined in his prophecy: see 3:17-21; 33:2-7. But in Israel, "this role meant that the prophet's fate was to be entrapped and hated in the house of his God. The people would show no gratitude for his work. They would treat him as a wild animal by trying to ensnare him" (Jack R. Riggs). The servant of God can expect to be hated. God's servants most certainly cannot expect to be regarded in the world, secular or religious, as "the ministers of Christ, and stewards of the mysteries of God" (1 Cor. 4:1).

Rejection of the word of God opens the door to fearful sin. This is the sense of the words that follow: "They have deeply corrupted themselves, as in the days of Gibeah" (v.9). See also 10:9. This cites the sad story in Judges 19-21. It has been aptly described as "the abominable atrocity of Gibeah" (M. F. Unger). It resulted in the near extinction of the tribe of Benjamin. Israel's sin would result in national disaster: "He will remember their iniquity, he will visit their sins".

3) THEY HAD REVERSED THE PLEASURE OF GOD, vv.10-17
The third reason for Israel's misery is that early promise had been dashed. These verses may be divided as follows: *(a)* God delighted in them initially (v.10); *(b)* God detested their conduct latterly (v.10); *(c)* God determined their judgment imminently (vv.11-17).

a) God delighted in them initially, v.10
"I found Israel like grapes in the wilderness; I saw your fathers as the firstripe in the fig tree at her first time". This eloquently expresses God's delight and anticipation. M. F. Unger puts it nicely: "At first, Israel was a delight to the Lord, like luscious grapes or first-ripe figs are to a hungry and thirsty traveler". Grapes are not usually found in the wilderness! There was now nothing for God: see 10:1. "Israel is an empty vine, he bringeth forth fruit unto himself". The reference to "the firstripe in the fig tree" reminds us of Matthew 21:18-19. For Israel as a vineyard, see Matthew 21:33-41.

b) God detested their conduct latterly, v.10
"But they went to Baal-peor, and separated themselves unto that shame; and their abominations were according as they loved". They "became detestable like the thing they loved" (RSV). This cites Numbers 25. In Balaam's four parables (Numbers 23-24), God described His people there in beautiful language. See, for example, Numbers 24:5-6. This was immediately followed by the chilling words, "And Israel abode in Shittim, and the people began to commit whoredom with the daughters of Moab...and Israel joined himself unto Baal-peor" (Num. 25:1-3). Jeremiah 2:1-8 makes an appropriate commentary here.

c) God determined their judgment imminently, vv.11-17
As the result of their capitulation to "the doctrine of Balaam" (Num. 31:16; Rev. 2:14), "the anger of the Lord was kindled against Israel" (Num. 25:3), and this is repeated here. The result is spelt out in detail:

i) **There would be no children, vv.11-14.** "As for Ephraim, their glory shall fly away as a bird, from the birth, and from the womb, and from the conception. Though they bring up their children, yet will I bereave them, that there shall not be a man left: yea, woe also to them when I depart from them!" (vv.11-12). The significance of this statement lies in the meaning of "Ephraim". See Genesis 41:52, "For God hath caused me to be *fruitful* in the land of my affliction". But now, Ephraim would be fruitful no longer: see also 13:15. The words, "their glory" refers, in context, to their children. The nation would be reduced either through slaughter (v.13), or barrenness (v.14). This prediction is all the more significant when we remember that the most abominable fertility rites were associated with Baal-worship. Some commentators suggest that the words "their glory" (v.11) have a wider meaning than Ephraim's children, and should be compared with 1 Samuel 4:21, "The glory has departed from Israel".

The words, "woe also to them when I depart from them!", might well have been endorsed by Samson when he discovered that "the LORD was departed from him" (Judges 16:20), and by Saul when he "enquired of the LORD" and "the LORD answered him not, neither by dreams, nor by Urim, nor by prophets" (1 Sam. 28:6).

The reference to Tyre (v.13) points us to Ezekiel chs.26-28. Tyre was ultimately destroyed in spite of its position and beauty, and Ephraim's pleasant situation would not prevent fearful carnage either. The words, "Ephraim, as I saw Tyrus, is planted in a pleasant place" have been otherwise rendered "Ephraim, as I saw [him], was *a* Tyre planted in a beautiful place" (JND). The slaughter of Ephraim's children ("Ephraim shall bring forth his children to the murderer ('slayer', JND)", leads Hosea to ask for mercy: "Give them, O LORD: what wilt thou give? give them a miscarrying womb and dry breasts". This has been variously understood, but Hosea is evidently saying that "it was better for a woman to be childless than to bring children into such a world" (quoted by F. A. Tatford). Tatford then continues: "Barrenness was preferable to the loss of the young at an age when they were emerging into full growth". It was a case of rather have no children at all than have children who would have to face the horrors of the coming judgment described in v.16: "yea, though they bring forth, yet will I slay even the beloved fruit of their womb". The women who "bewailed" and "lamented" when the Lord Jesus was being taken to Calvary were told, "Daughters of Jerusalem, weep not for me but weep for yourselves, and for your children. For, behold, the days are coming, in the which they shall say, Blessed are the barren, and the wombs that never bare, and the paps which never gave suck" (Luke 23:27-29).

ii) There would be no love, v.15. "All their wickedness is in Gilgal: for there I hated them: for the wickedness of their doings I will drive them out of mine house, I will love them no more: all their princes are revolters". The words, "I will love them no more", does not mean that the Lord had ceased to love them and would never do so again. See 11:8, and 14:4. They imply the cessation of the marriage relationship. Hence, "I will drive them out of mine house". They would no longer enjoy God's love and provision. Hosea's own experience in Chapters 1-3 illustrates the meaning of this verse. For the significance of Gilgal, see Hosea 4:15 and Amos 4:4. Gilgal, where prophets were trained under Elijah and Elisha (2 Kings 2:1; 4:38), and which had most sacred associations in the past, was now evidently notorious for idolatry.

iii) There would be no fruit, v.16. This is expressed in two ways. **Firstly,** Ephraim would be fruitless in horticultural terms, perhaps referring to the grapes and figs of the early days (v.10): "Ephraim is smitten, their root is dried up, they shall bear no fruit". Compare the happier situation described in Isaiah 37:31, "the remnant that is escaped of the house of Judah shall again take root downward, and bear fruit upward". The connection between roots and fruit, and between roots and branches (Hos. 14:5-6), has some very important lessons for *us* today. **Secondly,** Ephraim would be fruitless in family terms: "yea, though they bring forth, yet will I slay even the beloved fruit of their womb". People who deliberately reject God ultimately reap a bitter harvest.

iii) There would be no home, v.17. "My God will cast them away, because they did not hearken unto him: and they shall be wanderers among the nations". See Deuteronomy 28:63-68. Believers today are not "wanderers among the nations", but "strangers and pilgrims" (1 Pet. 2:11).

The lessons for ourselves are clear: disobedience and disloyalty to Christ, will rob us of spiritual fruitfulness, rob us of enjoyment of God's love, and rob us of the security and stability of our God-given citizenship. No wonder we read, "Woe also to them when I depart from them!" (v.12).

READ CHAPTER 10:1-15

"Israel is an empty vine"

Previous chapters have built up a picture of Israel's coming captivity: they are **derided** at the end of Chapter 7 ("this shall be their derision in the land of Egypt", v.16), **devoured** at the end of Chapter 8 "(I will send a fire upon his cities, and it shall devour the palaces thereof", v.14), and **dispossessed** at the end of Chapter 9 ("My God will cast them away, because they did not hearken unto him: and they shall be wanderers among the nations", v.17).

Now, in this chapter, they are **demeaned** by the yoke of slavery: "I will make Ephraim to ride ('draw', JND); Judah shall plough, and Jacob shall break his clods" (v.11). The chapter advances three reasons for Israel's sorry state in this way: *(1) God found them unfruitful (vv.1-3)*: "Israel is an empty vine, he bringeth forth fruit unto himself" (v.1); *(2) men found them unfaithful (vv.4-8)*: "They have spoken words, swearing falsely in making a covenant" (v.4); *(3) history found them unrighteous (vv.9-15)*: "O Israel, thou hast sinned from the days of Gibeah" (v.9).

1) GOD FOUND THEM UNFRUITFUL, vv.1-3

Israel had originally brought pleasure to God: "I found Israel like grapes in the wilderness" (9:10). But there was nothing for Him now: "Israel is an empty vine, he bringeth forth fruit unto himself" (v.1). Jeremiah charts the change: "I remember thee, the kindness of thy youth, the love of thine espousals, when thou wentest after me *in the wilderness*, in a land that was not sown. Israel was holiness unto the LORD, and the firstfruits of his increase... What iniquity have your fathers found in me, that they are gone far from me, and have walked after vanity, and are become vain?" (Jer. 2:1-6). The Thessalonian believers were so different: they "turned to God from idols" (1 Thess. 1:9).

The vine is a familiar picture of Israel. See, for example, see Psalm 80:8-16 ("Thou hast brought a vine out of Egypt: thou hast cast out the heathen, and planted it..."); Isaiah 5:1-7 ("Now will I sing to my wellbeloved a song of my beloved touching his vineyard..."); Isaiah 27:1-11 ("In that day sing ye unto her, A vineyard of red wine. I the LORD do keep it; I will water it every moment: lest any hurt it, I will keep it night and day". See also Ezekiel 15:1-8. But any mention of the subject would be incomplete without reference to the Lord Jesus. While Israel failed to bring pleasure to God, the Lord Jesus is "the true Vine". What delight He brought to God! He said, "And he that sent me is with me: the Father hath not left me alone; for I do always those things that please him" (John 8:29). Our privilege, on earth, as branches 'abiding in the vine', is to bring forth fruit for God's pleasure: "Herein is my Father glorified in that ye bear much fruit" (John 15:1-8).

Gesenius states that the Hebrew root for "empty", is used here intransitively (not taking or requiring a direct object), and means 'to be poured out, to be spread wide, used of a spreading tree'. The word (*baqaq*) had been variously translated: "unpruned" (JND); "luxuriant" (RV); "a spreading vine" (NIV). Albert Barnes *(Notes on the Old Testament: Hosea)* nicely explains the different renderings as follows: "Israel is 'an empty vine' or, in the same sense, 'a luxuriant vine', literally, 'one that poureth out': poureth itself out into leaves...luxuriant in leaves, emptying itself in them, and empty of fruit...For the more a fruit tree putteth out its strength in leaves and branches, the less and the worst fruit it beareth" (quoted by J. M. Flanigan (*What the Bible Teaches – Hosea*). In the goodnesss of God, Israel had certainly enjoyed some prosperity during the reign of Jeroboam II (see Hos. 1:1). "He restored the coast of Israel from the entering of Hamath unto the sea of the plain, according to the word of the LORD God of Israel, which he spoke by the hand of his servant Jonah, the son of Amittai, the prophet, which was of Gath-hepher. For the LORD saw the affliction of Israel...but he saved them by the hand of Jeroboam the son of Joash". More follows: "Now the rest of the acts of Jeroboam, and all that he did, and his might, how he warred, and how he recovered Damascus, and Hamath, which belonged to Judah, are they not written in the book of the chronicles of the kings of Israel?" (2 Kings 14:23-29).

But God had not been honoured, and, worse, idolatry had flourished. The improvement in national life had been attributed to idols, and every effort was made to secure their future patronage: hence, "according to the multitude of his fruit he hath increased the altars; according to the goodness of his land they have made goodly images ('pillars', RV, or 'obelisks', RV margin)" (v.1). God's provision for His people had been lavished on Baal and Ashtoreth, reminding us of New Testament censure: "Ye ask, and receive not, because ye ask amiss, that ye may consume it upon your lusts" (James 4:3). Justin Waldron points out that Paul warns against the same sin: "ye have been called unto liberty; only use not liberty for an occasion to the flesh" (Gal. 5:13). All of which should cause *us* to review our stewardship of the benefits which God bestows upon us. "Honour the LORD with thy substance, and with the firstfruits of thine increase: so shall thy barns be filled with plenty, and thy presses burst out with new wine" (Prov. 3:9-10).

Although Israel cried, "My God, we know Thee" (8:2), it was false profession. They paid lip-service to Jehovah, but gave their allegiance to Baal. In the words of this chapter, "their heart is divided" (v.2). They failed to "cleave unto the Lord" with "purpose of heart" (Acts 11:23). They were "double-minded", and therefore "unstable" in all their ways (James 1:8). It is impossible to have a divided heart, and walk with God. "No man can serve two masters" (Matt. 6:24). Paul's heart was not divided. He said, "For to me to live is Christ" (Phil. 1:21). The Saviour must be "Lord of all" (Acts 10:36). God made it clear that He will tolerate no rival in the affections and lives of His people, saying "thou shalt worship no other god: for the LORD, whose name is Jealous, is a jealous God" (Exodus 34:14).

> *What shall I give Thee, Master,*
> *Thou who didst die for me;*
> *Shall I give half or part of my heart,*
> *Or shall I give all to Thee?*
> *Jesus my Lord and Master,*
> *Thou didst give all for me;*
> *Not just a part or half of my heart,*
> *I will give all to Thee.*

But God found Israel guilty of a 'divided heart': "now shall they be found faulty ('guilty', RV)", and He would "break down their altars" and "spoil their images" (v.2).

The fulfilment of this prediction is recorded in 2 Kings 17:1-6. Hosea's prophecy was fulfilled to the letter - of course! For the last three years of its history, Samaria was under siege and without a king. Hoshea (the last king of Israel) had been captured and imprisoned by the Assyrians, and this dire situation wrung from Samaria the cry, "We have no king, **because we feared not the LORD**: what then should a king do to us? (v.3). Human leadership would be totally ineffective without a right relationship with God.

But it was all too late, and "in the ninth year of Hoshea the king of Assyria took Samaria, and carried Israel away into Assyria, and placed them in Halah, and in Habor by the river of Gozan, and in the cities of the Medes. For so it was that the children of Israel had sinned against the LORD their God, which had brought them out of the land of Egypt....and had feared other gods" (2 Kings 17:6-7).

The lesson is clear: "Be not deceived; God is not mocked: for whatsoever a man soweth, that shall he also reap" (Gal. 6:7).

2) MEN FOUND THEM UNFAITHFUL, vv.4-8
Israel had certainly become "a cake not turned" (7:8). They were unpalatable to God (vv.1-3), and unpalatable to Assyria (vv.4-8). "They speak (mere) words, swearing falsely in making a covenant" (v.4, JND). This refers to Hoshea's failure to honour his agreement to pay tribute to Assyria, and his attempt to forge an alliance with Egypt: "And the king of Assyria found conspiracy in Hoshea: for he had sent messengers to So king of Egypt, and brought no present to the king of Assyria, as he had done year by year: therefore the king of Assyria shut him up, and bound him in prison" (2 Kings 17:4). As noted above, Israel was then invaded and conquered (2 Kings 17:5-6). However, the underlying reason for the disaster was Israel's long-standing rebellion against God. See 2 Kings 17:7-23. Divine judgment, carried out by the Assyrian, would carpet the land with death: it would resemble "hemlock (a poisonous weed: translated "gall" elsewhere) in the furrows of the field" (v.4). The land would be desolate with empty shrines (vv.5-6), an empty throne (v.7) and empty altars (v.8).

Like Zedekiah (2 Chron. 36:11-13: Ezek. 17:15), Hoshea was not 'a man of his word', reminding us that our pledges and promises should reflect the character of God himself. Paul puts it like this: "But *as God is true*, our word toward you was not yea and nay (that is, marked by uncertainty), for the Son of God, Jesus Christ, who was preached among you by us...was *not* yea and nay, *but* in him was yea (absolute certainty). For *all the promises of God in him are yea, and in him Amen*, unto the glory of God by us" (2 Cor. 1:18-20). Paul's promises and Paul's preaching had the character of God whom he served, and the character of the word of God that he preached. Believers should "provide things honest in the sight of all men" (Rom. 12:17).

a) The empty shrines, vv.5-6
There would be no calves. "The inhabitants of Samaria shall fear because

of the calves ('calf', JND) of Beth-aven: for the people thereof shall mourn over it, and the priests thereof that rejoiced on it, for the glory thereof, because it is departed from it. It shall also be carried unto Assyria for a present to king Jareb: Ephraim shall receive shame, and Israel shall be ashamed of his own counsel". As noted in connection with Hosea 5:13, "king Jareb" is an adjectival expression, meaning, 'a contentious king' (JND footnote). As said earlier, George Adam Smith calls him, 'King Pick-Quarrel!' If our understanding is correct, his proper name was Tiglath-pileser (2 Kings 15:27-31).

We must notice the sad commentary on the spiritual state of God's people: "the inhabitants of Samaria shall **fear** because of the calves of Beth-aven". (As noted in connection with 4:15, **Beth-el,** the house of God, had become **Beth-aven**, the house of vanity). They "**feared not** the LORD" (v.3), and had no concern for His glory: but they feared, mourned, and had every concern for the glory of their lost calf. Chapter 8:6 may suggest that king Jareb (see 5:13) was not too impressed with his present. So much for their calf-worship: no wonder "Ephraim shall receive shame, and Israel shall be ashamed of his own counsel" (v.6).

b) The empty throne, v.7
There would be no king. "As for Samaria, her king is cut off as the foam (some render 'twigs' or 'chips') upon the water". Hoshea was left helpless when "the king of Assyria shut him up, and bound him in prison" (2 Kings 17:4). How glad we are that the throne in heaven is occupied. The Lord Jesus is "set (sat down) on the right hand of the throne of the Majesty in the heavens" (Heb. 8:1), enabling us to sing:

> He fills the throne - the throne above,
> He fills it without wrong;
> The object of His Father's love,
> The theme of heaven's song.

Because He is there, we may "come boldly unto the throne of grace, that we may obtain mercy, and find grace to help in time of need" (Heb. 4:16).

c) The empty altars, v.8
There would be no worshippers. "The high places also of Aven, the sin of Israel (see 1 Kings 12:28-33) shall be destroyed; the thorn and the thistle shall come up on their altars". It seems most appropriate that Hosea should

say "the thorn and the thistle" here: see Genesis 3:18. We must take steps to ensure that thorns and thistles do not grow on our "altars". While in Israel's case they were idolatrous altars, nevertheless our "altars" of rightful devotion, prayer and worship can fall into disuse through sin and neglect. According to Gesenius the word "thistle" (*dardar*) means 'a luxuriously growing but useless plant'. Young's Concordance has 'thistle, bramble'.

The horror of invasion and massacre (they knew what was coming: see v.14) would cause terror: "And they shall say to the mountains, Cover us; and to the hills, Fall on us". The Assyrians treated prisoners of war monstrously. The Lord Jesus cited this verse in speaking to the "daughters of Jerusalem" (Luke 23:30), and it is cited again in Revelation 6:16. The sheer terror caused by the Assyrians (here) and the Romans (in Luke 23:30), is a pale reflection of the universal terror which will be caused by the "wrath of the Lamb". How glad we should be that the Lord Jesus has "delivered us from the wrath to come" (1 Thess. 1:10). In this case, "the wrath to come" is the judgment of the 'great tribulation'. See 1 Thessalonians 5:1-11, and in particular the words, "God hath not appointed us to wrath, but to obtain salvation by our Lord Jesus Christ" (v.9).

3) HISTORY FOUND THEM UNRIGHTEOUS, vv.9-15
Israel's long-standing sin is stressed by the words, "O Israel, thou hast sinned from the days of Gibeah". See Hosea 9:9, and Judges chs.18-20. This implies that "the nation had persisted in sin, and had not advanced beyond their early wicked condition" (M. F. Unger). The fearful sin committed at Gibeah, which the Benjamites refused to acknowledge, resulted in civil war (Judges 19:22-30). Although twice defeated, the other tribes ultimately triumphed, and almost completely destroyed Benjamin: "there they (the other tribes) stood: the battle in Gibeah against the children of iniquity did not overtake them" (v.9). Now, just as the surrounding tribes assembled against Benjamin, so foreign nations would assemble against those very tribes which ultimately overcame Benjamin. Israel as a nation proved to be no better than Benjamin. "It is in my desire that I should chastise them ('At my pleasure will I chasten them', JND, or 'when I so decide', D. Kidner); and the people ('peoples', plural) shall be assembled against them, when they shall bind themselves (or, 'when they are bound', JND) in their two furrows" (v.10). This is not easily understood, and the word rendered "furrows" (*onah*) leaves commentators in disarray. It is generally said that it means 'iniquities'. However, Israel had persisted in her original sins of rejecting the house of David and practising calf-worship (see 1 Kings 12:26-30), and it could be

said that judgment would fall upon them as they continued in these two furrows. Support for this might be found in Jeremiah 2:13: "For my people have committed **two evils**; they have forsaken me the fountain of living waters, and hewed them out cisterns, broken cisterns, that can hold no water". On the other hand, the "two furrows" might refer to the two calves erected by Jeroboam (1 Kings 12:28).

The Lord now illustrates the course of divine chastisement by referring in four ways to agricultural work with 'bound' or 'yoked' animals:

a) The work they loved doing, v.11
"Ephraim is as an heifer that is taught, and **loveth** to tread out the corn". This was comparatively light work, and the beast was fed and provisioned: "Thou shalt not muzzle the ox when he treadeth out the corn" (Deut. 25:4). Rather than submitting to the yoke of the law and doing the will of God, Israel preferred a self-gratifying life. They chose to live "according to their own will and pleasure, like a heifer without yoke and muzzle" (J. Gill, quoted by J. M. Flanigan).

b) The work they would be doing, v.11
"But I passed over upon her fair neck (i.e., put a yoke upon her neck): I will make Ephraim to ride ('draw', JND; 'I will set a rider on Ephraim', RV); Judah shall plough, and Jacob shall break his clods". Light work now gives place to laborious toil and the discipline of the yoke. This describes the bondage imposed by captivity. The passage also anticipates the ultimate downfall of Judah, bringing the entire nation into captivity; hence "**Judah** shall plow, and **Jacob** shall break his clods".

c) The work they could be doing, v.12
Even at this late hour, Hosea appeals to them. It was still possible that predicted judgment could be averted: "Sow to yourselves in righteousness, reap in mercy; break up your fallow ground: for it is time to seek the LORD, **till** he come (we must persist in sowing righteousness) and rain righteousness upon you". See also Jeremiah 4:3. As M. F. Unger observes, this involved "repentance toward God, and required more than scratching the surface". Derek Kidner is worth quoting in full here: "The expression 'fallow ground' was extraordinarily well suited to describe a people doubly impervious to the good seed of the word of God, both by the tangled growth of worldly notions and preoccupations which had taken hold of them, and by the hard crust beneath it all, of wills and attitudes never broken into penitence". If **we**

have hardened our hearts in any way to the word of God, it is also, for us, "time to seek the LORD". There was little time left for Israel, and perhaps little time left before we "appear before the judgment seat of Christ; that every one may receive the things done in his body" (2 Cor. 5:10).

d) *The work they had been doing, v.13*
"Ye have ploughed wickedness, ye have reaped iniquity: ye have eaten the fruit of lies: because thou didst trust in *thy way*, in the multitude of thy mighty men". They would prove that "there is a way which seemeth right unto a man, but the end thereof are the ways of death" (Prov.14:12).

The chilling words that follow (vv.14-15) describe the consequences of their evil work. The horrors of a previous military campaign under Shalmaneser (Shalman for short) would be repeated. "*Therefore* shall a tumult arise among thy people, and all thy fortresses shall be spoiled, as Shalman spoiled Beth-arbel (possibly Arbela, near the western shore of Galilee) in the day of battle: the mother was dashed in pieces upon her children. So shall Bethel do unto you because of your great wickedness: in a morning ('at daybreak' RV/JND) shall the king of Israel utterly be cut off". They had "sown the wind": now they would "reap the whirlwind" (8:7). The day of reckoning would come.

READ CHAPTER 11:1-11

"How shall I give thee up...?"

The atmosphere of the book now changes. Whilst Israel had offended and rejected God's love, and would reap judgment of the greatest severity, His love for Israel had not altered. It has been nicely said that God "loves that which He is obliged to smite, and is obliged to smite that which He loves" (J. N. Darby). The nation would be restored, not out of dogged determination to honour ancient promises, but because the Lord loved His people.

G. Campbell Morgan is worth quoting in full here: "Here begins the last movement in the prophecy of Hosea. In these last four chapters the emphasis is upon one note, that of the love of God. Hosea, prophesying in the dark days of the declension and backsliding of the northern kingdom of Israel, had been brought into fellowship with God through tragedy in his own home, through which tragedy, the tragedy of wounded love, there had come to him an understanding of the Divine heart. This has been realised throughout, but in this last movement it comes into special prominence".

In this connection we should notice the following: *(1)* God's love for them in their redemption (vv.1-4); *(2)* God's love for them in their rebellion (vv.5-9); *(3)* God's love for them in their restoration (vv.10-11).

1) GOD'S LOVE FOR THEM IN THEIR REDEMPTION, vv.1-4

First of all, God recalls His love for them in national infancy. "When Israel was *a child*, then I loved him, and called my son out of Egypt" (v.1). God's relationship with His people rested on His love for them: "The LORD did not set his love upon you, nor choose you, because ye were more in number than any people ('peoples', JND); for ye were the fewest of all people ('peoples', JND): but because the LORD loved you..." (Deut. 7:7-8). Compare Isaiah 63:9, "In all their affliction he was afflicted, and the angel of his presence saved them: in his *love* and in his pity he redeemed them; and he bare them, and carried them all the days of old"; Jeremiah

31:3, "The LORD hath appeared of old unto me ['from afar unto me', JND], saying, Yea, I have *loved* thee with an everlasting love; therefore with kindness have I drawn thee"; Malachi 1:2-3, "I have *loved* you, saith the LORD. Yet ye say, Wherein hast thou *loved* us? Was not Esau Jacob's brother? saith the LORD: yet I *loved* Jacob, and I hated Esau..."

a) He called them in love, vv.1-2
We can justifiably ponder both verses (vv.1-2) as they relate to Israel, with their lessons for ourselves, and the first verse, quoted in the New Testament, as it relates to the Lord Jesus Christ.

i) The relevance to Israel. "When Israel was a child, then I loved him, and called my son out of Egypt". God chose Israel out of His love for them, and eventually the time came for Him to implement His sovereign choice. God's love for His people gave them a unique status: "I...called *my son* out of Egypt". They were, in fact, God's firstborn son. See Exodus 4:22. As such, they were doubly-privileged (Deut. 21:15-17), and therefore doubly-responsible (Isaiah 40:2).

Alas, Israel abused the great privilege bestowed upon them. This follows: "As they called them, so they went from them: they sacrificed unto Baalim, and burned incense to graven images" (v.2). The child grew up, and became rebellious. God's love was not reciprocated. They rejected His word. After "the initial call which brought them out of Egypt" (J. M. Flanigan), the nation turned away from the Lord who loved them and redeemed them. Through the prophets, God "pleaded with them, exhorted them, warned them, but they would not heed" (J. M. Flanigan). In Hosea's own words, "As they (the prophets) called them, so they went from them: they sacrificed unto Baalim ('unto the Baals', JND), and burned incense to graven images" (v.2). See also v.7: "though they called them to the most High, none at all would exalt him". Compare Jeremiah 7:25-26.

ii) The relevance to ourselves. This reminds us of New Testament teaching: "Whom he did foreknow, he also did predestinate to be conformed to the image of his Son... Moreover whom he did predestinate, them he also called", leading Paul to say that "neither death, nor life, not angels, nor principalities, nor powers, nor things present, nor things to come, nor height, nor depth, nor any other creature, shall be able to separate us from the love of God, which is in Christ Jesus our Lord" (Rom. 8:29-30; 38-39). God displayed His love for Israel in redeeming them from Egypt, and He has displayed His love for us in "the redemption that is in Christ Jesus" (Rom. 3:24). See also 1 John 4:10.

But what about our response to His love for us? H.A.Ironside has a challenging piece here: "What saint but will see in words so lovely the story of his own deliverance from sin and Satan, when first brought to the knowledge of Christ...**let us challenge our hearts as to what return we have made to love so deep and tender**".

iii) Its relevance to the Lord Jesus Christ. As noted above, the passage is quoted in the New Testament: "he (Joseph) took the young child and his mother by night, and departed into Egypt: and was there until the death of Herod: that it might be **fulfilled which was spoken of the Lord by the prophet, saying, Out of Egypt have I called my son"** (Matt. 2:14-15). Israel is called "my son". The Lord Jesus is called "my Son" (Heb. 1:5). But more than that, the Lord Jesus is called "my **beloved** Son" (Matt. 3:17; 17:5). In passing, and as noted above, Israel is called God's "firstborn" (Exod. 4:22), and the Lord Jesus is "the image of the invisible God, the firstborn of every creature" (Col. 1:15).

The Lord Jesus, **not** the church, is the **true Israel**. In order to escape death by famine, Israel found refuge in Egypt. In order to escape death by the sword, the Lord Jesus also found refuge in Egypt. Having come out of Egypt, Israel passed through the wilderness, and the Lord Jesus was "led up of the Spirit into the wilderness" (Matt. 4:1). But what a difference! So far as Israel was concerned, "many of them ('most of them', JND)...were overthrown in the wilderness" (1 Cor. 10:5), but the Lord Jesus was "not rebellious, neither turned away back" (Isaiah 50:5) when "tempted of the devil". Ultimately, after passing through the wilderness, Israel entered the promised land, and after passing through another wilderness, the Lord Jesus began His ministry in the same land. It is called "thy land, O Immanuel" (Isaiah 8:8).

This is not an exaggerated comparison: Matthew is precise; "that it might be **fulfilled** which was spoken of the Lord by the prophet saying, Out of Egypt have I called my Son". In the words of J. M. Flanigan: "How wonderful is the versatility of Holy Scripture that what was true of the nation so many centuries earlier has actually been fulfilled also in the Messiah".

b) He taught them in love, v.3
"I taught Ephraim also to go, taking them by their arms" or "It was I that taught

Ephraim to walk" (JND). God displayed His love for Israel in "coaxing and supporting the child's first staggering steps; picking him up when he tires or tumbles" (D.Kidner). God did this as they left Egypt. It was too early to expose them to the rigours of war so he "led them not through the way of the land of the Philistines, although it was near; for God said, Lest peradventure the people repent when they see war, and they return to Egypt" (Exodus 13:17). Just watch the tottering child by the Red Sea where Pharaoh's pursuing chariots made them "sore afraid" and they "cried out unto the LORD" (Exodus 14:10). The child was very weak indeed, to the extent that Moses felt the full blast of their unbelief: "hast thou taken us away to die in the wilderness?...it had been better for us to serve the Egyptians, than that we should die in the wilderness" (Exodus 14:11-12). But the Lord who loved them took "them by the arms" in reassurance and deliverance. He taught them to trust in Him, and they all sang heartily, "The LORD is my strength and my song, and he is become my salvation: he is my God, and I will prepare him an habitation; my father's God, and I will exalt him" (Exodus 15:2).

But it was all short-lived. "He saved them from the hand of him that hated them, and redeemed them from the hand of the enemy. And the waters covered their enemies: there was not one of them left. Then believed they his words; they sang his praise. They soon forgat his works; they waited not for his counsel" (Psalm 106:10-13). Alas, they never really learned the lesson. God's tender support and help was disregarded. He nursed and cared for them, but "they knew not that I healed them". His early promise went unrecognised: "If thou wilt diligently hearken to the voice of the LORD thy God, and wilt do that which is right in his sight, and wilt give ear to his commandments, and keep all his statutes, I will put none of these diseases upon thee, which I have brought upon the Egyptians: for I am the LORD that healeth thee" (Exodus 15:26).

God who loves us provides all the help we need in order to "walk worthy of the Lord unto all pleasing". To this end we have "the knowledge of his will in all wisdom and spiritual understanding" (Col. 1:9-10). He still teaches His people to walk: see Ephesians 2:10; 4:1; 4:17; 5:2; 5:8; 5:15; Col. 4:5.

c) *He drew them in love, v.4*
"I drew them with cords (or 'ropes') of a man, with bands (*aboth*, 'thick bands') of love". While it is said that this refers to "a considerate herdsman caring for his oxen" (J. M. Flanigan), the language suggests something far more tender. In the words of G. Campbell Morgan, "That can only be understood

as we remember the first part of the prophecy. Hosea knew what that meant. He had been commanded to go and love a woman who had broken his heart, and take her home again. Jehovah thus spoke under the figure of a husband". The verse emphasises the strength of His love ("cords...bands").

d) He fed them in love, v.4
"I was to them as they that take off the yoke on their jaws, and I laid meat unto them". George Adam Smith sees here "the team of draught oxen surmounting the steep road", followed by rest and refreshment at its summit. God did not overdrive His people; they came, for example, to Elim with its "twelve wells of water, and threescore and ten palm trees" (Exodus 15:27). He provided the manna. See Exodus 16:1-36. Merrill Unger puts nicely: "the Lord pictures Himself as a human husbandman loosing the straps under the jaws of the oxen, by which the yoke is fastened to the neck, and then giving food and drink to the beasts (Exod. 16:32), a simple yet tender figure of the divine loving-kindness shown to Israel". How glad we are that "his divine power hath given unto us all things that pertain unto life and godliness" (2 Pet. 1:3).

2) GOD'S LOVE FOR THEM IN THEIR REBELLION, vv.5-9
God's love for the nation in its infancy had not diminished, even in the face of their rebellion and backsliding. We should therefore notice *(a)* the consequences of their backsliding (vv.5-7); *(b)* the continuity of God's love (vv.8-9).

a) The consequences of their backsliding, vv.5-7
In His love for them, God did not compromise His righteousness. He must deal with their sin. "He shall not return into the land of Egypt, but the Assyrian shall be his king" (v.5). This is a most significant statement. God would not reverse the redemption of His people. He did not do it then, and He does not do it now. One consequence of alliance with Egypt was that some would return there (9: 3): we know from Jeremiah chs.41-44, that refugees from Judah did so. But there would be no *national* return to Egypt. God would use the Assyrian, as He did in connection with Judah, as "the rod of mine anger" (Isaiah 10:5). Three reasons for this follow:

i) "They refused to return", v.5.
That is, refused to return to God. As noted above, God had spoken to them, He had made His word clear, but they had consciously rejected it: "As they (the prophets) called them, so they went from them: they sacrificed unto Baalim ('unto the Baals', JND), and burned incense to graven images" (v.2).

ii) They preferred "their own counsels", v.6. This evidently refers either to their preference for idolatry, or to their penchant for unholy alliances: "Ephraim also is a silly dove without heart; they call to Egypt, they go to Assyria" (7:11). In consequence "the sword shall abide on his cities ('turn about in his circles', JND), and shall consume his branches, and devour them (*akal*, as in v.4 'laid meat')…" Judgment would fall not only upon their "cities" but upon their branches", which probably refers to "lesser towns and villages" or possibly "their mighty men, their nobles and princes" (J. M. Flanigan). According to M. F. Unger, the words "shall abide" (*hala hul*) or "turn about in his circles" (JND), mean to 'whirl, twist, writhe'. Unger therefore describes "the sword" as 'an insatiable monster'.

iii) They were "bent to backsliding from me" v.7. We cannot fail to notice that God's people were not guilty of a silly mistake, but of a deliberate policy. According to M. F. Unger, the word, "bent" (*tala*) means 'to hang, be inclined toward, be hung up on'. We describe someone as having a 'hang up'. Judah was no better: "Why then is this people of Jerusalem slidden back by a perpetual backsliding? They hold fast deceit, they refuse to return" (Jer. 8:5).

The saddest part of it all is that they were God's people: "***my*** people are bent to backsliding from me". Compare Jeremiah 2:13; "For ***my*** people have committed two evils; they have forsaken me the fountain of living waters, and hewed out for themselves cisterns, broken cisterns, that can hold no water". Sadly, "though they (the prophets) called them to the most High, none at all would exalt him". It would be equally tragic if we lived like that. Paul's "earnest expectation and…hope" was "that in nothing I shall be ashamed, but that with all boldness, as always, so now also Christ shall be magnified in my body, whether it be by life, or by death" (Phil. 1:20). Every believer should desire to "exalt him" in that way.

b) The continuity of God's love, vv.8-9
Jeremiah exclaimed, "It is of the Lord's mercies that we are not consumed, because his compassions fail not…great is thy faithfulness" (Lam. 3:22), and this is the atmosphere of these verses. God says four times in v.8, "How shall I?", and three times in v.9, "I will not". We cannot miss the depth of divine feeling expressed in these words: "How shall I give thee up, Ephraim? How shall I deliver thee, Israel? How shall I make thee as Admah? How shall I set thee as Zeboim? Mine heart is turned within me, my repentings are kindled together. I will not execute the fierceness of mine anger, I will not return to

destroy Ephraim: for I am God, and not man: the Holy One in the midst of thee: and I will not enter into the city". As F. A. Tatford rightly observes, "this was no concession to sin, and certainly no restriction of the punishment due. It was rather an intimation that, whatever Israel's experiences and whatever judgment fell upon them, He would not entirely obliterate them".

The enormity of Israel's sin merited judgment akin to the destruction of Admah and Zeboim (companion cities to Sodom and Gomorrah: see Deut. 29:23: why only Admah and Zeboim are mentioned is not clear). But although "the sword shall abide on his cities, and shall consume his branches, and devour them", the love of God for His people did not permit their total rejection and annihilation: "mine heart is turned within me, my repentings ('compassions', RV) are kindled together". God's anger was tempered by His compassion. This is not the language of impulse and emotion, but of deep unchangeable love. The strength of God's determination to preserve rather than destroy His people is expressed in the words, "For I am God, and not man; the Holy One in the midst of thee". God's love was not fickle and unreliable: He would not abandon the people whom He had chosen in love, even though they deserved destruction. Compare Isaiah 49:14-16: "But Zion said, the LORD hath forsaken me, and my Lord hath forgotten me. Can a woman forget the sucking child, that she should not have compassion on the son of her womb? Yea, they may forget, yet will I not forget thee. Behold, I have graven thee upon the palms of my hands; thy walls are continually before me". The closing words, "I will not enter into the city" (v.9) mean, in the words of J. M. Flanigan, "He would not enter into Samaria to consume them as He had done with Sodom and Gomorrah".

3) *GOD'S LOVE FOR THEM IN THEIR RESTORATION, vv.10-11*
In proof of what He has said, God now anticipates the future blessing of His people, as a result of which, "They shall walk after the LORD". We must briefly note the following:

i) *Reawakening, v.10.* "He shall roar like a lion". The lion's roar signals imminent judgment: see Jeremiah 25:30-38; Joel 3:16; Amos 1:2; 3:8. It anticipates here the judicial hand of God in tribulation days, which will be recognised as "the day of the LORD". It has to be said, however, most commentators say the verse refers to the lion's roar in calling back its young, and that it therefore describes God's call to His captive people. *C'est possible!*

ii) Regathering, vv.10-11. "The children shall tremble ('hasten' or 'come trembling', JND), from the west. They shall tremble (ditto) as a bird out of Egypt, and as a dove out of the land of Assyria (compare 7:11)". That is, they will come from all points of the compass. Compare 7:11-12. See Isaiah 60:8. The word translated "west" (*yam*) means 'the sea' which "must be the Mediterranean" (J. M. Flanigan). He continues: "The islands of the sea and those western countries of Europe which have had such a populace of Jewish people will all yield them up *when the lion roars for its young and they return to Zion* (see comments above)".

iii) Resettlement, v.11. "I will place them in their houses, saith the LORD". Compare Ezekiel 36:11, "I will settle you after your old estates, and will do better unto you than at your beginnings" (v.11). Justin Waldron rightly suggests that we should now read John 14:2-3; 1 Peter 1:4. A splendid idea!

Note: the competent authorities tell us that in the Hebrew Bible, the last verse in our Chapter 11 is the first verse in our Chapter 12, and this certainly seems preferable since the verse, as it stands in the AV, does bring Chapter 11 to an abrupt end on a different theme (J. M. Flanigan).

READ CHAPTER 11:12 - 12:14

"Turn thou to thy God"

After affirming His love for erring Israel in chapter 11:1-11, God resumes His lawsuit ("controversy", 4:1) against Israel in the concluding verse of the chapter (v.12) with particular reference to alliances with foreign powers. If only they would learn, like Jacob centuries before, that power does not lie in subtilty and deceit, but in submission and dependence on God! He appeals to them on this basis in 12:6, "Therefore turn thou to thy God: keep mercy and judgment, and wait on thy God continually". The chapter may be divided as follows: *(1)* perversity before God, 11:12 - 12:2; *(2)* power with God (12:3-6); *(3)* prosperity without God (12:7-9); *(4)* prophets from God (12:10-14).

1) PERVERSITY BEFORE GOD, 11:12 - 12:2

Both kingdoms are censured by God, although at first glance this does not seem to be the case at all: "Ephraim compasseth me about with lies, and the house of Israel with deceit: but Judah yet ruleth with God, and is faithful with the saints" (11:12). There are, however, differences in translation:

- *As it stands* in the AV, the translation is perfectly clear: its meaning is unmistakable, leading J. M. Flanigan to say: "Judah however, still had a monarchy which had divine approval. In that sense they still ruled "with God", and were faithful with those that were holy, the true prophets and priests". However, according to Derek Kidner (*The message of Hosea*, IVP The Bible Speaks Today) the AV translation is based, not on the Hebrew text, but on the Septuagint Version. Notwithstanding, the meaning above might well have support if this particular part of Hosea's prophecy was delivered during the reign of Hezekiah (see 1:1). It could be said indeed of this period that "Judah yet ruleth with God, and is faithful with the saints".

- *As against this*, scholars tell us that the Hebrew words in question refer to Judah as actually unbridled or unruly towards God, rather than obedient to Him, leading to the alternative rendering, "And Judah is unruly against God, even against the faithful Holy One" (NIV) or "According to others, 'And Judah is yet unsteadfast as regard God and the true Holy One'" (JND margin). We should notice that J. N. Darby does say, "according to others!" Gesenius states that the Hebrew word rendered "ruleth" (AV) was 'used of beasts which have broken the yoke, and wander freely'. Derek Kidner rightly observes that the words "against the faithful Holy One" (NIV) sound a little forced, and suggests that since the plural is used here, the 'holy ones', it might be better to freely translate, "still loyal to the idols he counts holy".

In support of this, it has to be said that it does seem rather unlikely that Hosea should say "Judah yet ruleth with God, and is faithful with the saints", when, at the same time, "the LORD also hath a controversy with Judah" (12:2). There we must leave it.

Israel's double dealing with God ("Ephraim compasseth *me* about with lies, and the house of Israel with deceit", 11:12) was matched by double-dealing with foreign powers: "Ephraim feedeth on wind, and followeth after the east wind: he daily increaseth lies and desolation; and they do make a covenant with the Assyrians, and oil is carried into Egypt (12:1). Needless to say, the oil in question was olive oil. "Israel was rich in olive oil, and it became a valuable export (Ezek. 27:17)" (J. M. Flanigan).

- **Israel's double dealing with God** is illustrated in 8:11-13; "Because Ephraim hath made many altars to sin, altars shall be unto him to sin. I have written unto him the great things of my law, but they were counted as a strange thing. They sacrifice flesh for the sacrifices of mine offerings, *and eat it*; but the LORD accepteth them not; now will he remember their iniquity, and visit their sins: they shall return to Egypt".

- **Israel's double dealing with foreign powers** is explained in 2 Kings 17:4: "And the king of Assyria found conspiracy in Hoshea: for he had sent messengers to So king of Egypt, and brought no present to the king of Assyria, as he had done year by year".

It is therefore clear, firstly, that lack of integrity with God will lessen integrity with our fellow men, and, secondly, that the policy of alliance with foreign powers was both futile ("Ephraim feedeth on wind", probably referring to Egypt), and perilous ("followeth after the east wind", undoubtedly referring to Assyria). The word "feedeth" ("feedeth on wind") denotes "feeding or pasturing of a flock" (J. M. Flanigan). But it amounted to nothing. The "east wind" is identified later in the prophecy (13:15-16), where clear reference is made to the Assyrian destruction of Samaria: "an east wind shall come, the wind of the LORD shall come up from the wilderness, and his spring shall become dry, and his fountain shall be dried up: he shall spoil the treasure of all pleasant vessels. Samaria shall become desolate..." Israel would certainly prove to its cost, that the "east wind" was the "hot, destructive sirocco from the scorching desert" (M. F. Unger). See also Ezekiel 19:12, where it is predicted that another "east wind", in this case Babylon, would dry up Judah.

For us, "the friendship of the world" is equally futile and perilous. Paul tells us that the "the fashion of this world passeth away" (1 Cor. 7:31). James says something similar: see James 1:11. He also tells us that "the friendship of the world is enmity with God" and that "whosoever therefore will be the friend of the world is the enemy of God" (James 4:4). John tells us that "all that is in the world, the lust of the flesh, the lust of the eyes, and the pride of life, is not of the Father, but is of the world. And the world passeth away, and the lust thereof: but he that doeth the will of God abideth for ever" (1 John 2:16-17).

Judah is not excluded from divine judgment: "The LORD hath also a controversy (as in 4:1, a legal word denoting a lawsuit) with Judah, and will punish Jacob according to his ways; according to his doings will he recompense him" (v.2). God deals in perfect equity with all His people. There are no favourites with Him.

2) POWER WITH GOD, 12:3-6
God now addresses both Ephraim and Judah together, as "Jacob". The reason is clear: the nation had endeavoured to achieve security by diplomacy and double-dealing, by "lies" and "deceit". In his early history, Jacob displayed these very characteristics, but turned, in later life, from his duplicity to complete dependence on God. This great event in Jacob's life is now recalled, and made the ground of an appeal: "Therefore (in view of Jacob's experience) turn thou to thy God..." (v.6). Reference is made to: *(a)* Jacob's babyhood (v.3a); *(b)* Jacob's manhood (vv.3b-6):

a) Jacob's babyhood, v.3a
"He took his brother by the heel in the womb", or "In the womb he took

his brother by the heel" (RV). Jacob means, 'taking hold of the heel': "And after that (the birth of Esau) came his brother out, and his hand took hold on Esau's heel; and his name was called Jacob" (Gen. 25:26). According to Gesenius (*Hebrew - Chaldee Lexicon to the Old Testament*), Jacob means, in addition to the above, 'supplanter, layer of snares'. For 'supplanter' see Genesis 27:36, "And he (Esau) said, Is he not rightly called Jacob? For he hath supplanted me these two times". As Derek Kidner observes, "for years his dealings with his fellows were to confirm all that was sinister in the name, as of one who steals up from behind to outwit and overreach you". According to a piece supplied by Justin Waldron, "In ancient Israel, a 'heel-catcher' was a double-dealer, someone who achieved their goals through crafty and dishonest means". In this respect, Jacob was a picture of his descendants in Hosea's day, as they endeavoured to achieve security by diplomacy and alliance. But God looked for a change in His people, in exactly the same way that Jacob became Israel. This brings us to:

b) Jacob's manhood, vv.3b-6
"And by his strength he had power with God (or "In his manhood he had power with God", RV): Yea, he had power over the angel, and prevailed: he wept and made supplication unto him: he found him at Bethel, and there he spake with us; even the LORD God of hosts; the LORD is his memorial" (vv.3b-5). This refers to Jacob at Peniel (Genesis 32:24-32), and at Bethel (Genesis 35:1-15). For the identity of the Angel, see for example, Exodus 3:2-4, Judges 6:20-22, Judges 13:17-22, Isaiah 63:9, Revelation 10:1).

i) God gave power to Jacob at Peniel. "Yea he had power ('he strove', RV: 'he wrestled', JND) over the angel, and prevailed: he wept and made supplication unto him". Jacob "prevailed" and became Israel ("for as a prince hast thou power with God, and hast prevailed", Gen. 32:28), by crying, "I will not let thee go, except thou bless me" (Gen. 32:26). Jacob did not become Israel by resisting God ("there wrestled a man **with him**"), but by dependence on Him. In the language of the New Testament: "My grace is sufficient for thee: for my strength is made perfect in weakness" (2 Cor. 12:9). Israel and Judah desperately needed to learn the lesson, **and so do we.** F. A. Tatford points out that "Hosea revealed what had not been previously disclosed in the Genesis record, viz, that Jacob wept in his supplication to the One with whom he had wrestled all night".

ii) God made promises to Jacob at Bethel. "He found him in Bethel, and there he spake with us". This evidently refers to Jacob's second encounter with the Lord at Bethel (Gen. 35:1-15). He had previously seen the Lord in a vision received at Bethel (Gen. 28:11-19) but it seems more likely that Hosea is now, for the following reasons, referring to the latter of the two occasions:

- **The chronological order.** Hosea refers to Peniel first, and then to Bethel, rather than the reverse, although the words, "he **found** him in Bethel seem more applicable to the first occasion since Jacob was **commanded** to go to Bethel on the second occasion. On the other hand, the explanation may well lie in the fact that just as the Lord Jesus gave sight to the man born blind and then sought and found him (John 9:35) in order to give him wonderful reassurance, so Jacob, having passed through the experience of Peniel, is assured at Bethel of the Lord's future blessing (T. Miller).

- **The reference to Peniel.** Genesis 35 evidently refers to what had happened in Genesis 32: "Thy name is Jacob: thy name shall not be called any more Jacob, but Israel shall be thy name" (Gen. 35:10), referring to the words of the Angel, "Thy name shall be called no more Jacob, but Israel" (Gen. 32:28).

- **The use of the plural.** In Hosea's words, "he (the Lord) found him in Bethel, and there he spake with **us**". On the first occasion (Genesis 28), Jacob was alone, but on the second (Genesis 35) he was accompanied by his family, and it is usually suggested that the promises were made, not to one man only, but also to his descendants.

We have noticed how Jacob became a 'prince with God', but what was God's interest in Jacob in the first place? Although he was a fugitive, fleeing because of deceit, Jacob was none the less the subject of divine promises, which were given to him in Genesis 28, and confirmed and amplified in Genesis 35. But before he could realise those promises, he had to learn dependence on God. The lesson is now clear: God's people, as Jacob, were in receipt of divine promises, which could only be enjoyed once they, too, had learned dependence on God alone. The people, who had made "a covenant with the Assyrians" and supplied oil to Egypt (probably as a bribe), are now therefore urged, "Turn thou to thy God, keep mercy and judgment, and wait on thy God continually" (v.6). He was perfectly able to protect and sustain them: He is "the LORD God of hosts: the LORD is his memorial (the name by which He was to be remembered)" (v.5). The title,

"LORD God of hosts" ('*Jehovah Elohim* of hosts'), conveys His immense resources. See, for example Daniel 4:35. In the words of J. M. Flanigan, "Jehovah was His memorial Name, the Name of Him which is, and which was, and which is to come (Rev. 1:4, 8), unchanging, self-existing, all-sufficient and immutable".

It is noticeable that Hosea emphasises that it was at **Bethel** that Jacob encountered the "the LORD God of hosts". As Derek Kidner observes, Hosea "called the chief shrine of northern Israel by its right name, Bethel, 'the house of God', instead of by its savage nickname 'Beth-aven', 'the house of wickedness'. For it was **God** whom Jacob had met there, **not** a golden calf (10:5; 13:2); and if Israel would learn from Jacob, this was the first lesson it must face".

Israel's God is **our** God. His resources are undiminished, and the exhortation (or, better, 'command') given to Israel is equally applicable to us: "Turn thou to thy God, keep mercy and judgment, and wait on thy God continually". Compare Micah 6:8. We must listen now to F. A. Tatford: "Turning to God involved more than a mere nominal act: it implied a complete change of life - the jettisoning of the deceit and dissimulation which had characterised them, the repentance for the injustice to neighbour and nation, and the acknowledgement of the duties due to God and man. They should hold fast to lovingkindness and justice, demonstrating the genuineness of their returning to God by a new integrity and uprightness. Moreover, instead of scheming and intriguing on their own behalf and demonstrating thereby their confidence in their own ability, they should show their confidence in God by waiting continually upon Him and allowing Him to act in the lives of themselves and in the nation as He pleased…there is no other way for the one who submits to the Divine will and surrenders his life to God". All this is illustrated in the history of Jacob.

3) PROSPERITY WITHOUT GOD, 12:7-9
But, as H. A. Ironside observes, "the nation was following the first ways of their father". God, who had called them to "keep mercy and judgment, and wait on thy God continually" (v.6) had to say of His people, "He is a merchant (*kenaan*: a Canaanite: compare Zech. 14:21), the balances of deceit are in his hand" (v.7). The words, "balances of deceit" and "loveth to oppress ('defraud', JND margin)", tell us about their business transactions. See also Amos 8:4-6. Such practices were an "abomination to the LORD" (Prov. 11:1). According to Homer, the Canaanites or Phoenicians were

infamous for their greed and commonly known as money-lovers. Israel had become "as much dishonest traffickers as the Canaanites whom they had been originally commanded to destroy" (F. A. Tatford). It has to be said that nothing seemed to have changed in the next 700 years: see John 2:16.

Although Jacob is not mentioned by name here, there is an evident allusion to him in the words, "And Ephraim said, Yet am I become rich (Hosea prophesied at a time of national prosperity), I have found me out substance (they said the same at Laodicia, Rev. 3:17): in all my labours they shall find none iniquity in me that were sin" (v.8). This certainly recalls the business contract between Jacob and Laban which Jacob successfully manipulated to his own advantage without giving the slightest sign that he was acting unlawfully. See Genesis 30:25-43. The Fraud Squad didn't stand a chance with Jacob! (Had he been pressed, Jacob might well have argued that it was only a case of 'tit for tat': Laban had deceived *him*. See Genesis 31:7). Israel thought that they were 'squeaky-clean', but God was perfectly aware of their deceit. They were His people, and He would correct them: "But I [that am] Jehovah *thy* God from the land of Egypt will again make thee to dwell in tents, as in the days of the solemn feast" (v.9, JND). See Leviticus 23:42. At first glance, this appears to refer to the Millennial Kingdom, but the context demands otherwise: their deceit would be rewarded by dispossession of the land, and they would become, again, a wandering people without permanent dwelling. Hence the words, "in tabernacles *as* in the days of the solemn feasts" (v.9, AV) not 'in tabernacles in the days of the solemn feasts'. Peter describes his first readers as "sojourners of the Dispersion" (1 Pet. 1:1 RV).

4) PROPHETS FROM GOD, 12:10-14
The final paragraph of this chapter emphasises that God had warned His people about the consequences of their sin and wickedness. Hosea has already referred to this: see, for example, 6:5; 9:7-8. There are two sub-paragraphs in this section of the chapter, both of which stress the divinely-given authority of the prophets, and the consequences of ignoring them:

a) *The prophets generally, vv.10-12*
"I have also spoken by the prophets, and have multiplied visions, and used similitudes, by the ministry of the prophets. Is there iniquity in Gilead? surely they are vanity: they sacrificed bullocks in Gilgal; yea, their altars are as heaps in the furrows of the fields" (vv.10-11). The prophets were men in receipt of God's word. "I have also spoken *to* the prophets" (JND) or "*unto*

the prophets" (RV). This is echoed in Hebrews 1:1: "God, who at sundry times and in divers manners **spake in time past unto the fathers by the prophets**..." We should notice the following:

i) The **source** of their ministry: "I have also spoken by the prophets..." (v.10). See 2 Peter 1:21: "no prophecy of the scripture is of any private interpretation (that is, the prophets did not tell the people what **they** thought God meant). For the prophecy came not in old time by the will of man: but holy men of God spake as they were moved by the Holy Ghost" or "men spake from God, being moved by the Holy Ghost" (RV).

ii) The **clarity** of their ministry. "I have also **spoken** by the prophets, and have **multiplied** visions, and **used** similitudes (parables), by the ministry of the prophets". As Jack R. Riggs points out, "The thought is that God has not only spoken, but that He has spoken clearly so that He could be understood".

iii) The **variety** in their ministry: "I have also spoken by the prophets, and have multiplied visions, and used similitudes (parables), by the ministry of the prophets" (v.10). Here is an example of the "divers manners" in which God spoke (Heb. 1: 1).

iv) The **forthrightness** of their ministry: "Is there iniquity in Gilead? Surely they are vanity: they sacrifice bullocks in Gilgal; yea their altars are as heaps in the furrows of the fields" (v.11).There was nothing neutral about their preaching; they got down to detail.

- **Gilead**, on the east of Jordan, was known for its iniquity: see Hosea 6:8-9. It would become "vanity" or 'nothing'. What Hosea "plainly predicted as their fate came to pass (2 Kings 15:29)". Here is the passage: "In the days of Pekah king of Israel came Tiglath-pileser king of Assyria, and took Ijon, and Abel-beth-maachah, and Janoah, and Kedesh, and Hazor, and **Gilead**, and Galilee, all the land of Naphtali, and carried them captive to Assyria".

- **Gilgal**, on the west of Jordan, was equally culpable, but for a different reason: "they sacrifice bullocks in Gilgal". Gilgal, where prophets were trained under Elijah and Elisha (2 Kings 2:1; 4:38), and which had most sacred associations in the past, was now evidently notorious for idolatry: "All their wickedness is in Gilgal: for there I hated them: for the wickedness of their doings" (Hosea 9:15). See also Hosea 4:15. Amos, contemporary with Hosea, refers to Gilgal as follows: "Come to Bethel, and transgress: at Gilgal multiply transgression; and bring your sacrifices every morning, and your tithes after three years" (Amos 4:4). Bullocks were evidently sacrificed at Gilgal "in an affront to the true God" (F. A. Tatford). As a result, "their altars are as heaps in the furrows of the fields". The present tense is used to denote the certainty of coming judgment. According to F. A. Tatford this means that "their altars would become like the heaped stones which the farmer piled up in the ploughed fields, and of no more value to the worshippers than such heaps". Alternatively, "as gathered and piled stones would dot a farmer's field, so Israel multiplied her stone altars across the land" (J. Waldron).

This is followed by a fourth, and rather unexpected, reference to Jacob: "And Jacob fled into the country of Syria ('Aram', RV), and Israel served for a wife, and for a wife he kept (*shamar*: rendered 'preserved in v.13) sheep" (v.12). (See Genesis 29). So, in a chapter which draws lessons from the life of Jacob, God cites his history again to illustrate the consequences of Israel's "lies" and "deceit" (11:12), witnessed by their sacrifices and altars. For his deceit, Jacob became an exile engaged in long and laborious toil. It would not be long before Israel followed suit.

b) A prophet particularly, vv.13-14

Having said, "I have also spoken by the prophets" (v.10), Hosea now says, "and by a prophet the LORD brought Israel out of Egypt, and by a prophet was he preserved" (v.13). The way in which the Lord had delivered and preserved the nation had been rewarded by the total rejection of His word (v.14). The value and importance of the prophetic office is emphasised by the fact that Moses is not mentioned by name: "By *a prophet* the Lord brought Israel out of Egypt, and by *a prophet* was he preserved". It was not so much **who** Moses was, but **what** Moses was. Compare 1 Corinthians 3:5, "Who then is Paul, and who is Apollos, but ministers by whom ye believed, even as the Lord gave to every man?" In this case Moses is described as "a prophet". The man used by God to deliver and preserve His people was the same man who predicted the awful consequences of rejecting the word of God. See, for example, Deuteronomy 28:15-68.

The awful crime of rejecting the prophetic word follows: "Ephraim hath provoked to anger most bitterly: therefore shall his blood (that is, his blood-guiltiness) be left upon him, and his reproach shall his Lord (strongly suggesting His continuing authority) return unto him" (RV). F. A. Tatford helpfully explains: "Moreover, their reproach - the insult offered to God by the idolatrous rites of Baalism - would recoil upon the people's heads". In New Testament language: "Be not deceived; God is not mocked: for whatsoever a man soweth, that shall he also reap" (Gal 6:7).

As Justin Waldron points out, "God still values highly obedience to the word of God: see James 1:22-25". It should also be said that it is still perilous for sinners and saints to reject God's word.

READ CHAPTER 13

"Thou hast destroyed thyself"

With this chapter we reach "the climax of Hosea's prophecies of doom, but not the climax of the book....That distinction is reserved for the next chapter" (Derek Kidner). While the ultimate blessing of Israel is assured (v.14), this chapter concludes on the most chilling note of all: "Samaria shall become desolate; for she hath rebelled against her God: they shall fall by the sword: their infants shall be dashed in pieces, and their women with child shall be ripped up" (v.16).

The chapter comprises four main paragraphs: *(1)* increasing sin (vv.1-3): "they sin more and more" (v.2); *(2)* incontestable rights (vv.4-8): "I am the LORD thy God from the land of Egypt" (v.4); *(3)* infinite grace (vv.9-14): "I will be thy king...save thee...ransom them from...the grave...redeem them from death" (vv.10, 14); *(4)* inevitable judgment (vv.15-16): "Samaria shall become desolate...they shall fall by the sword" (v.16).

1) INCREASING SIN, vv.1-3
These verses plot the progress of idolatry: *(a)* its commencement (v.1); *(b)* its course (v.2); *(c)* its conclusion (v.3).

a) Its commencement, v.1
"When Ephraim spake trembling, he exalted himself in Israel; but when he offended in Baal, he died", or "When Ephraim spoke, there was trembling; he exalted himself in Israel: but he trespassed through Baal, and he died" (JND). In the first case (AV), Ephraim is trembling as he speaks; in the second (JND/RV), others are trembling as he speaks. We ought to say that as a general rule, Ephraim (said to occur 37 times in Hosea), being the principal tribe and having the national capital (Samaria), stands for the entire nation. See Ezekiel 37:15-17. Similarly, the two tribes in the south, Judah and Benjamin are called, corporately, Judah. There are references

to an image of Baal in 2 Kings 3:2; 10:26-27. Calf-worship was evidently distinct from Baal-worship: see 2 Kings 10:29.

If we follow the Authorised Version ("When Ephraim spake trembling, he exalted himself in Israel; but when he offended in Baal, he died"), the starting point is Ephraim's humility, reminding us that "before honour is humility" (Prov. 15:33), and pointing us to the New Testament lesson: "Yea...all of you be clothed with humility: for God resisteth the proud, and giveth grace to the humble. Humble yourselves therefore under the mighty hand of God, that he may exalt you in due time" (1 Pet. 5:5-6).

If we follow the New Translation (JND) and the Revised Version ("When Ephraim spoke, there was trembling; he exalted himself in Israel: but he trespassed through Baal, and he died") then the starting point is not Ephraim's original humility which gave way to pride and self-assertion, but rather his exalted position which led to his decline and fall. Ephraim was certainly given priority over Manasseh (Gen. 48:17-20) and most definitely achieved eminence in Israel through Joshua. See Numbers 13:8. It was Joshua, Ephraim's most glorious son, who charged the nation with idolatry and urged them to forsake it (Joshua 24:14).

Sadly, another son of Ephraim, Jeroboam (1 Kings 11:26 RV), endeavoured to cement control of the ten tribes by placing golden calves in Bethel and Dan with the proclamation, "Behold thy gods, O Israel, which brought thee up out of the land of Egypt" (1 Kings 12:28).

But Hosea may well be referring to something more specific here. Some fifty years after Jeroboam, Ahab, newly married to Jezebel, "went and served **Baal,** and worshipped him. And he reared up an altar for Baal in the house of Baal, which he had built in Samaria" (1 Kings 16:31-32). In doing this, Ahab signed his own death-warrant, his family's death-warrant, and the nation's death-warrant: "when he offended in Baal, he died". As Derek Kidner points out "Ephraim 'died' assuredly as Adam did, although like Adam he went on living to all outward appearance". In personal terms, judgment duly fell on Ahab at Ramoth-Gilead (1 Kings 22:29-37). In family terms, judgment fell on his family (2 Kings 9:1-10; 10:1-11) at the hands of Jehu. The 'house of Ahab' certainly died, and in like manner Ephraim would die. Judgment was imminent.

In summary, we must notice some important lessons for ourselves here. The lessons are timeless:

- *In the first place*, we must beware of pride: the words "he exalted himself in Israel" have a nasty ring about them, and we must never forget the Lord's words to His disciples, "whosoever will be great among you, let him be your minister; and whosoever will be chief among you, let him be your servant" (Matt. 20:26-27). We should now read 1 Samuel 15:17.

- *In the second place*, self-importance and self-assertion are recipes for disaster: Ephraim "exalted himself in Israel", and "offended in Baal", and this is explained later in the chapter: "their heart was exalted; therefore have they forgotten me" (v.6). It could also be said, that the verse illustrates the oft-quoted (and oft-misquoted) words: "Pride goeth before destruction, and an haughty spirit before a fall" (Prov. 16:18).

- *In the third place*, we must never forget the New Testament injunction, "Little children, keep yourselves from idols" (1 John 5:21).

b) Its course, v.2

The warning above went unheeded: Ephraim learnt absolutely nothing from his history: "And now they sin more and more, and have made them molten images of their silver, and idols *according to their own understanding* (note this: it all began in *their* minds), all of it the work of the craftsmen: they say of them, Let the men that sacrifice kiss the calves". Sin never stands still. It is a 'slippery slope'. In pursuing idolatry, they deliberately transgressed the first and second commandments, and exhibited gross stupidity at the same time. Human beings, the crowning glory of God's creation, were kissing calves! It was sinful in the first place, and bizarre in the second. Other prophets expose the sheer stupidity of idolatry. See, for example, Isaiah 44:9-20. In this case, amongst other things, the carefully crafted idol has to remain "in the house". Jeremiah says something similar. After all the artisans have finished their work, the idol has to be "fastened with nails and with hammers, that it move not". Jeremiah continues: "They are as upright as the palm tree, but speak not: they must needs be borne, because they cannot go" (Jer. 10:3-5).

The course of our modern world is very much like the course of Israel's history. In Hosea's day, they were sinning "more and more", and we live today in a world where "evil men and seducers...wax worse and worse, deceiving, and being deceived" (2 Tim. 3:13).

c) Its conclusion, v.3

Hosea employs four figures to describe the cessation of national life:

"Therefore they shall be as the *morning cloud*, and as the *early dew* that passeth away, as the *chaff* that is driven with the whirlwind out of the floor, and as *the smoke* out of the chimney". As J. M. Flanigan observes, "Their idolatrous kingdom would not last, and the prophet employs four similes to illustrate how soon and how suddenly they would be scattered by the approaching captivity and exile…there was no future for them". Hosea's similes are worth pursuing. For example, "the *morning cloud* (some say 'morning mist')" with its apparent promise of rain (see Jude v.12), proves to be nothing but a false hope. Idolatry is certainly like that. The *dew* quickly passes away "leaving the land dry and desolate" (J. M. Flanigan). Idolatry is certainly like that as well. *Chaff* is worthless, and most unstable, and these people were as empty and as useless as chaff. The "whirlwind" of Assyrian invasion would certainly drive Israel out of his "floor". *Smoke* quickly dissolves in the air (Hosea isn't talking about industrial smoke), and F. A. Tatford puts it nicely in saying that "they were no more permanent than the smoke which escaped through the hole in the roof. Security and stability were no longer theirs". In exile, "the children of Israel would remain many days without a king…and without *an image*, and without an ephod, and without *teraphim*" (Hos. 3:4). The captivity and exile would effectively bring idolatry to an end.

2) INCONTESTABLE RIGHTS, vv.4-8
The Lord now proclaims His rights over Israel and His intention to assert those rights. We may summarise the section as follows: *(a)* His rights proclaimed (vv.4-6a); *(b)* His rights rejected (v.6b); *(c)* His rights asserted (vv.7-8).

a) His rights proclaimed, vv.4-6a
"Yet I am the LORD thy God from the land of Egypt, and thou shalt know no god but me: for there is no saviour beside me. I did know thee in the wilderness, in the land of great drought. According to their pasture so were they filled". The Lord had every right to their fidelity and devotion:

i) **Because He was their God**. "I am the LORD thy God". Sadly they had forgotten that He was the one true God and that He had said, "I am the LORD thy God, which have brought thee out of the land of Egypt, out of the house of bondage. Thou shalt have no other gods before me. Thou shalt not make unto thee any graven image…" (Exodus 20:1-4).

ii) **Because He was their Saviour-God.** "There is no saviour beside me".

Compare Isaiah 43:11, "I, even I, am the LORD; and beside me there is no saviour"; Isaiah 45:21, "There is no God else beside me; a just God and a Saviour; there is none beside me".

This had been displayed in their **deliverance from Egypt**: "I am the LORD thy God from the land of Egypt" (v.4), in their **preservation in the wilderness**: "I did know thee in the wilderness, in land of great drought" (v.5), and in **provision in the land**: "according to their pasture they so were filled" (v.6).

The God who said to Israel, "No God *but me*...no Saviour *beside me*", is *our* God. Like Israel, we have a Saviour-God. He is "God our Saviour" (Titus 1:3; 2:10; 3:4). We too have been delivered from bondage, preserved and provisioned in this wilderness-world, and brought into a wonderful inheritance where there is abundant provision currently and eternally available to us.

b) His rights rejected, v.6b

"They were filled, and their heart was exalted; therefore have they forgotten me". It was like the case of Uzziah who was "marvellously helped, till he was strong. But when he was strong, his heart was lifted up to his destruction" (2 Chron. 26:15-16). Moses had warned the people of this very danger: "For the LORD thy God bringeth thee into a good land...When thou hast eaten and art full, then thou shalt bless the LORD thy God for the good land which he hath given thee. Beware that thou forget not the LORD thy God, in not keeping his commandments, and his judgments, and his statutes... Lest when thou hast eaten and art full...then thine heart be lifted up, and thou forget the LORD thy God" (Deut. 8:7-20).

We must not fail to remember and recognise that "Every good gift and every perfect gift is from above, and cometh down from the Father of lights, with whom is no variableness, neither shadow of turning" (James 1:17).

c) His rights asserted, vv.7-8

"Therefore I will be unto them as a lion: as a leopard by the way will I observe them: I will meet them as a bear that is bereaved of her whelps, and will rend the caul ('covering', JND, evidently referring to the breast, perhaps the rib-cage) of their heart, and there will I devour them like a lion: the wild beast shall tear them". God's rights over His people would be displayed again, but this time in delivering them *to* their enemies. He had redeemed and preserved His people: He therefore had every right to punish their disobedience and unthankfulness.

The assembly at Corinth learnt the same lesson to their cost: "But let a man examine himself, and so let him eat of that bread, and drink of that cup. For he that eateth and drinketh unworthily, eateth and drinketh damnation (judgment) to himself, not discerning the Lord's body. For this cause many are weak and sickly among you, and many sleep" (1 Cor. 11:28-30). Ananias and Sapphira leant the same lesson (Acts 5:1-11).

The references to "lion…leopard…bear…wild beast" are undoubtedly employed to emphasise the severity of pending judgment. The strength of the lion, the swiftness of the leopard, the ferocity and fury of a bear who had lost her cubs are all implicit here. While this must refer to the coming Assyrian conquest, it is tempting to think that, at the same time, they could have a wider prophetic significance. Compare Daniel 7:1-7, where the *lion* represents the Babylonian empire (v.4); the *leopard* represents the Grecian empire (v.6); the *bear* represents the Medo-Persian empire (v.5), and the *"wild beast"* represents the Roman empire "which shall be diverse from all kingdoms, and shall devour the whole earth, and shall tread it down, and break it in pieces" (v.23). Do remember, however, that it is only "tempting to think" that this might be the case! Very tempting indeed! After all, the four "beasts" (back to Daniel ch.7) would all subjugate Israel.

3) INFINITE GRACE, vv.9-14
God's infinite grace comes at the end of the paragraph, although the AV rendering suggests that it comes at the beginning as well: "O Israel, thou hast destroyed thyself; but in me is thine help, I will be thy king: where is any other that may save thee in all thy cities? And thy judges of whom thou saidst, Give me a king and princes?" (vv.9-10). However, the RV (supported by JND) reads as follows: "It is thy destruction, O Israel, that thou art against me, against thy help. Where now is thy king, that he may save thee in all thy cities…?" Nevertheless, it must be said that the Authorised Version makes perfectly good sense!

This section of the chapter may be divided as follows: *(a)* present destruction (vv.9-13); *(b)* coming deliverance (v.14).

a) Present destruction, vv.9-13
i) The cause, vv.9-11. "O Israel, thou hast destroyed thyself" (v.9). Israel

was reaping what she had sown. Sadly, this could be said of many believers today. Disobedience brings catastrophic results. It all began with the rejection of divine rule, when the failure of Samuel's sons, and the desire to emulate surrounding nations, prompted the request, "Make us a king". (1 Sam. 8:6). But they wanted a king for another reason: "that our king may judge us, and go out before us, **and fight our battles**" (1 Sam. 8:20). Now there was no king to do anything. Hoshea was in prison for the last three years of Israel's existence (see 2 Kings 17:4-6), and this seems to be the most likely explanation of the question, "Where now is thy king...?" (v.10 RV). So much for "a king and princes". So much for confidence in men, rather than confidence in God (Psalm 118:8-9).

The words, "I gave thee a king in mine anger, and took him away in my wrath" (v.11) can certainly be read in connection with Saul. Samuel was told by God "they have rejected me, that I should not reign over them" (1 Sam. 8:7) and He gave them 'a king in his anger'. Saul was certainly removed in God's wrath (1 Sam. 16:1). But so was the last king of Judah (Zedekiah: see 2 Kings 25:7) and so was the last king of Israel (Hoshea: see 2 Kings 17:6). There will never be another throne in Samaria, but the throne of David will not be empty for ever: the Lord Jesus will sit "upon the throne of David, and upon his kingdom, to order it, and to establish it with judgment and with justice, from henceforth even for ever" (Isaiah 9:7).

ii) The consequences, vv.12-13. "The iniquity of Ephraim is bound up; his sin is hid. The sorrows of a travailing woman shall come upon him: he is an unwise son; for he should not stay long in the place of the breaking forth of children". We should notice:

- The record of his sin. The words "The iniquity of Ephraim is bound up; his sin is hid" (v.12) evidently refer to the record of Ephraim's sin. See, for example Hosea 9:9. It is said that Hosea alludes here to "the practice of maintaining records of important events (Ezra 4:14-19)" when "the documents were tied together and then stored in a depositary for safe keeping (Deut 32:34; Isaiah 8:16)" (F. A. Tatford).(Documents for production in court are treated in the same way today). In New Testament language, "after thy hardness and impenitent heart" thou "treasurest up unto thyself wrath against the day of wrath and revelation of the righteous judgment of God" (Rom. 2:5). "The New Testament makes it clear that an imperishable record is kept of the deeds of all mankind and that, at the final assize, sentence will be passed on the basis of the unerring records maintained in heaven

(Rev. 20:12)" (F. A. Tatford). Israel must not imagine that any apparent delay in divine judgment meant that "Jehovah had forgotten or had decided to overlook their iniquities" (J. M. Flanigan). We must not imagine that either.

- **The certainty of judgment on his sin**: "The sorrows of a travailing woman shall come upon him" (v.13). Birth pangs are unavoidable, and so was the pain caused by divine judgment. The same figure is also used in connection with the sufferings of Israel in the Great Tribulation: "Wherefore do I see every man with his hands on his loins, as a woman in travail, and all faces are turned into paleness? Alas! For that day is great, so that none is like it; it is even the time of Jacob's trouble, but he shall be saved out of it" (Jer. 30:6-7). See also 1 Thessalonians 5:3, "For when they shall say, Peace and safety; then sudden destruction cometh upon them, as travail upon a woman with child; and they shall not escape".

- **The fatality of his sin**. Hosea emphasises the fatality of the situation: "he is an unwise son; for he should not stay long in the place of the breaking forth of children" (v.13). We get a little help from Hezekiah here: speaking in similar circumstances (the Assyians were at the door), he said "This day is a day of trouble....for the children are come to the birth, and there is not strength to bring forth" (2 Kings 19:3). When Hezekiah prayed to God the threat was averted, but here Ephraim, by staying "long in the place of the breaking forth of children", made no effort to extricate himself from fatal circumstances. Although Hosea had cried, "It is time to seek the Lord" (10:12), Ephraim did nothing. In consequence, he would perish like an unborn child remaining in its mother's womb. Interestingly, the responsibility here is attributed to the child. "The wise child, in the prophet's view, would be eager to leave the womb and to preserve the lives of himself and his mother thereby. Ephraim, with supreme lack of judgment, was delaying his birth" (F. A. Tatford). He did this at the risk of death. It would be fatal.

b) Coming deliverance, v.14
But suddenly (as on other occasions in Hosea's preaching) the picture changes: death gives place to life: "I will ransom them from the power of the grave (*sheol*); I will redeem them from death: O death, I will be thy plagues; O grave, I will be thy destruction". While, according to Derek Kidner, the Hebrew "does not use the interrogative prefix", this verse *is* cited by Paul interrogatively: "O death, where is thy sting? O grave where is thy victory" (1 Cor. 15:55). In the New Testament setting, it refers to the resurrection of individual believers, but in Hosea, *it refers to national resurrection.* This

is demanded by the context. Compare Ezekiel 37:1-14. (For the record, some commentators, following the RSV, *do* accept that Hosea is speaking interrogatively here: "Shall I ransom them from the power of Sheol? shall I redeem them from Death?", and that the Lord is calling on "Death" and "Sheol" to visit Israel since "compassion ('repentance', AV) is hid from mine eyes").

The basis on which the nation will ultimately be restored is clearly stated in the words "I will **ransom** (*padah*, to free)...I will **redeem** (*gaal* with its association with *goel*, the kinsman-redeemer)". All blessing, in every age, individual or national, rests upon the redemptive work of Christ. Although national destruction stared Israel in the face, "the Lord's unchanging purpose to restore Israel was once more reiterated in the very vortex of the maelstrom of sin that was about to hurl the nation into ruin" (H. A. Ironside). God's purpose for His people would not alter, and the words, "repentance shall be hid from mine eyes", remind us of Paul's observation in connection with Israel, "For the gifts and calling of God are without repentance" (Rom. 11:29). But the millennial blessing of Israel was then far distant: the storm of divine judgment was about to break. So:

4) INEVITABLE JUDGEMENT, vv.15-16
Joseph named his second son Ephraim, "For God hath caused me to be fruitful in the land of my affliction" (Gen. 41:52). But not now: "Though he be fruitful among his brethren, an east wind shall come, the wind of the LORD shall come up from the wilderness, and his spring shall become dry, and his fountain shall be dried up: he shall spoil the treasure of all pleasant vessels. Samaria shall become desolate; for she hath rebelled against her God: they shall fall by the sword: their infants shall be dashed in pieces, and their women with child shall be ripped up". Ephraim would cease to be fruitful, both materially (v.15), and in progeny (v.16). We have already encountered "the east wind" (see 12:1). The Assyrians achieved notoriety by their cruelty and barbarity. But behind Assyria lay the hand of God: it was "an east wind.....*the wind of the LORD*".

But the hand that judged, is the hand that will restore, as the final chapter will prove.

READ CHAPTER 14

"Return unto the Lord thy God"

The preceding Chapters of Hosea leave us in no doubt about the justice of God's "controversy" with His people (4:1). There is no doubt, either, that although the guilt of the nation could not be excused, God retained His original love for them. This is emphasised particularly in Chapter 11 ("How shall I give thee up, Ephraim? How shall I deliver thee, Israel...mine heart in turned within me, my repentings are kindled together", v.8), let alone in the analogy of Hosea's own relationship with Gomer, and now underlies the tender appeal with which the prophecy terminates: "I will heal their backsliding, *I will love them freely*" (14:4).

The chapter is both a *bona fide* appeal to Israel at the time, and a description of ultimate national blessing following repentance. Since, however, it is addressed to people "bent to backsliding" (11:7), its application to ourselves is very clear. What is God's attitude to the backsliding Christian? The chapter reveals the heart of God, and may be divided as follows: *(1)* the return (vv.1-3); *(2)* the reception (vv.4-5a); *(3)* the result (vv.5b-8); *(4)* the resumé (v.9).

1) THE RETURN, vv.1-3
This section of the chapter sets out the pathway which the backslider must take in returning to God: we should notice: *(a)* depth of conviction (v.1); *(b)* desire for cleansing (v.2); *(c)* determination to continue (v.3).

a) Depth of conviction, v.1
There must be recognition of previous failure and decline: "O Israel, return unto the LORD thy God; for thou hast fallen by thine iniquity". Their sinful backsliding had not altered His relationship with them. He was still their God: "return unto the LORD *thy* God". He takes the initiative in effecting their restoration by engendering conviction of sin in their hearts and minds. Previous chapters, with their searching messages, may have illuminated areas of weakness and deficiency in *our* lives. Perhaps we have heard the

Saviour say, "I have somewhat against thee..." (Rev. 2:4). None of us are immune from the danger of backsliding.

b) Desire for cleansing, v.2
Conviction of sin is followed by confession, and desire for forgiveness and cleansing: "Take with you words, and turn to the LORD". He then tells them what to say: what follows are *His* words: "say unto him, Take away all iniquity, and receive us graciously ('accept that which is good', RV: JND margin): so will we render the calves of our lips". There had been a great deal of lip-service, and a great deal of religious ceremony, but now there must be reality. 'That which is good' is described by David as follows: "For thou desirest not sacrifice; else would I give it... the sacrifices of God are a broken spirit: a broken and a contrite heart, O God, thou wilt not despise" (Psalm 51:16-17). The word 'render' is the "term used for paying one's vows... in due gratitude for answered prayer" (Derek Kidner). See, for example, Psalm 116:14, "I will pay my vows unto the LORD now in the presence of all his people". Compare Eccl. 5:6. Here, in our current chapter, it is thanksgiving after cleansing. The verse is cited Hebrews 13:15, "By him therefore let us offer the sacrifice of praise continually, that is, *the fruit of our lips,* giving thanks to his name". We cannot fail to remember the teaching of the New Testament at this juncture: "If we confess our sins, he is faithful and just to forgive us our sins, and to cleanse us from all unrighteousness" (1 John 1:9).

It is tempting to contrast the words, so shall "we render the *calves* of our lips" with "The inhabitants of Samaria shall fear because of the *calves* of Beth-aven (10:5) and "Let the men that sacrifice kiss the *calves*" (13:2), However, according to Young's Concordance, different Hebrew words are used in each case. Here (14:2), the word *par* refers to a young bull; in 10:5, the word *eglah* evidently refers to a calf, particularly a heifer; in 13:2 the word *egel* appears to have the same meaning as *eglah.* It will not escape notice, however, that the word used here (*par*) refers to an animal of the highest value ('young bullocks', JND). Israel was to give her best to God. It will do so in the future, and we must do so now.

c) Determination to continue, v.3
"Asshur shall not save us; we will not ride upon horses: neither will we say any more to the work of our hands, Ye are our gods: for in thee the fatherless find mercy".

Ephraim had been previously described as "a silly (open to deception) dove without heart (senseless): they call to Egypt, they go to Assyria" (7:11). She is described in this way because her behaviour was senseless because it was useless: "They call to Egypt, they go to Assyria". Their 'shuttle diplomacy' is illustrated in 2 Kings 17:1-4. They attempted to avert a crisis by making an alliance elsewhere, only to find that the very God they had ignored and forgotten was waiting with His net: "I will spread my net upon them: I will bring them down as the fowls of the heaven" (Hos. 7:12). They looked south-west, and north-east, but they forgot to look up. Such conduct was intolerable to God: "I will chastise them, as their congregation hath heard" (Hos. 7:12).

But they were now to say, "Asshur shall not save us". No more recourse to Assyria. There was to be no more recourse to Egypt, with its horses. See Isaiah 31:1, "Woe to them that go down to Egypt for help; and stay on horses". Compare Deuteronomy 17:16, "he (the future king) shall not multiply horses to himself, not cause the people to return to Egypt, to the end that he should multiply horses". See also Song of Solomon 1: 9. There was to be no more idolatry: "Neither will we say any more to the works of our hands, Ye are our gods". See 1 John 5:20.

The reason follows: "**For in thee** the fatherless findeth mercy". There was no mercy in Assyria or in Egypt for the disappointed, destitute and helpless nation, and there was no consolation in idolatry. But, in the words of John MacArthur, "God repeatedly demanded mercy for the orphan (Exodus 22:22; Deut. 10:18), consequently Israel could expect to receive His compassion". The words, "in thee the fatherless findeth **mercy**" recall the birth of both Lo-ruhamah, "I will **no more have mercy** upon the house of Israel", and Lo-ammi, "for ye **are not my people,** and I will not be your God" (Hos. 1:6-9). But God will have mercy upon His people. See Hosea 2:1, "Say ye unto your brethren, Ammi; and to your sisters, Ruhamah". It must nevertheless be said that God's mercy is only displayed when there are "fruits meet for repentance" (Matt. 3:8).

2) *THE RECEPTION, vv.4-5a*
If vv.1-3 describe the mind and heart necessary for restoration after backsliding, then vv.4-5a describe the grace and kindness of God. The expression, "I will", occurs three times: *(a)* "I will heal their backsliding (v.4); *(b)* "I will love them freely (v.4); *(c)* "I will be as the dew unto Israel" (v5a).

a) "I will heal their backsliding", v.4
The Lord had said, "My people are bent to backsliding from me" (Hos. 11:7).

(We should notice that the words, "Israel slideth back as a backsliding heifer", employ a different word, *sarar,* meaning 'refractory'). Now He announces His willingness to restore them. Backsliding is a disease: it must be cured.

But, at the same time, we must not forget that backsliding involves spiritual loss. Abram was brought back to "the place where his tent (and altar) had been at the beginning" (Gen. 13:3-4), and Israel was ultimately brought back to Kadesh-Barnea (Num. 20:1), but not without loss of fellowship with God in the first place, and fearful loss of personnel and time in the second. But God remains intent on the highest good of His people, even though Israel had looked elsewhere for help in the past: "When Ephraim saw his sickness, and Judah saw his wound, then went Ephraim to the Assyrian, and sent to king Jareb, yet **could he not heal** you, nor cure you of your wound" (Hos. 5:13). Compare Hosea 6:1, "Come, and let us return unto the LORD: for he hath torn, and he will **heal** us: he hath smitten, and he will bind us up".

But this is not all. We might be tempted to feel that having once, or more, allowed our affections to be weaned away from God, any restoration can only be, at the very best, recovery of an inferior place in His love. Not so: the passage continues:

b) "I will love them freely", v.4
There is nothing grudging about God's welcome. It recalls the welcome given to the 'prodigal son', for whilst that parable is often used effectively in Gospel preaching, it is worth using it as an illustration of the restoration of a backsliding Christian. The welcome amounted to far more than readmission to the house as "one of thy hired servants": the father said, "bring forth the best robe and put it on him..." (Luke 15:19, 22).

J. M. Flanigan points out that the word "freely" (*nedabah*) is often translated 'freewill offering' and that it "also has the meaning of 'spontaneity, plentiful, abundant'". He continues: "The sad behaviour of the nation really meant that they merited nothing from the Lord, except chastisement. But He was slow to chide and ever ready to bless. Like a free gift to those who did not deserve it He would heal their backsliding. How gracious He was, and still is. His anger would very quickly turn away from a repentant people".

This particular verse is, of course, characteristic of Hosea's ministry, which was to shew God's love for His erring people. Nothing will bring our heavenly

Father greater pleasure, should we backslide, than to make us feel again the warmth of His love toward us.

c) "I will be as the dew unto Israel", v.5a
Isaac spoke of "the dew of heaven from above" (Gen. 27:39). It is looked upon as a blessing - a refreshment sent from God - and withheld in punishment when the conduct of His people merited judgment. See 1 Kings 17:1. The summer dew is most copious in Israel, and aids greatly in the cultivation of the land. Israel's goodness had been described earlier "as the early dew, it goeth away" (Hos. 6:4).

In these three ways, the Lord describes the blessing resting upon His people, **restored after backsliding**: they are not precluded from divine blessing.

The characteristics of the restored backslider are outlined next, and emphasise the abundance of divine grace:

3) THE RESULT, vv.5b-8
These verses describe eight ways in which the restored nation would flourish, and point to the way in which the restored backslider can enjoy the "dew" of divine blessing.

a) "He shall grow as the lily", v.5b
Or "he shall blossom as the lily" (JND). Solomon refers to the same species (*shoshannah*): "As the lily among thorns, so is my love among the daughters" (Song 2:2) Israel's moral and spiritual identification with her neighbours had made her anything but beautiful, but the nation will "worship the Lord in the beauty of holiness" (Psalm 29:2). We too, have the privilege of such worship. But we must take steps to ensure that He can regard us as "the lily among thorns". It would be tragic, in fact, disastrous, if He cannot see us in this way.

b) "And cast forth his roots as Lebanon", v5b
This emphasises stability. One observer has said of the area that "Firs grow, clinging as it were to the bare rock". The stability of a tree depends, of course, on its roots: no less the stability of the Christian. A good Old Testament commentary on the subject is found in Psalm 1:1-3: "Blessed is the man that walketh not in the counsel of the ungodly. Nor standeth in the way of sinners, nor sitteth in the seat of the scornful. But his delight is in the law of the LORD, and in his law doth he meditate day and night. And he shall be like a tree **planted** by the rivers of water, that bringeth forth his

fruit in his season; his leaf also shall not wither; and whatsoever he doeth shall prosper", and in Psalm 92:12-13: "The righteous shall flourish like a palm tree: he shall grow like a cedar in Lebanon. Those that be planted in the house of the LORD shall flourish in the courts of our God".

The New Testament has the following to say on the subject: "That Christ might dwell in your hearts by faith; that ye, being **rooted** and grounded in love..." (Eph. 3:17); "As ye have therefore received Christ Jesus the Lord, so walk ye in Him; **rooted** and built up in Him..." (Col. 2:6-7). A root is a God-given device that links supply with need. The words, "cast forth his roots as Lebanon", must be taken in conjunction with what follows:

c) "His branches shall spread", v.6
That is, as opposed to 11:6, "And the sword shall abide on his cities, and shall consume **his branches**". This emphasises expansion. We are frequently told by gardening experts that our ornamental and fruit trees must be fed by distributing the fertilizer over the area of ground beneath the tree approximating to its branch spread, for the simple reason that the visible growth of the tree corresponds with the unseen growth of the roots. If we ensure that our spiritual roots, that is, the unseen life of prayer, reading, study, and fellowship with God, are developing, then we can be certain that our public life and testimony will grow too. Compare Isaiah 37:31, "And the remnant that is escaped of the house of Judah shall again take root downward, and bear fruit upward". Notice Job 29:19, "My root was spread out by the waters, and the dew lay all night upon my branch".

d) "His beauty shall be as the olive tree", v.6
The olive tree speaks of witness in the power of the Holy Spirit. See Revelation 11:3-4, "And I will give power unto my two witnesses...these are the two olive trees, and the two candlesticks standing before the God of the earth". See also Zechariah 4:1-14. To quote Sir John Wolfenden, one time Director of the British Museum, "I think one of the most beautiful things in the world is just watching the wind ripple through an olive grove, so that the leaves turn over and shimmer" (Extracted from the Daily Telegraph Magazine). A beautiful character is essential to effective witness.

e) "His smell as Lebanon", v.7
Cedar is an odiferous wood, and aromatic shrubs grow extensively in the area; hence the reference. Compare Song of Solomon 4:11: "the smell of thy garments is like the smell of Lebanon". Paul describes the practical

fellowship of the assembly at Philippi as "an odour of a sweet smell, a sacrifice acceptable, well-pleasing to God" (Phil. 4:18). Solomon said that "Dead flies cause the ointment of the apothecary to send forth a stinking savour" (Eccl. 10:1). Our lives should be free of 'dead flies'. There were none, and there could be none, in the life of the Lord Jesus. See Ephesians 5:2.

f) "They that dwell under his shadow shall return", v.7
This has been otherwise rendered: "they shall return and sit under his shadow" (JND). It is tempting to say that this means that whereas, at the time of writing, Israel was dwelling under the shadow of idolatry (see 4:13, "They sacrifice upon the tops of the mountains, and burn incense upon the hills, under oaks and poplars and elms, **because the shadow thereof is good**"), they could (and will) enjoy "the shadow of the Almighty" (Psalm 91:1). But, in keeping with the general tenor of the passage, it seems more likely that Hosea refers here to the beneficial shadow cast by Israel. In the millennial age, both regathered Jews together with Gentile nations will enjoy the blessings afforded by restored Israel with all her stability and beauty described in this chapter and elsewhere.

g) "They shall revive as the corn, and grow as the vine", v.7
This has been otherwise rendered, "They shall revive as the corn, and blossom as the vine" (RV/JND). This indicates fruitfulness. God had already said, "I will hear, saith the LORD, I will hear the heavens, and they shall hear the earth: and the earth shall hear the corn, and the wine, and the oil; and they shall hear Jezreel" (2:21-22). Both passages anticipate millennial blessings. See, for example, Psalm 72:16, "There shall be an handful of corn in the earth upon the top of the mountains; the fruit thereof shall shake like Lebanon"; Micah 4:4, "But they shall sit every man under his vine and under his fig tree; and none shall make them afraid: for the mouth of the LORD of hosts hath spoken it".

h) "The scent thereof shall be as the wine of Lebanon", v.7
That is, the scent of 'the blossoming vine'. The word rendered "scent" is more correctly 'memorial' or 'renown' (JND). In the words of M. F. Unger, "The nation's fame in millennial blessing, is compared to the wine of Lebanon, which was celebrated for its aroma, flavour, and medicinal properties". The nation will be known for its unique character: Christians should be known in the same way.

J.N.Darby, and other writers of his period, suggest that v.8 gives a conversation between Ephraim and God, as follows:

Ephraim:	"What have I to do any more with idols?"
God:	"I have heard him and observed him".
Ephraim:	"I am like a green fir tree".
God:	"From me is thy fruit found".

Ephraim's attitude to idolatry is now reversed. Once it was said, "Ephraim is joined to idols: let him alone" (Hos. 4:17). But now, "What have I to do any more with idols?" Reference is made to the evergreen fir, rather than to a deciduous tree. This emphasises the consistency and continuity of the nation. See, again, Psalm 92:12-14: "they shall still bring forth fruit in old age; they shall be fat and flourishing ('green', AV margin)".

This happy condition will not be produced by natural genius: God says, "From ***me*** is thy fruit found". Once Israel was, "an empty vine, he bringeth forth fruit unto himself" (Hos. 10:1). Galatians 5:22 specifically states that "the ***fruit of the Spirit is*** love, joy, peace, longsuffering, gentleness, goodness, faith, meekness, temperance". The Lord Jesus emphasised that "As the branch cannot bear fruit of itself, except it abide in the vine; no more can ye, except ye abide in me. I am the vine, ye are the branches: He that abideth in me, and I in him, the same bringeth forth much fruit: for without me ye can do nothing" (John 15:4-5).

4) THE RESUMÉ, v.9

If, in any measure, we have backslidden, there is possibility of wonderful restoration. We must heed the final encouragement, and warning, of the prophecy: "Who is wise, and he shall understand these things? prudent, and he shall know them? for the ways of the LORD are right, and the just shall walk in them: but the transgressors shall fall therein" (v.9). Compare Psalm 107:43: Eccl. 12:13-14.

G. Campbell Morgan draws attention to the two words "wise" and "prudent", and observes that "the Hebrew word translated 'wise' means intelligent. But intelligence is not enough. Who is prudent? Prudent means acting according to intelligence. Prudent means squaring conduct with conviction". Campbell Morgan continues: "The man intelligent and prudent will come to certain convictions. Of these the first is that 'the ways of Jehovah are right'. This summarises everything. That being so, it follows that the righteous walk in them; and the wicked fall in them". Men fall into one of the two categories.

We are told that "the just shall live by his faith" (Hab. 2:4). Evidence of faith will be seen in a desire to "walk worthy of the Lord unto all pleasing"

(Col. 1:10). The pathway may attract ridicule, and even persecution, but "the ways of the LORD are right". The "way that seemeth right unto a man" leads to disaster (Prov. 14:12). We may have every confidence that "he leadeth me in the paths of righteousness for his name's sake" (Psalm 23:3). Our prayer should be constantly, "Teach my thy way, O LORD, and lead me in a plain path, because of mine enemies" (Psalm 27:11). The path of obedience is the path of blessing. But "the transgressors shall fall therein". "God's ways are straight and true, and we walk or fall according to our relationship with those ways" (Campbell Morgan).

In the words, again, of G. Campbell Morgan, the prophecy of Hosea "declares that sin separates from God, and blinds us, so that we lose the vision of Him. It shows that idolatry results from the loss of the vision of God". He continues, "We are living in fuller light than Hosea had. We see God as Hosea never saw Him. We see Him in Jesus. There seeing him, we know, as never before, that He can make no terms with sin; but we know that He stays at no sacrifice in order that He may heal our backsliding. If we are guilty of idolatry, what will cure us? The vision of Him, as He was seen in Jesus Christ".

"What have I to do any more with idols?"

Hast thou heard Him, seen Him, known Him?
Is not thine a captured heart?
Chief among ten thousand own Him,
Joyful choose the better part.

Idols once they won thee, charmed thee,
Lovely things of time and sense;
Gilded, thus does sin disarm thee,
Honeyed lest thou turn thee hence.

What has stripped the seeming beauty
From the idols of the earth?
Not the sense of right or duty,
But the sight of peerless worth.

Not the crushing of those idols,
With its bitter void and smart,
But the beaming of His beauty,
The unveiling of His heart.

Chapter 14

Who extinguishes their taper
Till they hail the rising sun?
Who discards the garb of winter
Till the summer has begun?

'Tis the look that melted Peter,
'Tis the face that Stephen saw,
'Tis the heart that wept with Mary,
Can alone from idols draw.

Draw, and win, and fill completely,
Till the cup o'erflow the brim;
What have we to do with idols,
Who have companied with Him?

Ora Rowan

"We know that the Son of God is come, and hath given us an understanding, that we may know him that is true, and that we are in him that is true, even in his Son Jesus Christ. This is the true God and eternal life. Little children, keep yourselves from idols". *(1 John 5:20-21)*

JOEL

by
John M Riddle

JOEL

Introduction

Read the whole book

Before addressing the prophecy of Joel in detail, we must make some general observations about the book. It commences with one of the briefest introductions in 'The Book of the Twelve'. "The word of the Lord that came to Joel the son of Pethuel" (1:1). According to F. A.Tatford, 'When the Old Testament canon was completed, the twelve Minor Prophets were included as one prophetical book. This, according to a rabbinical tradition, was lest any one of these smaller writings should be lost'.

1) THE POSITION OF THE BOOK

Joel was, in all probability, a ninth century prophet, and as we usually say when introducing our studies in the so-called 'minor prophets', it would be interesting to commence at the exodus from Egypt, and construct a complete table of the prophets sent by God. It would begin with Moses (Deut 18:15; 34:10) and Aaron (Exodus 7:1) and include a great number of men (and some women), some named and some unnamed. The 'writing prophets' alone cover five centuries, viz:

Fifth/sixth century prophets:	Haggai/ Zechariah/ Malachi/ Ezekiel/ Daniel:
Seventh century prophets:	Nahum/ Habakkuk/ Zephaniah/ Obadiah/ Jeremiah:
Eighth century prophets:	Hosea/ Amos/ Micah/ Isaiah:
Ninth century prophets:	Jonah, and as we shall see, in all probability, Joel.

Introduction

The ninth century (900 - 801 BC) brings us to the era of Elijah and Elisha. The tenth century included the unnamed prophet who cried against Jeroboam's altar, and the "old prophet in Bethel" (1 Kings 13). David was a prophet: see Acts 2:30. These examples prove that God was not exaggerating when He said, "Since the day that your fathers came forth out of the land of Egypt unto this day, I have even sent unto you all my servants the prophets, **daily** rising up early, and sending them" (Jer. 7:25). Whilst the oft-quoted words in Acts 14:17 do not refer to the prophets, we can **apply** them in that way, and say that God "left not himself without a witness" so far as the prophetic testimony was concerned. This should encourage us today: He will continue to maintain testimony to "all the counsel of God" (Acts 20:27), and even when Jerusalem becomes the darkest moral blot on earth, He will give power to His "two witnesses...these two prophets" (Rev. 11:3-12). When the Lord Jesus was here, people in the city of Nain "glorified God, saying, That a great prophet is risen up among us" (Luke 7:16), but He had to say, "a prophet hath no honour in his own country" (John 4:44). This leads us to consider, in more detail:

2) THE PERIOD OF THE PROPHECY

Since we do not have a note of the kings in whose reign Joel prophesied, we have to look elsewhere in attempting to date the prophecy. Perhaps we ought to say that the absence of definite information means that God does not intend us to pursue our enquiries in this direction, but rather to concentrate on what He does tell us!

Although some commentators think otherwise, it is usual to regard Joel as one of the earliest, if not actually the very first, of the writing prophets. The absence of references to Assyria and Babylonia, let alone the Exile which commenced in 606 BC or thereabouts, points to a much earlier date than some commentators suggest. As J. Sidlow Baxter observes, 'surely it is almost incredible that if Joel prophesied *after* the onsets of these mighty powers he should leave them unmentioned, the more so if, as some assert, that he wrote after the Babylonian exile itself had occurred!'

If, as seems to be the case, the references to "Tyre and Sidon and all the coasts of Palestine" (the Philistines) and to the Egyptians and Edomites (3: 4, 19) point to past events, then it is worth noting that the Philistines, with others, invaded Judah in the reign of Joram the son of Jehoshaphat (See 2 Chron. 21:16-17; 22:1), and that the Edomites "revolted from under the dominion of Judah" in Joram's reign (2 Chron. 21:8-10). Joram reigned between 889-883 BC. Perhaps, however, this should not be regarded as 'hard evidence' since the Joel references could possibly refer to the future.

Although Kings and Chronicles do not record, in so many words, a locust invasion of the epic proportions described by Joel (1:4-20), it is worth noting that Joram was a wicked king, and "made Judah, and the inhabitants of Jerusalem to go a whoring, like to the whoredoms of the house of Ahab", in consequence of which the Lord said, "Behold, with a **great plague** will the Lord smite thy people, and thy children, and thy wives, and all thy goods: and **thou** shalt have great sickness by disease of thy bowels" (2 Chron. 21:13-15). It is noteworthy that this prediction came in the form of "a writing to him from Elijah" (v.12). (So Elijah was also a 'writing prophet!'). It should be said, after all this (!), that this in only an 'attempt' to date the prophecy.

3) THE PROPHET HIMSELF
"The word of the Lord...came to **Joel** the son of Pethuel". Joel means 'Jehovah is God' or 'Jehovah is strength', and his name reflected God's character as the judge of the nations: "The Lord also shall roar out of Zion, and utter his voice from Jerusalem; and the heavens and the earth shall shake" (3:16). His name is shared by some twelve others in the Old Testament. According to F. A. Tatford, the name Pethuel means 'enlargement of God'.

The conduct of some people in the Old Testament totally belied their marvellous names. The sons of Samuel, Joel and Abiah, are a case in point. As we have seen Joel means 'Jehovah is strength', or 'Jehovah is God', and Abiah means 'whose father is Jehovah'. But the conduct of Joel, Samuel's son, made it abundantly clear that Jehovah was not *his* God, and the conduct of Abiah made it equally clear that Jehovah was not *his* father. In view of the fact that James refers to "that worthy name by which ye are called" (James 2:7), we do well to examine our own lives.

4) THE PLACE
The prophecy makes it tolerably certain that Joel exercised his ministry in or near Jerusalem. It is the inhabitants of that city whom he addresses (2:23). It is Jerusalem which he sees in danger (2:9). It is in Zion that the "alarm" is to be sounded (2:1, 15). It is in Mount Zion and in Jerusalem that deliverance shall be in the after-days (2:32). It is the captivity of Judah and Jerusalem which is then to be ended (3:1); and it is Judah and Jerusalem which shall "dwell for ever" (3:20). The ten-tribed northern

kingdom is not once mentioned. F. A.Tatford observes that 'Because of the accuracy of his references to the temple and its activities and to the ministry of the priests, it is sometimes suggested that he was personally a priest, but there is no real support for this in the pages of his book'.

5) THE PROPHECY
The book can be summarised as follows: *(a)* desolation (1:1-20); *(b)* invasion (2:1-11) *(c)* contrition (2:12-17); *(d)* restoration (2:18-27); *(e)* regeneration (2:28-32); *(f)* retribution (3:1-21).

a) Desolation, 1:1-20
The prophecy commences by describing the devastation caused by a locust plague of gigantic proportions. Moses had warned Israel that this would be one of the results of disobedience: "Thou shalt carry much seed out into the field, and shalt gather but little in; for the *locust (arbeh)* shall consume it...All the trees and fruit of thy land shall the *locust* (a different word entirely: see JND margin) consume" (Deut. 28:38, 42). Hence, "That which the palmerworm hath left, hath the locust eaten; and that which the locust hath left, hath the cankerworm eaten; and that which the cankerworm hath left, hath the caterpillar eaten" (Joel 1:4). These are said to be the 'shearer' (*gazam*: as in Amos 4:9), 'swarmer' (*'arbeh*), 'lapper' (*yelek*), and 'stripper' (*hasil*).

The section carries a warning of worse things to come: "Alas for the day! For the day of the Lord is at hand, and as a destruction from the Almighty shall it come" (v.15), and this follows:

b) Invasion, 2:1-11
The precise meaning of the section is not easily determined. J. Sidlow Baxter is convinced that the passage describes a second locust invasion, and his arguments should be carefully considered. There is no doubt that Joel is describing an invasion, and that the invasion bears all the characteristics of a vast plague of locusts. This does seem to be the natural sense of the passage.

Consideration should also be given, however, to the suggestion that the passage describes an invasion by a northern army ("him that cometh from the north", 2:20, JND) whose irresistible progress is described in terms of a locust plague. George Williams (*The Student's Commentary on the Holy Scriptures*) puts it as follows: 'Most probably at the time the prophecy was given by God to Joel, the whole country was utterly devastated and ruined by a plague of locusts, and this fact was used to illustrate the divine judgments that were about to be inflicted on the land, and to have their climax in the dread "day of the Lord" at the close of Judah's history. This period of judgment (ch.1) was to introduce that Great Day (ch. 2). These judgments would be so exceptional as to be without previous experience (2:1-2, compare 1:2-3). Here is an instance, not unusual in prophetic teaching, of the Spirit of God using an event such as this plague of locusts to awaken the conscience of the people at the moment, and, at the same time, to make use of them to picture a future event of much greater moment'.

It is not without significance that the Deuteronomy passage cited above continues by saying, "The Lord shall bring a nation against thee from far, from the end of the earth, as swift as the eagle flieth; a nation whose tongue thou shalt not understand" (Deut 28:49). The expression "the day of the Lord" (1:15; 2:1; 3:14) points to the end-time when Israel will certainly be invaded by a gigantic army from the north (Ezekiel chs. 38-39). Alternatively, the passage could refer, in the first place, to the Assyrian invasions of Judah, which are a shadow of the final end-time invasion of the land from the north.

c) Contrition, 2:12-17
These verses are quite self-explanatory: "Turn also now, saith the Lord, turn ye even to me with all your heart, and with fasting, and with weeping, and with mourning: and rend your heart, and not your garments, and turn unto the Lord your God: for he is gracious and merciful, slow to anger, and of great kindness, and repenteth him of the evil" (vv.12-13). While, at first glance, the closing words of the section seem to indicate a human army rather than a locust plague ("Spare thy people, O Lord, and give not thine heritage to reproach, that the heathen should rule over them: wherefore should they say among the people, Where is their God?", v.17), this could mean that it was possible that Judah could become so weakened by the plague, that their enemies would be able to defeat and dominate them.

While these verses are a *bona fide* appeal to God's people at the time, they do remind us of the future repentance of the nation. See Zechariah 12:10-14.

d) Restoration, 2:18-27
Following their repentance, God would abundantly bless His people: "Then will the Lord be jealous for his land, and pity his people. Yea, the Lord will answer and say unto his people, Behold, I will send you corn, and

wine, and oil, and ye shall be satisfied therewith: and I will no more make you a reproach among the heathen" (vv.18-19). The section describes the material blessings that the Lord was ready to give Israel at the time, but they are described in terms which fit her ultimate millennial blessings.

e) Regeneration, 2:28-32
At this point, Joel clearly passes from current or imminent events, of which it could be said that 'coming events cast their shadow before them', to end-time events themselves. "And it shall come to pass afterward, that I will pour out my Spirit upon all flesh (the context suggests, not "all flesh" universally, but "all flesh" of Israel nationally); and your sons and your daughters shall prophesy, your old men shall dream dreams, your young men shall see visions: and also upon the servants and upon the handmaids in those days will I pour out my Spirit" (vv.28-29). The "great and terrible day of the Lord" (v.31) is certainly still a future event. As we shall see, while the passage is quoted in Acts 2:16-21, events of the day of Pentecost did not fulfil the prophecy.

f) Recompense, 3:1-21
The restoration of Israel (v.1) will be accompanied by retribution on the nations which had been responsible for her suffering and dispersion (vv.2-26). The military forces of the world will assembly in the valley of Jehoshaphat (v.12), only to fall under divine judgment. Compare Revelation 16:13-16. There will be "Multitudes, multitudes in the valley of decision" (3:2, 12-14). The word "decision" means 'something decided', hence 'judgment'. We can therefore read 'the valley of punishment' (Gesenius). Then the Lord, having returned to the mount of Olives (Zech. 14:3-4), will "roar out of Zion, and utter his voice from Jerusalem; and the heavens and the earth shall shake: but the Lord will be the hope of his people, and the strength of the children of Israel" (v.16).

The judgment of the nations will be followed by divine blessing upon God's people when "Judah shall dwell for ever, and Jerusalem from generation to generation" (vv.17-21).

The overall lessons for ourselves from the book are clear. Sin and disobedience in our lives will inevitably bring divine chastening upon us, but thorough repentance will bring recovery and blessing. We can therefore say that the prophecy of Joel certainly lies within the scope of Romans 15:4: "For whatsoever things were written aforetime were written for our learning, that we through patience and comfort of the scriptures might have hope".

READ CHAPTER 1:1-20

"That which the palmerworm hath left hath the locust eaten..."

In introducing the prophecy of Joel, we suggested that the book may be divided as follows: *(1)* desolation (1:1-20); *(2)* invasion (2:1-11); *(3)* contrition (2:12-17); *(4)* restoration (2:18-27); *(5)* regeneration (2:28-32); *(6)* retribution (3:1-21). We must now turn our attention to the details of the book. The prophecy commences with a grim picture. But Joel has better things in store for us, and the book ends with renewal and blessing: "the mountains shall drop down new wine, and the hills shall flow with milk, and all the rivers of Judah shall flow with waters...Judah shall dwell for ever, and Jerusalem from generation to generation. For I will cleanse their blood that I have not cleansed: for the Lord dwelleth in Zion" (3:18-21).

1) DESOLATION, 1:1-20
The chapter clearly falls into two major sections: *(a)* the introduction to the message (vv.1-3); *(b)* the burden of the message (vv.4-20).

a) The introduction to the message, vv.1-3
The introduction refers to *(i)* the communication of God's word *to* Joel (v.1) and *(ii)* the communication of God's word *by* Joel (vv.2-3).

i) The communication of God's word to Joel, v.1. "The word of the Lord that came to Joel the son of Pethuel". Nothing is known of Joel personally. The book contains no direct information regarding his background, character or occupation. But the omission is important. In some instances, God has revealed details of His servants, but not in this case, reminding us that He uses both well-known and lesser-known people. God can use every one of His people. It is therefore important to be "a vessel unto honour...prepared unto every good work" (2 Tim. 2:21). The assurance that we really do have the word of God is vitally important. Joel therefore introduces the book with a common prophetic formula to attest his credentials. He declares that the message recorded was nothing less than the word of the Lord. Paul was able to say of the Thessalonians: "from you sounded out the word of the **Lord**" (1 Thess.1:8).

It is worth noticing how the Lord used the preaching of this little-known man in the ministry of his fellow-prophets, of whom we know far more. It has been pointed out that Amos (1:2) evidently commences his prophecy with a passage from Joel (3:16), and closes it with a passage from Joel. Compare Amos 9:13 with Joel 3:18. In one of his passages dealing with coming judgment, Isaiah evidently borrows a sentence from Joel. Compare Isaiah 13:6 with Joel 1:15. Perhaps, however, we should be a little cautious here, and say that while the prophets were undoubtedly familiar with the preaching of their predecessors (see, for example, Daniel 9:2), God could have revealed His word directly to them in identical language.

ii) *The communication of God's word by Joel, vv.2-3.* What had happened - or was happening at the time - was to be conveyed to others. Four generations are mentioned: "Hear this, ye **old men**, and give ear, all ye inhabitants of the land. Hath this been in your days, or even in the days of your fathers? Tell ye **your children** of it, and let your children tell **their children**, and their children **another generation**". Compare Deuteronomy 6:2. See also 2 Timothy 2:2, "Thou therefore, my son, be strong in the grace that is in Christ Jesus. And the things that thou hast heard of **me** among many witnesses, the same commit **thou** to **faithful men**, who shall be able to teach **others** also". The nature of this unprecedented calamity (or series of calamities: see 2:25, "the years that the locust hath eaten"), something the older men had never seen before, was 'to be recounted to future generations, presumably, as a warning of the judgments which fall upon a sinful people' (F. A. Tatford).

Joel was quite unlike Jonah who, having received "the word of the Lord" acted quite differently: he "rose up to flee" (Jonah 1:1, 3). Our contributor Justin Waldron asks the question, 'Are we willing to communicate the message God has given to us?' and draws attention to our ambassadorial responsibilities: "Now then we are ambassadors for Christ, as though God did beseech by us: we pray in Christ's stead, be ye reconciled to God" (2 Cor. 5:20). Note the omission of "you" in the quotation.

b) *The burden of the message, vv.4-20*
In this passage, Joel describes the situation current at the time, whereas in the next section of the prophecy (2:1-11) he refers to coming events and

uses the future tense. Chapter 2 commences with the words: "Blow ye the trumpet in Zion; and sound an alarm in my holy mountain!" (2:1). An alarm warns of imminent danger, not to mark something that has already taken place. Hence the verse continues: "Let all the inhabitants of the land tremble; for the day of Jehovah cometh, for it is nigh at hand".

The past or present tense is used in the current verses: "howl...because of the new wine...for it *is* cut off from your mouth, for a nation *is* come up upon my land...He **hath** laid my vine waste...The meat-offering and the drink-offering *is* cut off from the house of the Lord...The field *is* wasted... the harvest of the field *is* perished. The vine *is* dried up...*Is* not the meat cut off before our eyes...The seed *is* rotten under their clods...How *do* the beasts groan!...O Lord, to thee will I cry: for the fire **hath** devoured the pastures of the wilderness".

With this in mind, we must now address the circumstances at the time of writing. Judah was reeling under the effects of a gigantic locust invasion (v.4) coupled with drought (v.20). The nation was faced with famine. We should notice the following: *(i)* the means of the desolation (v.4); *(ii)* the reason for the desolation (v.5); *(iii)* the distress over the desolation (vv.6-8); *(iv)* the results of the desolation (vv.9-20).

i) **The means of the desolation, v.4.** "That which the palmerworm ('the shearer') hath left, hath the locust ('the swarmer') eaten; and that which the locust hath left, hath the cankerworm ('the lapper') eaten; and that which the cankerworm hath left hath the caterpiller ('the stripper') eaten" (v.4). Some say chewing, swarming, crawling and consuming. The locusts are called "a nation" in the same way that the ants are described as "a *people* not strong...the conies are but a feeble *folk*" (Prov. 30:25-26).

The four names ("palmerworm...locust...cankerworm...caterpiller") could suggest that there had been four successive swarms (perhaps different sorts of locusts), and what one had left, the next had devoured. Alternatively, the four names could relate to different stages in the growth of the insects. This is not the place for a technical study, nor for quoting the numerous - and most interesting - descriptions of locust invasions. We allude to some of these in our next study. As J. Waldron observes, 'Israel had witnessed an unparalleled plague of locusts sent in judgment upon Egypt (Exodus 10:15). Now, because of their disobedience, the same God had sent locusts on Judah'.

Some have suggested that the fourfold description of the invading horde points to "the times of the Gentiles". See Daniel 2 & 7, which describe the four world powers which would devastate Israel. George Williams espouses this view: 'The development of the locust exhibits four stages. These four stages are expressed in four Hebrew words here translated "palmerworm, locust, cankerworm, caterpillar". The last stage is the most destructive of them all. Possibly they prefigure the four military monarchies of Babylon, Persia, Greece and Rome which successively devastated Judah as locusts destroy a land (v.4)'. However, in the first place, the insect invasion(s) were undoubtedly actual and historical. But it is not unreasonable to take the whole book as a picture of God's dealings with His people, in which case the restoration of the "years that the locust hath eaten, the cankerworm, and the caterpiller, and the palmerworm, my great army which I sent among you" (2:25), plus deliverance from a final invasion (2:1-11), could well refer to Israel's blessing once the times of the Gentiles have run their course.

ii) The reason for the desolation, v.5. "Awake, ye drunkards, and weep; and howl, all ye drinkers of wine, because of the new wine; for it is cut off from your mouth". This may well indicate one reason for the disciplinary hand of God. The people had become self-indulgent. Joel is evidently referring, not so much to the alcoholics in society, but to the nation generally who had become insensible to God's claims. They had used the provision of God for self-gratification. Moses had warned Israel against this: "And it shall be, when the LORD thy God shall have brought thee into the land which he sware unto thy fathers...to give thee great and goodly cities, which thou buildest not, and houses full of all good things, which thou filledst not, and wells digged, which thou diggedst not, vineyards and olive trees, which thou plantedst not; when thou shalt have eaten and be full; then beware lest thou forget the Lord, which brought thee forth out of the land of Egypt, from the house of bondage" (Deut. 6:10-12). We too should be warned.

The important point at this stage is to note that the invasion was not simply a 'natural disaster': it was intended to awaken the nation to its spiritual condition (vv.13-14). See also Haggai 1:3-11 and Amos 4:6-13, where reference is made to "the palmerworm" (*gazam*). See v.9. Barrenness is permitted to impress the implications of the situation; to create awareness of the position; to awaken concern and repentance. Compare 1 Corinthians 11:30-31: "For this cause many are weak and sickly among you, and many sleep...For if we would judge ourselves, we should not be judged". Spiritual barrenness is allowed by God to bring about repentance.

*iii) **The distress over the situation, vv.6-8***. The distress is twofold: the Lord first expresses His distress (vv.6-7), and then calls upon His people to recognise their distress:

- ***The Lord's distress, vv.6-7***. "A nation is come up upon my land, strong, and without number, whose teeth are the teeth of as lion, and he hath the cheek teeth of a great lion. He hath laid my vine waste, and barked my fig tree: he hath made it clean bare, and cast it away; the branches thereof are made white". Both the vine and the fig are symbols of Israel. The fact that they were God's people did not exclude them from divine judgment. The words, "A nation is come up upon *my* land...He hath laid *my* vine waste, and barked *my* fig tree" indicate that however much Israel deserved divine judgment, it was painful to the Lord who "doth not afflict willingly" (Lam. 3:33).

- ***The nation's distress, v.8.*** God's people were to "Lament like a virgin girded with sackcloth for the husband of her youth". The land is described as a betrothed young woman, who has just been bereaved of her bridegroom. As M. F. Unger points out, 'Such a betrothed young woman was regarded as married (Deut. 22:23-24; Matt. 1:19), and she is cited as an example of deepest grief, for she was at a period of life when affections are the strongest and therefore sorrow at bereavement is consequently the keenest'. Fellowship and companionship have been severed. Perhaps *we* have to say:

> *Where is the blessedness I knew*
> *When first I saw the Lord?*
> *Where is the soul-refreshing view*
> *Of Jesus and His Word?*
>
> *What peaceful hours I once enjoyed!*
> *How sweet their memory still!*
> *But they have left and aching void*
> *The world can never fill.*

The realisation that our fellowship with God has been impaired and that we have lost the enjoyment of His presence, should cause *us* to "lament" as well.

There should be nothing so grievous to us than distance from Christ. John, "the disciple whom Jesus loved", was "leaning on Jesus' bosom" when Peter "beckoned to him, that he should ask who it should be of whom he (the Lord Jesus) spake" (John 13:23-24). The disciple so close to the Lord

Jesus was the right man to ask! He is best able to speak to us when we are close to Him.

iv) The results of the desolation, vv.9-20. The evidence of famine conditions, brought about by the locust devastation and drought, furnishes criteria by which we can judge whether or not *we* are experiencing spiritual famine. If this is the case there will be:

- Absence of worship, v.9. "The meat-offering and the drink-offering is cut off from the *house of the Lord*; the priests, the Lord's ministers, mourn". There was nothing for God. This matter is mentioned three times in the chapter: "Gird yourselves, and lament, ye priests: howl, ye ministers of the altar: come, lie all night in sackcloth, ye ministers of my God: for the meat-offering and the drink-offering is withholden from the *house of your God*" (v.13); "Is not the meat cut off before our eyes, yea, joy and gladness from the *house of our God?*" (v.16). The threefold reference to the Lord's house in this way emphasises the seriousness of the matter. The Lord was not receiving the worshipful offerings of His people.

Famine in the land meant famine in the house of God. Because the personal lives of Israel were impoverished, there was nothing for God. Can it be said of us that "the meat-offering and the drink-offering is cut off from the house of the Lord?" Spiritual famine in our lives will mean that we are unable to "offer up spiritual sacrifices, acceptable to God by Jesus Christ" (1 Pet. 2:5).

- Absence of fruit, vv.10-12. "The field is wasted, the land mourneth; for the corn is wasted: the new wine is dried up, the oil languisheth. Be ye ashamed, O ye husbandmen; howl, O ye vinedressers, for the wheat and the barley; because the harvest of the field is perished. The vine is dried up, and the fig tree languisheth; the pomegranate tree, the palm tree also, and the apple tree, even all the trees of the field, are withered". The word "ashamed" (v.11) signifies, not so much a sense of humiliation or dishonour for wrongdoing, but rather the idea of frustration or loss of face (F. A. Tatford).

If there is no spiritual fruit in our lives, then there is something seriously wrong. Do we display the "fruit of the Spirit" which is "love, joy, peace, longsuffering, gentleness, goodness, faith, meekness, temperance" (Gal. 5:22-23)? Our assemblies should be places of fruitfulness. Do notice the context of this passage with its emphasis on "one another": "by love serve *one another*... take heed that ye be not consumed *one of another*...Let us not be desirous of vain glory, provoking **one another**" (Gal. 5:13, 15, 26). In the millennial age it will be said, "the pastures of the wilderness do spring, for the tree beareth her fruit, the fig tree and the vine do yield their strength" (2:22). Our lives should be like that now!

While these verses describe the absence of fruit generally, we should notice the references to the "new wine" and to the "vinedressers", reminding us that since it is "wine that maketh glad the heart of man" (Psalm 104:15) another feature of famine conditions is:

- **Absence of joy, vv.10-16.** In fact, vv.10-12 conclude with, "**joy** is withered away from the sons of men". Those who drank wine "howl" (v.5); those who prepared wine "howl" (v.11); those who offered wine "howl" (v.13). In summary, there was no joy in **personal** life (vv.5,12); no joy in **service** (v.13); no joy in **worship**: "Gird yourselves, and lament, ye priests: howl ye ministers of the altar...Is not the meat cut off before our eyes, yea, **joy and gladness** from the house of our God" (vv.13,16).

If we have lost "the joy of the Lord", there is something seriously wrong in our lives. It is further evidence of spiritual famine. Is the word of God 'the joy and rejoicing of our hearts' (Jer. 15:16)?. Have we the "joy of the Holy Ghost?" See Rom. 14:17 ("For the kingdom of God is not meat and drink; but righteousness, and peace, and joy in the Holy Ghost"; 1 Thess. 1:6 ("Ye...received the word in much affliction, with joy of the Holy Ghost"). Can we still say of the Lord Jesus that because we love Him, though unseen, we "rejoice with joy unspeakable?" (1 Pet. 1:8). In the millennial age, it will be said "Fear not, O land; be glad and **rejoice**: for the Lord will do great things" (2:21) and "the mountains shall drop down **new wine**" (3:18). Our lives should be like that now!

At this point in the message, Joel calls for repentance: "Gird yourselves (meaning 'prepare to do the work of repentance'), and lament, ye priests: howl, ye ministers of the altar: come, lie all night in sackcloth, ye ministers of my God: for the meat-offering and the drink-offering is withholden from the house of your God. Sanctify ye a fast (everything, however legitimate, must give place to re-establishing a right relationship with God) call a solemn assembly, gather the elders (the leaders of God's people should fulfil their role, and lead the people by example in the right direction) and all the inhabitants of the land into the house of the Lord, and cry (not 'speak' but 'cry') unto the Lord" (vv.13-14). This speaks for itself. The matter is intensely serious. In the

New Testament, the church at Ephesus was called upon to repent: "Remember therefore from whence thou art fallen, and **repent**" (Rev. 2:5). Like Judah, the church at Laodicea had become "wretched... miserable... poor... blind... naked", and the Lord Jesus calls on them to repent: "As many as I love, I rebuke and chasten: be zealous therefore, and **repent**" (Rev. 3:17-19).

Failure to repent (vv.13-14) would leave the way open to irresistible invasion. "Alas for the day! for the day of the Lord is at hand, and as a destruction from the Almighty shall it come" (v.15). When God ceases to receive the devotion and obedience of His people, they are not only at risk to defeat and barrenness, they are open to severe judgment. It was so at Ephesus: "Remember therefore from whence thou art fallen, and repent, and do the first works; or else I will come unto thee quickly, and **will remove thy candlestick out of his place**, except thou repent" (Rev. 2:5). It was so at Laodicea: "So then because thou art lukewarm... **I will spue thee out of my mouth**" (Rev. 3:16).

- Absence of resources, v.17. "The seed is rotten under their clods, the garners are laid desolate, the barns are broken down; for the corn is withered". As F. A. Tatford observes, 'There was no harvest to gather... the unused storehouses and barns fell into a pitiable state of dilapidation and disrepair. What use were granaries without grain?'

If our spiritual storehouses are empty, there is something seriously wrong. It is absolutely necessary for continuity of life and testimony that we are "nourished up in the words of faith and of good doctrine" (1 Tim. 4:6). If we have no 'gospel seed', things have reached a very low ebb. "He that goeth forth and weepeth, bearing precious seed, shall doubtless come again with rejoicing, bringing his sheaves with him" (Psalm 126:6). But supposing we do not have, and enjoy, the "precious seed?" Unlike natural seed, God's word is imperishable. It does not carry a 'shelf life!' But we can lose its value in our lives and in our service. In the millennial age, "the floors shall be full of wheat, and the fats shall overflow with wine and oil" (2:24) Our lives should be like that now!

- Absence of pasture, vv.18-20. "How do the beasts groan! The herds of cattle are perplexed, because they have **no pasture**; yea, the flocks of sheep are made desolate. O Lord, to thee will I cry: for the fire hath devoured **the pastures** of the wilderness". 'A country devastated by locusts appears as swept by fire' (George Williams).

Has the word of God ceased to be "green pastures" (Psalm 23:2) to us? Has our Bible reading become a chore, and we really get nothing at all from it? This is a 'storm signal' that something is desperately wrong. The "Good Shepherd" will enable us to "go in and out, and find pasture" (John 10:9). In the millennial age, it will be said, "Be not afraid, ye beasts of the field: for the pastures of the wilderness do spring" (2:22). Our lives should be like that! While these verses describe the absence of pasture generally, they also point to one of the contributory causes. The locust plague was accompanied by drought. So:

- **Absence of rainfall, v.20.** The beasts of the field cry also unto thee: for the rivers of waters are dried up". This was always a sign of divine displeasure. See, for example, 1 Kings 17:1. The Lord Jesus said, "If any man thirst, let him come unto me and drink. He that believeth on me, as the scripture hath said, out of his belly (inner man) shall flow rivers of living water. But this spake he of the Spirit, which they that believe on him should receive" (John 7:37-39). In the millennial age, the rains will fall and therefore the rivers will flow again: "Be glad, then, ye children of Zion, and rejoice in the Lord your God: for he hath given you the former rain moderately, and he will cause to come down for you the rain, the former rain, and the latter rain in the first month" (2:23). In consequence, "all the rivers of Judah shall flow with water" (3:18). Our lives should be like that now!

As we have noticed, at the *heart of these verses* lie two most important matters: an appeal for repentance (vv.13-14), and a warning of worse to come (v.15). Both are emphasised in the next sections of the book (2:1-11; 2:12-17).

READ CHAPTER 2:1-17

"The day of the Lord cometh"

In our introduction, we suggested that the prophecy may be divided as follows: *(1)* desolation (1:1-20); *(2)* invasion (2:1-11); *(3)* contrition (2:12-17); *(4)* restoration (2:18-27); *(5)* regeneration (2:28-32); *(6)* retribution (3:1-21).

1) DESOLATION, 1:1-20
In this connection we noticed that Joel describes the situation at the time of writing. Judah was reeling under the effects of a gigantic locust invasion (v.4) coupled with drought (v.20). The nation was faced with famine. The chapter describes *(i)* the means of the desolation (v.4); *(ii)* the cause of the desolation (v.5); *(iii)* the distress over the desolation (vv.6-7); *(iv)* the results of the desolation (vv.8-20). In applying the passage to ourselves, we noticed that the evidence of famine in Jerusalem and Judah vividly depicts famine in the soul. When God's word is disobeyed, there will be absence of fellowship with God (v.8), absence of worship (v.9), absence of fruit (vv.10-12); absence of joy (vv.10-16), absence of supplies (v.17), absence of pasture (vv.18-20), and absence of rainfall (v.20). At the heart of these searching verses lies an appeal for repentance (vv.13-14), and a warning of worse to come (v.15). These are emphasised in our current passage (2:1-17): the warning of worse to come is emphasised in vv.1-11 and the appeal for repentance is emphasised in vv.12-17. This brings us to:

2) INVASION, 2:1-11
Having said, "Alas for the day! for the day of the Lord is at hand, and as a destruction from the Almighty shall it come" (1.15), that "day" is now described: "Blow ye the trumpet in Zion, and sound an alarm in my holy mountain: let all the inhabitants of the land tremble: for the day of the Lord cometh, for it is nigh at hand" (v.1). An alarm warns of imminent danger, not to mark something that has already taken place. While the present tense is generally used in 1:4-20 to describe the locust plague and its effects, the future tense is now employed in the Authorised Version: "The appearance

of them is as the appearance of horses; and as horsemen, so **shall** they run. Like the noise of chariots on the tops of mountains **shall** they leap... they **shall**...they **shall**...they **shall**...the earth **shall** quake before them; the heavens **shall** tremble". However, it ought to be pointed out that the RV and JND continue to use the present tense here, which could suggest a further phase of the locust plague described in Chapter 1.

In the words of J. Sidlow Baxter (*Explore the Book*): 'If we now read on through Chapter 2, we shall find that the first eleven verses in it are a most gripping and awesome picture of this still further and greater trouble which was about to break on the nation. This is too clear to need comment...Then follows the description of the strange, dread army which was to overrun the land. It is enough to strike fear into any heart. This visitation, whatever its nature, was to be so grave and extraordinary that it could be described by no less an expression than "the day of Jehovah" - an expression which comes not only in verse 1, but again in verse 11, where we read, "The day of the Lord is great and very terrible; and who can abide it?". Quite clearly, the "day" anticipated in 1:15 is now described in detail.

We now have to address two problems in the passage: *(a)* the use of the expression, "the day of the Lord"; *(b)* the identity of the invader.

a) "The day of the Lord"
The Scriptures reveal that the "day of the Lord" will occur at the end-time, and therefore still lies in the future. The New Testament, as well as the Old Testament (see, for example, Joel 3:14), makes this clear: "But of the times and seasons, brethren, ye have no need that I write unto you. For yourselves know perfectly that the day of the Lord so cometh as a thief in the night" (1 Thess. 5:2); "The Lord is not slack concerning his promise (that is, that Christ will return)...but is longsuffering to us-ward, not willing that any should perish...But the day of the Lord *will* come as a thief in the night" (2 Pet. 3:9-10).

We are told here, however, that "the day of the Lord is **at hand**" (1.15), and that the trumpet was to be blown in Zion because "the day of the Lord cometh, for it is **nigh at hand**" (2:1). We have, therefore, to ask the question, 'If the "day of the Lord" will take place at the end-time, how can it possibly occur in Joel's lifetime? Or in Zephaniah's lifetime for that matter: see Zeph. 1:14-18.

In our introduction, we quoted George Williams (*Student's Commentary on the Holy Scriptures*), and the time has come to refer again to the same comment: 'Most probably at the time the prophecy was given by God to Joel, the whole country was utterly devastated and ruined by a plague of locusts, and this fact was used to illustrate the divine judgments that were about to be inflicted on the land, and to have their climax in the dread "day of the Lord" at the close of Judah's history. This period of judgment (ch.1) was to introduce that Great Day (ch.2). These judgments would be so exceptional as to be without previous experience (2:1-2, compare 1:2-3). Here is an instance, not unusual in prophetic teaching, of the Spirit of God using an event such as this plague of locusts to awaken the conscience of the people at the moment, and, **at the same time, to make use of them to picture a future event of much greater moment'.** Perhaps we could therefore say that the locust invasion is deliberately described in terms which can be understood both literally and figuratively.

In other words, it is an example of the much quoted words, 'coming events cast their shadow before them'. For example, the Assyrian invasion, described in detail in Isaiah 10:28-34, suddenly gives place to a glowing description of the glories of Messiah's kingdom in Isaiah 11:1-6. The past suddenly merges with the future, for the simple reason that at the end-time, another 'Assyrian invasion' will take place. See Micah 5:5-6. The future enemy will come from the same area as his historical predecessor. A further example occurs in the New Testament. The destruction of Jerusalem in AD 70 is merged with the return of the "Son of man" (Luke 21:20-28). Once again, the past suddenly merges with the future, because at the end-time Jerusalem will again be besieged by armies (see Zechariah 12:2-3; 14:1-2), at which point the Lord will return to deliver His people (Zech. 14:3).

We therefore suggest that although "the day of the Lord", which includes a period of unparalleled judgment on earth, has not yet come, past events (as here in Joel's lifetime) which pre-figure this coming judgment are also described by the same expression.

b) The identity of the invader
If the invasion described in vv.1-11 prefigures future judgment, we have to decide whether Joel is actually referring here to a *literal* locust invasion which prefigures a future invasion, or to the advance of a conventional army under the *figure* of a locust plague. The arguments look like this:

i) A locust army

J. Sidlow Baxter champions this view. In his commentary (*Explore the Book*) he sets out his arguments, and concludes that these verses actually describe *a literal locust plague*. His arguments should not be lightly dismissed. He writes as follows: 'Some argue that while the description has its **ground** in a locust plague, the language is too ominous to be limited by it. These locusts of chapter 2 (they say) are really the *"nations"* of chapter 3. Certain features in the description, it is said, imply a human army. The invaders are said to be "a great people and a strong" (v.2). They assault cities and terrify the people (vv.6-7). They are to be destroyed in a way which is inapplicable to locusts (v.20). The priests are urged to pray that the *"nations"* may not "rule over" Israel (v.17). The scourge is from the **north** (v.20), whereas locusts usually swarm Palestine from the south. All these things, it is argued, indicate something more than a locust plague'. Baxter adds that if vv.1-11 are really an allegory, then opinions vary considerably on what is actually being allegorised.

He continues: 'The idea that the description exceeds that of a locust plague breaks down on fuller knowledge, as we shall see. So does the idea that certain details are not applicable to locusts; for they invade towns just as Joel says, while Joel's further word about their stealing into houses "like a thief" certainly fits locusts more than a military assault! Moreover, Joel's account of the damage inflicted on the land is agricultural rather than military (v.3), and there is not even a hint of that which goes with a military invasion - massacre and plunder. But the allegorical theory is finally disproved by verses 4-7 where Joel says the invaders are *like* horsemen, and sound *like* chariots, and scale the wall *like* men of war. It has been aptly observed that Joel would never have compared a *real* army with itself!' (The terrifying results of locust plague are described in the addendum).

Baxter continues further: 'Yet even more than this, both the apocalyptic and allegorical theories are surely proved wrong by a comparison of verses 11 and 25; for in the one the invaders are called **Jehovah's** army, and in the other Jehovah Himself says: "I will restore unto you the years that **the locust** hath eaten, the cankerworm and the caterpillar and the palmerworm, my **great army** which I sent among you". Could language make it plainer, that the threatened **further** calamity, in chapter 2:1-11, was to be of the same kind - though in even severer degree - as that which had already taken place?'.

ii) A conventional army

If the passage really describes hostile nations, particularly northern enemies, then vv.2-10 suggest the advance of a ruthless, well-disciplined and perfectly organised army of irresistible and overwhelming force. It moves through the land without meeting any insurmountable difficulty. In the wake of its steady advance lies a train of utter destruction. Weapons are completely ineffective against it, and whether in countryside or town, no defence is able to impede its progress. This is how Peter C. Craigie (*The Twelve Prophets*) puts it: 'Just as a line of locusts marches steadily in ranks across a garden land, leaving behind it a wilderness without vegetation, so the apocalyptic army's advance (he evidently relates this to the future) defoliates the land. And so the awesome description continues: a totally unstoppable force, orderly and sinister, treads steadfastly across the land, missing no corner, conquering all resistance, overcoming every defensive barricade, so that even the cosmos seems to tremble, and the light of sun and moon are obscured'.

But it has to be said that the description of the invasion here does seem to fit locusts far more accurately than it does men! But having said this, we return to George Williams' observation that the Spirit of God uses 'this plague of locusts to awaken the conscience of the people at the moment, and, at the same time, to make use of them **to picture a future event of much greater moment'.** With this in mind, we could conclude that the passage foreshadows an invasion from the north at the end-time. A bold imagination might find material to suggest the onslaught of highly-trained infantrymen, and the use of mechanised divisions. In this connection, Ezekiel describes an invasion coming from the "north parts" (Ezek. 38:15), which points to a revival of the great Assyrian power. The question is asked "Art thou he of whom I have spoken in old time by my servants the prophets of Israel, which prophesied in those days many years that I would bring thee against them?" (Ezek. 38:17). The similarity between v.10, "the earth shall quake before them; the heavens shall tremble: the sun and the moon shall be dark, and the stars shall withdraw their shining" and 3:15 is too close to be coincidental. It is therefore certainly not beyond the realm of possibility that the invasion described here is a clear picture of events at the end time, when the invader will be defeated by Israel's Messiah: "this man shall be the peace, when the Assyrian shall come into our land…thus shall he deliver us from the Assyrian, when he cometh into our land, and when he treadeth within our borders" (Micah 5:5-6).

The imminence of invasion is coupled with an appeal for repentance and mourning, which brings us to:

3) CONTRITION, 2:12-17
This section of the chapter opens with a strong plea. The call to repentance and mourning here should not be confused with the mourning described by Zechariah: "In that day shall there be a great mourning in Jerusalem... And the land shall mourn, every family apart" (Zech. 12:11-14). It will not be said then, "Who knoweth if he will return and repent, and leave a blessing behind him" (v.14). The nation will "look on him whom they have pierced... In that day there shall be a fountain opened to the house of David and to the inhabitants of Jerusalem for sin and for uncleanness" (Zech. 12:10; 13:1).

The appeal, "turn ye even to me", emphasises the reason for divine judgment on the nation in this way. God's people had forsaken Him. In His words through Jeremiah, "they have turned unto me the back, and not the face" (Jer. 32:33). We must now consider the response required of God's people *(a)* generally (vv.12-14); *(b)* particularly (vv.15-17).

a) Generally, vv.12-14
"Therefore also now, saith the Lord, turn ye even to me with all your heart, and with fasting, and with weeping and with mourning: and rend your heart, and not your garments, and turn unto the Lord your God: for he is gracious and merciful, slow to anger, and of great kindness, and repenteth him of the evil. Who knoweth if he will return and repent, and leave a blessing behind him; even a meat-offering and a drink offering unto the Lord your God?" God's people were to exhibit three things: *(i)* sincerity; *(ii)* self-denial; *(iii)* sorrow (v.12).

i) Sincerity. "Turn ye unto me with all your heart". Cosmetic sincerity would not do: "rend your heart, and not your garments" (v.13). (For rent garments, see Joshua 7:6; 1 Sam. 4:12). God wanted reality, not externality. David knew only too well what God required: "For thou desirest not sacrifice; else would I give it: thou delightest not in burnt-offering, The sacrifices of God are a broken spirit: a broken and a contrite heart, O God, thou wilt not despise" (Psalm 51:16-17). The Lord Jesus quoted Isaiah 29:13 in saying, "This people draweth nigh unto me with their mouth, and honourest me with their lips; but their heart is far from me" (Matt. 15:8). The tendency to cover an alienated heart with religious formality is condemned throughout Scripture. See, for example, 1 Sam. 15:22; Isaiah 1:11-20; Jer.7:4; Micah 6:6-8.

ii) Self-denial. "Turn ye unto me...with fasting". Fasting is not a means to holiness - it is the fruit of holiness. Fasting involves, not the denial of sinful things in our lives - that goes without saying - but the denial of legitimate things in our lives in order that we may be undistracted in our devotion and prayer. Fasting does not stand alone. Luke tells us that at Antioch, fasting was associated with worship and devotion: "As they ministered to the Lord, and fasted" (Acts 13:2), and with prayer: "And when they had fasted and prayed, and laid their hands on them (Barnabas and Saul), they sent them away" (Acts 13:4). See also Matthew 17:21. Fasting is not commanded in the New Testament, but it was evidently practised. It does remind us of the need to curtail the untoward place that legitimate things can have in our lives. Fasting is basically saying 'No' to our own interests. It expresses the need for self-discipline. In the context of Joel 2, it expressed the reality of their attitude to the Lord.

iii) Sorrow. "Turn ye unto me...with weeping, and with mourning". There were no 'crocodile tears' at Corinth: "Ye sorrowed to repentance: for ye were made sorry after a godly manner...For godly sorrow worketh repentance to salvation not to be repented of...For behold this selfsame thing, that ye sorrowed after a godly sort" (2 Cor. 7:9-11). It should be remembered that Paul refers here to sorrow in the assembly at Corinth because they had tolerated sin in their midst. See 1 Cor. 5:1-2.

It must be stressed again that the Lord looked for thorough repentance and the renewal of devotion to Him, rather than religious formality: "rend your **heart** and not your garments, and turn unto the **Lord your God** (v.13). The sincerity, self-denial and sorrow of God's people in this way (v.12) would not fall on deaf ears: "He is gracious and merciful, slow to anger, and of great kindness, and repenteth him of the evil. Who knoweth if he will return and repent, and leave a blessing behind him; even a meat offering and a drink offering unto the Lord your God?" (vv.13-14). For the "meat offering" and the "drink offering" see 1:9 where neither could be offered. The priests were not able to worship: the locusts had consumed the ingredients for both offerings. But now there was the possibility of worshipping the Lord again in this way.

We should notice the reference to God repenting (v.13). It must be borne in mind that divine repentance is altogether different from human repentance. "God is not a man, that he should lie; neither the son of man, that he should repent" (Num. 23.19). However, the Lord does repent! But He does not repent as men and women repent, for the simple reason that He has never done wrong. With the Lord, repentance is not a change of mind and will, but a response consistent with a change of conduct on the part of a nation as in the case of Nineveh: "And God saw their works, that they turned from their evil way; and God repented of the evil, that he had said that he would do unto them; and he did it not" (Jonah 3.10).

We should also notice the precise wording: "Who knoweth if he will return and repent...?" (v.14). Similar language is used by Zephaniah, although it must be pointed out that the context is rather different: "it may be that ye shall be hid in the day of the Lord's anger" (Zeph. 2:3). Joel does not guarantee deliverance. While the Lord is "longsuffering to us-ward" (2 Pet. 3:9), that does not mean that He will continue to defer judgment *ad infinitum*.

b) Specifically, vv.15-17

These verses emphasise that the entire nation was to seek God in repentance and confession. For the second time in the chapter (cf. v.1), the alarm is sounded: "Blow the trumpet in Zion" (v.15). The entire nation is to gather: "sanctify a fast, call a solemn assembly: gather the people, sanctify the congregation". This was no carnival. It was to be marked by solemnity and sanctification. The nation was called to do business with God. Everybody was to feel the weight of the occasion. None were to be exempted. The burden was to be felt by all:

i) ***The leadership was addressed.*** "Assemble the elders" (v.16). Paul knew exactly what he was doing when, having arrived at Miletus, "he sent to Ephesus, and called the elders of the church" (Acts 20:17). Crises lay ahead: "I know this, that after my departing shall grievous wolves enter in among you, not sparing the flock. Also of your own selves shall men arise, speaking perverse things, to draw away disciples after them. Therefore watch and remember, that by the space of three years I ceased not to warn every one night and day with tears" (Acts 20:29-31). These were the men who were to 'watch for the souls' of God's people (Heb. 13:17).

ii) ***The families were addressed.*** "Gather the children, and those that suck the breasts" (v16). Family life was not to take precedence over the call to national repentance. All too often, it seems, families are made an excuse for absenteeism. This is not to say that the Lord's people should dispense with commonsense in raising their families, but this was a crisis. The urgency and importance of obeying God and maintaining a right relationship with

Him should lie at the heart of a believer's family life. Paul said of Timothy, "from a child thou hast known the holy scriptures, which are able to make thee wise unto salvation" (2 Tim. 3:15).

iii) The young couples were addressed. "Let the bridegroom go forth of his chamber, and the bride out of her closet" (v.16). We are now confronted with the deepest human joy. Jeremiah refers on several occasions to "the voice of mirth, and the voice of gladness, the voice of the bridegroom and the voice of the bride" (Jer. 7:34; 16:9; 25:10; 33:11). Moses made it very clear that this was most important. Read Deuteronomy 24:5. But the joys of married life should not take precedence over spiritual responsibilities.

iv) The priests were addressed. "Let the priests, the ministers of the Lord, weep between the porch and the altar (the place of access, and the ground of access), and let them say, Spare thy people, O Lord, and give not thine heritage to reproach, that the heathen should rule over them: wherefore should they say among the people, Where is their God?" (v.17). In the Old Testament, the priests represented the nation before God, but in the New Testament all believers are priests. See 1 Pet. 2:5, 7. A responsibility to intercede therefore rests upon every one of us. The threat to our existence should bring us on our knees to God. The priests were to plead the love of God, "Spare thy people, O Lord, and give not thine heritage to reproach", and the honour of God, "Wherefore should they say among the people (a plural word, referring to the Gentile nations), Where is their God?". Compare Exodus 32:12; Psalm 42:3, 10; 79:10; Micah 7:10.

In our next study, we will meet the restoring grace of God: "I will restore to you the years that the locust hath eaten…" (2:25).

Addenda

i) The ravages of a locust plague

These descriptions of a locust plague are taken from the *Journal of Sacred Literature,* October 1865: 'A writer recorded: "Our garden finished, they (the locusts) continued toward the town, devastating one garden after another. Whatever one is doing one hears their noise from without, like the noise of armed hosts, or the running of many waters. When in an erect position their appearance at a little distance is like that of a well-armed horseman". Another writer says: "To strength incredible for so small a creature, they add saw-like teeth, admirably calculated to eat up all the herbs in the land". Another says: "After eating up the corn, they fell upon the vines, the pulse, the willows, and even the hemp, notwithstanding its great bitterness". And another says: "For eighty or ninety miles they devoured every green herb and every blade of grass". And another says: "The gardens outside Jaffa are now completely stripped, even the bark of the young trees having been devoured, and look like a birch-tree forest in winter". And still another: "The fields finished, they invade towns and houses, in search of stores. Victual of all kinds, hay, straw, and even linen and woollen clothes and leather bottles, they consume or tear in pieces. They flood through the open, unglazed windows and lattices; nothing can keep them out". W. M. Thomson tells us that when the millions upon millions of locust eggs hatch, the very dust seems to waken to life, and the earth itself seems to tremble with them; and later, when the vast new breed have acquired wings, the very heavens seem tremulous with them. And as for Joel's likening of the locusts to "dawn scattered on the mountains," G. A. Smith says: "No one who has seen a cloud of locusts can question the realism even of this picture; the heavy gloom of the immeasurable mass of them, shot by gleam of flight where a few of the sun's imprisoned beams have broken through or across the storm of lustrous wings. This is like dawn beaten down upon the hilltops, and crushed by rolling masses of cloud, in conspiracy to prolong the night'".

ii) Locusts in the book of Revelation
Whilst it is *not* suggested that the two passages refer to the same events, it is rather striking that when the "fifth angel sounded" and "the bottomless pit" was opened, "there arose a smoke out of the pit, as the smoke of a great furnace; and the sun and the air were darkened by reason of the smoke of the pit. And there came out of the smoke locusts upon the earth" (Rev. 9:2-3). They were certainly no ordinary locusts! Read the rest of the passage (Rev. 9:3-11).

READ CHAPTER 2:18-27

"The Lord will do great things"

It is worth recalling that the prophecy of Joel may be divided as follows: *(1)* desolation (1:1-20); *(2)* invasion (2:1-11); *(3)* contrition (2:12-17); *(4)* restoration (2:18-27); *(5)* regeneration (2:28-32); *(6)* retribution (3:1-21).

1) DESOLATION, 1:1-20
The prophecy commences with Joel's description of conditions in the land at the time of writing. Judah was reeling under the devastating effects of a locust invasion (v.4) coupled with drought (v.20). The nation was faced with famine. If famine deprived Judah of the ability to worship, destroyed the fruitfulness of the land, and robbed the people of their joy, then spiritual famine in our lives will have the same spiritual results.

2) INVASION, 2: 1-11
While some commentators suggest that these verses describe the advance of a conventional army under the figure of a locust plague, it seems more probable that they refer to the imminence of a further locust plague of such gigantic proportions that it merits the title "the day of the Lord". This invasion is "nigh at hand" (2:1) rather than "in those days, and at that time, when I shall bring again the captivity of Judah and Jerusalem" (3:1). But having said this, there can be little doubt that, through Joel, the Spirit of God uses 'this plague of locusts to awaken the conscience of the people at the moment, and, *at the same time*, to make use of them to picture a future event of much greater moment' (George Williams). The locust invasion is called "the day of the Lord" because it is a shadow of events at the end-time.

3) CONTRITION, 2: 12-17
In view of the threat of such a terrifying invasion, the nation is called to thorough-going repentance: "Therefore also now, saith the Lord, turn ye even to me with all your heart, and with fasting, and with weeping, and with mourning" (2:12). There was to be sincerity ("with all your heart"); self-denial

("with fasting"); sorrow ("with weeping, and with mourning"). No one was excluded: the leadership was addressed ("assemble the elders"); the families were addressed ("gather the children, and those that suck the breasts"); the young couples were addressed ("let the bridegroom go forth of his chamber, and the bride out of her closet"); the priests were addressed ("Let the priests… weep between the porch and the altar" (vv.16-17). This brings us to:

4) RESTORATION, 2:18-27
We can divide these verses in the following way: *(a)* the reason for blessing (vv.18-19); *(b)* the removal of the invader (v.20); *(c)* the renewal of the land (vv.21-27).

a) The reason for blessing, vv.18-19
We have already noticed that God's people should not automatically trade on the Lord's grace and mercy: "Who knoweth if he will return and repent, and leave a blessing behind him; even a meat-offering and a drink-offering unto the Lord your God?" (2:14). Nevertheless the promise of restoration is clearly made: "Then will the Lord be jealous for his land, and pity his people. Yea, the Lord will answer and say unto his people, Behold, I will send you corn, and wine, and oil, and ye shall be satisfied therewith: and I will no more make you a reproach among the heathen". This reiterates the promise made to Solomon: "If I shut up heaven that there be no rain, or if I command the locusts (*chagab*) to devour the land, or if I send pestilence among my people; if my people, which are called by my name, shall humble themselves, and pray, and seek my face, and turn from their wicked ways; then I will hear from heaven, and will forgive their sin, and will heal their land" (2 Chron. 7:13-14).

The reason for promised blessing does not lie in the virtue of God's people - they are completely unworthy of His favour - but with God's concern for His own glory, and His deep concern for their welfare: "Then will the Lord be jealous for his land, and pity his people". Not a word about their personal merit! This is stressed by Ezekiel: "But I had pity for mine holy name, which the house of Israel had profaned among the heathen, whither they went. Thus saith the Lord God; I do not this for your sakes, O house of Israel, but for my holy name's sake, which ye have profaned among the heathen, whither ye went. And I will sanctify my great name, which was profaned among the heathen…and the heathen shall know that I am the Lord, saith the Lord God, when I shall be sanctified in you before their eyes" (Ezek.36:21-23). Christians sing:

Chosen not for good in me,
Wakened up from wrath to flee:
Hidden in the Saviour's side,
By the Spirit sanctified;
Teach me, Lord, on earth to show,
By my love, how much I owe.

At least three things are promised here. Following true repentance ("rend your heart, and not your garments", v.13), the Lord will *(i)* be "jealous for his land": He will act for them against their enemies (v.18); *(ii)* "send corn, and wine, and oil" (v.19); *(iii)* no longer make them "a reproach among the heathen" (v.19).

i) The Lord will be "jealous for his land", v.18. Jealousy is one of the attributes of God. God is jealous in three ways, and in this particular instance He is:

- *Jealous for His people*. He is jealous over the welfare of His people. Compare the following: "I am jealous for Jerusalem and for Zion with a great jealousy" (Zech.1:14); "I was jealous for Zion with great jealousy, and I was jealous for her with great fury" (Zech. 8:2). In both cases, His people were oppressed by the Gentile powers. See also Ezek. 36:5-6; 38:19; Zeph.3:8. He is jealous for His people in the sense that He is against those who harm them. But He is also:

- *Jealous of His own glory*. "Now will I bring again the captivity of Jacob, and have mercy on the whole house of Israel, and will be jealous for my holy name" (Ezek. 39:25). Compare Isaiah 48:11 ("My glory will I not give to another") and 1 Cor. 1:26-29 ("For ye see your calling, brethren, how that not many wise men after the flesh, not many mighty, not many noble, are called: but God hath chosen the foolish things of the world...the weak things...and base things...and things which are despised...and things which are not...that no flesh should glory in his presence"). Then He is:

- *Jealous over the affections of His people*. He states quite categorically, "I the Lord thy God am a jealous God" (Exod. 20:5); "thou shalt worship no other god: for the Lord, whose name is Jealous, is a jealous God" (Exod.34:14.) In both cases idolatry is condemned. Compare Deut. 32:16 ("They provoked him to jealousy with strange gods"); Deut. 32:21 ("They have moved me to jealousy with that which is not God"); Psalm 78:58

("they...moved him to jealousy with their graven images"). Ezekiel saw, in a vision, an idol in the temple at Jerusalem which he calls "the image of jealousy, which provoketh to jealousy...this image of jealousy" (Ezek. 8:3,5).

All this contributes to the New Testament warning: "Little children, keep yourselves from idols" (1 John 5:21). Is the Lord jealous of anything, or anybody apart from Himself, in our lives? Paul, speaking as their spiritual father, was deeply concerned over the spiritual welfare of the Corinthians: "I am jealous over you with **godly jealousy**: for I have espoused you to one husband, that I may present you as a chaste virgin to Christ" (2 Cor.11:2). How concerned are we about **our** loyalty to Him?

ii) The Lord will "send corn, and wine, and oil", v.19. True repentance ("turn unto the Lord your God", v.13) would reverse the barrenness of the land. This is amplified in vv.21-27. The reference to "corn, and wine, and oil" reminds us that it is "wine that maketh glad the heart of man, and oil to make his face to shine, and bread which strengtheneth man's heart" (Psalm 104:15). There is nothing 'unsatisfactory' about God's blessings. We cannot be other than "satisfied therewith". See, for example, John 6:35.

iii) The Lord will no longer make them "a reproach among the heathen", v.19. True repentance will bring recognition on the part of others that God is with them. The priests were to cry, "Spare thy people, O Lord, and give not thine heritage to reproach, that the heathen should rule over them: wherefore should they say among the people, Where is their God?" (v.17). Once downcast and defeated through the ravages of the locust plague, Judah would be able to look her neighbours in the face without fear and shame. In New Testament language (which should be true of every assembly), men would be constrained to say, "God is in you of a truth" (1 Cor. 14.25).

b) The removal of the invader, v.20
"But I will remove far off from you the northern army, and will drive him into a land barren and desolate, with his face toward the east sea, and his hinder part towards the utmost sea, and his stink shall come up, because he hath done great things".

The description of the removal and destruction of the locusts certainly agrees with historical records. For example: "When they come to water, be it a mere puddle or a river, a lake or the open sea, they never attempt to go round it, but unhesitatingly leap in and are drowned, and their dead bodies, floating on the surface, form a bridge for their companions to pass over. The scourge thus often comes to an end, but it often happens that the decomposition of millions of insects produces pestilence and death. History records a remarkable instance which occurred in the year 125 before the Christian era. The insects were driven by the wind into the sea in such vast numbers that their bodies, being driven back by the tide upon the land, caused a stench which produced a fearful plague whereby eighty thousand persons perished in Libya, Cyrene, and Egypt". (*Van-Lennep's Bible Lands,* quoted by J. Sidlow Baxter, *Explore the Book - Joel*).

There can be no doubt that this was a *bona fide* promise at the time. True repentance would signal the end of the locusts' destructive work. We must remember that the Lord used the locusts to chasten His people. They are described as "his army" (v.11) and "my great army which I sent among you" (v.25). In this instance it was through the locusts that the Lord "executeth his word" (v.11) in dealing with His people, with the intention of turning them to Him in confession and repentance.

Conditions in the assembly at Corinth underline the same lesson: "But let a man examine himself, and so let him eat of that bread, and drink of that cup. For he that eateth and drinketh unworthily, eateth and drinketh damnation (condemnation) to himself, not discerning the Lord's body. **For this cause** many are weak and sickly among you, and many sleep. For if we would judge ourselves, we should not be judged" (1 Cor. 11:28-31). We should take a hard look at our own circumstances and, if necessary, ask the question, 'Is our present weakness the result of failure on our part, and has the Lord allowed this to happen in order to convict us of our need to turn to Him in thorough-going repentance?' Today, in many places, it has to be said: "That which the palmerworm hath left hath the locust eaten; and that which the locust hath left hath the cankerworm eaten; and that which the cankerworm hath left hath the caterpillar eaten" (1:4). We sorely need to heed the Lord's injunction, "turn ye even to me with all your heart, and with fasting, and with weeping, and with mourning" for "Who knoweth if he will return and repent, and leave a blessing behind him...?" (Joel 2:12-14). Jeremiah similarly points the way to recovery: "Let us search and try our ways, and turn again to the Lord. Let us lift up our heart with our hands unto God in the heavens" (Lam.3:40-41).

At this point we must remind ourselves that if the earlier verses in this chapter (vv.1-10) describe the imminent arrival of a literal plague of locusts (described as "the northern army", v.20), which was, at the same time, a shadow of events at the end-time, then the removal of the insects must also depict events at the end-time. Ezekiel describes an invasion "out of the north parts" (38:15) and predicts that the invader will "fall upon the mountains of Israel" (39:4) "which have always been waste" (38:8). Joel describes the location of the invader's destruction as "a land barren and desolate" (2:20). He also relates that "his stink shall come up, and his ill savour shall come up" (2:20) which corresponds with Ezekiel's description, "I will give unto Gog a place there of graves in Israel, the valley of the passengers ('passers-by', JND) on the east of the sea: and it shall stop the noses of the passengers ('passers-by')" (39:11). The correspondence between the two passages is remarkable.

We should add that since the invasion described by Ezekiel will evidently take place when Israel has returned to the land and is dwelling there in peace (Ezek.38:8), it cannot apparently refer to the invasion described by Daniel, when "the king of the north" will "plant the tabernacles of his palace **between the seas** in the glorious holy mountain; yet shall he come to his end, and none shall help him" (Dan.11:45). It should be said that not all prophetic students would agree with this conclusion!

c) The renewal of the land, vv.21-27
Repentance would mark the end of the locust plague and usher in a period of great blessing for the land. 'If the locusts had done *great things* (v.20) in the havoc wrought by them, God will also do...*great things* (v.21) in restoring fertility to the soil' (*The Twelve Prophets,* edited by Dr. A. Cohen). Once again, there can be no doubt that this was a *bona fide* promise at the time. But, equally, there can be no doubt that the reversal of the ravages of the locust plague points forward to millennial conditions after the ravages of war at the end-time, when "the Lord will answer and say unto his people, behold, I will send you corn and wine, and oil, and ye shall be satisfied therewith: and I will no more make you a reproach among the heathen" (v.19), and "my people shall never be ashamed" (v.27). It will be at this time that the promise will be fulfilled, "I will pour out my Spirit upon all flesh; and your sons and your daughters shall prophesy, your old men shall dream dreams, your young men shall see visions: and also upon the servants and upon the handmaids in those days will I pour out my Spirit" (vv.28-29).

The features described here beautifully depict the spiritual blessings which follow a right relationship with the Lord. There should be millennial conditions in our hearts and lives, and in our assemblies *now!* In studying Chapter 1 we noticed that the features of famine conditions, brought about by the locust devastation, furnish criteria by which we can judge whether or not *we* are in famine conditions. Now we have criteria by which we can judge whether or not we are in spiritual prosperity. John prayed that Gaius might "prosper and be in health, even as thy soul prospereth" (3 John 2). The verses now before us illustrate what it is like to be in good spiritual health. We must now take note of the "great things" (v.21) which the Lord would do for the land and for His people. We should notice the encouraging note on which these verses begin: "Fear not...Be not afraid" (vv.21-22). The future was assured.

i) **There would be renewal of pasture.** "Be not afraid, ye beasts of the field: for the pastures of the wilderness do spring" (v22). During the locust plagues, which seem to have extended over a considerable time (v.25), herds and flocks suffered though lack of pasture: "How do the beasts groan! The herds of cattle are perplexed, because they have no pasture; yea, the flocks of sheep are made desolate" (1:18). When spiritual life is barren, the word of God ceases to be "green pastures" (Psalm 23:2) to our souls. Bible reading becomes a mere routine, if we read the Scriptures at all. But the renewal of spiritual life, when we turn to the Lord, will enable us to say, "O how I love thy law! it is my meditation all the day" (Psalm 119:97).

ii) **There would be renewal of fruitfulness.** "The tree beareth her fruit, the fig tree and the vine do yield their strength" (v.22). As a result of the locust plagues, "the vine is dried up, and fig tree languisheth...even all the trees of the field, are withered" (1:12). The evidence of spiritual life is seen in spiritual fruitfulness. The "fruit of the Spirit is love, joy, peace, longsuffering, gentleness, goodness, faith, meekness, temperance" (Gal. 5:22-23). Compare Psalm 1:3: 2 Pet.1:8.

iii) **There would be the renewal of joy**. "Be glad then, ye children of Zion, and rejoice in the Lord your God" (v.23). No longer would it have to be said that "joy is withered away from the sons of men" (1:12). Joy in the Lord is one feature of healthy spiritual life. Love for Christ and joy in Him are closely linked: "Whom having not seen, ye love; in whom, though now ye see him not, yet believing, ye rejoice with joy unspeakable and full of glory" (1 Pet. 1:8). John wrote that our "joy may be full" (1 John 1:4). No more howling! (See 1:5,11,13). Justin Waldron asks 'What about our joy in prayer (Phil.1:4); in devotion (Phil. 2:17); in each other (Phil. 4:1); in studying the word of God (Jer.15:16); in trials (James 1:2)?'

iv) There would be renewal of rainfall. "He hath given you the former rain moderately, and he will cause to come down for you the rain, the former rain, and the latter rain in the first month" (v.23). The drought would end. No longer would the rivers be "dried up" (1:20). The withdrawal of rain and dew was a sign of divine displeasure (see Deut. 28.23-24; 1 Kings 17:1). In the millennial age, the Lord will "come down like rain upon the mown grass: as showers that water the earth" (Psalm 72:6). The bestowal of rain and dew was therefore a sign of divine pleasure and blessing. When this is enjoyed, our spiritual lives will be "like a watered garden, and like a spring of water, whose waters fail not" (Isaiah 58:11). Compare Jeremiah 31:12. The expression "the former rain moderately (literally 'in righteousness') means 'the rain in just measure, as the ground naturally requires' (Gesenius). 'It will not come down in torrents and swamp the soil' (*The Twelve Prophets*). The "former rain, and the latter rain" fall in October and April ("the first month") respectively.

v) There would be renewal of harvests. "And the floors shall be full of wheat, and the fats shall overflow with wine and oil. And I will restore to you the years that the locust hath eaten...my great army which I sent among you. And ye shall eat in plenty, and be satisfied" (vv.24-26). As a result of the locust plagues, "the corn is wasted: the new wine is dried up, the oil languisheth...the seed is rotten under their clods (rotting in the earth, or 'the grains shrivel under their hoes'), the garners are laid desolate, the barns are broken down; for the corn is withered" (vv.10,17). But now, abundant harvests! This reminds us that a right relationship with the Lord will result in abundant spiritual supplies. We will be "nourished up in the words of faith and of good doctrine" (1 Tim. 4:6). Like the millennial priests, our souls will be satiated "with fatness" (Jer. 31:14). We can say without doubt that God loves to give "good measure, pressed down, and shaken together, and running over!" (Luke 6:38).

vi) There would be renewal of worship. "And ye shall...praise the name of the Lord your God, that hath dealt wondrously with you" (v.26). The locust plague had robbed the Lord's people, particularly the priests, of joy in worship. See 1:9,13,16. There was no "joy and gladness" in the house of God (v.16). But now the Lord would receive the praise of His people.

The passage ends with the promise of ongoing security and blessing. "My people shall never be ashamed. And ye shall know that I am in the midst of Israel, and that I am the Lord your God, that hath dealt wondrously with you: and my people shall never be ashamed. And ye shall know that I am in the midst of Israel and that I am the Lord your God...and my people shall never be ashamed" (vv.26-27). No longer will the nations say, "Where is their God?" (v.17) and no longer will His people be "a reproach among the heathen" (v.19). The repetition of the words, "my people shall never be ashamed", emphasises the permanence of divine blessing. The people who were called upon to "Lament like a virgin girded with sackcloth for the husband of her youth" (1:8), will enjoy the presence of the Lord. He will be "in the midst of Israel".

Our enjoyment of the Lord's presence and the Lord's promises enables us to say with Paul, "I am not ashamed" (Rom. 1:16; 2 Tim. 1:12). Peter writes on the subject as follows: "Wherefore also it is contained in the scripture, Behold, I lay in Sion a chief corner stone, elect, precious: and he that believeth on him shall not be confounded" ('put to shame', RV)" (1 Pet. 2:6).

Looking back over the passage, it could be said, in summary, that turning to the Lord wholeheartedly (v.12) will secure His blessing in the following ways. *(i) Barrenness will give place to fullness*: "I will send you corn, and wine, and oil" (v.19); provision is made for the renewal of offerings to God, and for the satisfaction of men. *(ii) Oppression will give place to liberty*: "I will remove far off from you the northern army" (v.20). God's people will no longer be at the mercy of the northern invader: He will act on their behalf. *(iii) Misery will give place to joy:* "rejoice" (v.21); "rejoice" (v.23); "praise" (v.26): no longer "howl" (1:5,11, 13). *(iv) Reproach will give place to honour:* "I will no more make you a reproach among the heathen" (v.19): "my people shall never be ashamed" (vv.26-27). *(v) Distance will give place to nearness:* "And ye shall know that I am in the midst of Israel" (v.27). Compare 3:17,21.

READ CHAPTER 2:28-32

"I will pour out my Spirit upon all flesh"

We have said that the prophecy of Joel may be divided as follows: *(1)* desolation (1:1-20); *(2)* invasion (2:1-11); *(3)* contrition (2:12-17); *(4)* restoration (2:18-27); *(5)* regeneration (2:28-32); *(6)* retribution (3:1-21).

1) DESOLATION, 1:1-20
The prophecy commences with Joel's description of conditions in the land at the time of writing. Judah was reeling under the devastating effects of a locust invasion (v.4) coupled with drought (v.20). The passage illustrates the effects of spiritual famine in our lives. We must remember that "whatsoever things were written aforetime were written for *our* learning" (Rom. 15:4). Compare 1 Cor. 10:11.

2) INVASION, 2:1-11
While some commentators suggest that these verses describe the advance of a conventional army under the figure of a locust plague, it seems more probable that they refer to the imminence of a further locust plague of such gigantic proportions that it merits the title "the day of the Lord". This invasion was "nigh at hand" (2:1) rather than "in those days, and at that time, when I shall bring again the captivity of Judah and Jerusalem" (3:1). But having said this, there can be little doubt that, through Joel, the Spirit of God uses 'this plague of locusts to awaken the conscience of the people at the moment and, *at the same time*, to make use of them to picture a future event of much greater moment' (George Williams). The locust invasion is called "the day of the Lord" because it is a shadow of events at the end-time.

3) CONTRITION, 2:12-17
In view of the threat of such a terrifying invasion, the nation is called to thorough-going repentance: "Therefore also now, saith the Lord, turn ye even to me with all your heart, and with fasting, and with weeping, and with mourning" (2:12). No one was exempted: the elders, families, newly-weds

and priests were all involved in national repentance and intercession. If disobedience has brought famine conditions into our lives, then thorough-going repentance on our part will bring restoration and blessing. God can still restore "the years that the locust hath eaten" (2:25) in our lives. He is the God of recovery.

4) RESTORATION, 2:18-27
There can be no doubt that this was a *bona fide* promise at the time. True repentance would signal the end of the locusts' destructive work. We must remember that the Lord used the locusts to chasten His people. They are described as "his army" (v.11) and "my great army which I sent among you" (v.25). In this instance it was through the locusts that the Lord "executeth his word" (v.11) in dealing with His people, with the intention of turning them to Him in confession and repentance.

At the same time we should say that if the earlier verses in this chapter (vv. 1-10) describe the imminent arrival of a literal plague of locusts (described as "the northern army", v.20), which was, at the same time, a shadow of events at the end-time, then the removal of the insects must also depict events at the end-time. In this connection, Ezekiel describes an invasion "out of the north parts" (38:15) and predicts that the invader will "fall upon the mountains of Israel" (39:4). There can be no doubt that the reversal of the ravages of the locust plague is expressed in language that beautifully anticipates Israel's deliverance from coming invasion, when "the Lord will answer and say unto his people, behold, I will send you corn and wine, and oil, and ye shall be satisfied therewith: and I will no more make you a reproach among the heathen" (v.19), and "my people shall never be ashamed" (v.27).

The features described here also beautifully depict the spiritual blessings which follow a right relationship with the Lord. There should be millennial conditions in our hearts and lives and in our assemblies *now!* In studying Chapter 1 we noticed that the features of famine conditions, brought about by the locust devastation, furnish criteria by which we can judge whether or not *we* are in famine conditions. In these verses we have criteria by which we can judge whether or not we are in *spiritual prosperity*. This brings us to:

5) REGENERATION, 2:28-32
We are told that Joel 2:28 marks the beginning of Chapter 3 in the Hebrew text. See J. N. Darby's marginal note. The words, "And it shall come to pass afterward" mark the commencement of a passage which clearly describes

events at the end-time. We have noticed that the language used to describe both the ravages caused by the locust plagues and the promised restoration following national repentance, is deliberately suited both to circumstances at the time of writing, and also to the future. But now the prophecy proceeds to describe future events alone. A cursory glance at our current passage, let alone Chapter 3, will be sufficient to prove the point.

The order in which events are mentioned calls for comment. Joel begins by describing the outpouring of the Holy Spirit, which will evidently bring about national regeneration (vv.28-29), and then follows by describing unprecedented cosmic disturbances (vv.30-31) coupled with a colossal invasion by Israel's enemies, from whose clutches a remnant will be delivered (v.32). This invasion will be divinely-initiated ("I will also gather all nations", 3:2) and will be divinely-defeated ("I will enter into judgment with them there on account of my people", 3:2, JND).

Very clearly, this is not the order of events given elsewhere in the Scriptures. Through Ezekiel, the Lord describes the return of Israel to the land, and continues: "Then will I sprinkle clean water upon you, and ye shall be clean: from all your filthiness, and from all your idols, will I cleanse you. A new heart also will I give you, and a new spirit will I put within you...and I will put my Spirit within you, and cause you to walk in my statutes, and ye shall keep my judgments, and do them" (Ezek. 36:25-27). Through Zechariah, the Lord describes the destruction of the nations which will surround Jerusalem, and adds: "And I will pour upon the house of David, and upon the inhabitants of Jerusalem, the spirit of grace and of supplications; and they shall look upon me whom they have pierced, and they shall mourn for him" (Zech. 12:10).

The explanation for the reversal of the usual order of events is accounted for by the fact that having described the blessings of repentant Israel (2:18-27), culminating in national regeneration (2:28-29), Joel then describes the sequence of events which will lead to their ultimate blessing in this way (2:30-32). This will involve divine retribution on the nations of the world because of their hostility towards God's people, and therefore towards God Himself. The end-time will therefore be marked by the blessing of God's people, and the defeat of their enemies.

Very clearly, our current passage (2:28-32) falls into two sections: *(A)* the bestowal of the Spirit (vv.28-29); *(B)* the deliverance of the remnant (vv.30-32).

A) *The bestowal of the Spirit, vv.28-29*
"And it shall come to pass afterward, that I will pour out my Spirit upon all flesh; and your sons and your daughters shall prophesy, your old men shall dream dreams, your young men shall see visions: and also upon the servants and upon the handmaids in those days will I pour out my Spirit". This emphasises the deity of the Holy Spirit. How could countless multitudes of people enjoy the blessing of the Holy Spirit simultaneously in this way if this were not the case? We must now consider: *(a)* the bestowal of the Spirit at Pentecost; *(b)* the bestowal of the Spirit at the end-time.

a) *The bestowal of the Spirit at Pentecost*
Peter explained events on the day of Pentecost by quoting Joel 2:28-29: "And it shall come to pass in the last days, saith God, I will pour out of my Spirit (Joel has "I will pour out my Spirit") upon all flesh; and your sons and your daughters shall prophesy, and your young men shall see visions, and your old men shall dream dreams: and on my servants and on my handmaidens will I pour out in those days my Spirit; and they shall prophesy" (Acts 2:17-18). Peter evidently quoted the Joel passage to emphasise that the immense blessing on the day of Pentecost was in accordance with the highest favour promised for Israel. It is noteworthy that Peter did not say, 'But that which was spoken by the prophet Joel is fulfilled': rather, "But this is that (of that sort) which was spoken by the prophet Joel". As F. A. Tatford observes, 'It is frequently stated that the apostle Peter expressly claimed that the descent of the Holy Spirit at Pentecost was the fulfillment of Joel's prophecy...but the accompanying details, which the apostle quoted (i.e. reference to the cosmic disturbances), were not, of course, fulfilled at Pentecost...Peter merely implied that what had transpired at Pentecost was of the same nature as the events foretold by Joel, and it is obvious that the complete fulfillment awaits the outpouring of the Holy Spirit in the millennium". See Ezekiel 39:29, "Neither will I hide my face any more from them: for I have poured out my Spirit upon the house of Israel, saith the Lord God". Notice that Peter omitted the words, "for in mount Zion and in Jerusalem shall be deliverance, as the Lord hath said, and in the remnant whom the Lord shall call". He draws attention to the Lord Jesus (Acts 2:22-24).

ii) *The bestowal of the Spirit at the end-time*
Having "washed away the filth of the daughters of Zion, and...purged the blood of Jerusalem from the midst thereof, by the spirit of judgment, and by the spirit of burning" (Isaiah 4:4), God's people will experience the out-pouring of God's Holy Spirit. It is rather significant to notice that the

preceding section ends with the twice-repeated words, "and my people shall never be ashamed" (vv.26-27), and the new section commences with reference to the pouring out of the Spirit. This, surely, is no coincidence. God's people will "never be ashamed", because they will enjoy the ministry of the Holy Spirit. "I will **pour out** my Spirit" indicates something quite different to the way in which the Holy Spirit came upon certain individuals in the Old Testament, enabling them to do certain things, and remaining on them for limited periods. We enjoy this **now**: "hope maketh not **ashamed**; because the love of God is **shed abroad in our hearts by the Holy Ghost**, which is given unto us" (Rom 5: 5). Did Paul have Joel 2:26-28 in mind when he wrote this? We should now consider:

- **The scope.** We have to decide whether this is universal, or whether this future blessing belongs only to Israel. The context might suggest that the prophecy relates only to Israel. The words "all flesh" appear to be qualified by "**your** sons and **your** daughters...**your** old men...**your** young men". Quite clearly, there would be no divisions when it comes to this blessing: male and female, young and old, masters and servants will all be included. When Joshua asked Moses to rebuke Eldad and Medad for prophesying "in the camp", Moses answered, "Would God that all the Lord's people were prophets, and that the Lord would put his spirit upon them!" (Num. 11:26-29). He would not have to say that here! However, it is difficult to escape the fact that the words "all flesh" (compare Luke 3:6) mean what they say, and that believing Gentiles as well as believing Jews will be blessed in this way. Perhaps the words "all flesh" have exactly this meaning, but it will be in Israel that there will be prophecy, dreams and visions.

- **The people**. All sections of society will be included. The inclusion of sons and daughters, old and young, servants and handmaids, serves to remind us that every believer today is indwelt by the Holy Spirit, for "if any man have not the Spirit of Christ, he is none of his" (Rom. 8:9). But it also reminds us that "the manifestation of the Spirit is given to every man to profit withal. For to one is given...to another...to another" (1 Cor. 12:7-11).

- **The result**. The passage emphasises the communication of God's word. "Your sons and your daughters shall prophesy, your old men shall dream dreams, your young men shall see visions" (v.28). God's people will be in receipt of His word. F. A. Tatford observes that 'it has always been the case that it is the older who meditate (and perhaps ruminate) and ponder, dreaming of what might have been and of what might still be. But it is the younger who seem to catch the glimpse of life's potentialities and, with the vigour and inspiration of youth go forth, conquering and to conquer'. Compare Ezra 4:10-13. Perhaps the point emphasised here is that the nation will have new life, and that this life will be demonstrated by the active enjoyment of God's word. M. F. Unger observes that prophecy, dreams and visions were the three ways in which the Lord revealed Himself and His will in the Old Testament: "Hear now my words: If there be a prophet among you, I the Lord will make myself known to him in a vision, and will speak to him in a dream" (Num. 12:6). W. E. Vine defines a dream as 'a vision in sleep, in distinction from a waking vision'.

But who are the people who will benefit from His outpouring of the Spirit? The answer follows:

B) *The deliverance of the remnant, vv.30-32*

While, as we have seen, "all flesh" suggests both Jew and Gentile, it certainly includes the former. Paul tells us that "all Israel shall be saved" (Rom. 11:26). The words "all Israel" do not mean the entire nation without further distinction, but the true Israel (see Romans 2:28-29) as indicated here: "And it shall come to pass, that **whosoever shall call on the name of the Lord shall be delivered**: for in mount Zion and in Jerusalem shall be deliverance, as the Lord hath said, and in the remnant whom the Lord shall call ('and for the residue whom Jehovah shall call', JND)" (v.32).

The believing remnant in Israel at the end-time will be delivered from "the great and terrible day of the Lord" (v.31), and in this connection we must notice the following:

i) *The title given to the judgment.*

Preachers often distinguish between "the day of the Lord" and "the great and terrible day of the Lord", suggesting that the latter refers to the most intensive judgments associated with the "day of the Lord". In His 'Olivet Discourse', the Lord Jesus said: "Immediately after the tribulation of those days shall the sun be darkened, and the moon shall not give her light, and the stars shall fall from heaven, and the powers of the heavens shall be shaken: and then shall appear the sign of the Son of man in heaven: and then shall all the tribes of the earth mourn, and they shall see the Son of man coming in the clouds of heaven with power and great glory" (Matt. 24:29-30). (Compare Revelation 6:12-17). This leads us to suggest that "the great and terrible day of the Lord" refers to the public return of the Lord Jesus to earth as "King of kings and Lord of lords"

(Rev.19:16) to execute judgment on the world that had rejected Him. The "great and terrible day of the Lord" is not therefore the great tribulation, but the consuming judgment that the Lord Jesus will exercise at His public return. See Revelation 19:11-17.

ii) The signs preceding the judgment. "And I will shew wonders in the heavens and in the earth, blood, and fire, and pillars of smoke. The sun shall be turned into darkness, and the moon into blood, before the great and terrible day of the Lord come". See also Joel 3:14-16. We can now see why the locust plague is described as "the day of the Lord": "the earth shall quake before them; the heavens shall tremble: the sun and the moon shall be dark, and the stars withdraw their shining" (Joel 2:1, 10).

As we have seen, the Lord Jesus put these phenomena "*immediately after the tribulation of those days"* (that is, after the time to which Matt. 24:21, Dan. 12:1 etc. refer), and *just before His appearing in glory.* Thus we read, "And *then* shall appear the sign of the Son of man in heaven: and then shall all the tribes of the earth mourn, and they shall see the Son of man coming in the clouds of heaven with power and great glory" (Matt. 24:29-30).

These verses (vv.30-31) should be compared with Revelation 6:12-13: "And I beheld when he had opened the sixth seal, and, lo, there was a great earthquake; and the sun became black as sackcloth of hair, and the moon became as blood; and the stars of heaven fell to the earth".The effect on men is clear. These were the portents of coming judgment: all men, great and small, "hid themselves in the dens and in the rocks of the mountains; and said to the mountains and rocks, Fall on us, and hide us from the face of him that sitteth on the throne, and from the wrath of the Lamb: for the great day of his wrath is come; and who shall be able to stand" (Rev. 6:16-17). Features of the "great and terrible day of the Lord" will be seen prior to that event.

iii) The deliverance from the judgment. As already noted: "And it shall come to pass, that whosoever shall call on the name of the Lord shall be delivered: for in mount Zion and in Jerusalem shall be deliverance, as the Lord hath said, and in the remnant whom the Lord shall call ('and for the residue whom Jehovah shall call', JND)" (v.32). It is not without significance that Paul refers to this passage in saying, "For the scripture saith, Whosoever believeth on him shall not be ashamed. For there is no difference between the Jew and the Greek: for the same Lord over all is rich unto all that call upon him. *For whosoever shall call upon the name of the Lord shall be saved*" (Rom. 10:11-13). While, in context, Joel is referring to the deliverance of the repentant and believing remnant in Israel at the end-time, Paul *applies* the text to the mercy of God towards Jew and Gentile at the present time.

In this connection, it should be noted that reference is made to mount Zion and Jerusalem (v.32) We know that ultimately, Jerusalem will be surrounded by enemies and at the 'eleventh hour' there will be deliverance. See Zech. 14:1-3. Compare Joel 3:16. As M. F. Unger points out, the words "as the Lord hath said" (v.32) refer, not to other prophets (Joel was evidently one of the first writing prophets), but to what the Lord has just said through him: "whosoever shall call on the name of the Lord shall be delivered".

The *whole period*, terminating with "the great and terrible day of the Lord", will be one of intense pressure on Israel. Jeremiah refers to this: "Alas! For the day is great so that there is none like it: it is even the time of Jacob's trouble, but he *shall be saved out of it*" (Jer. 30:7). See also Dan. 12:1, "There shall be a time of trouble, such as never was since there was a nation even to that same time: and at that time *thy people shall be delivered*, every one that shall be found written in the book". The Lord Jesus referred to this time as follows: "And except those days should be shortened, there should no flesh be saved: but for *the elect's sake* those days shall be shortened" (Matt. 24:22). This brings us to the final section of the prophecy which we have entitled:

6) RETRIBUTION, 3:1-21
The chapter describes events in "the day of the Lord" in more detail, and concludes with a description of the millennial blessings of God's people.

READ CHAPTER 3:1-21

"Multitudes, multitudes in the valley of decision"

We now come to the final section of the prophecy of Joel. As noted throughout our studies, the book may be divided as follows: *(1)* desolation (1:1-20); *(2)* invasion (2:1-11); *(3)* contrition (2:12-17); *(4)* restoration (2:18-27); *(5)* regeneration (2:28-32); *(6)* retribution (3:1-21). While past studies have been introduced with a summary of the preceding sections, on this occasion we will make a prompt start with the verses before us. Hopefully, we now have an outline of the prophecy firmly in our minds! This brings us to:

6) RETRIBUTION, 3:1-21
As noted at the end of our last study, this chapter commences by describing events in "the day of the Lord" in more detail, and concludes with a description of the millennial blessings of God's people. The passage may therefore be divided as follows: *(A)* the destruction of Israel's enemies (vv.1-16); *(B)* the description of Israel's blessings (vv.17-21).

A) The destruction of Israel's enemies, vv.1-16
Before giving attention to the details of the passage, we should notice the following: *(i)* its connection with the previous verses; *(ii)* its connection with the regathering of Israel; *(iii)* its connection with the locust invasion.

i) **Its connection with the previous verses.** There can be little doubt that this passage amplifies the preceding verses: "And I will shew wonders in the heavens and in the earth, blood, and fire, and pillars of smoke. The sun shall be turned into darkness, and the moon into blood, before the great and the terrible day of the Lord come. And it shall come to pass, that whosoever shall call upon the name of the Lord shall be delivered: for in mount Zion and in Jerusalem shall be deliverance, as the Lord hath said, and in the remnant whom the Lord shall call" (2:30-32). It should be noted that the current verses also refer to *(a)* cosmic disturbances: "The sun and the moon shall be darkened, and the stars shall withdraw their shining" (v.15): compare 2:30-31; *(b)* "the day of the Lord" (v.14): compare 2:31; *(c)* the deliverance of God's besieged people: "the Lord will be the hope of his people, and the strength of the children of Israel" (v.16): compare 2:32. The two passages – in the previous chapter and in this chapter – are linked by the words, "For, behold, in those days, and in that time" (3:1).

ii) Its connection with the regathering of Israel. The events described in vv.1-16 prepare the way for the restoration of the nation: "For, behold, in those days, and in that time, when I shall bring again the captivity of Judah and Jerusalem, I will gather all nations, and will bring them down into the valley of Jehoshaphat, and will plead with them there for my people and for my heritage Israel" (vv.1-2).

iii) Its connection with the locust invasion. The passage enables us to understand the language used to describe the locust plagues in the earlier part of the prophecy. We said then that there can be little doubt that, through Joel, the Spirit of God uses 'this plague of locusts to awaken the conscience of the people at the moment and, *at the same time*, to make use of them to picture a future event of much greater moment' (George Williams). Bearing this in mind, it has to be said that the current passage does not therefore represent a sudden change of direction in the prophecy. The locust invasion is described by the Lord as "his army" and "my great army" (2:11, 25). At the end-time, He will gather another army: "I will also gather all nations" (3:2). The two armies have several things in common, including a common reason for their existence. If the locust army swarmed over the land because Israel (Judah in particular) had sinned against the Lord in disobeying His word, then the fearful sufferings of His people during the great tribulation will be the result of their apostasy at the end-time. The "abomination of desolation" (the image of the beast in the rebuilt temple at Jerusalem: Matt. 24:15; Rev. 13:14-15) is 'the abomination *causing* desolation' (JND margin: 'desolation is an active word'). The two invasions take place on account of similar moral and spiritual conditions.

The passage (vv.1-16) refers, briefly, to the recovery of God's people (v.1) and then, in more detail, to the retribution on the nations (vv.2-16).

a) The recovery of the nation, v.1
"For, behold, in those days, and in that time, when I shall bring again the captivity of Judah and Jerusalem". Nothing further is said at this juncture. The relevant details are given in vv.17-21. However, we cannot leave this verse without saying that the Scriptures proclaim the coming restoration of Israel with a loud and clear voice. An example occurs in the book of Ezekiel:

"Therefore thus saith the Lord God; Now will I bring again the captivity of Jacob, and have mercy upon the whole house of Israel, and will be jealous for my holy name...When I have brought them again from the people, and gathered them out of their enemies' lands, and am sanctified in them in the sight of many nations; then shall they know that I am the Lord their God, which caused them to be led into captivity among the heathen: but I have gathered them unto their own land, and have left none of them any more there. Neither will I hide my face any more from them: for I have poured out my Spirit upon the house of Israel, saith the Lord God" (Ezek. 39:25-29).

b) The retribution on the nations, vv.2-16
We must notice here: *(i)* the rendezvous (v.2); *(ii)* the reasons (vv.2-8); *(iii)* the rallying call (vv.9-11); *(iv)* the reaping (vv.12-14); *(v)* the roar (vv.15-16).

i) The rendezvous, v.2
"I will also gather all nations, and I will bring them down into the **valley of Jehoshaphat**". See also v.12: "Let the heathen be wakened, and come up to the **valley of Jehoshaphat**: for there will I sit to judge all the heathen round about". It is evidently to this location that v.14 refers, "Multitudes, multitudes in the valley of decision". Jehoshaphat means 'whom Jehovah judges', so there is a play upon words here: God's judgment will take place in the valley of 'God judges'. F. A. Tatford points out that there is no valley known by that name in the vicinity of Jerusalem, but that the name probably alludes to the great victory in Jehoshaphat's day over the Moabites and the Ammonites in the valley of Berachah (2 Chron. 20:26). Berachah means 'blessing', which it will be for **God's people**. The location is otherwise known as Armageddon (Rev. 16:13-16).

ii) The reasons, vv.2-8
God had said, "I will bless them that bless thee, and curse him that curseth thee" (Gen. 12:3) and "he that toucheth you toucheth the apple of his eye" (Zech. 2:8). We must notice:

- **God's people scattered**. "**My** people...*my* heritage Israel, whom they have scattered among the nations, and parted *my* land" (v.2). 'They have partitioned the Lord's land of Palestine' (M. F. Unger).

- **God's people degraded.** "And they have cast lots for my people; and have given a boy for an harlot, and sold a girl for wine that they might drink" (v.3). 'That is, given a harlot a Jewish boy for a slave, instead of paying her with money for her prostitution...So valueless did they consider a Jewish maiden that they would sell her for a drink of wine, ironically, for perhaps just enough to intoxicate them and make them hilariously happy' (M. F. Unger). In maltreating and wronging His people these foreigners ("What have ye to do with me, O Tyre and Zidon, and all the coasts of Palestine" or 'all the districts of Philistia', JND) had done despite to the Lord himself. "Will ye render *me* a recompence? and if ye recompense *me*, swiftly and speedily will I return your recompence upon your own head" (v.4). In the words of "the King", "Inasmuch as ye did it not to one of the least of these, ye did it not unto me. And these shall go away into everlasting punishment" (Matthew 25:41-46). The Lord Jesus said to Saul of Tarsus, "Why persecutest thou *me*" (Acts 9:4). Compare Isaiah 63:9.

- ***God's name profaned.*** "Ye have taken my silver and my gold, and have carried into your temples my goodly pleasant things" (v.5). Nebuchadnezzar did this (Dan. 1:2), and proclaimed, he thought, the superiority of his god over Jehovah.

- ***God's people deported.*** "The children also of Judah and the children of Jerusalem have ye sold unto the Grecians (literally, the *Javanim*, or 'the sons of the Javanites) that ye might remove them far from their border" (v.6). These were probably Greek traders who imported Jewish slaves into Greece from Phoenicia (M. F. Unger). The principle of sowing and reaping (Gal. 6:7) is found everywhere in Scripture, including these verses: "Behold, I will raise them out of the place whither ye have sold them. And will return your recompence upon your own head: and I will sell your sons and your daughters into the hand of the children of Judah, and they shall sell them to the Sabeans, to a people far off: for the Lord hath spoken it" (vv.7-8). F. A. Tatford quotes S. R. Driver, 'The punishment' would be 'awarded according to the *lex talionis*' (meaning, the law of retaliation). F. A. Tatford continues: 'The Phoenicians and Philistines had sold the Jews into slavery to the Greeks. God declared that He would sell their people to the Judahites, so that they in turn might sell them to the Sabeans, or men of Sheba - a distant nation dwelling in the south-west of Arabia... God's dealings are always just and equitable, and as the enemy had dealt with Israel, so would He deal with them'. With this in view, we come to:

iii) The rallying of the armies, vv.9-11
"Proclaim ye this among the Gentiles; Prepare for war, wake up the mighty men, let all the men of war draw near; let them come up: beat your plowshares into swords, and your pruninghooks into spears: let the weak say, I am strong. Assemble yourselves, and come, all ye heathen, and gather yourselves together round about". This amplifies the earlier words, "***I will gather*** all nations" (v.2).

This should be compared with Revelation 16:16, "And **he gathered them** together into a place called in the Hebrew tongue Armageddon". God will use demon power to gather the nations (Rev. 16:14-16). See also Zech. 14:2-3, "*I will gather* all nations against Jerusalem to battle; and the city shall be taken, and the houses rifled, and the women ravished; and half the city shall go forth into captivity, and the residue of the people shall not be cut off from the city. Then shall the Lord go forth, and fight against those nations, as when he fought in the day of battle".

These verses describe a military invasion: "Prepare war, wake up the mighty men, let all the men of war draw near; let them come up: beat your plowshares into swords, and your pruninghooks into spears". (The reverse will take place in the millennial reign: see Isaiah 2:4). The nations will invade with confidence of victory: "Let the weak say, I am strong". Compare 1 Kings 20:11 ("Let not him that girdeth on his harness boast himself as he that putteth it off"); 1 Cor. 10:12 ("Let him that thinketh he standeth take heed lest he fall"). For the believer, the reverse is true: "And he said unto me, My grace is sufficient for thee: for my strength is made perfect in weakness... Therefore I take pleasure in infirmities, in reproaches, in necessities, in persecutions, in distresses for Christ's sake: for when I am weak, then am I strong" (2 Cor. 12:9-10).

The words, "Assemble yourselves, and come, all ye heathen, and gather yourselves together round about: thither cause thy mighty ones to come down, O Lord" (v.11) are thought-provoking. They evidently place the human invaders on one side, and the angelic powers on the other.

iv) The reaping, vv.12-14
"Let the heathen be wakened, and come up to the valley of Jehoshaphat: for there will I sit to judge all the heathen round about. Put ye in the sickle, for the harvest is ripe: come, get you down; for the press is full, the fats overflow; for their wickedness is great. Multitudes, multitudes in the valley of decision: for the day of the Lord is near in the valley of decision". We should notice:

- **The posture of the judge.** "There will I *sit* to judge all the heathen round about" (v.12). Compare Revelation 14:14, "And I looked, and behold a white cloud, and upon the cloud one *sat* like unto the Son of man"; Psalm 2:2-4, "The kings of the earth set themselves, and the rulers take counsel together, against the Lord, and against his anointed, saying, Let us break their bands asunder, and cast away their cords from us. He that *sitteth* in the heavens shall laugh".

- *The execution of judgment.* "Put ye in the sickle, for the harvest is ripe" (v13). Compare Revelation 14:14-16, "And I looked, and behold a white cloud, and upon the cloud one sat like unto the Son of man, having on his head a golden crown, and in his hand a sharp **sickle**...And he that sat on the cloud thrust in his **sickle** on the earth; and the earth was reaped".

It is evidently a grape harvest throughout: "Come, get you down; for the press is full, the fats overflow; for their wickedness is great" (v.13). Revelation 14 proceeds in the same way: "And another angel came out from the altar...and cried to him that had the sharp sickle, saying, Thrust in thy sharp sickle, and gather the clusters of the vine of the earth; for her grapes are fully ripe" (vv.17-20). See also Isaiah 63:1-6: note the words "I have trodden the winepress alone" (v.3). For "the fats overflow", see Revelation 14: 19-20: "And the winepress was trodden without the city, and blood came out of the winepress, even unto the horse bridles, by the space of a thousand and six hundred furlongs". (The words "even unto the horse bridles" probably refer to 'the blood spurting, or splattering, as high as the horse bridles' and the distance, "a thousand and six hundred furlongs", probably refers to 'the distance from Dan to Beersheba, the whole length of the present land of Israel' (J. Allen, *What the Bible Teaches- Revelation*).

The winepress is described: "Multitudes, multitudes in the valley of decision: for the day of the Lord is near in the valley of decision" (v14). The word "decision" means 'something decided', hence 'judgment'. We can therefore read 'the valley of punishment' (Gesenius). In our last study, we noted that "the great and terrible day of the Lord" appears to refer to the public return of the Lord Jesus to earth as "King of kings and Lord of lords" (Rev. 19:16) to execute judgment on the world that had rejected Him. It therefore refers to the most intensive judgments associated with the "day of the Lord" - to the consuming judgment that the Lord Jesus will exercise at His public return. See Revelation 19:11-17.

v) The roar, vv.15-16
"The sun and the moon shall be darkened, and the stars shall withdraw their shining (see 2: 30-31). The Lord also shall roar out of Zion, and utter his voice from Jerusalem; and the heavens and the earth shall shake: but the Lord will be the hope of his people, and the strength of the children of Israel". We have already noted that Matthew 24: 29 identifies the precise time that "the sun and moon shall be darkened, and the stars shall withdraw their shining". It will be: "***immediately after the tribulation of those days***".

"The Lord also shall *roar* out of Zion", that is, on His enemies, but "the Lord will be the *hope* ('refuge', JND, with the footnote 'stronghold' or 'fortress') of his people, and the *strength* of the children of Israel" (v.16). The Lord's people then, as always, will say, "God is our refuge and strength, a very present help in trouble" (Psalm 46:1). The following verses show how He will prove to be the "hope" and "strength" of His people. The Lord's people today are waiting for the *"shout!"* (1 Thess. 4:16). This brings us to:

B) The description of Israel's blessings, vv.17-21
Divine blessing will be seen in three areas *(a)* in their relationship with God (v.17); *(b)* in the productivity of the land (v.18); *(c)* in the effect on the nations (vv.19-21).

a) Relationship with God, v.17
"So shall ye know that I am the Lord your God dwelling in Zion, my holy mountain: then shall Jerusalem be holy, and there shall no strangers pass through her anymore". We should notice: *(i)* divine presence; *(ii)* divine purity; *(iii)* divine protection.

i) Divine presence. "I am the Lord your God dwelling in Zion". Compare Ezekiel 48:35, "The name of the city from that day shall be, the Lord is there".

ii) Divine purity. "I am the Lord your God dwelling in Zion, my holy mountain: then shall Jerusalem be holy" Compare Zechariah 14:20-21, "In that day shall there be upon the bells of the horses, HOLINESS UNTO THE LORD; and the pots in the Lord's house shall be like the bowls before the altar. Yea, every pot in Jerusalem and in Judah shall be holiness unto the Lord of hosts".

iii) Divine protection. "There shall no strangers pass through her anymore". Compare Luke 21:24, "Jerusalem shall be trodden down of the Gentiles, *until* the times of the Gentiles be fulfilled".

b) Productivity of the land, v.18
These verses describe the effect of divine blessing on the land itself. Compare Amos 9:13: "The plowman shall overtake the reaper, and the treader of grapes him that soweth seed; and the mountains shall drop sweet wine, and all the hills shall melt". Divine blessing will be seen:

i) On the mountains. "The mountains shall drop new *wine*". Without forgetting that this will be literally fulfilled, it is a picture of spiritual joy and gladness: "wine that maketh glad the heart of man" (Psalm 104:15). Nehemiah said to the people of his day, "the joy of the Lord is your strength" (Neh. 8:10). Compare 1 Pet. 1:6-8.

ii) On the hills. "The hills shall flow with milk". This suggests spiritual nourishment and satisfaction (F. A. Tatford). Peter refers to "the sincere milk of the word, that ye may grow thereby" (1 Pet. 2:2). The land will be, as promised, "a good land and a large…flowing with milk and honey" (Exodus 3:8).

iii) On the rivers. "All the rivers of Judah shall flow with water, and a fountain shall come forth of the house of the Lord, and shall water the valley of Shittim (meaning 'the valley of acacias' - which grow in dry soil)". This suggests spiritual life and power (J. Waldron). See John 7:38-39. F. A. Tatford observes that 'in the summer practically all Israel's rivers and streams dry up', but not any more! M. F. Unger puts it as follows: 'So copious will be those blessings springing from fellowship and worship of the Lord that the refreshing and fertilizing waters (cf. Ezek.47:1-12; Zech. 14:8); Psalm 46:4) are pictured extending to Shittim, on the border between Moab and Israel, beyond Jordan (Num. 25:1; 33:49; Josh. 2:1; Mic. 6:5). Even the parched wastelands shall be fertilized into life by the millennial blessing streaming from Jerusalem and the Temple". Rivers certainly flowed from the assembly at Thessalonica! See 1 Thess. 1:8.

c) The effect on the nations, vv.19-21
The closing verses of the prophecy describe the effect of "the Lord…dwelling in Zion" (v.17) upon Egypt and Edom (v.19) and on Judah and Jerusalem (vv.20-21).

i) On Egypt and Edom, v.19. "Egypt shall be a desolation, and Edom shall be a desolate wilderness, for the violence against the children of Judah, because they have shed innocent blood in their (Judah's) land". Under divine judgment, they will be totally unlike the well-watered land of Judah (v.18).

ii) On Judah and Jerusalem, vv.20-21. "But Judah shall dwell for ever, and Jerusalem from generation to generation. The words "For I will cleanse their blood that I have not cleansed" could mean that God will 'vindicate His people, who had been massacred by their inveterate foes' (F. A. Tatford), but more probably that they will be cleansed from their guilt so that the Lord may dwell among them. The permanence of the nation, "Judah shall **dwell for ever**" (v.20), is assured because "the Lord **dwelleth** in Zion" (v.21).

Hosea, Joel, Amos, Obadiah

AMOS

by
John M Riddle

AMOS

INTRODUCTION

Read the whole book
"You only have I known of all the families of the earth: therefore I will punish you for all your iniquities" (Amos 3:2). This is the 'key verse' of the book. It stresses that privilege determines responsibility. 'Israel had been supremely favoured, and was therefore supremely responsible' (J. Sidlow Baxter). As C. I. Scofield points out, 'It is noteworthy that Jehovah's controversy with the Gentile cities which hated Israel is brief: "I will send a fire." But Israel had been brought into the place of privilege and so of responsibility, and the Lord's indictment is detailed and unsparing.' This is a solemn lesson for us all: "Unto whomsoever much is given, of him shall much be required" (Luke 12:48).

1) THE PERIOD
"The words of Amos, who was among the herdmen of Tekoa, which he saw concerning Israel in the days of Uzziah king of Judah, and in the days of Jeroboam the son of Joash king of Israel, two years before the earthquake" (1:1). The names of Uzziah, king of Judah, and Jeroboam, king of Israel, enable us to place the date of this prophecy between 800BC and 750BC. Other contemporary prophets were Isaiah (see 1:1), Hosea (see 1:1) and probably Jonah (see 2 Kings 14:23-27). The earthquake evidently took place during the reign of Uzziah: see Zech 14:5, "Ye shall flee, like as ye fled from before the earthquake in the days of Uzziah king of Judah". According to Josephus *(Antiquities 9.10.4.)*, this earthquake took place when Uzziah was struck with leprosy for attempting to usurp the priest's office (2 Chron 26:16-21), but this is not confirmed by the scriptures.

"Jeroboam's long reign was marked by peace and prosperity (see 2 Kings 14:23-29), and the material prosperity had a disastrous effect on the people. They sank into a life of profligacy, luxury, cruelty and deceit. The poor were oppressed and justice was lacking. Immorality was shamelessly practised.

They lived in the enjoyment of the material with very little thought for the spiritual" (Bernard Osborne). In Jeroboam's reign the nation became wealthy, but only in the hands of the commercial barons. The rich became richer, and the poor became poorer. See Amos 2:6; 6:3-6; 8:4-6. Religion prospered, but there was no time for the word of God. See, for example, Amos 5:21-27; 7:10-17. Amos certainly wasn't welcome in Israel (7:10-13).

2) THE PLACE

Amos was from Tekoa, meaning 'the pitching of tents' (Gesenius). He therefore came from 'away down south, from the wild country (see 2 Chron 20:20) west of the Dead Sea, the wide stretch of open land known as the wilderness of Judaea' (J. Sidlow Baxter). Baxter continues (writing in 1952): 'the sparse ruins of the little Judaean town, Tekoa, are identifiable even today, some six miles south of Bethlehem'. Joab used the services of a "wise woman" from Tekoah to secure the repatriation of Absalom (2 Sam 14:2). Now we have a 'wise man' from Tekoa!

According to Jamieson, Fausset and Brown, 'The region being sandy, was fitter for pastoral than for agricultural purposes. Amos therefore owned and tended flocks, and collected sycamore figs'. Amos was a 'cross-border' prophet. Although he was a native of Judaea, he was called to prophesy in the northern kingdom (Israel), which never had one good king. Micah was a local preacher, but Amos was sent further afield for the simple reason that there were no faithful servants of God in Israel. The fact that the Lord used a man from the south was an indictment of the moral and spiritual bankruptcy of the northern kingdom.

3) THE PROPHET

Amos means 'burden'. He describes himself and his ministry in 7:14-15: "I was no prophet, neither was I a prophet's son; but I was an herdman, and a gatherer (cultivator) of sycomore fruit (the fig-like fruit of a tree resembling a mulberry in form and foliage): and the Lord took me as I followed the flock, and the Lord said unto me, Go, prophesy unto my people Israel." We should notice his honesty and humility: he did not conceal his humble origins. He made no attempt 'to hide his past life and employment. His exaltation to prophetic rank did not spoil him' (Robert Lee, *'The Outlined Bible'*)

Amos was a countryman. He was from "among the herdmen (*noqed*) of Tekoa" (1:1). The word "herdman" means 'sheepmaster' and occurs in that form in 2 Kings 3:4. A different word (*boger*) is used in 7:14. His rural background can be seen in his preaching. He refers, for example, to "a cart... full of sheaves" (2:13), a trap set for birds (3:5) and a shepherd taking "out of the mouth of the lion two legs, or a piece of an ear" (3:12). Amos did not 'preach over the heads of the people, but employed terms quite familiar to all of them' (Robert Lee). This reminds us that God doesn't put all his servants into the same mould. He uses people with different personalities and different backgrounds. As J. Sidlow Baxter observes, Amos 'is a great encouragement to thousands of Christians today who have had no academic or theological training. God is sovereign in His choice of servants. He is not tied to any bishop's hands. He is not bound to any set of officials. He is not restricted in His workings to any recognized ministerial order.' The only authority which Amos possessed was His calling by God, but it was the highest authority in the universe.

Notice too that Amos did not 'mince his words'. He was not afraid to address the upper-class ladies of Samaria as 'cows': "Hear this word, ye kine of Bashan, that are in the mountain of Samaria, which oppress the poor, which crush the needy, which say to their masters, Bring, and let us drink" (4:1). We get the impression from this that it was the women who 'wore the trousers.' (Perhaps current fashions have made this expression a little outdated!). Listen to the way in which Amos replied to "Amaziah the priest of Bethel": "Thus saith the Lord; thy wife shall be an harlot in the city, and thy sons and thy daughters shall fall by the sword, and thy land shall be divided by line; and thou shalt die in a polluted land: and Israel shall surely go into captivity forth of his land" (7:17). Do remember that Amos was in hostile territory when he said this: he 'went to the main centre of Israel's golden-calf worship, Bethel, and there, like a solitary Luther, he denounced the prelate and the priests and the state idolatry, under the very shadow of "the king's chapel"...Bethel was Israel's Canterbury: the head priest of Bethel was Israel's primate' (J. Sidlow Baxter). The analogy is too close for comfort. But Amos was a man of deep conviction who could not be swayed or over-awed by his circumstances. He refused to be turned from the work the Lord had given him.

4) THE PROPHECY
Amos and Hosea both addressed the Northern Kingdom, but were quite different in approach. In Amos, sin is an outrage of divine *law*, and God **commands** return. In Hosea, sin is an outrage of divine *love*, and God **pleads** for return. 'Hosea's ministry was one of *love*, whilst Amos' ministry was one of *light.* Amos is not known for his sympathy or warmth, but for his

sense of justice and right. Not a sob is to be found in his book for the nation of wicked apostates, and there is only a sigh for the poor'.

The prophecy of Amos may be divided into five distinct sections. *(a)* eight burdens, (1:1 - 2:16); *(b)* three messages (3:1 - 5:17); *(b)* two woes (5:18 - 6:14); *(d)* five visions (7:1 - 9:10); *(e)* the restoration (9:11-15).

a) The burdens, 1:1 - 2:16
Although the word "burden" is not actually used (it certainly occurs elsewhere: see, for example, Isaiah 15:1, 17:1, 19:1) it does seem appropriate here since it usually signifies 'a grievous or threatening oracle' (Gesenius) or a message 'burdened with the news of coming retribution' (J. Sidlow Baxter), and this describes the passage exactly.

It should be noted that Amos caught the attention of the people right away by speaking first against their enemies (Robert Lee). In this connection we should notice the narrowing scope of the eight messages: *(i)* unrelated nations (Damascus, Gaza, Tyre); *(ii)* related nations (Edom, Ammon, Moab); *(iii)* a brother nation (Judah); *(iv)* Israel herself. Each sentence is accompanied by a full explanation ("for three transgressions...and for four") and the whole section demonstrates that the Lord remains in perfect control of the international situation: no nation is permitted to exceed the allotted place in His purposes or to avoid payment for its wickedness.

b) The messages, 3:1 - 5:17
Whilst this section commences with reference to the entire nation ("Hear this word that the Lord hath spoken against you, O children of Israel, against the whole family which I brought up from the land of Egypt...You only have I known of all the families of the earth", 3:1-2), it is addressed particularly to the northern kingdom, with its political capital Samaria (see 3:9, 4:1, 6:1, 8:14), and its religious capital Bethel (4:4; 5:5-6; 7:10-13). However, Judah, is not exempt: "Woe to them that are at ease in Zion and that are secure in the mountain of Samaria" (6:1 JND). As J. A. Motyer observes, 'Had he left out Judah he would have lost all credibility with his Israelite audience, as a tendentious and biased person.'

The section comprises three messages all of which commence in the same way: "Hear this word" (3:1, 4:1, 5:1). Each of the messages has the same structure. They begin with judgment deserved, 3:1-10; 4:1-11; 5:1-15, and continue with judgment decreed, and in each case this is introduced with the word "therefore", 3:11-15; 4:12-13; 5:16-17. Broadly speaking, the section looks like this: *(i) a "word" of warning* (3:1-15): "Shall a trumpet be blown in the city, and the people not be afraid?" (3:6); *(ii) a "word" of rebuke* (4:1-13): "I have...yet have ye not" (vv.6-11); *(iii) a "word" of counsel* (5:1-17); "Seek" (vv.4, 6, 8, 14). Bethel is mentioned in each section (3:14; 4:4; 5:5-6).

c) The woes, 5:18 - 6:14

This section of the prophecy censures Israel's self-confidence. *(i)* They were sure that the Lord would vindicate and deliver them, only to learn that He would intervene against them: "**Woe** unto you that desire the day of the Lord! to what end is it for you? The day of the Lord is darkness, and not light" (5:18). The reason follows: "I hate, I despise your feast days, and I will not smell in your solemn assemblies" (5:21). *(ii)* "**Woe** to them that are at ease in Zion, and trust in the mountain of Samaria, which are named chief of the nations, to whom the house of Israel came!" (6:1). They were sure that their position as "chief of the nations" guaranteed uninterrupted pleasure, only to hear the Lord say, "I abhor the excellency of Jacob, and hate his palaces (6:8), and to discover that another "nation" would afflict them" (6:14). The passage emphasises the danger of self-sufficiency.

d) The visions, 7:1 - 9:10

Of the five visions, the first four are introduced in the same way: "Thus hath the Lord God shewed unto me" (7:1, 7:4, 8:1) or "Thus he shewed me" (7:7). The final vision is introduced by the words, "I saw the Lord" (9:1). J. Sidlow Baxter suggests that there is a clear progression in their meaning: "Thus, in these five visions we have, successively, judgment averted (grasshoppers), restrained (fire), determined (plumbline), imminent (summer fruit), and executed (the Lord standing upon the altar). The altar in question is at Bethel, not Jerusalem. Jeroboam the son of Nebat established this altar and stood by it (1 Kings 12:32, 13:1). Now the Lord stands on it in judgment. Note: "the king's chapel" (meaning 'sanctuary) at Bethel (7:13) and "the temple" (8:3) and are one and the same.

e) The restoration, 9:11-15

'It is inconsistent with any theology centering on the name Jehovah, and resting on the covenant, to blacken the whole sky with the clouds of wrath, and to forget mercy and hope' (J. A. Motyer).

The expression, "Behold, the days come saith the Lord", does not only occur in connection with Israel's desolation and abject misery (8:11-12), but also in connection with its restoration and glory. The "sinful nation" having been utterly destroyed (9:8), and the true "grain", or godly remnant, preserved (9:9), God "will...raise up the tabernacle of David that is fallen, and close up the breaches thereof" (9:11). The terms of the Davidic covenant will be fulfilled in Christ who will sit "upon the throne of David, and upon his kingdom, to order it, and to establish it with judgment and with justice from henceforth even for ever" (Isaiah 9:7). In that day, Israel will expand its borders and "possess the remnant of Edom, and of the heathen that are called by my name, saith the Lord that doeth this" (9:12). The restoration of the people will be accompanied by unprecedented material prosperity. The people of whom God had to say, "Ye have built houses of hewn stone, but ye shall not dwell in them; ye have planted pleasant vineyards, but ye shall not drink wine of them" (5:11), will "build the waste cities, and inhabit them; and they shall plant vineyards, and drink the wine thereof; they shall also make gardens, and eat the fruit of them" (9:14). Though their past is marked by rebellion and failure, their present condition by dispersion and difficulty, the future which awaits Israel is one of glorious blessing. Never again will they fail, and never again will they lose possession of their land: "And I will plant them upon their land, and they shall no more be pulled up out of their land which I have given them, saith the Lord thy God" (9:15).

In conclusion we should note that Amos is cited on two occasions in the New Testament: 5:25-26 are cited by Stephen in Acts 7:42-43, and 9:11 by James in Acts 15:15-17. The first is cited in connection with rebellion of Israel, and second with the restoration of Israel.

READ CHAPTER 1:1 - 2:3

"For three transgressions...and for four"

"The words of Amos, who was among the herdmen of Tekoa, which he saw (compare Isaiah 1:1) concerning Israel in the days of Uzziah king of Judah, and in the days of Jeroboam the son of Joash king of Israel, two years before the earthquake. And he said, The Lord will roar from Zion (David's city, 1 Kings 8:1), and utter his voice from Jerusalem (Solomon's city, 1 Kings 10:26-27); and the habitations of the shepherds shall mourn, and the top of Carmel shall wither" (1:1-2). The words, "which he saw" (v.1), can be explained by Psalm 89:19, "Then thou spakest in a vision". See also Lamentations 2:9. The introduction to the prophecy touches on three things:

i) The occupation of the prophet
He was "among the herdmen of Tekoa" (v.1). According to M. F. Unger (*Unger's Commentary on the Old Testament*), the term used for shepherds here (A.V. 'herdmen': Hebrew *noqed*) is unusual, and 'suggests that the sheep herded by Amos were not the common variety, but a dwarfed variety, prized for its wool'. More personal details are given in 7:14-15. A different word (*boger*) is translated "herdman" in 7:14.

ii) The occasion of the prophecy
As we noted in our introduction, the names of Uzziah, king of Judah, and Jeroboam, king of Israel, enable us to place the date of this prophecy between 800BC and 750BC. The reference to the earthquake (see also Zech. 14:5) must be significant, and probably indicated approaching divine judgment in the same way that earthquakes, among other terrifying things, will precede consuming divine judgment at the end-time. See Matt. 24:7-8; Rev. 6:12. Since earthquakes are very common in the area, this particular earthquake must have been exceptionally severe.

iii) The outline of the prophecy
The message of the book is introduced with the words, "The Lord will roar

from Zion, and utter his voice from Jerusalem; and the habitations of the shepherds (Hebrew *raah*: the usual word for shepherds) shall mourn, and the top of Carmel shall wither" (v.2). It is noteworthy that the Lord speaks from Jerusalem, just as He will at the end-time: "The Lord also shall roar out of Zion, and utter his voice from Jerusalem" (Joel 3:16). He does not speak from one of the northern shrines (Dan or Bethel, where the golden calves were situated), but from 'the place where men were directed by the Lord to worship' (M. F. Unger). As in the book of Joel, it is the "roar" of divine judgment, which would be seen in consuming drought: "the habitations ('pastures', JND) of the shepherds shall mourn, and the top of Carmel (meaning 'park' or 'fruitful place') shall wither". The references to roaring from Zion (David's city, 1 Kings 8:1), and speaking ("utter his voice") from Jerusalem (Solomon's city, 1 Kings 10:26-27), may represent Hebrew poetry, with its correspondence of ideas rather than words.

After the general introduction, the message of Amos is in two major parts which can be broadly described as follows: *(i)* judgments on the nations (chs.1-2) and *(ii)* judgments on Israel (chs.3-9).

The opening two chapters of the prophecy proclaim eight judgments which fall into two major divisions. The first six judgments are pronounced against Israel's neighbours: Damascus, Gaza, Tyrus, Edom, Ammon, and Moab. The last two judgments are pronounced against God's people themselves: Judah and Israel. Since the preaching of Amos was directed against the northern kingdom in particular, it is significant to notice the progression of these judgments: *(i)* unrelated nations (Damascus, Gaza, Tyre); *(ii)* related nations (Edom, Ammon, Moab); *(iii)* a brother nation (Judah); *(iv)* Israel herself.

In considering these chapters, we must notice: *(1)* some general principles of judgment, and *(2)* specific causes of judgment.

1) GENERAL PRINCIPLES OF JUDGMENT
These are: *(a)* that judgment must fall upon all men; *(b)* that God is cognisant of the affairs of all nations; *(c)* that there is a limit to human sin; *(d)* that there is a law of sowing and reaping; *(e)* that privilege determines responsibility.

a) Judgment must fall on all men
These judgments illustrate Romans 2:12, "For as many as have sinned without law (Damascus, Gaza, Tyrus, Edom, Ammon, and Moab) shall perish

also without law: and as many as have sinned under law (Judah and Israel) shall be judged by law". It is important to notice that those nations without the word of God and the prophets of God are not therefore absolved from moral responsibility. They may not have the testimony of God's word, but they do have the testimony of conscience. With this in mind, it is noticeable that judgment is pronounced against those nations "without law" on account of their conduct towards other men, particularly God's own people, but judgment is pronounced against Judah and Israel on account of their conduct towards God. It should also be noted that five of the six Gentile nations are held responsible for their treatment of God's people (cf. 1:3, 6, 9, 11, 13), reminding us that God had said "I will bless them that bless thee, and curse him that curseth thee" (Gen. 12:3), and that "he that toucheth you toucheth the apple of his eye" (Zech. 2:8).

The certainty of judgment is emphasised by the fact that each oracle commences with the words, "Thus saith the Lord" (1:3, 6, 9, 11, 13, 2:1, 4, 6), and that in five cases they conclude with either, "saith the Lord" or "saith the Lord God".

b) *God is cognisant of the affairs of all nations*
He is not a tribal deity. He is "the Judge of all the earth" (Gen. 18:25). All men are accountable to Him. He will judge all nations. The eight cases surveyed in these two chapters are therefore of relevant interest: they allow us to see something of God's dealings with the nations at all times. We are not to think that these are isolated cases, for He remains in perfect control of the international situation: no nation is permitted to exceed the allotted place in His purposes or to avoid payment for its wickedness.

c) *There is a limit to human sin*
The recurring phrase "for three transgressions…and for four" indicates that the nations had reached and exceeded a limit. The fourth and most heinous crime, which crowns the preceding iniquities, is cited. As our contributor Justin Waldron points out, "this phrase also shows the omniscience of God". We must remember that "Neither is there any creature that is not manifest in his sight: but all things are naked and opened unto the eyes of him with whom we have to do" (Heb. 4:13).

"Three" suggests a limit. "And he left them, and went away again, and prayed the **third** time, saying the same words" (Matt. 26:44): "For this thing I besought the Lord **thrice**, that it might depart from me" (2 Cor. 12:8).

Chapter 1

d) The law of sowing and reaping
The section illustrates Galatians 6:7: "Be not deceived; God is not mocked: for whatsoever a man soweth, that shall he also reap." Hence, "let us not be weary in well doing: for in due season we shall reap, if we faint not. As we have therefore opportunity, let us do good unto all men, especially unto them who are of the household of faith" (Gal 6:9-10).

In this connection, we should notice that God does not deal with the nations in a purely arbitrary fashion, but advances adequate reasons for the severity of His judgments upon them. He pronounces His sentences with a full explanation in each case.

Notice, too, that in all cases (apart from the judgment pronounced on Israel) divine retribution is described as "fire" (1:4, 7, 10, 12, 14, 2:2, 5). This reminds us that the Lord Jesus will "be revealed from heaven with his mighty angels in flaming fire...." (2 Thess. 1:7-8).

e) Privilege determines responsibility
This is illustrated in the extensive description of judgment against Israel and against "the whole family". Compare Isaiah 40:2, "Speak ye comfortably to Jerusalem, and cry unto her, that her warfare is accomplished, that her iniquity is pardoned: for she hath received of the Lord's hand **double** for all her sins".

It has been pointed out (T. Miller) that the five things detailed above occur in the same order in the Epistle to the Romans: for *(a)* above, see 1:18; for *(b)* above, see 1:21-32; for *(c)* above, see 2:2; for *(d)* above, see 2:5-6; for *(e)* above, see 2:17-24.

2) PARTICULAR CAUSES OF JUDGMENT
The eight pronouncements can be divided into four pairs as follows: crimes against **national life** (Damascus and Gaza); offences against **brotherly kindness** (Tyre and Edom); offences against **the helpless** (Ammon and Moab); offences against **divine revelation** (Judah and Israel).

a) Damascus, 1:3-5
i) **The crime**: "For three transgressions of Damascus, and for four, I will not turn away the punishment thereof; because they have threshed **Gilead** with threshing instruments of iron" (v.3). Threshing is something planned, thorough, and systematic. It carries the idea of cruelty and unsparing

destruction. It has been said that the purpose of threshing is to extract the crop, perhaps conveying here the idea of commercial profit before human welfare.

This was foretold by Elisha: "And he settled his countenance steadfastly, until he was ashamed: and the man of God wept. And Hazael said, Why weepest thou my lord? And he answered, Because I know the evil that thou wilt do unto the children of Israel: their strong holds wilt thou set on fire, and their young men wilt thou slay with the sword, and wilt dash their children, and rip up their women with child" (2 Kings 8:11-12). As always, the word of God proved accurate: "In those days (during the reign of Jehu) the Lord began to cut Israel short: and Hazael smote them in all the coasts of Israel; from Jordan eastward, all the land of **Gilead**, the Gadites, and the Reubenites, and the Manassites, from Aroer, which is by the river Arnon, even **Gilead** and Bashan" (2 Kings 10:32-33). We are also told that "the king of Syria oppressed them...Neither did he leave of the people to Jehoahaz but fifty horsemen, and ten chariots, and ten thousand footmen; for the king of Syria destroyed them, and had made them like the dust by **threshing**" (2 Kings 13:4-7).

ii) The punishment: "But I will send a fire into the house of Hazael, which shall devour the palaces of Ben-hadad. I will break also the bar of Damascus, and cut off the inhabitants from the plain of Aven, and him that holdeth the sceptre from the house of Eden: and the people of Syria shall go into captivity unto **Kir**, saith the Lord" (vv.4-5). This was fulfilled about fifty years later: "The king of Assyria went up against Damascus, and took it, and carried the people of it to **Kir**, and slew Rezin" (2 Kings 16:9).

The expression "bar of Damascus" evidently refers to its gate (compare Jer. 51:30) and therefore to its defences, indicating that the city would fall. Aven (literally 'the valley of Aven' or the 'plain of Aven') means 'wickedness' (possibly 'emptiness') and was presumably near Damascus. The "house of Eden" ('Beth-Eden') means 'the house of delight' (JND). It would prove to be otherwise under divine judgment. Kir is unidentified, but it was apparently the place from which the Syrians originated (Amos 9:7), leading J. A. Motyer to write, 'To this unknown place, having blotted history with their inhumanities, they return'.

b) Gaza, 1:6-8
i) The crime: "For three transgressions of Gaza, and for four, I will not

turn away the punishment thereof; because they carried away captive the whole captivity, to deliver them up to Edom" (v.6). The expression, "the whole captivity" could mean 'an entire population' in the sense of 'whole communities' (NIV). Gaza was 'the southernmost city of the Philistine Pentapolis, and the key to Palestine on the south; hence, it was viewed as the representative of the whole nation' (M. F. Unger). The words "to deliver them up" suggest slave-trading, and it is possible that Amos refers here to the invasion of Judah by the Philistines and the Arabians described in 2 Chron. 21:16-17, although the incident to which Amos refers could have been in the nature of 'border warfare, in which defenceless Judaean villages were overpowered, and the inhabitants sold to the Oriental tribes through the medium of the Edomites' (Ellicott's Commentary). Edom, the implacable and inveterate enemy of God's people, was either the buyer or the middleman in this fearful traffic in human beings.

ii) The punishment: "But I will send a fire on the wall of Gaza, which shall destroy the palaces thereof: and I will cut off the inhabitant from Ashdod, and him that holdeth the sceptre from Ashkelon, and I will turn my hand against Ekron: and the remnant of the Philistines shall perish, saith the Lord God" (vv.7-8). Four of the five Philistine cities are named. Gath is omitted, possibly because it sheltered David (1 Sam 27:1-3). References to divine judgment upon the Philistine cities are found in Jeremiah 47:1-7; Zephaniah 2:4; Zechariah 9:5-7.

In summary, as noted above, the first two oracles refer to nations, Syria (represented by Damascus) and the Philistines (represented by Gaza), who were intent on the destruction of God's people. They remind us of another enemy of God's people: "the devil, as a roaring lion, walketh about, seeking whom he may devour" (1 Pet. 5:8).

c) Tyre, 1:9-10
i) The crime: "For three transgressions of Tyrus, and for four, I will not turn away the punishment thereof; because they delivered up the whole captivity to Edom, and remembered not the brotherly covenant" (v.9). The "brotherly covenant" refers to the excellent relationship between Hiram and David, and between Hiram and Solomon: "Hiram was ever a lover of David" (1 Kings 5:1); "Hiram and Solomon made a league together" (1 Kings 5:12). Perhaps, however, we should also remember Hiram's aggrieved tone of voice in saying; "What cities are these which thou hast given me my brother?" (1 Kings 9:13).

Tyre was 'a great Phoenician coastal emporium that was famous for its commerce and wealth' (M. F. Unger). The city is likened to a ship (Ezek. 27:1-11) and the passage continues by describing its markets: see Ezek. 27:12-25. Judah traded there in "wheat of Minnith, and Pannag, and honey, and oil, and balm" (Ezek. 27:17). But the city also traded in Judaean slaves: "They delivered up the whole captivity to Edom" (v.9). They were 'guilty of the same crime of complicity with the slave trade with Edom as were the Philistines (v.6)...in selling whole communities of captives to Edom, apparently handling the business end of the shameful traffic, and considering themselves bound by no ties of honour, disregarding the treaty of brotherhood' (M. F. Unger). Their greed for profits overruled any thought of mercy and kindness.

This reminds us of the brotherly relationships which should exist between the Lord's people. It was conspicuously absent at Corinth (1 Cor. 6:1-7). In the circumstances, two courses were open to the Lord's people: *(i)* to 'rest' the matter with wise men in the assembly (vv.4-5); *(ii)* to leave the matter and "rather take wrong" (v.7). Strife among brethren occurred in the Old Testament: "There was a strife between the herdmen of Abram's cattle and the herdmen of Lot's cattle", causing Abram to say to Lot: "Let there be no strife, I pray, between thee and me, and between my herdmen and thy herdmen; for we be **brethren**" (Gen. 13:7-8). The New Testament refers to the "brotherly covenant" between believers today as follows: "Seeing ye have purified your souls through the Spirit unto unfeigned love of the **brethren**, see that ye love one another with a pure heart fervently" (1 Pet. 1:22); "Let **brotherly** love continue" (Heb. 13:1).

ii) The punishment: "But I will send a fire on the wall of Tyrus, which shall devour the palaces thereof" (v.10). The city surrendered to Nebuchadnezzar after a thirteen-year siege (585-573 BC), and was eventually destroyed by Alexander the Great in 332 BC.

d) Edom, 1:11-12
i) The crime: "For three transgressions of Edom, and for four, I will not turn away the punishment thereof; because he did pursue his brother with the sword (see Num. 20:14-21; Deut. 2:8), and did cast off (some say 'stifled') all pity, and his anger did tear perpetually, and he kept his wrath for ever" (v.11). The two nations were descended from twin brothers (Jacob and Esau), and the reference to "the sword" describes Edom's traditional attitude towards Israel, rather than alluding to any specific instance of hostility. Edom's anger burned in the heart. It was on-going malice, not a

sudden outburst of temper, but a smouldering, persistent anger. He nursed enmity. The animosity of Edom reminds us that men hate what God chooses. This is clear from Obadiah vv.10-14, which refers to Edomite hatred at the destruction of Jerusalem. When Jerusalem fell, the Edomites cried, "Rase it, rase it, even to the foundation thereof" (Psalm 137:7).

James describes this attitude as follows: "But if ye have bitter strife and enmity in your heart, glory not and lie not against the truth. This wisdom descendeth not from above but is earthly, sensual, devilish. For where envying and strife is there is confusion and every evil work" (James 3:14-16). We must beware of adopting an Edomite attitude towards fellow-believers. Our contributor Justin Waldron makes the following contrasts: Edom "did pursue his brother with the sword", and Paul warns us that "if ye bite and devour one another, take heed that ye be not consumed one of another" (Gal. 5:15); Edom "did cast off all pity", and Paul urges us to be "kind one to another, tenderhearted, forgiving one another, even as God for Christ's sake hath forgiven you" (Eph. 4:32); Edom's "anger did tear perpetually, and he kept his wrath for ever", whereas Paul tells believers, "Let not the sun go down upon your wrath" (Eph. 4:26). If *we* forget "the brotherly covenant" (v.9), we too may end up pursuing our "brother with the sword" (v.11).

ii) The punishment: "But I will send a fire upon Teman, which shall devour the palaces of Bozrah" (v12). Teman was named after one of Esau's grandsons (Gen. 36:11). Its destruction is described in Obadiah vv.8-9. Bosrah (or Bozrah) was evidently one of the royal cities of Edom (Gen. 36:33). The Lord Jesus will evidently destroy His enemies in that region before entering Jerusalem in triumph. See Isaiah 63:1-6.

In summary, we have two peoples, Tyre and Edom, who had no regard at all for brotherly kindness. This is a solemn lesson for us all.

e) Ammon, 1:13-15
i) The crime: "For three transgressions of the children of Ammon, and for four, I will not turn away the punishment thereof; because they have ripped up the women with child of Gilead, that they might enlarge their border" (v.13). The books of Judges (3:13; 10:7-18; 11:4-33) and 1 Samuel (11:1-11; 14:47) refer to Ammonite incursions, and particular reference is made to Gilead in Judges 10:8; 11:5; 1 Sam. 11:1.

The Ammonites committed terrible atrocities in the interests of territorial expansion. Spiritual ambition is good. See Rom. 15:20; 2 Cor. 5:9; 1 Thess. 4:11, where "strived", "labour" and "study" all translate one word (*phileotimeomai*), meaning 'aim' or 'ambition'. But the Ammonites were consumed by ambition that stopped at nothing to achieve its object. Ambition can destroy others. Even Christians can destroy the future by failing to bestow kindness and care upon fellow-believers. (This can also apply to their attitude towards unbelievers as well). The Lord is so different: "He shall feed his flock like a shepherd: he shall gather the lambs with his arm, and carry them in his bosom, and shall gently lead those that are **with young**" (Isaiah 40:11).

ii) The punishment: "I will kindle a fire in the wall of Rabbah (modern Amman), and it shall devour the palaces thereof, with shouting in the day of battle, with a tempest in the day of the whirlwind: and their king shall go into captivity, he and his princes together, saith the Lord" (vv.14-15). See Jeremiah 49:3.

f) Moab, 2:1-3
i) The crime: "For three transgressions of Moab, and for four, I will not turn away the punishment thereof; because he burned the bones of the king of Edom into lime" (v.1). The Moabites desecrated the past. They exhibited a malice that continued into the grave. Burning the bones of the king of Edom was the final insult.

Sadly, some Christians never let past matters rest. They continue to cast aspersions upon the character of fellow-believers who have been "absent from the body" for years!

ii) The punishment: "But I will send a fire upon Moab, and it shall devour the palaces of Kirioth (called 'Kir of Moab', Isaiah 15:1): and Moab shall die with tumult, with shouting and with the sound of the trumpet: and I will cut off the judge (perhaps referring to the king, or to his representative) from the midst thereof, and will slay all the princes thereof with him, saith the Lord" (vv.2-3). According to the Moabite Stone, Moab's national god, Chemosh, was located at Kir.

In summary, we have two peoples who were guilty of crimes against the helpless. Ammon destroyed the future, and Moab desecrated the past.

In our next study, we will consider the oracles concerning Judah and Israel (2:4-16).

READ CHAPTER 2:4-16

The "transgressions" of Judah and Israel

As we have already noticed, the opening chapters of the prophecy illustrate some general principles of judgment, as well as detailing specific reasons for judgment.

i) General principles

Amongst other things, the eight judgments illustrate New Testament teaching that "as many as have sinned without law (Damascus, Gaza, Tyrus, Edom, Ammon and Moab) shall perish also without law: and as many as have sinned under law (Judah and Israel) shall be judged by law" (Rom. 2:12). Bearing this in mind, it is noticeable that judgment is pronounced against those nations "without law" on account of their conduct towards other **men**, whereas judgment is pronounced against Judah and Israel on account of their conduct towards **God**. The length of the pronouncement against Israel emphasises the biblical principle that privilege determines responsibility. This was stressed by the Lord Jesus: "For unto whosoever much is given, of him shall much be required" (Luke 12:48). Paul refers to the privileges of the Jewish people as follows: "What advantage then hath the Jew? Or what profit is there in circumcision? Much every way chiefly, because that unto them were committed the oracles of God" (Rom. 3:1-2). See also Romans 9:4-5.

ii) Particular causes

We have already surveyed the crimes and punishment of Judah and Israel's neighbours, and this brings us to Judah and Israel themselves. The very fact that they are numbered with the surrounding nations indicates that they had lost their distinctive character. The people who should not have been "reckoned among the nations" (Num. 23:9) had merged with the world. Compare Isaiah 22 where "the burden of the valley of vision", concerning Judah and Jerusalem, is located in the 'foreign nations' section of the prophecy (chs. 13-23). Because Jerusalem had become like the nations, she is treated as one of them. She had no confidence in the living God, and behaved in the same way as her neighbours. The ongoing warning to God's people is expressed in the New Testament: "And be not conformed to this world: but be ye transformed by the renewing of your mind, that ye may prove what is that good, and acceptable, and perfect, will of God" (Rom. 12:2).

While in the prophecies of Isaiah, Jeremiah and Ezekiel, the word of the Lord to Israel precedes the 'foreign nations' section in each case, this order is reversed in the book of Amos. It has been suggested that this was to win 'a sympathetic hearing' (M. F. Unger) on the part of Israel, who would be quite ready to listen to the condemnation of their neighbours, even though they were quite oblivious to their own guilt. The messages of divine judgment on Damascus, Gaza, Tyrus, Edom, Ammon and Moab would have been music to their ears, and so would the condemnation of Judah. But having gained their attention, the Lord suddenly confronts them with their own sin! Nathan adopted this approach when confronting David (see 2 Sam. 12:1-12). Paul did the same: having described the sins of the pagan world, he turns to the cultured Gentile: "Therefore thou art inexcusable, O man, whosoever thou art that judgest: for wherein thou judgest another, thou condemnest thyself; for thou that judgest doest the same things" (Rom. 2:1). We must now consider:

1) JUDAH, vv.4-5
As in the six preceding cases, Amos draws attention to Judah's crimes (v.4), and then describes their punishment (v.5).

a) Their crimes, v.4
"For three transgressions of Judah, and for four, I will not turn away the punishment thereof; because they have despised the law of the Lord ('rejected the law of the Lord', R.V.), and have not kept his commandments, and their lies caused them to err, after which their fathers have walked". If Judah "**despised** the law of the Lord", then the Psalmist should speak for us all in saying, "O how I *love* thy law! It is my meditation all the day" (Psalm 119:97).

It has been observed that "Judah, even with the temple of God in their midst, rejected the law which they professed to keep". The writer (unidentified) then raises the following questions: "Did Judah, as many professing believers today, regard the law as having little or no relevance to their day? Had it become 'out of date' and 'boring'? And if out of date (for 'times have changed, and we are more enlightened'), why bother to keep commandments that were not revered? They were, in fact, no better than their neighbours". We live in an age when even in so-called 'Christian circles' the word of God is despised and rejected. How often decisions are made at church synods without any reference whatsoever to the Scriptures. As a result, to give the most fearful example, sodomy has invaded the highest strata of 'church' government in major denominations.

The words, "their lies caused them to err", refer to their false gods. Habakkuk tells us that the "molten image" is "a teacher of lies" (Hab. 2:18). They had rejected "the *law* of the Lord" in favour of "*lies*". They had "changed the truth of God into a lie, and worshipped and served the creature more than the Creator, who is blessed for ever. Amen" (Rom. 1:25). At the end-time, men and women will believe "a lie" (Satan's masterpiece of deception) because they "believed not the truth" (2 Thess. 2:8-12). Obedience to the word of God is a great preservative. Hence the necessity to "Preach the word; be instant in season, out of season; reprove, rebuke, exhort with all longsuffering and doctrine" (2 Tim. 4:2). We live at a time when so many professing Christians do not "endure sound doctrine; but after their own lusts… heap to themselves teachers, having itching ears" who "turn away their ears from the truth… unto fables" (2 Tim. 4:3-4). It has to be said that in many cases, the Lord's people today face, not 'new lies, but the old ones dressed up'. In fact, like Israel, the things "after the which their fathers have walked". Just think of Israel's idolatrous history! See, for example, Joshua 24:14.

b) *Their punishment, v.5*
"I will send a fire upon Judah, and it shall devour the palaces of Jerusalem". This was fulfilled in the fall of the city to the Chaldeans, circa 586 B.C. "The Chaldeans burned the king's house, and the houses of the people, with fire, and brake down the walls of Jerusalem" (Jer. 39:8).

2) *ISRAEL, vv.6-16*
For the last time in these eight oracles, Amos draws attention to their crimes (vv.6-12), and then describes their punishment (vv.13-16). Since, however, this is the longest oracle, there is room for expansion, and we will adopt the approach taken by Richard Catchpole at Cheshunt on 15th June 2005: *(a)* Israel's perversity (vv.6-8); *(b)* Israel's privileges (vv.9-12); *(c)* Israel's punishment (vv.13-16).

a) *Israel's perversity, vv.6-8*
"For three transgressions of Israel, and for four, I will not turn away the punishment thereof; because they sold the righteous for silver, and the poor for a pair of shoes; that pant after the dust of the earth on the head of the

poor, and turn aside the way of the meek: and a man and his father will go in unto the same maid, to profane my holy name: and they lay themselves down upon clothes laid to pledge by every altar, and they drink the wine of the condemned in the house of their god". We must notice *(i)* their injustice (v.6); *(ii)* their inhumanity (v.7); *(iii)* their immorality (v.7); *(iv)* their indulgence (v.8); *(v)* their idolatry (v.8).

i) Their injustice. They "sold the righteous for silver, and the poor for a pair of shoes" (v.6). The words, "they sold the righteous for silver" remind us that the Lord Jesus, "the Holy One and the Just" (Acts 3:14), was sold for thirty pieces of silver (Zech. 11:12-13; Matt. 26:15; 27:9-10).

Both parts of this statement evidently refer to injustice in the legal system. In the first case, those with a righteous cause were condemned by Israel's judges who had been suitably bribed. This was a direct violation of the law. Israel's "judges and officers" were to "judge the people with just judgment" and to that end they were told, "Thou shalt not wrest judgment; thou shalt not respect persons, neither take a gift: for a gift doth blind the eyes of the wise, and pervert the words of the righteous" (Deut 16:18-19). In the second case, 'a poor man, being helpless and defenceless, had no recourse but to submit himself to injustice' (M. F. Unger). According to M. F. Unger, 'the verse means either that a bribe as small as a pair of shoes (sandals commonly made of wood) was enough to save a verdict, or that a debt that small was enough to bring a man before a judge, so covetous had the Lord's people become'.

Assembly elders must not "wrest judgment. It is not unknown in assembly life for one standard to be applied to family and friends, and quite another standard in the case of other believers. There must be no favouritism in the assembly, and no partiality when applying divine truth. Whilst money may not 'change hands' amongst believers, it is sadly possible to influence others by flattery and praise. In this way, "a gift doth blind the eyes of the wise, and pervert the words of the righteous".

ii) Their inhumanity. They "pant after the dust of the earth on the head of the poor, and turn aside the way of the meek" (v.7). M. F. Unger suggests that the preferable meaning seems to be 'that unscrupulous creditors begrudged the poor oppressed debtor, even to the very dust that he sprinkled on his head as a mourner, thus vividly underscoring their covetousness for real estate'. The meek were an easy prey for people bent on promoting their own interests. See James 5:6. The Lord required His people to "do justly, and to love mercy, and to walk humbly with thy God" (Micah 6:8), but these requirements were conspicuously lacking in Israel.

This has a clear voice for us today: "Hereby perceive we the love of God because he laid down his life for us: and we ought to lay down our lives for the brethren. But whoso hath this world's good, and seeth his brother have need, and shutteth up his bowels of compassion from him, how dwelleth the love of God in him?" (1 John 3:16-17). See also James 2:15-16. We are to "support the weak" (Acts 20:35; 1 Thess. 5:14).

iii) Their immorality. "A man and his father will go in unto the same maid, to profane my holy name" (v.7). The "maid" was undoubtedly a temple prostitute. See Hosea 4:14. The believers at Corinth were warned against such liaisons. See 1 Corinthians 6:13-20. Immorality is a sin against the holiness of God, and we must never forget the injunction, "For this is the will of God, even your sanctification, that ye should abstain from fornication" (1 Thess. 4:3).

iv) Their indulgence. "They lay themselves down upon clothes laid to pledge by every altar, and they drink the wine of the condemned in the house of their god" (v.8). They kept the outer garment taken in pledge as a surety against a loan, even though, it was to be returned before nightfall, since it was the poor man's only covering. See Exodus 22:25-27; Deut 24:10-13. But these heartless people used the clothes of their victims as a groundsheet on which they lay drinking wine confiscated from those they had unjustly condemned. The "wine of the condemned" was evidently either wine taken as fines (according to the NIV), or 'wine purchased with money taken from those who had been unjustly fined as the result of crooked legal proceedings' (M. F. Unger). There was little hope of leading "a quiet and peaceable life in all godliness and honesty" (1 Tim. 2:2) with people like that about.

v) Their idolatry. They laid "themselves down...by every altar" and drank "in the house of their god" (v.8), reminding us that Israel "built them high places in all their cities, from the tower of the watchmen to the defenced city. And they set them up images and groves in every high hill, and under every green tree: and there they burnt incense in all the high places, as did the heathen whom the Lord carried away before them; and wrought wicked things to provoke the Lord to anger: for they served idols, whereof the Lord had said unto them, Ye shall not do this thing" (2 Kings 17:9-12). It is for good reason that John wrote, "Little children, keep yourselves from idols" (1 John 5:21).

These things should remind us that *we* are not beyond making shipwreck of our spiritual lives. But this is not all. The verses that follow blacken the picture even further by referring to Israel's ingratitude. So:

b) Israel's privileges, vv.9-12
Their behaviour described above was even more culpable in view of the way in which the Lord had blessed them. Their privileges may be summarised as follows *(i)* they had witnessed God's power (v.9); *(ii)* they had enjoyed God's leadership (v.10); *(iii)* they had heard God's voice (v.11).

i) They had witnessed God's power, v.9.
"Yet destroyed I the Amorite (see Gen. 14:16) before them, whose height was like the height of the cedars, and he was as strong as the oaks; yet I destroyed his fruit from above, and his roots from beneath". The Amorites were descended from Canaan, the son of Ham (Gen. 10:15-20). This appears to be a general designation for the inhabitants of the land, both east and west of Jordan. Rahab knew all about the defeat of the Amorites to the *east* of Jordan: "We have heard… what ye did unto the two kings of the Amorites, that were on the other side Jordan, Sihon and Og, whom ye utterly destroyed" (Joshua 2:10). See also Joshua 24:8. It is said of Og, "so they smote him, and his sons, and all his people, until there were none left him alive (Num. 21:35). Through Israel, the Lord certainly "destroyed his fruit from above, and his roots from beneath". Compare Malachi 4:1 where there is no possibility of regrowth (no "root"), and no trace of past growth (no "branch"). The spies described the inhabitants of the land to the *west* of Jordan as "men of a great stature" (Num. 13:32). In the words of Amos, they were "like the height of the cedars", but the Lord was higher! They were "as strong as the oaks", but the Lord was stronger!

But in spite of all this, the behaviour of God's people was deplorable. As the Lord's people we must "adorn the doctrine of God our Saviour in all things" (Titus 2:1), and Paul continues by reminding us that "the grace of God that bringeth salvation hath appeared to all men, teaching us that, denying ungodliness and worldly lusts, we should live soberly, righteously, and godly, in this present world" (Titus 2:11-12).

ii) They had enjoyed God's leadership, v.10.
"Also I brought you up from the land of Egypt, and led you forty years through the wilderness, to possess the land of the Amorites". This is a most comprehensive statement, covering events at the beginning of the journey from Egypt to Canaan, events during the journey, and events at the end of the journey.

We have every reason to identify ourselves with each stage of Israel's journey from Israel to Canaan. In the first place, "Christ our passover is sacrificed for us" (1 Cor. 5:7), and we have been "redeemed...with the precious blood of Christ, as of a lamb without blemish and without spot" (1 Pet. 1:19). In the second place, "he hath said, I will never leave thee, nor forsake thee" (Heb. 13:5). In the third place, we enjoy a marvellous inheritance already, for we have been "blessed... with all spiritual blessings in heavenly places in Christ" (Eph. 1:3), and look forward to possessing the "inheritance" described by Peter: "incorruptible, and undefiled, and that fadeth not away, reserved in heaven for you" (1 Pet. 1:4).

Centuries before, "an angel of the Lord came up from Gilgal to Bochim, and said, I made you to go up out of Egypt, and have brought you unto the land which I sware unto your fathers; and I said, I will never break my covenant with you. And ye shall make no league with the inhabitants of this land; ye shall throw down their altars: but ye have not obeyed my voice: why have ye done this?" (Judges 2:1-2). Nothing had changed in the intervening years. But are **we** "obedient children?" (1 Pet. 1:14).

*iii) **They had heard God's voice, v.11.*** "And I raised up of your sons for prophets, and of your young men for Nazarites. Is it not even thus, O ye children of Israel? saith the Lord. But ye gave the Nazarites wine to drink; and commanded the prophets, saying, Prophesy not". In short, they despised the voice of God, which they had clearly heard ("Is it not even thus, O ye children of Israel? Saith the Lord", v.11), whether it reached them through the **voice** of the prophet, or through the **life** and devotion of the Nazarite, of whom it is said, "All the days of his separation he is holy unto the Lord" (Num. 6:8). The Nazarites set them an example in purity: "Her Nazarites were purer than snow, they were whiter than milk". Purity is beautiful, and the same passage continues, "they were more ruddy in body than rubies, their polishing was of sapphire" (Lam. 4:7). Sin is ugly. But neither the prophets nor the Nazarites were acceptable in Israel's society:

- **The prophets** were silenced. Amos himself was told by Amaziah, the priest of Bethel, to "flee...away into the land of Judah, and there eat bread, and prophesy there: but prophesy not again any more at Bethel" (7:12-13). The word of God was unpopular in Israel then (compare Hosea 9:7), just as it is increasingly unpopular in the United Kingdom now. The warning by David Suchet (*Daily Express*, November 26th 2009) that 'Christianity is being marginalised by other religions in Britain', is undoubtedly correct. The message of the Bible has become politically incorrect in our society generally, and even more tragically, it has become politically incorrect in so-called Christian circles. But perhaps the Lord has to say to *us,* "Despise not prophesyings" (1 Thess. 5:20). Do *we* accept "all the counsel of God?" (Acts 20:27).

- *The Nazarites* were encouraged to break their vows. See Numbers 6:3-4. We can almost hear a voice saying, 'Surely one little drink will do no harm' or 'Oh, come on now, it's Christmas'. Even Christians need to guard against stumbling a fellow-believer: "Judge this…that no man put a stumblingblock or an occasion to fall in his brother's way" (Rom. 14:13).

Our privileges are no less than Israel's privileges. We have been delivered from the thraldom of sin; we have enjoyed His gracious ways with us in the wilderness of this world, in spite of our many failures; we have enjoyed the help of His servants whom the Lord has given "for the perfecting of the saints" (Eph. 4:12). In fact, we have every reason to sing:

> *Count your many blessings, name them one by one,*
> *And it will surprise you what the Lord hath done.*

c) Israel's punishment, vv.13-16

Having confronted Israel with her sins, in the face of all His goodness towards them, the Lord expresses His displeasure: "Behold, I am pressed under you, as a cart is pressed that is full of sheaves" (v.13). Amos, a countryman, uses the sight of a loaded cart groaning under the sheaves to describe the effect of Israel's harvest of transgression upon the Lord. An alternative rendering puts it rather differently: 'Behold, I will press upon you, as a cart presseth that is full of sheaves' (JND). Both translations emphasise the certainty of judgment: "Therefore the flight shall perish from the swift, and the strong shall not strengthen his force, neither shall the mighty deliver himself: neither shall he stand that handleth the bow; and he that is swift of foot shall not deliver himself; neither shall he that rideth the horse deliver himself. And he that is courageous among the mighty shall flee away naked in that day, saith the Lord" (vv.14-16). The first rendering (AV) suggests that the pressure of their sin (v.13) would bring upon them the pressure of judgment (vv.14-16), and the second (JND) that the Lord who had blessed them in the past (vv.9-11) would now burden them with judgment. All human effort and resource would be powerless against it: there would be no escape. "Neither native ability (v.14) nor acquired skill (v.15) nor outstanding qualities (v.16) will avail anything" (J. A. Motyer). They would reap what they had sown. Although not mentioned by name, the Assyrian would come and prove too strong for Israel. He would be an adversary against whom nothing would prevail.

READ CHAPTER 3:1-15

"You only have I known of all the families of the earth"

We have noticed that the book of Amos commences with eight judgments, with two major sub-divisions. The first six judgments are pronounced against Israel's neighbours: Damascus, Gaza, Tyrus, Edom, Ammon and Moab, and the last two against God's people themselves, Judah and Israel.

In this chapter the Lord commences His pronouncements against Israel in detail, although it is significant that the passage commences with reference to "the whole family which I brought up from the land of Egypt" (v.1), perhaps reminding us that what God has to say to one group of people is applicable to all His people: "He that hath an ear, let him hear what the Spirit saith unto the churches" (Rev. 2:7 etc). We must notice at least five important lessons in these verses, of which the last leads to the pronouncement of judgment on the nation: *(1)* privilege determines responsibility (vv.1-2); *(2)* sin mars fellowship (v.3); *(3)* warnings cannot be ignored (vv.4-6); *(4)* God reveals his purposes (v.7); *(5)* God's word must be communicated (vv.8-15).

1) PRIVILEGE DETERMINES RESPONSIBILITY, vv.1-2

a) The privilege, vv.1-2a
"Hear this word that the Lord hath spoken against you, O children of Israel, against the whole family which I brought up from the land of Egypt, saying, You only have I known of all the families of the earth." As noted in our introduction, the words "Hear this word" or "Hear ye this word", occur at 3:1, 4:1 and 5:1.

The words, "you only have I known", refer to God's predetermination. The words of Moses should be read in this connection: "For thou art a holy people unto the Lord thy God: the Lord thy God hath chosen thee to be a special people unto himself above all people that are upon the face of the earth. The Lord did not set his love upon you, nor choose you, because ye were more in number than any people: for ye were the fewest of all people; but because the Lord loved you" (Deut. 7:6-8). The Psalmist said, "He sheweth his word unto Jacob, his statutes and his judgments unto Israel. He hath not dealt so with any nation: and as for his judgments, they have not known them. Praise ye the Lord" (Psalm 147:19-20). With this in mind, Balaam prophesied "Lo the people shall dwell alone, and shall not be reckoned among the nations" (Num. 23:9).

Similar language is used of believers today: "For whom he did **foreknow**, he also did predestinate to be conformed to the image of his Son" (Rom. 8:29); "But ye are a **chosen** generation, a royal priesthood, an holy nation, a peculiar people: that ye should shew forth the praises of him who hath called you out of darkness into his marvellous light" (1 Pet. 2:9). God chose Israel for the same purpose: "This people have I formed for myself; they shall shew forth my praise" (Isaiah 43:21). The New Testament speaks of our "high", "holy", and "heavenly" calling (Phil. 3:14; 2 Tim. 1:9; Heb. 3:1).

b) The responsibility, v.2b
The words which follow, "therefore I will punish you for all your iniquities", make strange reading until we realise that privilege determines responsibility. A similar passage occurs in Isaiah 40:2, "Speak ye comfortably to Jerusalem and cry unto her that her warfare is accomplished, that her iniquity is pardoned: for she hath received of the Lord's hand double for all her sins". Whilst the word "double" can certainly be understood to describe the fullness of divine judgment upon Israel, there may be a reference to the Israel's place as God's firstborn. The firstborn son had a double portion of his father's inheritance. As God's firstborn, the double privilege was matched by double responsibility. The principle can be seen in the New Testament so far as Israel is concerned. The gospel is "to the Jew first, and also to the Greek" (Rom 1:16), and "indignation and wrath, tribulation and anguish" is "upon every soul of man that doeth evil, of the Jew first, and also of the Gentile; but glory, honour, and peace to every man that worketh good, to the Jew first, and also to the Gentile" (Rom. 2:9-10).

The principle is clearly demonstrated in the teaching of the Lord Jesus: "Woe unto thee Chorazin! Woe unto thee Bethsaida! For if the mighty works, which were done in you, had been done in Tyre and Sidon, they would have repented long ago in sackcloth and ashes. But I say unto you, It shall be more tolerable for Tyre and Sidon at the day of judgment, than for you" (Matt. 11:21-22). The Lord Jesus continued by addressing Capernaum in the same way (Matt. 11:23-24). See also Matthew 12:41-42.

For unregenerate men and women there will be degrees of punishment contingent on privilege. The Lord Jesus made this clear: "And that servant, which knew his lord's will, and prepared not himself, neither did according to his will, shall be beaten with many stripes. But he that knew not, and did commit things worthy of stripes, shall be beaten with few stripes. For unto whomsoever much is given, of him shall much be required" (Luke 12:47-48).

The principle, "unto whomsoever much is given, of him shall much be required", is applicable to believers as well, especially to Bible teachers: "My brethren, be not many masters (teachers), knowing that we shall receive the greater condemnation" (James 3:1). A priest was required to bring a greater sin-offering than the other Israelites (Lev. 4:3). He, above all people, was well aware of the character of God. Matthew Henry puts it like this: 'If they be but as bad as others, they shall be punished worse than others, because it is justly expected that they should be so much better than others'.

2) SIN MARS FELLOWSHIP, v.3
The statement, "You only have I known of all the families of the earth: therefore I will punish you for all your iniquities" is followed by the question, "Can two walk together, except they be agreed (or 'except by making an arrangement')?" The Lord desired to be in the closest fellowship with His people. He had said, "If ye walk in my statutes, and keep my commandments, and do them...I will walk among you, and will be your God, and ye shall be my people" (Lev. 26:3-12). But His people failed to keep their covenant responsibilities, and fellowship had been destroyed. In consequence, He was obliged to punish their iniquities.

There can be no doubt that the human race was created for God's pleasure and to enjoy fellowship with Him. This is apparent from the beginning of human history: "And they heard the voice of the Lord God walking in the garden in the cool of the day; and Adam and his wife hid themselves from the presence of the Lord God amongst the trees of the garden" (Gen. 3:8). Sin prevented their "walk together". But God's intentions can never be thwarted. The Lord Jesus said of the faithful believers at Sardis, "They shall walk with me in white: for they are worthy" (Rev. 3:4). In the meantime, there have been men who walked with God, and this is particularly said of Enoch (Gen. 5:22) and Noah (Gen. 6:9). The 'Enoch chapter' in the New Testament commences with the words, "As ye have received of us how ye ought to walk and to please God" (1 Thess. 4:1).

It is so important for us to remember that sin mars fellowship. Hence "Be ye not unequally yoked together with unbelievers: for what fellowship hath righteousness with unrighteousness? and what communion hath light with darkness? and what concord hath Christ with Belial? or what part hath he that believeth with an infidel? and what agreement hath the temple of God with idols?" (2 Cor. 6:14-16). When fellowship with God is interrupted, provision is made for restoration: "If we confess our sins, he is faithful and just to forgive us our sins, and to cleanse us from all unrighteousness" (1 John 1:9). We must never forget that if "I regard iniquity in my heart, the Lord will not hear me" (Psalm 66:18).

3) WARNINGS CANNOT BE IGNORED, vv.4-6
These verses develop the words, "I will punish you for all your iniquities" (v.2). Three pictures are used here to emphasise the seriousness of warnings:

a) The roar of a lion, v.4
"Will a lion roar in the forest, when he hath no prey? will a young lion cry out of his den, if he have taken nothing?" The lesson lies in the two cries of the lion.

i) "Will a lion **roar** in the forest, when he hath no prey?" This has been described as the 'pouncing roar' of the lion. It has been said that he has four feet off the ground when he roars like this! He does not roar otherwise. As J. A. Motyer points out, 'The Lion is still roaring (3:8), therefore the prey has not yet been seized. There is still a chance to come to terms. Hope has not yet vanished'.

ii) "Will a young lion **cry** out of his den, if he have taken nothing?" This is the low 'grumbling cry' of the lion as the prey is devoured.

The lesson is clear. In the first case, danger is imminent. In the second case, it is too late!

b) The preparation of a trap, v.5
"Can a bird fall in a snare upon the earth, where no gin (perhaps referring to a noose) is for him? Shall one take up a snare from the earth, and have taken nothing at all?" Again, the lesson is in two connected parts:

i) "Can a bird fall in a snare upon the earth, where no gin is for him?" In the words of J. A. Motyer, "the dropping flight of the bird bespeaks the baited trap". Unsuspected danger looms. Capture and destruction lie ahead.

ii) "Shall one take up a snare from the earth, and have taken nothing at all?" The trap has been sprung. The victim is caught. 'Will the snare spring up from the earth when nothing at all hath been taken?' (JND).

Again, the lesson is clear. In the first case, danger is imminent. In the second case, it is too late!

c) *The blowing of a trumpet, v.6*
"Shall a trumpet be blown in the city, and the people not be afraid? Shall there be evil in a city, and the Lord hath not done it?" For the third time, the lesson is in two parts:

i) "Shall a trumpet be blown in the city, and the people not be afraid?" The trumpet is blown to warn the city. So the opportunity exists for the nation to have dealings with God

ii) "Shall there be evil in a city, and the Lord hath not done it?" The enemy is in the city. The word "evil" refers to the terrible aftermath. 'Calamity never falls without the directive hand of God' (J. A. Motyer).

Once more, the lesson is clear. In the first case, danger is imminent. In the second case, it is too late!

Before the three pictures are interpreted, and we learn how the lion has roared and how the trumpet has sounded, *we* too must remember that warnings cannot be ignored. Very clearly, the figures employed conveyed warnings of imminent danger: God's people faced captivity and loss of inheritance. The New Testament warns believers of spiritual danger: "If any man defile the temple of God, him shall God destroy" (1 Cor. 3:17); "He that soweth to his flesh shall of the flesh reap corruption" (Gal. 6:8). We must never forget that "we must all appear before the judgment seat of Christ; that every one may receive the things done in his body, according to that he hath done, whether it be good or bad" (2 Cor. 5:10). See also 1 Cor. 3:15.

4) GOD REVEALS HIS PURPOSES, v.7
"Surely the Lord God will do nothing, but he revealeth his secret unto his servants the prophets". All that God intends to do He has revealed in His word. See, for example, Romans 16:25-26; Ephesians 3:1-8.

The true prophet is a man who "stood in the counsel of the Lord and hath perceived and heard his word" (Jer. 23:18). This was the case at Antioch: "As they ('certain prophets and teachers') ministered unto the Lord, and fasted, the Holy Ghost said, Separate me Barnabas and Saul for the work whereunto I have called them" (Acts 13:2). The Lord communicates His word to men and women who are in fellowship with Him. Here are some more examples:

i) "Shall I hide from Abraham that thing which I do" (Gen. 18:17). Abraham was the "friend of God" (James 2:23). See also 2 Chron. 20:7; Isaiah 41:8.

ii) "And the Lord spake unto Moses face to face, as a man speaketh to his friend" (Exodus 33:11). "Hear now my words: If there be a prophet among you, I the Lord will make myself known to him in a vision, and I will speak unto him in a dream. My servant Moses is not so, who is faithful in all mine house. With him will I speak mouth to mouth, even apparently, and not in dark speeches" (Num. 12:6-8).

iii) "Henceforth I call you not servants; for the servant knoweth not what his Lord doeth: but I have called you friends; for all things that I have heard of my Father I have made known unto you" (John 15:15).

It was the disciple who leant "on Jesus' bosom" who learnt the identity of the betrayer (John 13:21-26), and it was through that same man that the Lord Jesus showed "unto his servants things which must shortly come to pass" (Rev. 1:1). It is also worthwhile remembering that it was after the first recorded prayer meeting (Dan. 2:17-18) that the meaning of Nebuchadnezzar's dream was revealed to Daniel, leading him to say, "Blessed be the name of God for ever and ever...He revealeth the deep and secret things" (Dan. 2:22), and leading Nebuchadnezzar to say, "Of a truth it is, that your God is a God of gods, and a Lord of kings, and a revealer of secrets, seeing thou couldest reveal this secret" (Dan. 2:47). Pharaoh was so impressed with Joseph that he called him "Zaphnath-paaneah", meaning 'the revealer of secrets' (Gen. 41:45).

It is important to remember that while Scriptures are complete, and there is nothing to be added to "the faith once delivered unto the saints" (Jude v.3), we do need to be constantly in His presence seeking daily help and guidance, knowing that He will never direct us in opposition to His own word. It is also worth saying that there are many matters on which we do not have to pray for guidance, for the simple reason the word of God is perfectly clear! It is therefore most important to be thoroughly acquainted with the Scriptures!

5) GOD'S WORD MUST BE COMMUNICATED, vv.8-15
These verses tell us about the compelling power of God's word (v.8), and then the content of God's word to Israel (vv.9-15).

a) The compelling power of God's word, v.8
If the Lord imparts His word to His servants (v.7), then His servants are to impart His word to others (v.8), and they are to do so with deep conviction. "The lion hath roared, who will not fear? The Lord God hath spoken, who can but prophesy?" Jeremiah knew all about this: "Then I said, I will not make mention of him, nor speak any more in his name. But his word was in mine heart as a burning fire shut up in my bones, and I was weary with forbearing, and I could not stay" (Jer. 20:9), and so did Paul: "For though I preach the gospel, I have nothing to glory of: for necessity is laid upon me: yea, woe is unto me, if I preach not the gospel" (1 Cor. 9:16). See also Acts 4:20: "For we (Peter and John) cannot but speak the things which we have seen and heard". Paul was "pressed in spirit" (AV) or 'constrained by the word' (RV) (Acts 18:5).

b) The content of God's word to Israel, vv.9-15
Judgment would fall in three areas of national life in which Israel found security and satisfaction: it would destroy *(i)* their military security (vv.9-12); *(ii)* their religious security (vv.13-14); *(iii)* their material security (v.15).

i) **Military security, vv.9-12.** In these verses, the word "palaces" occurs four times (vv.9, 10, 11). It also occurs several times in Chapters 1 & 2, and means "fortress" or "stronghold". Their military strength would evaporate. We should notice the following:

- The external witnesses: "Publish in the palaces of Ashdod, and in the palaces of the land of Egypt, and say, Assemble yourselves upon the mountains of Samaria, and behold the great tumults in the midst thereof, and the oppressed in the midst thereof" (v.9). Ashdod and Egypt, people who 'had no special revelation, and who had never experienced special redemption' (J. A. Motyer) are invited to sit in judgment upon people who had enjoyed both, but whose social injustice and oppression had sunk to a lower level than that of their two pagan neighbours. Sadly, it is not unknown for God's people to act in a way that attracts the condemnation of non-believers.

- *The internal weakness:* "For they know not to do right, saith the Lord God, who store up violence and robbery in their palaces" (v.10). Israel was militarily strong (see 2 Kings 14:23-27), but it was rotten at the core: "They know not to do right". First appearances can be deceptive. "Bitterness, and wrath, and anger, and clamour, and evil speaking…with malice" (Eph. 4:31), together with lack of loving care (1 John 3:17; James 2:15-16), will weaken and ultimately destroy an assembly.

- *The eventual destruction.* "Therefore thus saith the Lord God; An adversary there shall be even round about the land; and he shall bring down thy strength from thee, and thy palaces shall be spoiled" (v.11). The destruction of the nation would be so complete that not much would remain: in fact what would be left is compared to the remains of a sheep ("two legs, or a piece of an ear") retrieved from the mouth of a lion. (Note: "two legs", no longer able to walk; "a piece of an ear", no longer able to hear). The rich inhabitants of Samaria, accustomed to luxury would find themselves in the jaws of the Assyrian lion, and there would not be much left to be "taken out" of his mouth (v.12). Such would be the end of the people that "dwell in Samaria in the corner of a bed, and in Damascus in a couch" or "that sit in Samaria in the corner of a couch (footnote: 'the best place of the divan in the houses of the rich'), and upon the damask of a bed" (JND). The people who reclined 'on the silken cushions of a bed' (RV) would end up like the remains of a sheep in a lion's mouth! There is a probable allusion here to Exodus 22:13, where a torn carcass was evidence that a beast had taken an animal entrusted to a neighbour for safe-keeping. In these circumstances, the neighbour did not have to pay compensation, perhaps implying here that the Lord was not in any way negligent over the destruction of Israel. Compare Genesis 31:39.

ii) Religious security, vv.13-14. Their religious security would be unavailing: "Hear ye, and testify in the house of Jacob, saith the Lord God, the God of hosts (none can withstand Him), that in the day that I shall visit the transgressions of Israel upon him I will also visit the altars of Bethel: and the horns of the altar shall be cut off, and fall to the ground".

Bethel, with all its sacred associations in the past (Gen. 28:11-22; 35:1-15) had become a centre of idolatry: "Come to Bethel, and transgress" (Amos 4:4). Jeroboam the son of Nebat had placed one of his two golden calves there (1 Kings 12:25-33). As J. A. Motyer points out, 'Heresy…never stands idle. Jeroboam built an altar in Bethel (1 Kings 12: 32, but Amos speaks of altars'. Israel went to Bethel and Gilgal, but they did not seek the Lord

(Amos 5:4-5). Grasping the "horns of the altar" did not do Joab much good (1 Kings 2:28), and it would be no good running to the altars at Bethel in time of distress. Israel's false religion would avail nothing. "Bethel shall come to nought" (Amos 5:5). See Hosea 8:5-6, 10:5-6.

iii) Material security, v.15. Their godless material security would be destroyed: "And I will smite the winter house with the summer house; and the houses of ivory shall perish, and the great houses shall have an end, saith the Lord". Notice the emphasis on "houses": "the winter house...the summer house...the houses of ivory...the great houses". 'False religion with all its display ends in total collapse of shrine and society alike' (J. A. Motyer).

READ CHAPTER 4:1-13

"Prepare to meet thy God, O Israel"

This chapter contains the second of the three messages delivered by God through Amos to Israel: "Hear this word" (v1): compare 3:1 and 5:1. The passage can be divided into three sections: *(1)* the conduct of God's people (vv.1-5); *(2)* the response to God's people (vv.6-11); *(3)* the appeal to God's people (vv.12-13).

1) THE CONDUCT OF GOD'S PEOPLE, v.v1-5
In the previous chapter, judgment was pronounced on three areas of national life in which they found their security and satisfaction: *(i)* military security (3:9-12); *(ii)* religious security (3:13-14); *(iii)* material security (3:15). The last two of these are now amplified. Their material security is re-examined with reference to the wealthy Samaritan women, and their religious security is re-examined with reference to the well-attended shrines at Bethel and Gilgal.

a) The wealthy Samaritan women, vv.1-3
We should notice *(i)* their luxurious living (v.1); *(ii)* their disregard for others (v.1); *(iii)* their coming humiliation (vv.2-3)

i) Their luxurious living. The luxurious houses described in the first message, "the winter house...the summer house...the houses of ivory... the great houses" (3:15), were inhabited by luxury-loving women. "Hear this word, ye kine of Bashan, that are in the mountain of Samaria, which oppress the poor, which crush the needy, which say to their masters, Bring, and let us drink" (v.1). It has been said that 'Amos was not trained as a prophet: he was a simple herdsman and a farmer. When he wanted to get the point across to the indulgent women of Israel, he called them *fat cows*'. Bashan, in the north of the country (the modern Golan Heights), was renowned for its cattle. See Psalm 22:12 ("the strong bulls of Bashan"); Ezekiel 39:18 ("fatlings of Bashan"). The expression "kine of Bashan" may well refer 'both to the luxury that the wealthy women enjoyed, and to a certain voluptuousness and sensuality which their extravagant life-style afforded them' (supplied by J. Waldron).

Amos notes the influence exercised by these women over their husbands: "which say to their masters ('their lords', JND), Bring, and let us drink". As J. A. Motyer observes, "How Amos must have enjoyed the irony of calling the husbands of these matriarchs 'their lords'…It is clear who lorded it in these marriages!" He adds that this points to "self-determination, whereby no-one can side-step the mandate of the mistress. And all is done so that there may be drink in the house: not done for necessity, but for luxury; not done for life, but for kicks".

These women evidently used the same word (*adon*) as Sarah who referred to Abraham as "my lord" (Gen. 18:12). See 1 Peter 3:6. But Sarah was "one of the holy women…who trusted in God" (1 Pet. 3:5), which could not be said of "the kine of Bashan". There is no resemblance here to the respective roles of husbands and wives described in Ephesians 5:22-33 and 1 Peter 3:7. Divine order in marriage had been perverted amongst the upper classes in Israel, and the home served mammon rather than God. The home of Aquila and Priscilla was quite different (Rom. 16:3-4). Lest we should think that Amos was biased against women, notice what he has to say later about high society in both Zion and Samaria. See 6:4-6. It is not without significance that having spoken of the husbands of these women as "lords" (JND), Amos immediately refers to "the Lord God" (*Adonahy Jehovah*). If they had recognised *Him* as their Lord, they would have been given to holiness rather than sinfulness (vv.1-2)

ii) *Their disregard for others*. It was material prosperity that was rotten at the core. They "oppress the poor…crush the needy" (v.1). It has been suggested that while the women may not have directly oppressed God's people and that it was the husbands who actually exploited the poor and needy, it was the wives who plotted the whole sorry business from behind the scenes. Their incessant demands for luxuries drove their pathetic husbands to these injustices.

We must remember that God's people are to be characterised by the exact opposite: they should have "the same care one for another" (1 Cor. 12:25). Note the injunctions, "Look not every man on his own things, but every man also on the things of others" (Phil 2:4); "Bear ye one another's burdens, and so fulfil the law of Christ" (Gal 6:2).

iii) Their coming humiliation. "The Lord God hath sworn by his holiness, that, lo, the days shall come upon you, that he will take you away with hooks, and your posterity with fishhooks. And ye shall go out at the breaches, *every cow at that which is* before her; and ye shall cast *them* into the palace, saith the Lord" (vv.2-3), or 'and ye shall go out by the breaches, every one straight before her, and ye shall be cast out to Harmon, saith Jehovah' (JND). Note the italicised words in the A.V.

The words, "The Lord God hath sworn by his holiness", prompt J.A.Motyer to ask what it is that moves God, who 'in the totality of His nature is unutterably and perfectly moral', to utter such an oath, with the answer, 'A society and a religion organised on the basis of human self-pleasing'. Self-pleasing and self-indulgence are abhorrent to God.

Amos, the man from the country, now employs a new figure of speech. The cows of Bashan are now seen as fish. Israel is the fish pond and although not named here, Assyria is the angler. 'When the Assyrians depopulated and exiled a conquered community, they led the captives away on journeys of hundreds of miles, with the captives naked and attached together with a system of rings and fishhooks pierced through their lower lip. God would make sure that they were led in this humiliating manner through the broken walls of their conquered cites' (supplied by J.Waldron). The words, "the palace" ('ye shall be cast out to Harmon', JND) possibly refer to the enemy's fortress or palace, but 'the meaning is not ascertained' (JND footnote).

b) The well-attended shrines, vv.4-5
"Come to Bethel, and transgress; at Gilgal multiply transgression; and bring your sacrifices every morning, and your tithes after three years: and offer a sacrifice of thanksgiving with leaven, and proclaim and publish the free offerings: for this liketh you, O ye children of Israel, saith the Lord God". There was a proliferation of religious observances - "for this liketh you, O ye children of Israel, saith the Lord God" - but their religious practices were nothing more than self-indulgence. Israel's religion was a combination of external correctness (note the references to the various Levitical offerings) and idolatry (practised at Bethel with its plurality of altars, 3:14). With this in mind, we should notice:

i)   The places. "Come to Bethel, and transgress; at Gilgal multiply transgression". These were places of former blessing. **Bethel**, meaning the house of God, was the place of God's presence and of fellowship with

Him. It was the place where God revealed Himself to Jacob. See Genesis 28:10-22; 35:1-15. **Gilgal** was the first place of encampment on entering Canaan. See Joshua 4: 19. It was there that circumcision was re-introduced, that the Passover was kept, and where Israel ate the old corn of the land (Joshua 5:2-12). Joshua's headquarters was located at Gilgal (Joshua 9:6, 10:6, 14:6).

But God does not bless 'for old times' sake'. Just listen to this: "But go ye now unto my place which was in Shiloh, where I set my name at the first, and see what I did to it for the wickedness of my people Israel. And now, because ye have done all these works...therefore will I do unto this house, which is called by my name, wherein ye trust, and unto the place which I gave to you and to your fathers, as I have done to Shiloh" (Jer. 7:12-14). We must not forget that current blessing demands current godliness.

ii) The changed status of those places. Following the secession of Jeroboam, Bethel became a centre of idolatry. See 1 Kings 12:25-33. One of the two golden calves was sited there; it became a place of sacrifice, and the centre of a new priestly system. The word of God which said, "Thou mayest not sacrifice the passover within any of thy gates...but at the place which the Lord thy God shall choose to place his name in" (Deut. 16:5-6), was rejected for reasons of political expediency. Jeroboam did not want his subjects to go to Jerusalem. If they did that, they might defect!

iii) These places now witnessed a combination of truth and error. "Bring your sacrifices every morning (but no reference to the evening sacrifice: see Exodus 29: 39)...your tithes after three years (see Deut. 14:28)... offer a sacrifice of thanksgiving with leaven" (see Lev.7:13), but it was only to "multiply transgression". They offered their sacrifices and brought their tithes with Jeroboam's description of the golden calves ringing in their ears: "Behold thy gods, O Israel, which brought thee up out of the land of Egypt" (1 Kings 12: 28). Any combination of truth and error, is error.

All this speaks with a loud voice to us. We can 'go through the motions', dotting our i's and crossing our t's, but it is all quite pointless if the Lord does not have the pre-eminence in our lives. More than 'pointless', it is positively obnoxious to Him.

iv) The supposed worship at these places was an empty acknowledgement of God. There was no repentance: their worship was nothing more than self-gratification: "For this liketh you, O ye children of Israel, saith the Lord God". Compare 5:21-24, "I hate, I despise your feast days, and I will not smell in your solemn assemblies. Though ye offer me burnt-offerings and your meat-offerings, I will not accept them: neither will I regard the peace-offerings of your fat beasts. Take thou away from me the noise of thy songs: for I will not hear the melody of thy viols". It has been rightly said that 'it is always wrong to measure worship by how much it pleases us'.

It was an attempt at ceremonial correctness, but without spiritual reality. There was religious strength, but nothing for God. Their worship was certainly not "in spirit and in truth" (John 4:23). In it all, they were far from the Lord.

2) THE RESPONSE TO GOD'S PEOPLE, vv.6-11
The Lord now describes His disciplinary measures and their object. Israel had been actively religious, and He had been active too with the object of securing their repentance and return to Him. But to no avail: "Yet have ye not returned unto me, saith the Lord" (vv.6, 8, 9, 10, 11). We should note the following:

i) The Lord cared sufficiently for His erring people to chasten them with a view to their recovery.

ii) In the Hebrew language, the word 'return' signifies far more than nominal acknowledgement: it means 'a return which reaches right up to (and does not stop short of) its mark' (J. A. Motyer). Motyer then quotes E. B. Pusey: 'God does not half-forgive, so neither must man half-repent'.

iii) But the nation failed to see the Lord's correcting hand in it all. Notice that in what follows we have the Lord, in accordance with Deut 28:15-68, implementing the curses of the covenant. He is the covenant-keeping God - in every way. God spoke to Israel in various ways and with increasing intensity, culminating with earthquakes, from which they were "as a firebrand plucked out of the burning" (v.11).

a) By famine, v.6
"And I also have given you cleanness of teeth in all your cities, and want of bread in all your places: yet have ye not returned unto me, saith the Lord". Tooth-picks were not required because there was no food to lodge between their teeth. The 'prodigal son' must have known what 'cleanness of teeth'

was like, and he did return to his father (Luke 15:17-19). Famine in *his* life had the desired effect.

The word of God is intended to be "more than our necessary food" (Job 23:12), but if it ceases to feed our souls, and we therefore fail to gain its nourishment, something is terribly wrong. It is a sign of spiritual malaise. The godly man 'delights in the law of the Lord" (Psalm 1:2). If the scriptures have no appeal to us, then we are far from the Lord. This should be a strong 'wake-up' call.

b) By drought, vv.7-8
"And I also have withholden the rain from you, when there were yet three months to the harvest: and I caused it to rain upon one city, and caused it not to rain upon another city: one piece was rained upon, and the piece whereupon it rained not withered. So two or three cities wandered unto one city, to drink water; but they were not satisfied: yet have ye not returned unto me, saith the Lord". So it was selective drought. 'The word "rain" here (*geshem*) denotes the period when copious showers were most needed, three months before the harvest. They were the spring rains that fell in the latter half of February until April (Hos. 6:3; Joel 2:23)' (M. F. Unger).

Rain is a sign of God's blessing, and rain (and dew) withheld is a sign of divine displeasure. See, for example, Deut. 28:23-24; 1 Kings 17:1. Note the words "wandered...not satisfied". According to M. F. Unger, the word "wandered" means 'staggered' or 'tottered'. They endeavoured to satisfy themselves by enjoying the blessing of others, but they 'did not get enough to drink' (NIV).

c) By blight, v.9
"I have smitten you with blasting and mildew: when your gardens and your vineyards and your fig trees and your olive trees increased, the palmerworm (the locust in its form as 'the shearer') devoured them: yet have ye not returned unto me, saith the Lord". See Deuteronomy 28:22. Expectations were unfulfilled. The promised harvests did not materialise, with all the attendant frustration and disappointment.

d) By death, v.10
"I have sent among you the pestilence after the manner of Egypt: your young men have I slain with the sword, and have taken away your horses: and I have made the stink of your camps to come up unto your nostrils: yet

have ye not returned unto me, saith the Lord". There was loss of potential: "Your young men have I slain with the sword". There was loss of power: "and have taken away your horses". It appears that the words, "the stink of your camps", refer to the stench of dead bodies.

In this case, the young men had been slain as the result of Israel's idolatry and waywardness. It has to be said, however, that while in some cases the loss of young men and women by assemblies is attributable to lack of pastoral care and good leadership (as in Israel), this is not always the case. One thing is clear, while 'aging assemblies' have certainly been revived, and continue to flourish, as the result of believers moving into the area, every assembly ought to pray, "Give me children, or else I die" (Gen. 30:1), and then take steps to ensure that they do not become like Mephibosheth, who became lame when his nurse allowed him to fall (2 Sam. 4:4). We must never cease to pray that the Lord will give our local assemblies young men like Joshua, "a young man" who "departed not out of the tabernacle" (Exodus 33:11), and like "the young men of the princes of the provinces" through whom the Lord defeated the Syrians (1 Kings 20:13-21).

e) By earthquake, v.11
"I have overthrown some of you, as God overthrew Sodom and Gomorrah, and ye were as a firebrand plucked out of the burning: yet have ye not returned unto me, saith the Lord." The Lord had finally spoken to His people in the most devastating way of all, comparable with the destruction of Sodom and Gomorrah. They had *almost* suffered complete destruction and their survival is likened to "a firebrand plucked out of the burning". But the Lord still had to say, "Yet have ye not returned unto me".

Far from describing the anger of a vengeful God, these verses (vv.6-11) are an appeal to His people. He had dealt with them in this way, not to destroy them, but to secure their return to Him. But because, after all this, they had not returned to Him, the Lord announces further judgments, and makes a further appeal to them. This brings us to:

3) THE APPEAL TO GOD'S PEOPLE, vv.12-13
"Therefore thus will I do unto thee, O Israel: and because I will do this unto thee, prepare to meet thy God, O Israel" (v.12). We should notice *(a)* the announcement (v.12); *(b)* the appeal (v.12); *(c)* the affirmation (v.13).

a) The announcement, v.12

God states His intention to continue these judgments: "Therefore thus will I do unto thee, O Israel". We know that they would culminate in national destruction (3:11-15), with the resultant lamentation: "The virgin of Israel is fallen; she shall no more rise: she is forsaken upon her land; there is none to raise her up" (5.1-3).

b) The appeal, v.12
"And because I will do this unto thee, prepare to meet thy God, O Israel". The oft-quoted words - "prepare to meet thy God" - are usually quoted as a warning to sinners of inevitable judgment if they reject His word, and this does seem to be a logical conclusion in view of the preceding verses. But it is also worth considering them differently. After all, what preparation *can* be made to meet an angry God! Surely the only preparation possible is repentance! This is certainly the message in the next chapter: "For thus saith the Lord unto the house of Israel, Seek ye me, and ye shall live: but seek not Bethel, nor enter into Gilgal...Seek the Lord, and ye shall live; lest he break out like a fire in the house of Joseph, and devour it, and there be none to quench it in Bethel" (5:4-6).

It has been pointed out that "Wherever the idea of meeting God is found in the Bible, it has a connotation of grace. The nearest parallel to this verse in Amos is Exodus 19:17, where Moses leads out the people from the camp 'to meet God'" (J. A. Motyer). See also Genesis 18:2; 19:1; Exodus 5:3; Numbers 23:3; Zechariah 2:3.

c) The affirmation, v.13
The Lord affirms His ability to impart stability and safety to His people. Repentance - preparing to meet God - would give them a security not found in their strongholds ("palaces", AV), in their religion, or in their material prosperity. Their security would be vested in "the Lord, the God of hosts". He is incomparable: "For, lo, he that formeth the mountains, and createth the wind, and declareth unto man what is his thought, that maketh the morning darkness, and treadeth upon the high places of the earth, the Lord, The God of hosts, is his name". Compare 5:8; 9:6. He is all-powerful; able to deliver His people. They had sought their own security. He alone could be their true security. Note the covenant name: "The **Lord** (Jehovah), The God of hosts, is his name".

We should notice (i) His omnipotence: "He that formeth the mountains, and createth the wind"; (ii) His omniscience: "and declareth unto man what is his thought (that is, man's thought: compare Psalm 139:2); (iii) His omnipresence: "that maketh the morning darkness, and treadeth upon the high places of the earth" (Amos 4:13).

Why should Israel resort to Bethel or Gilgal when they could enjoy the presence and blessing of the true God? Why should we seek satisfaction elsewhere when the eternal God is our refuge, and underneath are the everlasting arms"? (Deut. 33:27). Our Saviour is "the true God, and eternal life" (1 John 5:20).

READ CHAPTER 5:1-15

"Seek ye me, and ye shall live"

This chapter contains the third of the three messages delivered by God through Amos to Israel: "Hear this word" (v.1): compare 3:1 and 4:1. The chapter comprises two lamentations in view of coming judgment: "Hear this word which I take up against you, even a **lamentation** (*qinah*, meaning 'a mournful song'), O house of Israel" (v.1); "Alas! Alas! and they shall call the husbandman to mourning, and such as are skilful of **lamentation** (*nehi*, meaning 'wailing, or 'a song of wailing') to wailing (*misped*, another word for 'wailing')" (v.16).

i) The first lamentation (vv.1-15) arises from divine judgment on Israel's *civil injustice.* This is emphasised as follows: "Ye who turn judgment to wormwood, and leave off righteousness in the earth, seek him that maketh the seven stars and Orion" (vv.7-8); "They hate him that rebuketh in the gate, and they abhor him that speaketh uprightly. Forasmuch therefore as your treading is upon the poor...they afflict the just, they take a bribe, and they turn aside the poor in the gate from their right...it is an evil time" (vv.10-13).

ii) The second lamentation (vv.16-27) arises from divine judgment on Israel's *religious hypocrisy.* This is emphasised as follows: "I hate, I despise your feast days, and I will not smell in your solemn assemblies. Though ye offer me burnt-offerings and your meat-offerings, I will not accept them... Take thou away from me the noise of thy songs...But let judgment run down as waters, and righteousness as a mighty stream" (vv.21-24).

In both sections of the chapter, Amos **commences** with a lamentation (vv.1-3;16-20), **continues** with the reason for the lamentation (vv.4-13; 21-26), and **concludes** with either an appeal (vv.14-15) or a statement of inevitable judgment (v.27). It is most noticeable that while there is the possibility of grace and mercy in the first case (vv.15-16), there is no mention of this in the second (v.27), and this emphasises the Lord's particular abhorrence of religious hypocrisy.

1) THE FIRST LAMENTATION, vv.1-15
As already noted, this arises from divine judgment on Israel's civil injustice. The section may be divided as follows: *(A)* he laments the death of the nation (vv.1-3); *(B)* he expresses God's desire for the nation (vv.4-9); *(C)* he describes the injustice of the nation (vv.10-13); *(D)* he makes an appeal to the nation (vv.14-15).

A) He laments the death of the nation vv.1-3
"Hear this word which I take up against you, even a lamentation, O house of Israel". It can be summarised like this: *(i)* the nation will *fall*: "The virgin of Israel is fallen; she shall no more rise" (v.2); *(ii)* the nation will be *forsaken*: "She is forsaken upon her land; there is none to raise her up" (v.2); *(iii)* the nation will be *few*: "The city that went out by a thousand shall leave an hundred, and that which went forth by an hundred shall leave ten, to the house of Israel" (v.3). As Peter C. Craigie (*The Twelve Prophets*, Volume 1) points out, 'Normally, one only employs a lament *after* the death has occurred. And yet the words are addressed to an assembled crowd of Israelites, apparently alive and kicking'.

These verses underline the solemn lesson that rebellion against God leaves people helpless and hopeless. The nation, described as "the virgin of Israel", untouched and unviolated (M. F. Unger), would be invaded and carried into captivity. Referring now to the reduction in numbers, it has been said that 'the city that would have sent out a thousand soldiers would now only be able to send out a hundred' and 'only a handful of ragged war-weary men will be left of Israel's proud army' (supplied by Justin Waldron). All this has a solemn message for us today, and we must seriously ask how much *we* are responsible for local spiritual weakness and reduced numbers. Lamentation over closed assemblies is all too common.

It should be said that the glowing description of restoration and renewal at the end of the prophecy (9:11-15) does not mean that Amos has contradicted himself! When he says that the "virgin of Israel is fallen; she shall no more rise", he refers to the cessation of the northern kingdom, Israel, as opposed to Judah in the south. Israel, the northern kingdom, will never be reconstituted. Samaria, its capital, has no future. The ten northern tribes will ultimately enjoy divine blessing, but *not* as a separate kingdom. Hence the dirge here.

In view of coming judgment, Amos was prospectively singing a lament at the funeral of Israel.

B) He expresses God's desire for the nation, vv.4-9

Against this dark background, Amos speaks about the possibility of *life.* He had been lamenting the *death* of the nation, but this sad prospect brought no pleasure to the Lord. The Lord wanted the nation to *live.* Hence we read: "For thus saith the Lord unto the house of Israel, **Seek ye me**, and ye shall *live*" (v.4); "**Seek the Lord**, and ye shall *live*" (v.6); "**Seek him** that maketh the seven stars and Orion…" (v.8). (It should be stressed that these verses refer to *national life*, although we must not ignore their personal application). Later in the chapter, we hear Amos say, "**Seek good**, and not evil, that ye may *live*" (v.14). The sequence needs no explanation. If they genuinely sought the Lord, then they would obviously seek those things that please Him. They would seek good, and not evil"

To summarise the section: *(a)* they were to seek the Lord as their covenant-keeping God (vv.4-6): He was *Jehovah* ("the Lord", AV); *(b)* they were to seek Him as the Creator-God (vv7-9).

a) They were to seek Him as the covenant-keeping Lord, vv.4-6

They were warned against trusting in places, rather than in the Lord. After all, Bethel, Gilgal and Beer-sheba were places with an illustrious history. Surely God was to be found there. But this was not the case. They were to "seek the Lord" for two reasons: *(i)* because national survival depended on it (vv.4-5); *(ii)* because preservation from judgment depended on it (v.6).

i) Because national survival depended on it.

"For thus saith the Lord unto the house of Israel, Seek ye *me*, and ye shall *live:* but seek *not* Bethel, nor enter into Gilgal, and pass not to Beer-sheba: for Gilgal shall surely go into *captivity,* and Bethel shall come to *nought*" (vv.4-5). These people evidently thought that in order to please the Lord all they needed to do was to go to the right places, and that was all. Never mind about righteous living. They were so wrong. Terribly wrong! **We can fall into the same trap.** Of course we ought to go to places where Christ is honoured, and where the word of God is taught and practised. But simply being there is not enough. We are to be "obedient children" (1 Pet. 1:14) in every department of our lives. Spiritual strength doesn't just lie in being in the right place, but in living the right way, and in a personal relationship with the Lord: "Let him that glorieth glory in this, that he understandeth and knoweth me, that I am the Lord which exercise lovingkindness, judgment, and righteousness, in the earth" (Jer. 9:24).

The words, "Seek ye me, and ye shall live", should be read in conjunction with the following: "My soul thirsteth *for God*, for the living God" (Psalm 42:2); "O God, thou art my God; early will I seek thee: my soul thirsteth *for thee*, my flesh longeth *for thee* in a dry and thirsty land, where no water is" (Psalm 63:1); "My soul longeth, yea, even fainteth for the courts of the Lord: my heart and my flesh crieth out *for the living God"* (Psalm 84:2).

The words, "But seek not Bethel...Gilgal...Beer-sheba", remind us that places with an illustrious history can suffer fearful decline.

- Bethel was a place with sacred associations: Jacob said of Bethel, "Surely the Lord is in this place; and I knew it not" (Gen. 28:16); "Jacob...built there an altar, and called the place El-beth-el: because there God appeared unto him" (Gen. 35:7); "And Jacob called the place where God spake with him, Bethel" (Gen. 35:15); Bethel was therefore the place of divine presence and revelation: it was where God spoke. But *not* now: there was *no* revelation and *no* promise. There was a golden calf there (1 Kings 12:28-29).

- Gigal was the first place of encampment in the land, and it was there that the twelve stones were erected which had been taken from the bed of Jordan. Circumcision was re-instituted there: the first passover in the land was kept there: they ate the fruit of Canaan there: Joshua's headquarters were there. Gilgal stood for the possession of the land. But *not* now: dispossession was imminent.

- Beersheba figured in the lives of Abraham, Isaac and Jacob. It was there that Abraham was addressed by Abimelech and Phichol: "God is *with thee* in all that thou doest" (Gen. 21:22). It was there that the Lord promised His presence with Isaac: "And the Lord appeared unto him the same night, and said, I am the God of Abraham thy father: fear not, for I am *with thee*" (Gen. 26:23-24). It was there that the Lord promised His presence to Jacob: "And God spake unto Israel in the visions of the night, and said, Jacob, Jacob...I will go down *with thee* into Egypt" (Gen. 46:1-4). Beersheba, meaning 'the well of the oath' because of the covenant between Abraham and Abimelech, stood for the assurance of God's presence. But *not* now: there was no sense of His presence.

So they went, they thought, to the right places. But they were only *places:* they had become places of pilgrimage, with a nominal acknowledgement of God, but nothing else. Israel had lost all that the shrines stood for, because they did not seek the Lord *Himself.* This is the lesson of Ephesus. The believers would have certainly said, 'we are in the right place', but the Lord Jesus said: "I have somewhat against thee, because thou hast left thy first love" (Rev. 2:4). Orthodoxy without devotion to Christ was met with severe censure: "Remember therefore from whence thou art fallen, and repent, and do the first works; or else I will come unto thee quickly, and will remove thy candlestick out of his place, except thou repent" (Rev. 2:5).

Having noticed that they were to "seek the Lord" because it was a matter of life or death, Amos now gives the second reason why they were to "seek the Lord":

ii) Because preservation from judgment depended on it, v.6. "Seek ye the Lord, and ye shall live; lest he break out like a fire in the house of Joseph, and devour it, and there be none to quench it in Bethel". (The expression, "house of Joseph" refers to Israel, the northern kingdom, bearing in mind that Ephraim, Joseph's younger son, often stands for the nation as a whole. Samaria, Israel's capital city, was in the territory of Ephraim). Bethel, with all its past associations, and with its golden calf, would not be able to save them. The shrine would avail nothing. In the words of Isaiah, they were to "Seek… the Lord while he may be found, call…upon him while he is near" (Isaiah 55:6). But why such severity? Does nominal acknowledgement of God without true and sincere devotion in Him *really* merit such sweeping judgment?

The reasons for the severity of divine judgment follow: "Ye who turn judgment to wormwood, and leave off righteousness in the earth" (v.7). This is actually the beginning of a longer sentence but it does serve to emphasise that when people do not "seek the Lord" they decline morally, and fall into all kinds of sinful practices. Judgment is then inevitable. They had forgotten that "Righteousness exalteth a nation, but sin is a reproach to any people" (Prov. 14:34). They went to the right places, but it effected no change in their conduct. This is the solemn message of 1 John: "If we say that we have fellowship with him, and walk in darkness, we lie, and do not the truth" (1 John 1:6); "He that saith, I know him, and keepeth not his commandments, is a liar, and the truth is not in him" (1 John 2:4).

b) They were to seek Him as the Creator-God, vv.7-9
The reference to God's mighty power in creation at this point in the chapter

is probably explained by Israel's idolatry. Amos refers to this as follows: "Ye have borne the tabernacle of your Moloch and Chiun your images, the star of your god, which ye made to yourselves" (v.26). We are told that this verse refers to Saturn, and we may therefore conclude that these verses emphasise that Israel was to worship the Creator of the stars, not imaginary gods! "Ye who turn judgment to wormwood (a bitter and poisonous plant), and leave off righteousness in the earth ('cast down righteousness to the earth', JND), **Seek him that maketh the seven stars** ('Pleiades', JND) **and Orion**, and turneth the shadow of death into the morning, and maketh the day dark with night: that calleth for the waters of the sea, and poureth them out upon the face of the earth: The Lord is his name: that strengtheneth the spoiled against the strong, so that the spoiled shall come against the fortress". The "seven stars" are elsewhere called Pleiades (Job 9:9; 38:31). The constellation of Pleiades 'in its rising and setting marked the commencement and termination of the season of navigation' (M. F. Unger). Put another way, its rising before daybreak heralds the arrival of spring. Orion (known as 'the hunter') is 'an outstanding southern constellation' (M. F. Unger). Some say that the rising of Orion after sunset signals the onset of winter: others that it releases 'the earth from the bonds of winter'. God's power in the celestial and terrestrial creation is matched by His power in the affairs of men. 'He causeth destruction to break forth suddenly upon the strong, and bringeth destruction upon the fortress' (v.9, JND; see also RV). The power of the omnipotent God, whom they had failed to obey, would sweep them away. How necessary to "seek the Lord!".

C) He describes the injustice of the nation, vv.10-13
Their recourse to Bethel, Gilgal and Beer-sheba had no moral effect whatsoever. They went to these places, but that was all. Their empty religious profession was accompanied by moral bankruptcy. It was a cloak for evil conduct. There was no spiritual reality. We have already noticed this: "Ye who turn judgment to wormwood, and leave off righteousness in the earth, seek him that maketh the seven stars and Orion…" (vv.7-8).

Perhaps we ought to ask ourselves about our conduct. If, for example, our lives are not affected in any way by our attendance at the Lord's Supper, then our presence means very little, if anything at all. To seek God in sincerity will produce moral character and divine likeness. We will be "the children of light" (John 12:36).

We should notice the expression "in the gate" (vv.10, 12, 15). The "gate" was the law-court in ancient cities. It has been said that 'Judicial decisions for each community were taken at the gate of the city, where the heads of families and other elders assembled to hear witnesses, arbitrate disputes, decide controversies, and generally dispense justice. The space on the inner side of the gate, together with rooms or alcoves in the gate area itself, were used as courtrooms' (supplied by Justin Waldron). The best Old Testament example is found in Ruth 4:1-2. But a sorry picture of Israel's justice greets us in these verses:

i) **They despised the truth.** "They hate him that rebuketh *in the gate*, and they abhor him that speaketh uprightly" (v.10). Compare 2:12, "Ye… commanded the prophets, saying, prophesy not". People do like to hear what they like to hear. We certainly live in the age described by Paul: "The time will come when they will not endure sound doctrine" (2 Tim. 4:3). "Itching ears" do not relish "sound doctrine". The faithful Bible teacher can expect a rough ride. In Hosea's day they were saying, "The prophet is a fool, the spiritual man is mad" (Hos. 9:7).

ii) **They dispensed with compassion.** "Forasmuch therefore as your treading is upon the poor, and ye take from him burdens (exactions) of wheat" (v.11). In New Testament language, there was no "care one for another" (1 Cor. 12:25). Assemblies should be caring communities: see James 2:15-16; 1 John 3:17-18. Those responsible for such inequity would not enjoy their ill-gotten gains: "Ye have built houses of hewn stone, but ye shall not dwell in them; ye have planted pleasant vineyards, but ye shall not drink wine of them" (v.11).

iii) **They dispensed with justice.** "For I know your manifold transgressions and your mighty sins: they afflict the just, they take a bribe, and they turn aside the poor *in the gate* from their right" (v.12). The judiciary could be manipulated. Money talked! There was no impartiality. James 2:1-13 now becomes compulsory reading! We would not (hopefully!) contemplate bribery and corruption for one moment, but we could easily become "partial" (James 2:4). For example, it is not unknown for people to demand high standards from other believers, but to conveniently lower them for members of their own families! Moreover, it would be unwise to protest in Israel: "Therefore the prudent shall keep silence in that time; for it is an evil time" (v.13). It was safer to keep your mouth shut, because you never knew what might happen if you protested. Something like, 'You wouldn't want to spoil your prospects, now, would you?'

All this had to go if they were going to genuinely and sincerely "seek the Lord". Having noticed how Amos *(a)* laments the death of the nation (vv.1-3); *(b)* expresses God's desire for the nation (vv.4-9); *(c)* describes the injustice of the nation (vv.10-13), we must now notice, that:

D) He makes an appeal to the nation, vv.14-15

He calls for change: "Seek good, and not evil, that ye may *live*: and so the Lord, the God of hosts, shall be with you, as ye have spoken. Hate the evil, and love the good, and establish judgment *in the gate*" (vv.14-15). Compare 1 Thessalonians 5:21-22: "Prove all things; hold fast that which is good. Abstain from all appearance of evil". The Lord Jesus "*loved* righteousness, and *hated* iniquity" (Heb. 1:9).

Do notice the words, "and so the Lord, the God of hosts, shall be with you, *as ye have spoken*" (v.14), or 'and so the Lord, the God of hosts, shall be with you, *as ye say*' (JND). So they wanted God's presence: they expected Him to be with them. They wanted the right thing, but as things were, they were wrong in their expectation. How could He be with them in the current circumstances? A 'sea change' was necessary if this was to be the case: "Seek good, and not evil...Hate the evil, and love the good". Compare Psalm 24:3-6, "Who shall ascend into the hill of the Lord? or who shall stand in his holy place? He that hath clean hands, and a pure heart; who hath not lifted up his soul unto vanity, nor sworn deceitfully. He shall receive the blessing from the Lord, and righteousness from the God of his salvation. *This is the generation of them that seek him*, that seek thy face, O Jacob, Selah".

The appeal for change is accompanied by the possibility of blessing: "It may be that the Lord God of hosts will be gracious unto the *remnant* of Joseph" (v.15). Compare Joel 2:14. This is where Amos started: "The city that went out by a thousand shall leave an hundred, and that which went forth by an hundred shall leave ten, to the house of Israel" (v.3). We have already noted that Joseph stands for the northern kingdom. See our comments against v.6. However, J. A. Motyer points out that it is specifically stated on three occasions that "the Lord was with Joseph" (Gen. 39:2; 39:21; 39:23), all of them referring to a period in his life 'when hope had sunk beyond the horizon'. As "the Lord, the God of hosts" (v.14) and "the Lord God of hosts" (v.15), the Lord was perfectly able to deliver His people or, to use the language here, be "gracious unto the remnant of Joseph". He had not "forgotten to be gracious" (Psalm 77:9). J. A. Motyer nicely observes that "the 'may be' of grace rightly rebukes complacent human hearts, but in the divine heart there is no 'may be'. The God of grace cannot forget to be gracious". But we must remember that this was dependent on the repentance of the people. In Isaiah's words, "Let the wicked forsake his way, and the unrighteous man his thoughts: and let him return unto the Lord, and he will have mercy upon him; and to our God, for he will abundantly pardon" (Isaiah 55:7).

2) THE SECOND LAMENTATION, vv.16-27
As already noted, this arises from divine judgment on Israel's religious hypocrisy, and we will deal with this in our next study.

READ CHAPTER 5:16-27

"Let judgment run down as waters"

We have already noticed that this chapter comprises two lamentations in view of coming judgment: "Hear this word which I take up against you, even a *lamentation*, O house of Israel" (v.1); "Alas! alas! and they shall call the husbandman to mourning, and such as are skilful of *lamentation* to wailing" (v.16). We also noted the difference between the two lamentations:

i) The first lamentation (vv.1-15) arises from divine judgment on Israel's *civil injustice.* This is emphasised as follows: "Ye who turn judgment to wormwood, and leave off righteousness in the earth, seek him that maketh the seven stars and Orion" (vv.7-8); "They hate him that rebuketh in the gate, and they abhor him that speaketh uprightly. Forasmuch therefore as your treading is upon the poor...they afflict the just, they take a bribe, and they turn aside the poor in the gate from their right...it is an evil time" (vv.10-13).

ii) The second lamentation (vv.16-27) arises from divine judgment on Israel's **religious hypocrisy**. This is emphasised as follows: "I hate, I despise your feast days, and I will not smell in your solemn assemblies. Though ye offer me burnt-offerings and meat-offerings, I will not accept them...Take thou away from me the noise of thy songs...But let judgment run down as waters, and righteousness as a mighty stream" (vv.21-24).

1) THE FIRST LAMENTATION, vv.1-15
We noted that this section of the chapter may be divided as follows: *(a) he laments the death of the nation (vv.1-3)*: "The virgin of Israel is fallen; she shall no more rise" (v.2); *(b) he expresses God's desire for the nation (vv.4-9)*: "Seek ye me, and ye shall live: but seek not Bethel...Gilgal... Beers-sheba" (v.5); *(c) he describes the injustice of the nation (vv.10-13)*: "I know your manifold transgressions and your mighty sins" (v.12); *(d) he makes an appeal to the nation (vv.14-15)*: "Seek good, and not evil,

that ye may live... it may be that the Lord God of hosts will be gracious unto the remnant of Joseph" (v.15).

2) THE SECOND LAMENTATION, vv.16-27
As already pointed out, this arises from divine judgment on Israel's religious hypocrisy. In this section of the chapter Amos does four things: *(a)* he anticipates their national sorrow (vv.16-17); *(b)* he asserts that God will be with them (vv.18-20); *(c)* he abhors their religious practices (vv.21-26); *(d)* he announces their coming captivity (v.27).

a) He anticipates their national sorrow, vv.16-17
"Therefore the LORD (*Jehovah*), the God of hosts (*Elohim Tsebahoth*), the Lord *Adonai*, the sovereign Lord), saith thus: Wailing shall be in all streets; and they shall say in the highways, Alas! alas! and they shall call the husbandman to mourning, and such as are skilful of lamentation to wailing. And in all vineyards shall be wailing: for I will pass through thee (not "pass over", Exodus 12:13) saith the LORD". The same expression ("pass through") is used in connection with divine judgment on Egypt (Exodus 12:12). There is nothing but "wailing...wailing...wailing". It has been said that divine judgment on Israel would be so widespread that they would run out of professional mourners, and have to hire farmers to do the job. The title "God of hosts" should be noticed. The title "LORD of hosts" is used in connection with divine support for God's people, whereas "God of hosts is used in connection with their judgment.

b) He asserts that God will be with them, vv.18-20
Having noted that these people wanted the presence of God (v.14), Amos tells them that they would have it, but *not* in the way they expected: "Woe unto you that desire the day of the LORD! to what end is it for you? the day of the LORD is darkness, and not light. As if a man did flee from a lion, and a bear met him; or went into the house, and leaned his hand on the wall, and a serpent bit him. Shall not the day of the LORD be darkness, and not light? even very dark, and no brightness in it?". They desired "the day of the LORD", evidently thinking that it would a day of judgment on their **enemies**. But it would be a day of judgment upon **them**! They would find no joy (vv.16-17), no light (v.18) and no escape (v.19). The outstanding feature of "the day of the LORD" will be its darkness (v.20). Compare Zephaniah 1:15. The "day of the LORD", whether at the end-time (1 Thess. 5:2-3), or at any other time, is always a time of divine judgment. It must be said, however, that strictly speaking, "the day of the LORD" includes the millennium, and it could be

that these people were selecting what suited them, and conveniently closing their eyes to the judgment associated with the period.

The expression, "the day of the LORD", reminds us that we do need to distinguish between various 'days' mentioned in the New Testament. There are four:

- **'Man's day'.** See 1 Corinthians 4:3, "But with me it is a very small thing that I should be judged of you, or of man's judgment", where the words, "man's judgment", are literally, 'man's day' (*anthropinos hemera*), and we therefore learn that Paul was not concerned about the light men could throw upon his service. The term 'man's day' only occurs here. 'It denotes the period during which world government has been put into man's hands' (J. M. Davies). We live at the moment, therefore, in 'man's day'.

- **"The day of Jesus Christ".** See Philippians 1:6. It is elsewhere called "the day of Christ" (Phil. 1:10; 2:16), "the day of our Lord Jesus Christ" (1 Cor. 1:8), "the day of the Lord Jesus" (1 Cor. 5:5; 2 Cor. 1:14), and "that day" (2 Tim. 4: 8). These passages all refer to the Lord's coming for His church ('the rapture'), and to His review and reward of our work for Him. This will take place in heaven.

- **"The day of the Lord".** See 1 Thessalonians 5:2. Unlike "the day of Christ", this refers to events on earth, and includes divine judgment on wicked men, together with the millennial reign of the Lord Jesus. 2 Thessalonians 2:2 calls for special comment. The AV reads "that ye be not soon shaken in mind, or be troubled by spirit, nor by word, nor by letter as from us that the day of Christ is at hand", whereas the revised text reads 'that ye be not soon shaken in mind…as that the day of the Lord is present' (RV/JND). The Old Testament prophecies abound with references to "the day of the LORD", *most* of which refer to events at the end-time, and *some* of which describe current or imminent events, but which point forward to events at the end-time. Prophetic students often say that 'coming events cast their shadow before them'.

- **"The day of God".** This expression occurs only in 2 Peter 3:12, and refers to the eternal state: "Seeing then that all these things shall be dissolved, what manner of persons ought ye to be in all holy conversation and godliness, looking for and hastening unto the coming of the day of God, wherein ('by reason of which', JND) the heavens being on fire shall be dissolved, and the elements shall melt with fervent heat?"

Chapter 5A

c) He abhorred their religious practices, vv.21-26
We have already noticed that they went to the right places (v.5), but they were wrong, and that they wanted the right thing (v.14), but they were wrong. Now we must notice that they worshipped in the right way, but they were wrong! There was plenty of orthodox religion (vv.21-23), but no righteousness (v.24). The whole thing was a shameful sham. We should notice at least four things in these solemn verses

i) He detested their religion. "I hate, I despise your feast days, and I will not smell in your solemn assemblies. Though ye offer me burnt-offerings and your meat-offerings, I will not accept them: neither will I regard the peace-offerings of your fat beasts. Take thou away from me the noise of thy songs; for I will not hear the melody of thy viols" (vv.21-23). It was orthodox. But it was devoid of reality. As J. A. Motyer observes, 'they went in for religion in a big way at Gilgal. They took their religious duties seriously, the *feasts* at which attendance was by law obligatory, and the *solemn assemblies*, 'red letter' days on the 'church calendar' which must be observed (v.21); they entered fully into their religious privileges, bringing *burnt offerings*, *cereal offerings* and *peace offerings* symbolic of their status as God's people and their fellowship with Him and with each other (v.22); they gave full expression to their religious joys, singing *songs* to the accompaniment of *harps* (v.23). Somehow the vivacity of it all and the thrill of it all communicates itself. One can almost hear the singing. But God could not! All He heard was noise!'

Isaiah knew all about it: "To what purpose is the multitude of your sacrifices unto me? saith the LORD: I am full of the burnt-offerings of rams, and the fat of fed beasts…the new moons and sabbaths, the calling of assemblies, I cannot away with…Your new moons and appointed feasts my soul hateth" (Isaiah 1:11-14).

Notice the significant omissions by Amos: the 'sweet-savour offerings' are mentioned ("burnt-offerings…meat-offerings…peace-offerings"), together with "songs" and "melody", but there is no mention of sin-offerings or trespass-offerings. In New Testament language, there was no self-examination (1 Cor. 11:28), and no recognition of the fact that "if we would judge ourselves, we should not be judged" (1 Cor. 11:31).

ii) He desired righteousness. "But let judgment run down as waters, and righteousness as a mighty stream" (v.24). Micah reads similarly: "He showed thee, O man, what is good; and what doth the LORD require of thee, but to do justly, and to love mercy, and to walk humbly with thy God?" (Micah 6:8).

James emphasises the lesson: "If any man among you seem to be religious (*threskos,* outwardly religious), and bridleth not his tongue, but deceiveth his own heart, this man's religion is vain. Pure religion and undefiled before God and the Father is this, To visit the fatherless and widows in their affliction, and to keep himself unspotted from the world" (James 1:26-27).

The word translated "run down" (*galal*, meaning 'roll') derives from the same Hebrew word which gives Gilgal (meaning 'circle' or 'wheel') its name. See Joshua 5:8-9: "And it came to pass, when they had done circumcising all the people...the LORD said unto Joshua, This day have I rolled away (*galal)* the reproach of Egypt from off you. Wherefore the name of the place is called Gilgal unto this day". As J. A. Motyer observes, "It is as if the Lord is saying, 'Yes, you have been to Gilgal, but there is a rolling you have forgotten, the rolling of justice and righteousness'". Religion without righteousness is more than meaningless, it is sheer hypocrisy. Moreover, 'A momentary flow of justice and righteousness will not do; these virtues are to keep on in the social order like a stream that does not dry up with summer heat' (supplied by Justin Waldron).

iii) He describes their insincerity. "Have ye offered unto me sacrifices and offerings in the wilderness forty years, O house of Israel?" (v.25): or 'Did ye bring unto me sacrifices and offerings in the wilderness?' (JND/RV). Amos does not appear to give us the answer to the question, unless it carries its own answer! It is often said that 'to ask the question is to answer it'. In other words, the answer is self-evident. This seems to be the case here, but we must look at the possible answers:

- '*Yes*, you did "bring unto me sacrifices and offerings in the wilderness"', in which case the question implies that there was a time when God's people obeyed Him, but that this had now changed. They had become idolatrous. There had been a terrible deterioration in their worship. Support for this may well be found by simply reading vv.25-26 together: "Have ye offered unto me sacrifices and offerings in the wilderness forty years, O house of Israel? ***But*** ye have borne the tabernacle of your Moloch..."

- '*No*, you did not "bring unto me sacrifices and offerings in the wilderness"', in which case the answer is incorrect! Sacrifices and offerings were certainly made in the wilderness. See, for example, Numbers 10:12-20. Some commentators assert that because Israel was in the wilderness 'their circumstances in life made such formal worship impossible' (Peter C. Craigie), but this was evidently not the case.

- '**Yes**, you did "bring...sacrifices and offerings in the wilderness", but you did **not** bring them **"unto me"**. In other words, even in the wilderness they were 'going through the motions', but there was no reality about their worship, just as there was no reality about their worship in the days of Amos (vv.21-24). The constant murmuring and disobedience of God's people in the wilderness proclaimed the insincerity of their worship. Just think about events at Sinai (see Exodus 32:1-35), and at Shittim (see Numbers 25:1-3) where "they joined themselves also unto Baal-peor, and ate the sacrifices of the dead (that is, the sacrifices offered to dead idols)" (Psalm 106:28). The reference to the "forty years" really says it all: it was forty years of wandering because of unbelief. 'Unbelief kept them out of the land for forty years, and unbelief would take them out of the land', v.27 (T. Miller).

The third answer appears to suit the context, and was evidently understood in this way by Stephen in his address to the religious leaders in Jerusalem (see Acts 7:1-53). The quotation from Amos occurs in the section of his argument in which he traces the history of idolatry in Israel. Here are Stephen's words: "And they made a calf in those days, and offered sacrifice unto the idol, and rejoiced in the works of their own hands. Then God turned, and gave them up to worship the host of heaven; as it is written in the book of the prophets, O ye house of Israel, have ye offered to me slain beasts and sacrifices by the space of forty years in the wilderness? Yea, ye took up the tabernacle of Moloch, and the star of your god Rempham, figures which ye made to worship them: and I will carry you away beyond Babylon" (Acts 7:41-43).

Perhaps it should be said that Stephen does not mean that having made the golden calf (v.41), God immediately "gave them up to worship the host of heaven" (v.42), but that this was the ultimate result of their idolatry at Sinai. Similarly, Stephen does not mean that Israel were carrying "the tabernacle of Moloch, and the star of your god Rempham" through the wilderness, and offering Levitical sacrifices at the same time. Rather that 'the worship of the planetary powers, for which the nation lost its liberty and suffered deportation, was the climax of that idolatrous process which began in the wilderness' (F. F. Bruce).

This is very solemn. If we are right in saying that the question, "Have ye offered unto me sacrifices and offerings in the wilderness forty years, O house of Israel?" (v.25), means 'did you really offer sacrifices **to me** in the wilderness', implying that their worship was formal and superficial, then their superficiality ultimately led **to outright idolatry.** This is now described (v.26). Let **us** be warned. If our worship is ceremonially correct but lacking in reality, it will not be long before even the outward form is cast aside.

iv) He describes their resultant idolatry. "But ye have borne the tabernacle of your Moloch and Chiun your images, the star of your god, which ***ye made*** to yourselves" (v.26). While, evidently, they had not practised this in the wilderness, they were certainly doing it in the days of Amos, along with their "feast days...solemn...assemblies....burnt-offerings...meat-offerings...peace-offerings...songs...viols" (vv.21-23).

At this point we need some technical help, but it has to be said that the 'technical help' available is not always easy to follow!

- "But ye have borne the tabernacle of your Moloch". According to F. F. Bruce (*The Book of the Acts*), "the tabernacle of Moloch" (or, as Amos has it, "the tabernacle of *your* Moloch") can be rendered 'Sakkut your king'. We are told that the Hebrew word rendered "tabernacle" in this verse (*sikkuth*) has strong connections with an Akkadian word (*sakkut*), referring to the planet Saturn. F. F. Bruce also states that the word "Moloch" is 'probably Hebrew *melek*, meaning "king", used as a divine title'. To the layman, this all looks very complicated, and seems to involve some alteration of the original text, something that should be regarded with great caution, even though the RV does read: 'Yea, ye have borne Siccuth your king'.

On reflection, and bearing in mind that the word "tabernacle" here (*sikkuth*) means 'a booth or tent' (Gesenius), it seems better to follow the Authorised Version as it stands. The Old Testament refers to the Sukkiims (2 Chron. 12:3), meaning 'dwellers in tents' (Gesenius). Let's go further and say that it also seems better to take Moloch as it stands, rather than assuming that the original Hebrew word meaning Moloch somehow got changed to another word (*melek*) meaning 'king'. On balance, it does seem that the Authorised Version makes perfectly good sense without requiring an amendment to the original text! It simply means that Israel had made a house, box or tent in which the idol was placed. Moloch (or Molech) was the god of Ammon. Solomon built a "high place" to Molech, and to Chemosh (1 Kings 11:7). We are told that the idol was made of brass, with extended arms. It was heated and children were placed in the arms and burnt to death. According to Adam Clark, 'Moloch was generally understood to be the sun'.

- "And Chiun your images". Possibly the plural here ("images") refers to the many images made to represent Chiun. Piecing together various shreds of information, it appears (according to Gesenius) that Chiun could be the Egyptian name for Saturn, which was worshipped in Assyria under the name Kaiwan, but other scholars suggest that the word actually refers to the pedestal on which the idol (Moloch, or Molech) stood. According to M.F.Unger the word 'Chuin' evidently comes from a root meaning 'to set firmly'.

- "The star of your god". Stephen calls this "the star of your god Remphan" (Acts 7: 43). According to F. F. Bruce, Remphan (it has various other spellings) 'seems to be a form of *repa*, an Egyptian name of Saturn, used by Septuagint (LXX) translators (those who translated the Hebrew Old Testament into Greek) to replace Kaiwan, an Assyrian name for the same planet. There is nothing unusual about the word "star". It means what it says! Perhaps M. F. Unger is right in saying that '"the star of *your* god" probably refers to the representation of the planet Saturn on the head of the image of the idol'.

There can be no doubt that the people who heard Amos, and Stephen, preach would have been able to follow all this without difficulty. Leaving aside the detail which is interesting, if not particularly profitable, it does seem that Israel was evidently worshipping the 'astral deities' (in this case, the sun and Saturn), rather than "him that maketh the seven stars and Orion, and turneth the shadow of death into the morning, and maketh the day dark with night... The LORD is his name" (v.8).

d) *He announces their coming captivity, v.27*
"Therefore will I cause you to go into captivity beyond Damascus, saith the LORD, whose name is the God of hosts". The words "beyond Damascus" point to Assyria, which lay to the north-east of Damascus. Idolatry ends in captivity. Notice that Stephen said, "beyond **Babylon**" (Acts 7:43), whereas Amos said, "beyond **Damascus**". This was not a mistake on Stephen's part, as some suggest. Amos deals with the Northern Kingdom, and refers to the captivity described in 2 Kings 17:6. Stephen 'updates' the quotation to take in the *final* captivity - to Babylon.

As J. A. Motyer observes, 'The gods of Assyria occupied the hearts of Israel long before the armies of Assyria occupied its streets and towns..."the LORD, whose name is the God of hosts" will not be mocked'.

"Little children, keep yourselves from idols" (1 John 5:21).

READ CHAPTER 6:1-14

"They are not grieved for the affliction of Joseph"

Chapter 5 is addressed to the nation generally, with particular reference to its religious veneer, which served only to cover its moral and spiritual bankruptcy. It can be summed up in the following way:

i) They went to the **right places**, but they were **wrong**. The people were evidently making pilgrimages to Bethel, Gilgal and Beersheba, all of which had sacred associations in the past, but there was nothing sacred about them now, and certainly nothing sacred about the people who went there. They were commanded to "seek the LORD, and ye shall live; lest he break out like a fire in the house of Joseph, and devour it, and there be none to quench it in Bethel. Ye who turn judgment to wormwood, and leave off righteousness in the earth, Seek him that maketh the seven stars and Orion…" (5:6-8).

ii) They wanted the **right things**, but they were **wrong.** They wanted the presence of God: "Seek good, and not evil, that ye may live: and so the LORD, the God of hosts, shall be with you, as ye have spoken ('as ye say', JND)" (5: 14). But what they said they wanted, and how they behaved, were quite incompatible (vv.10-13). They could only have what they *said* they wanted if they obeyed the injunction, "Hate the evil, and love the good, and establish judgment in the gate" (v.15). Only then could it be said, "it may be that the LORD God of hosts will be gracious unto the remnant of Joseph" (v.15).

iii) They worshipped with the **right sacrifices**, but they were **wrong**. They certainly practised orthodox religion (together with idolatry: the two together are called 'syncretism'): the Lord refers to their "burnt-offerings…your meat-offerings…peace-offerings" (v.22), but it was sheer hypocrisy: "Judgment" and "righteousness" were required (v.24). Without these, their 'worship' was devoid of reality.

Chapter 6 is addressed, at least initially, to one particular class of people:

the rich ruling class. "Woe to them that are at ease in Zion, and trust in the mountain of Samaria, which are named chief of the nations, to whom the house of Israel came!" or 'Woe to them that are at ease in Zion, and to them that are secure in the mountain of Samaria, the notable men of the chief of the nations, to whom the house of Israel come!' (RV). We have already noticed that the wealthy *women* have been censured: "Hear this word, ye *kine* of Bashan" (4:1-3). Now we have an address to the rich *men* in Israel: to the acknowledged leaders: "to whom the house of Israel come (present tense)" (6:1, RV).

The chapter commences with security and comfort (vv.1-6), and concludes with destruction and captivity (vv.7-14). The three main paragraphs may be entitled *(1)* idle leaders (vv.1-6); *(2)* inescapable judgment (vv.7-11); *(3)* irreversible law (vv.12-14).

1) IDLE LEADERS, vv.1-6
The leadership is marked by *(a)* self-satisfaction, or pride (vv.1-2); *(b)* self-indulgence, or indolence (vv.3-6).

a) Self-satisfaction, vv.1-2
i) The scope of the message. "Woe to them that are at ease *in Zio*n, and trust in the mountain of *Samaria* ('and to them that are secure in the mountain of Samaria', RV)" (v.1). Jerusalem (Zion) is mentioned before Samaria! While the prophecy of Amos relates particularly to Israel, with its capital city Samaria, Judah and Jerusalem are not excluded. Compare, "Thus saith the Lord; For three transgressions of Judah, and for four, I will not turn away the punishment thereof" (2:4); "Hear this word that the LORD hath spoken against you, O children of Israel, against the whole family which I brought up from the land of Egypt" (3:1). Jeremiah makes the same point: "Hast thou seen that which backsliding Israel hath done?...And her treacherous sister Judah saw it...feared not...hath not turned unto me with her whole heart, but feignedly, saith the LORD" (Jer. 3:6-10). We learn at least one important lesson here - **we must never hide behind ministry addressed to other people!**

ii) The people in the message. "Woe to them that are *at ease* in Zion, and trust ('*are secure*' or '*careles*s', JND margin) in the mountain of Samaria, which are named chief of the nations (that is of Judah and Israel), to whom the house of Israel came (or 'come', RV)" (v.1). As already noted, this evidently refers to the rich leaders, who are called 'the notable men of the chief of the nations' (RV) or 'the renowned of the first of the nations' (JND).

The words "chief of the nations" (AV/RV) were evidently a proud boast. That is, they (the wealthy leaders) were the notable (AV) or renowned (JND) of the most renowned and notable kingdom. In other words, they said, 'There is no one like us!' Perhaps this boast was based on the long reigns of Uzziah (Judah) and Jeroboam (Israel). Both are mentioned in the introduction (1:1). Uzziah (Azariah) reigned for fifty-two years (2 Kings 15:1-2) and Jeroboam for forty-one years (2 Kings 14:23-29). The statement "to whom the house of Israel come (not 'came', AV)", is evidently a proud boast to boost morale, and impress the populace! In other words 'what fortunate people you are to have leaders like us!'

iii) The warning in the message. "Pass ye unto Calneh (on the river Tigris); and from thence go ye to Hamath the great (on the river Orontes in northern Syria); then go down to Gath of the Philistines: be they better than these kingdoms? (i.e. better than Israel and Judah) or their border greater than your border?" (v.2) J. A. Motyer suggests that this is a piece of government propaganda: 'these places are not worthy of comparison with ***us***: we are ***better*** and ***greater***: we are "better" in affluence, and our "border" indicates our territorial advantage. In other words, the answer to the question in v.2 is 'No, they are not better than us - ***we*** are the tops!'

But the context suggests something rather different. Read it like this: "Pass ye unto Calneh, and see; and from thence go ye to Hamath the great; then go down to Gath of the Philistines: be they better than these kingdoms? or their border greater than your border? Ye that put far away the evil day, and cause the seat of violence to come near... Therefore now shall they go captive with the first that go captive" (vv.2-7). In this case, the answer is 'Yes, these kingdoms are better than Judah and Israel, just look at the conduct of Judah and Israel's leaders! They deserve to go into captivity'. As M. F. Unger points out, 'Israel in her rebellious degeneracy was much worse and far more guilty than these nations, which had already been punished. How much less could Israel not expect to be punished?'

We must now compare the picture of the complacent and proud leadership here with what the New Testament requires in assembly leaders: "Not a novice, lest being lifted up with pride he fall into the condemnation of the devil" (1 Tim. 3:6); "A bishop (overseer) must be blameless, as the steward of God" (Titus 1:7); "Neither as being lords of God's heritage, but being ensamples to the flock" or 'neither as lording it over the charge allotted to you, but making yourselves ensamples to the flock' (1 Pet 5:3, RV). Compare 2 Sam 23:3, "The God of Israel said, the Rock of Israel spake to me, He that ruleth over men must be just, ruling in the fear of God".

There is no room for pride or complacency in assembly leaders. It is a work rather than a position: "Take care of the church of God" (1 Tim. 3:5); "feed (tend) the church of God" (Acts 20:28); "which labour among you" (1 Thess. 5:12). That is not to say that assembly leaders are not to be honoured and respected for their work: "Esteem them very highly in love for their work's sake" (1 Thess. 5:12). But to say 'what good elders we are' or 'our assembly is one of the best', is courting disaster. "Yea, all of you be subject one to another, and be clothed with humility: for God resisteth the proud, and giveth grace to the humble" (1 Pet. 5:5). The question is:

> *Is* **He** *satisfied? Is* **He** *satisfied? Is* **He** *satisfied with me?*
> *Have I done my best? will I pass the test?*
> *Is* **He** *satisfied with me?*

b) Self-indulgence, vv.3-6
This section describes the opulence and excesses of the rulers. Self-indulgent leadership will bring destruction. So far as they were concerned "the evil day" was "far away". But in actual fact they were causing "the seat (or 'habitation') of violence to come near" (v.3).

Their action was precipitating calamity. In terms of Israel's future (the northern kingdom), this could refer either to the dark spectre of Assyria, or to the disintegration of the nation after Jeroboam's death. Jeroboam reigned for forty-one years: in the next forty years six kings reigned: **Zechariah** (six months), Jeroboam's son, who died at the hand of **Shallum**; he reigned for one month, and died at the hand of **Menahem**; Menahem reigned for ten years and was guilty of terrible violence: see 2 Kings 15:16: during his reign Pul (Assyria) invaded; Menahem was succeeded by his son **Pekahiah**; he reigned for two years and died at the hand of **Pekah**, who reigned for twenty years, during which Tiglath-pileser (Assyria) invaded, died at the hand of **Hoshea**; Hoshea reigned for nine years, and during his reign Shalmaneser (Assyria) invaded and deported Israel 'lock, stock and barrel'.

A description of the self-indulgence of the leadership follows (vv.4-6): we should notice: *(i)* what interested them (vv.4-6a); *(ii)* what did not interest them (v.6b).

i) What interested them, vv.4-6a
"That lie…stretch themselves…eat…chant…invent…drink…anoint". There is nothing athletic here! Fasting and self-denial are conspicuous by their absence! Bodily wellbeing is placed before godliness. Bodily appetites are paramount. The motto was "Take thine ease, eat drink and be merry" (Luke 12:19). Let's look at it like this:

- "That lie upon beds of ivory and stretch themselves upon their couches" (v.4). There's not a trace of Psalm 4:4, "Stand in awe, and sin not: commune with your own heart upon your bed", or of Psalm 16:7, "My reins also instruct me in the night season", or of Joshua 1:8, "Thou shalt meditate therein ('this book of the law') day and night". Romans 13:11-14 is now compulsory reading.

- "That eat of the lambs out of the flock, and calves out of the midst of the stall" (v.4). Nothing but the best. Only young animals with tender flesh. No mutton! Nothing 'chewy!' No trace of 1 Corinthians 10:31 here: "Whether therefore ye eat or drink, or whatsoever ye do, do all to the glory of God", or 1 Timothy 4:4-5: "For every creature is good, and nothing to be refused, if it be received with thanksgiving: for it is sanctified by the word of God and prayer". Romans 14:17 must now be read.

- "That chant to the sound of the viol ('the lute', JND), and invent to themselves instruments of musick, like David" or 'that sing idle songs to the sound of the viol' (v.5, RV). (Amos would not approve of 'Top of the Pops'). No trace of Ephesians 5:19 here, "Speaking to yourselves in psalms and hymns and spiritual songs, singing and making melody in your heart to the Lord" or 1 Corinthians 14:15, either: "I will sing with the spirit, and I will sing with the understanding also".

- "That drink wine in bowls" (v.6). Looks like a binge: not by the glass, but "in bowls". No trace of Ephesians 5:18 here: "And be not drunk with wine, wherein is excess; but be filled with the Spirit".

- That "anoint themselves with the chief ointments" (v.6). There was nothing of Philippians 4:18 here: "An odour of a sweet smell, a sacrifice acceptable, well-pleasing to God", or of 2 Corinthians 2:15 either: "We are unto God a sweet savour of Christ."

ii) What did not interest them, v6b

They were "not grieved for the affliction of Joseph". (Note other references to Joseph: 5:6, "the house of Joseph"; 5:15, "the remnant of Joseph"). This refers to the way in which Joseph was treated by his brothers: "And they took him, and cast him into a pit...and they sat down to eat bread" (Gen. 37:24); "And they said one to another, we are verily guilty concerning our brother, in that we saw the anguish of his soul when he besought us, and we would not hear" (Gen. 42:21). The word "affliction" carries the idea of 'destruction' or 'breaking'. There was no interest in the care and welfare of others. The rulers were given to self-indulgence. Compare Isaiah 62:9.

Israel's self-indulgent leaders had no care for the overall testimony. They had no interest in others. But what of assembly leaders?

- They are not to be self-indulgent. It could not be said of Israel's leaders: "given to hospitality...not given to wine...not greedy of filthy lucre" (1 Tim. 3:2-3). It should be noted that material prosperity is not in itself censured in scripture: it is a wrong attitude to material prosperity that is censured. So: "But they that *will be* rich ('that will to be rich', margin: set their hearts on being rich) fall into temptation and a snare...for the love of money is the root of all evil: which while some coveted after they have erred from the faith, and pierced themselves through with many sorrows" (1 Tim. 6:9-10).

- They are not to be oblivious of the Lord's people. It could not be said of Israel's leaders, taking "care of the house of God" (1 Tim. 3: 5). Israel's shepherds were certainly living up to Ezekiel's description: "Woe be to the shepherds of Israel that do feed themselves! Should not the shepherds feed the flocks?...The diseased have ye not strengthened, neither have ye healed that which was sick, neither have ye bound up that which was broken, neither have ye brought again that which was driven away, neither have ye sought that which was lost..." (Ezek. 34:2-4). They were quite unlike the "good shepherd" who "giveth his life for the sheep" (John 10:11). The Lord Jesus is not only the "good shepherd", the "great shepherd" (Heb. 13:20), and the "chief shepherd (1 Pet. 5:4), He is the 'pattern shepherd'. "He calleth his own sheep by name, and leadeth them out...he goeth before them...they know his voice". Under His tender care, the sheep "go in and out, and find pasture". Moreover, He continues by saying, "I...know my sheep, and am known of mine" (John 10:3,4, 9, 14). What an example to assembly shepherds!

2) INESCAPABLE JUDGMENT, vv.7-11

Israel's godless society would be utterly destroyed. Not that they would have described themselves as 'godless'. To the contrary, they would argue, they went to great lengths in their worship, but it was "a form of godliness, but denying the power thereof " (2 Tim. 3:5). It was obnoxious to God.

i) Their luxury would end. The wealthy self-indulgent leaders would be the first to be enslaved: "Therefore now shall they go captive with the first that go captive" (v.7). Their feasting and banqueting would come to an end: "The banquet of them that stretched themselves shall be removed" (v.7): instead of stretching themselves on couches, they would trudge away to captivity.

ii) Their pride would be judged. "The Lord (*Adonai*, the Sovereign) GOD (*Jehovah*) hath sworn by himself, saith the LORD (*Jehovah*) the God of hosts (*Elohim Tsebahoth*), I abhor the excellency ('or pride', RV margin: 'pride', JND) of Jacob, and hate his palaces: therefore will I deliver up the city (literally, 'I will shut up the city', by enemy siege', M. F. Unger) with all that is therein" (v.8). Both James and Peter refer to Proverbs 3:34 in saying "God resisteth the proud, but giveth grace to the humble" (James 4:6; 1 Pet. 5:5). In the words of J. A. Motyer, when 'God swears "by himself" He commits the totality of His nature (the holy One, the Redeemer, and Judge), the totality of His status as the world's Sovereign Lord, and the totality of His effective power as the Omnipotent'. He does this in blessing (Heb. 6:13), or in judgment, as here.

iii) Their numbers would be decimated. The horrifying results of the coming siege are described: "And it shall come to pass, if there remain ten men in one house, that they shall die" (v.9). It has been suggested that this is an allusion to Genesis 18:32. The Amplified Version renders vv.10-11 as follows: "And when a man's uncle or kinsman, he who is to make a burning to cremate and dispose [of his pestilence-infected body], comes in to bring the bones out of the house, and shall say to another still alive in the farthest parts of the house, 'Is there anyone else with you?' and he shall say 'No'; then shall the newcomer say 'Hush' hold your [cursing] tongue! We dare not so mention the name of the LORD [lest we invoke more punishment]". M. F. Unger suggests that the survivor in the house is told to hold his tongue from mentioning the name of the Lord with thankful praise, but whatever the exact meaning of the text, one thing is very clear: there is a deep conviction that the Lord is ***against*** them: no longer will they bandy about His name in empty 'worship'.

iv) Their ruin was irresistible. "For, behold, the Lord **commandeth**…and **he** will smite the great house with breaches, and the little house with clefts" (v.11). It should be noted that leaders involve others in their successes and failures. In this case, the doom of the leadership would be shared by those they purport to lead. The big houses of the leaders and the little houses of the ordinary people would both be smashed.

3) IRREVERSIBLE LAW, vv.12-14

"Shall horses run upon the rock? will one plough there with oxen?" We are told by the textual critics that there has been some emendation of the Hebrew text, and that the RSV rendering 'Do horses run upon rocks? Does one plough the sea with oxen?' is 'as sensible and undoubtedly correct' (J. A. Motyer). Once again it has to be said that we should be very cautious when faced with these 'emendations of the text'. However, in this case, the point of the verse is not in doubt. It would be absurd and pointless to reverse natural laws, but they had stupidly reversed the moral law: "Ye have turned judgment into gall, and the fruit of righteousness into hemlock (or 'wormwood', 5:7)". (James 3:8-12) makes a similar comparison.

The result of attempting to use animals on the rocks would be disastrous (for a start, you would injure the horse), and the result of reversing moral laws was equally disastrous. However, there often seems to be some short-term success when God's moral laws are flouted, but in the long-term, judgment must fall:

i)   The short-term. "Ye which rejoice in a thing of nought, which say, Have we not taken to us horns by our own strength?" (v.13). This probably refers to recent military successes of Jeroboam. It is said that there is a play on words here. By treating the Hebrew consonants, two place names emerge, as indicated in the Amplified Version: "Ye who rejoice in Lodebar (or a thing of nought), who say, Have we not by our own strength taken Karnaim (or horns of resistance) for ourselves?" This is called 'paronomasia', and is particularly noticeable in Micah 1:10-15. However, taking the text as it stands, Israel's triumphs were empty: the opposition they had encountered was nothing when compared with the looming might of Assyria (v.14).

ii) The long-term. But such military success would be shortened: the reversal of the moral law would bring inevitable consequences. "Be not deceived; God is not mocked: for whatsoever a man soweth, that shall he also reap" (Gal. 6:7). Hence we read: "But, behold, I will raise up against you a nation (the Assyrians), O house of Israel, saith the LORD, the God of hosts; and they shall afflict you from then entering in of Hamath (in the north) unto the river of the wilderness (in the south - probably near the Gulf of Aquaba: some say, 'the brook of the Arabah')". (v.14).

People face nothing but disaster when they dispense with moral values. Their maintenance ensures continuity and security. "Righteousness exalteth a nation: but sin is a reproach to any people" (Prov.14:34).

READ CHAPTER 7:1-17

"The Lord took me"

This chapter of the book contains an auto-biographical section (vv.10-17). Thus far, we have listened to the preaching of Amos, with more to follow, but our knowledge of the man himself has been rather limited. This is about to change, and what Amos is to tell us about himself contains some most important lessons.

Looking back over the previous chapters, we have noted that the prophecy commences with eight messages (1:1 - 2:16), reminding us that the Lord is in complete command of international affairs. He is not a mere tribal deity. All nations, whether Jew or Gentile, are subject to His control. The prophecy then focuses on Israel, the northern kingdom (although not always exclusively, see 3:1; 6:2), with three messages, all of which commence with the same formula, "Hear this word" (3:1; 4:1; 5:1). The third message, which includes two lamentations (5:1, 16), leads to the pronouncement of "Woe" twice on the nation (5:18; 6:1), and the coming judgment is then portrayed in a series of five visions given to Amos, the first three of which are described in our current chapter (7:1, 4, 7). The remaining two visions are introduced in 8:1 and 9:1, but before we reach them, Amos relates his encounter with Amaziah, the priest of Bethel.

Bearing this in mind, we can divide the chapter as follows: *(1)* the advocacy of Amos (vv.1-9): twice we hear him say, "O Lord GOD...by whom shall Jacob arise, for he is small?" (vv.2, 5); *(2)* the accusations against Amos (vv.10-13): Amaziah's two accusations (vv.10, 11) were not only inaccurate, they were deliberately falsified; *(3)* the answer of Amos (vv.14-17).

1) THE ADVOCACY OF AMOS, vv.1-9
As noted above, the chapter commences with the first three of five visions. In introducing the book, we noticed that of "the five visions, the first four are introduced in the same way: "Thus hath the Lord GOD shewed unto me" (7:1,

7:4, 8:1) or "Thus he shewed me" (7:7). The final vision is introduced by the words, "I saw the Lord" (9:1)". We also noted J. Sidlow Baxter's suggestion that there is a clear progression in their meaning: "Thus, in these five visions we have, successively, judgment averted (grasshoppers), restrained (fire), determined (plumbline), imminent (summer fruit), and executed (the Lord standing upon the altar). The altar in question is at Bethel, not Jerusalem. Jeroboam the son of Nebat established this altar and stood by it (1 Kings 12:32, 13:1). Now the Lord stands on it in judgment". We will look at the three visions here in order. It is often said that the first three visions refer to Assyrian invasions under Pul (2 Kings 15:19), Tiglath-pileser (2 Kings 15:29), and Shalmaneser (2 Kings 17:3), but this is not easily proved. These invasions appear to have taken place after the days of Amos. On the other hand, the visions could be predictive.

a) The first vision, vv.1-3
The details are easily divided: *(i)* the vision itself (v.1); *(ii)* the intercession of Amos (v.2); *(iii)* the response by the Lord (v.3).

i) **The vision itself.** "Thus hath the Lord GOD shewed unto me; and, behold, he formed grasshoppers (probably referring to a variety of locust) in the beginning of the shooting up of the latter growth; and, lo, it was the latter growth after the king's mowings" (v.1). The "king's mowings" were evidently some kind of tax paid to the king. The consumption of the second crop would be disastrous for the common people. According to Deuteronomy 28:38, locusts were evidence of divine discipline. See also Joel 1:1-7; Amos 4:9. The fact that Amos saw God 'forming' the grasshoppers, or locusts, indicates His control of creation. 'He is in absolute control, doing what He will, when He will, and how He will' (R. Catchpole).

ii) **The intercession of Amos**. "And it came to pass, that when they had made an end of eating the grass of the land, then I said, O Lord GOD, forgive, I beseech thee: by whom shall Jacob arise? For he is small" (v.2). Amos had a tender heart, and interceded for God's people. Compare Paul's tears: "For out of much affliction and anguish of heart, I wrote unto you with **many tears**" (2 Cor 2:4). Sometimes we can be so hard!

Richard Catchpole (at Cheshunt 29.06.05) draws attention to the features of Amos' prayer: he prayed **briefly** (see Eccl. 5:1-2); **reverently** ("Lord GOD"); **earnestly** ("O Lord GOD"); **humbly** (no complaint or argument, referring to God's people as 'Jacob' rather than as 'Israel'); **effectively** (God was not indifferent to His prayer, see v.3). It has been suggested that Amos might have referred to God's people as 'Jacob', in view of the promises made to the patriarch himself. See Genesis 28:10-22.

iii) The response by the Lord. "The LORD repented for this: it shall not be, saith the LORD" (v.3). It must be borne in mind that divine repentance is altogether different from human repentance. "God is not a man, that he should lie; neither the son of man, that he should repent" (Num 23:19). However, the Lord does repent! But He does not repent as men and women repent, for the simple reason that He has never done wrong. With the Lord, repentance is either a response consistent with a change of conduct on the part of those threatened with divine judgment, or in response to the intercession of others on the part of those threatened with divine judgment.

God's mercy towards Nineveh is a good example of the first case: "And God saw their works, that they turned from their evil way; and God repented of the evil, that he had said that he would do unto them; and he did it not" (Jonah 3:10). God's mercy towards Israel here is a good example of the second case, to which we can add His mercy towards Israel as the result of the advocacy of Moses: "And the Lord ***repented*** of the evil which he thought to do unto his people" (Exodus 32:14). We should also remember that divine repentance can be exercised in the opposite direction. See Genesis 6:5-7.

Perhaps this is a good opportunity to address the question, 'Does prayer really change things, or will the will of God be done regardless of our prayers? The words, "Known unto God are all his works from the beginning of the world" (Acts 15:18), must be a ***fixed point*** in considering the subject! From the human standpoint, it may appear that the Lord's response to Amos' intercession represents an ***apparent*** change of mind, but in actual fact He acting consistently with His own mercy and grace. Judgment is "his strange work...his strange act" (Isaiah 28:21). See Psalm 106:44-45, "Nevertheless he regarded their affliction, when he heard their cry: and he remembered for them his covenant, and repented according to the multitude of his mercies". He "delighteth in mercy" (Micah 7:18). He delights to answer the prayers of His people in a manner which is consistent with His mercy and grace. Intercession is not a means of bringing about something that God does not want to do! The will of God is accomplished in harmony with the prayers of His people. Prayer is a very wonderful thing!

b) The second vision, vv.4-6

Again, the details are easily divided: *(i)* the vision itself (v.4); *(ii)* the intercession of Amos (v.5); *(iii)* the response by the Lord (v.6).

i) The vision itself. "Thus hath the Lord GOD shewed unto me: and, behold, the Lord GOD called to contend by fire, and it devoured the great deep, and did eat up a part" (v.4). For "the great deep", see Genesis 7:11; 8:12. It evidently refers to the subterranean water reservoirs. This would mean perennial drought. The reference to fire reminds us that "God is a consuming fire" (Deut. 4:24).

ii) The intercession of Amos. "Then said I, O Lord GOD, cease, I beseech thee: by whom shall Jacob arise? For he is small" (v.5). See our comments above (v.2).

iii) The response by the Lord. "The LORD repented for this: This also shall not be, saith the Lord GOD" (v.6).

c) The third vision, vv.7-9

Once again, the details are easily divided: *(i)* the vision itself (v.7); *(ii)* the interpretation by the Lord (v.8); *(iii)* the imminence of judgment (v.9).

i) The vision itself. "Thus he shewed me: and, behold, the Lord stood upon a wall made by a plumbline, with a plumbline in his hand" (v.7)

ii) The interpretation by the Lord. "Amos, what seest thou? And I said, A plumbline. Then said the Lord, Behold, I will set a plumbline in the midst of my people Israel: I will not again pass by them any more" (v.8). The Lord "stood upon a wall made by a plumbline" (that is, on the basis of perfect righteousness), with a plumbline in his hand" (that is, He measured His people by the standard of perfect righteousness), and His people had come to the point at which He could "not again pass by them any more." No more prayer. They had 'sinned unto death' (1 John 5:16). Compare Jeremiah 7:16, "Therefore pray not for this people...for I will not hear thee".

iii) The imminence of judgment. "And the high places of Isaac shall be desolate, and the sanctuaries of Israel shall be laid waste; and I will rise against the house of Jeroboam with the sword" (v.9). The reference to Isaac strongly suggests that since, like Isaac, they were the people of the promise, they thought that they were quite immune from judgment. It was an attitude that said, 'This could never happen to *us*! See also v.16.

2) THE ACCUSATIONS AGAINST AMOS, vv.10-13
In these verses we should notice *(a)* what Amaziah said to Jeroboam (vv.10-11); *(b)* what Amaziah said to Amos (vv.12-13).

a) What Amaziah said to Jeroboam, vv.10-11
i) "Then Amaziah the priest of Bethel sent to Jeroboam king of Israel, saying, Amos hath conspired against *thee* in the midst of the house of Israel: the land is not able to bear all his words" (v.10). Amaziah totally *misrepresented* Amos: he made no reference to the fact that Amos was the Lord's messenger (vv.8-9). He depicted Amos as just a 'rabble-raiser' from Judah!

ii) "For thus Amos saith, Jeroboam shall die by the sword, and Israel shall surely be led away captive out of their own land" (v.11). Amaziah *misquoted* Amos. The prophet actually said that the Lord would "rise against *the house* of Jeroboam with the sword" (v.9). Jeroboam "slept with his fathers" (2 Kings 14:29), but Zachariah, his son, was assassinated by Shallum (2 Kings 15:8-10). God's word, as ever, was marked by pin-point accuracy! Paul was misrepresented and misquoted. See, for example, Romans 3:8. So was the Lord Jesus. See, for example, Mark 14:57-58. We can expect the same.

b) What Amaziah said to Amos, vv.12-13
"O thou seer, go, flee thee away into the land of Judah, and there eat bread, and prophesy there: But prophesy not again any more at Bethel: for it is the king's chapel (sanctuary), and it is the king's court (JND, 'the house of the kingdom')". It was a religious ban imposed by a false priest. The religious world today says in effect, "Flee away". But we face worse. Amaziah said, "Go, flee thee away into the land of Judah, and *there* eat bread, and prophesy *there*". He made no attempt to extend the ban and silence Amos in Judah as well. This is not the case today. In the name of 'political correctness', which is nothing but a front for satanic opposition, we can expect attempts to silence all who preach the Gospel and who maintain the sacred truths of Scripture. In effect, Amos told Amaziah: "We ought to obey God rather than men" (Acts 5:29) and that may well have to be our position in the not too distant future.

3) THE ANSWER OF AMOS, vv.14-17
We may divide the prophet's answer into three sections: *(a)* his circumstances (v.14); *(b)* his calling (v.14); *(c)* his commission (v.15-17).

a) His circumstances, v.14

"I was no prophet, neither was I a prophet's son; but I was an herdman, and a gatherer (cultivator) of sycomore fruit (the fig-like fruit of a tree resembling a mulberry in form and foliage): and the LORD took me as I followed the flock" (vv.14-15). (The word "herdman" means 'shepherd' in 1:1, but 'ploughman' in 7:14). Amos was a countryman, and his rural background can be seen in his preaching. He refers, for example, to "a cart...full of sheaves" (2:13), a trap set for birds (3:5) and a shepherd taking "out of the mouth of the lion two legs, or a piece of an ear" (3:12). Amos had no pretensions or delusions of grandeur about himself. He had:

i) No formal training. "I was no prophet". He had no connection with the schools of the prophets which certainly existed at the time. Reference is made to "the sons of the prophets" at Bethel and elsewhere in the days of Elijah and Elisha (2 Kings 2:3; 4:38).

ii) No family tradition. "Neither was I a prophet's son." Amos was not a prophet himself, and did not spring from a prophetic family.

We therefore learn that it is not where a man comes from that is important, but where a man is going. Abraham came from Ur of the Chaldees, and was evidently an idol-worshipper! Saul of Tarsus was the arch-persecutor of the church! It is important to remember that whilst a Christian family background is a great privilege, believers without that background are not necessarily disadvantaged.

Although Amos appeared to be quite unqualified as God's spokesman he was able to speak with authority: "But the **LORD took me** as I followed the flock". As J. Sidlow Baxter observes, Amos 'is a great encouragement to thousands of Christians today who have had no academic or theological training. God is sovereign in His choice of servants. He is not tied to any bishop's hands. He is not bound to any set of officials. He is not restricted in His workings to any recognized ministerial order'. The only authority which Amos possessed was His calling by God, but it was the highest authority in the universe.

This illustrates 1 Cor 1:26-27, "For ye see your calling, brethren, how that not many wise men after the flesh, not many mighty, not many noble, are called. **But God hath chosen** the foolish things of the world to confound the wise; and **God hath chosen** the weak things of the world to confound the things that are mighty; and base things of the world, and things which are despised **hath God chosen**: yea, and things which are not, to bring to nought things that are, that **no flesh should glory in his presence**".

b) His calling, v.14
Amos therefore recognised the sovereign hand of God, and was deeply convicted of his place in God's purposes: "But the **LORD took me** as I followed the flock". The call and commission of Amos were his only credentials. As already noted, he received no formal training: "I was no prophet". The call of God was firmly established in his heart. This will give us boldness in the face of opposition. As we have seen, Amos faced religious opposition (vv.10-13), but he was certainly bold! See vv.16-17.

For ourselves, the calling and commission of God do not necessarily involve a spectacular burst into the public eye. In fact, it is seldom like that at all! But at the same time our calling should have a transforming effect in our lives. See, for example 1 Pet 2:9, "But ye are a chosen generation, a royal priesthood, an holy nation, a peculiar people, that ye should shew forth the praises of him that hath **called you** out of darkness into his marvelous light"; 2 Tim.1:8-9, "Be not thou therefore ashamed of the testimony of our Lord, nor of me his prisoner: but be thou partaker of the afflictions of the gospel according to the power of God; who hath saved us, and called us with an holy **calling,** not according to our works, but according to his own purpose and grace, which was given us in Christ Jesus before the world began." We should notice:

i) "The **LORD** took me". This is the divine title *Jehovah*. The name embraces the past, present and future, although not in that order. 'It is a combination in marvellous perfect of the three periods of existence in one word, the future, the present, and the past. First, *Yehi*, "he will be" (long tense). Second, *hove*, "being", participle. Third, *hahyah*, "he was", short tense used in the past' (Thomas Newberry). Compare Rev. 1:4, "Grace be to you and peace, from him which is, and which was, and which is to come; and from the seven spirits which are before his throne". See also Rev. 4:8. The Lord Jesus is "the same yesterday, and today, and for ever" (Heb. 13:8).

The words, "And the **LORD** took me", therefore emphasise the greatness of God. Amos was deeply conscious of the grandeur and majesty of "the living and true God" who had called him. The God of Amos is *our* God. How much do *we* appreciate His greatness and glory?

ii) "The LORD *took me*". This speaks of possession. Like Amos, we belong to Him. We are not our own, but "bought with a price" (1 Cor. 6:20). Paul's desire was to "apprehend that for which I am apprehended of Christ Jesus" (Phil. 3:12). The word "apprehended" means 'to lay hold of; then, to lay hold of so as to possess as one's own, to appropriate' (W. E. Vine). We must not miss the amazing contrast here. "The **LORD** took *me*..." It is intensely personal. Is it too much to say that Amos said this with a deep sense of wonder in his heart and voice? Surely we can be forgiven if this seems a little speculative! There was certainly a sense of wonder in Paul's mind and heart in Ephesians 3:8 and Galatians 2:20.

We could expand this by saying, 'The LORD took me as I was' and 'used me as I am'. Amos did not become a robot. God did not obliterate his personality. The book begins, "The words of **Amos**...thus saith the **LORD**" (1:1, 3). Although the message came from the Lord, it was expressed in the words of Amos. He was a countryman, and his preaching discloses his rural background. This reminds us that God does not 'carbon-copy' his servants. He uses people with different personalities and different backgrounds. We must be ourselves in the service of God! It has been nicely said that 'God makes originals, not duplicates!' In the words of W.T.P. Wolston, 'Nobody can preach like me, and I can't preach like anybody else!'

iii) "The LORD took me *as I followed the flock*". One qualification for Christian service, whether this involves leaving secular occupation or not, is diligence in daily work. Believers should regard their secular work as service for God. See Col. 3:22-23; "Servants, obey in all things your masters according to the flesh; not with eyeservice as men pleasers, but in singleness of heart, fearing God; knowing that of the Lord ye shall receive the reward of the inheritance; for *ye serve the Lord Christ."*

c) His commission, v.15-17
i) In general terms. "And the LORD said unto me, *Go prophesy* unto my people Israel" (v.15). This was not 'an optional extra' for Amos, but a divine command. This involved consecrated feet ("go") and consecrated lips ("prophesy"). Compare Matthew 28:19, "*Go* ye therefore, and *teach* (make disciples) all nations".

This involved communion with God, for the true prophet "stood in the counsel of the LORD, and hath perceived and heard his word" (Jer. 23:18). The false prophets "speak a vision of their own heart, and not out of the mouth of the

LORD" (v.16). As a true prophet, Amos could say, "Surely the Lord GOD will do nothing, but he revealeth his secret unto his servants the prophets. The lion hath roared, who will not fear? The Lord GOD hath spoken, who can but prophesy?" (Amos 3:7-8). The "prophets and teachers" at Antioch were in the same position: "As they ministered unto the Lord and fasted, the Holy Ghost said, Separate me Barnabas and Saul for the work whereunto I have called them" (Acts 13:1-2).

ii) In particular terms. "And the LORD said, Go, prophesy unto my people *Israel*" (v.15). Amos was sent away from Tekoa (in Judah) to Israel in the north. This is clear from the beginning: "The words of Amos, who was among the herdmen of Tekoa, which he saw concerning Israel" (1:1). Amos was not sent to his native Judah or, like Jonah, to Nineveh. His preaching was not directed, like Obadiah's, against Edom. We must therefore notice:

- **The sphere of the servant.** Amos was appointed to a specific sphere of service: "my people *Israel*". Compare 1 Cor. 12:18, "But now hath God set the members every one of them in the body, as it hath pleased him". This does not mean that we have no interest in other spheres of service and it is worth pointing out that the ministry of Amos took note of the entire situation. Hence references to Judah (see, for example, 2:4-5) and to the "whole family" 3:1). The apostles at Jerusalem had a deep interest in the service of Paul and Barnabas: "when they saw that the gospel of the uncircumcision was committed unto me, as the gospel of the circumcision was unto Peter…they gave to me and Barnabas **the right hands of fellowship**; that we should go unto the heathen, and they unto the circumcision" (Gal. 2:7-9). A man with conviction about his calling and commission from God will not be given to compromise or be easily diverted from his service

- **The heart of the servant.** "Go, prophesy unto *my* people Israel". How often we forget that our fellow-believers are **God's** people! This does not mean that we are obliged to agree with every view and every practice amongst believers. But our hard-hearted attitudes would be softened if we remembered that every child of God is precious to Him. It was this that engendered an interceding heart within Amos (see vv.1-6).

- **The faithfulness of the servant.** His obedience to the divinely-given commission is evident from his words, "Now therefore hear thou the word of the LORD…Therefore thus saith the LORD" (vv.16-17). It is always necessary to refer back to our authority, and to be true to it. In his divinely-appointed sphere of service, Amos proved faithful. He did not shrink from unpalatable ministry (compare 1 Sam. 3:17): "Now therefore hear thou the word of the LORD: Thou sayest, Prophesy not against Israel, and drop not thy word against the house of Isaac (see comments at v.9). Therefore thus saith the LORD; Thy wife shall be an harlot in the city, and thy sons and thy daughters shall fall by the sword, and thy land shall be divided by line; and thou shalt die in a polluted land: and Israel shall surely go into captivity forth of his land".

Like John the Baptist, Amos was no "reed shaken with the wind" (Luke 7:24). He did not bow under pressure from anybody, and he certainly didn't vary his preaching to suit his audience. Like John, who called the Pharisees and Sadducees "a generation of vipers", Amos was not intimidated by the religious fraternity. He was not "tossed to and fro, and carried about with every wind of doctrine" (Eph. 4:14). John said, "He that sent me...said unto me" (John 1:33) and Amos said, "The LORD took me...and the LORD said unto me". Both men met opposition head on with this conviction.

When the pressure begins to mount on us, will we do the same?

READ CHAPTER 8:1-14

"I will send a famine in the land"

Throughout his preaching, Amos had constantly warned of coming captivity: "An adversary there shall be even round about the land; and he shall bring down thy strength from thee, and thy palaces shall be spoiled" (3:11); "But ye have borne the tabernacle of your Moloch and Chuin…Therefore will I cause you to go into captivity beyond Damascus" (5:27); "I will raise up against you a nation…and they shall afflict you" (6:14); "Israel shall surely go into captivity forth of his land" (7:17).

Chapters 8 & 9 bring us to the edge of that captivity, and then take us beyond it. The two chapters may be summarised as follows: *(i)* retribution on the land (8:1-14); *(ii)* removal from the land (9:1-10); *(iii)* restoration to the land (9:11-15).

This chapter may be divided as follows: *(1)* the sign of coming retribution (vv.1-3); *(2)* the causes of coming retribution (vv.4-6); *(3)* the certainty of coming retribution (v.7); *(4)* the description of coming retribution (vv.8-14).

1) THE SIGN OF COMING RETRIBUTION, vv.1-3
"Thus hath the Lord GOD (*Adonahy Jehovah*) shewed unto me: and behold a basket of summer fruit" (v.1). This is the fourth of five visions given to Amos in chapters 7-9, and it might be helpful at this juncture to recall them again. As we have already noted twice in these studies, J. Sidlow Baxter observes that there is a clear progression in their meaning: "judgment averted (grasshoppers: 7:1-3); restrained (fire: 7:4-6); determined (plumbline: 7:7-9); imminent (summer fruit: 8:1-3); executed (the Lord standing on the altar: 9:1-10)". It is significant that the third and fourth visions, which have a common theme ("I will not again pass by them any more") are separated by the total rejection of the word of God and the servant of God (7:10-13). Israel's judgment was sealed by their rejection of God's word. As Peter C. Craigie observes, 'One can in fact practise evil so persistently that a death

sentence is inevitably proclaimed... For a short time in his ministry Amos had been able to say: "Seek ye the LORD, and ye shall live" (5:6). Now all he could say was "It's too late; you must die"'.

Israel's national history began with the words, "When I see the blood, *I will pass over you*, and the plague shall not be upon you to destroy you" (Exodus 12:13). Centuries went by, during which the Lord had faithfully spoken to His people: "Since the day that your fathers came forth out of the land of Egypt unto this day, I have even sent unto you all my servants the prophets, daily rising up early, and sending them" (Jer. 7:25). But now, after all that time, He has to say, "I will not again *pass by them* any more". What a sad testimony to Israel's perpetual waywardness!

The chapter therefore commences with imminent judgment. Harvest time had come, reminding us of the oft-quoted words, "The harvest is past, the summer is ended, and we are not saved" (Jer. 8:20). In common with the third vision (7:7-9), the solemn pronouncement is made as noted above: "The end is come upon my people of Israel; *I will not again pass by them any more*" (v.2). Amos makes no further intercession. It is as if the Lord had said to him, "Therefore pray not thou for this people...for I will not hear thee" (Jer. 7:16). Israel had 'sinned unto death' (1 John 5:16).

We usually think of harvest as a time of rejoicing: "He that goeth forth and weepeth, bearing precious seed, shall doubtless come again with rejoicing, bringing his sheaves with him" (Psalm 126:6). But we should also remember that the law of sowing and reaping operates banefully as well as beneficially. This is clearly expressed in the New Testament: "Be not deceived; God is not mocked: for whatsoever a man soweth, that shall he also reap. For he that soweth to his flesh shall of the flesh reap corruption; but he that soweth to the Spirit shall of the Spirit reap life everlasting. And let us not be weary in well doing: for in due season we shall reap, if we faint not" (Gal. 6:7-9).

Harvest, as an emblem of judgment, is solemnly depicted in Revelation 14:14-20: "And I looked, and behold a white cloud, and upon the cloud one sat like unto the Son of man, having on his head a golden crown, and in his hand a sharp sickle. And another angel came out of the temple, crying with a loud voice to him that sat on the cloud, Thrust in thy sickle, and reap: for the time has come for thee to reap; for the harvest of the earth is ripe. And he that sat on the cloud thrust in his sickle on the earth; and the earth was reaped".

Normally, "a basket of summer fruit" would have been a pleasant sight, but on this occasion Amos was told that it was a picture of Israel. The "basket of summer fruit" was ready for eating, and Israel was ripe for judgment. The Lord would spare them no longer. Like the fruit in the basket, they would be consumed. Instead of "joy in harvest" (Isaiah 9:3), the harvest here would resemble the downfall of Damascus: "In the day shalt thou make thy plant to grow, and in the morning shalt thou make thy seed to flourish: but the harvest shall be a heap in the day of grief and desperate sorrow" (Isaiah 17:11). It would certainly be a time of "desperate sorrow" for Israel: "And the songs of the temple shall be howlings in that day, saith the Lord GOD: there shall be many dead bodies in every place; they shall cast them forth with silence" (v.3). 'So great would be the slaughter that it would be impossible to have the customary rites, much less the professional mourners' (M. F. Unger).

It has been pointed out that there is evidently a play here on words of a similar sound in Hebrew: "behold a basket of summer fruit (*qayis*)...The end (*qes*) is come upon my people Israel" (vv.1-2). On a technical note, we would normally associate the word "temple" ('palace', RV/JND) with the temple in Jerusalem, but here it evidently refers to "the king's chapel ('sanctuary', JND)" at Bethel (7:13).

2) THE CAUSES OF COMING RETRIBUTION, vv.4-6
These can be summarised as follows: *(a)* God's people were maltreated (v.4); *(b)* God's interests were a nuisance (v.5); *(c)* God's laws were flouted (vv.5-6).

a) God's people were maltreated, v.4
"Hear this, O ye that swallow up the needy, even to make the poor (*ani*, emphasising their oppression) of the land to fail". The business barons treated the poor "as means and not ends... something to become the means of the highest possible profits" (J. A. Motyer). The wording of this verse makes appalling reading: "Ye that swallow up the needy, even to make the poor of the land to fail", meaning to do away with them by appropriating what little they possessed. J. A. Motyer suggests that Amos sees 'this class - the class of independent but unaffluent people - simply disappearing from the land'. The law 'called upon God's people to extend an open hand of generosity to the poor (Deut. 15:7-11; cf. Psalm 72:12-13), but the stingy Israelites were trying to eliminate them' (supplied by J. Waldron).

As we noted in connection with a similar passage in 5:11, there was no "care one for another" (1 Cor. 12:25), reminding us that assemblies should be caring communities: see James 2:15-16; 1 John 3:17-18. How much do *we* really care about the welfare of fellow-believers?

b) God's interests were a nuisance, v.5
"When will the new moon be gone, that we may sell corn? and the sabbath that we may set forth wheat?" The Lord's interests got in the way of the main purpose in life of the big businessmen. Their overriding objective was to make money. 'These oppressors were eager for the monthly festivals (the new moons) and the weekly sabbaths to end so that they could get back to work cheating their fellow-countrymen and making big profits. These holidays were days of rest and worship, but the Israelite workaholics did not enjoy them, though they observed them (nominally) as good religious people' (supplied by J. Waldron).

These people had their counterparts in the days of Malachi: "Ye said also, Behold, what a weariness is it! (the necessity for sacrifice) and ye have snuffed at it, saith the LORD of hosts" (Mal. 1:13). What place do God's interests have in *our* lives? Do we just keep up appearances? Do the demands (privileges do mean responsibilities) of assembly fellowship cause us resentment and frustration? It would be very sad if it could be said of us, "This people draweth nigh unto me with their mouth, and honoureth me with their lips; but their heart is far from me" (Matt. 15:8). This was certainly the case here. They evidently observed the new moons, marking the beginning of the months, and the sabbaths, but their hearts were elsewhere. Centuries later, the apostle John wrote, "For this is the love of God, that we keep his commandments: and his commandments are not grievous (*barus*, meaning 'burdensome')" (1 John 5:3). On this basis, the business barons in Israel had no love for God!

There is something terribly wrong if any of the Lord's people treat His word as a nuisance. If this is the case, we have grounds, surely, for querying their possession of spiritual life. The believer will gladly hearken to the Lord's voice in saying, "This book of the law shall not depart out of thy mouth; but thou shalt meditate therein day and night, that thou mayest observe to do according to all that is written therein: for then shalt thou make thy way prosperous, and then shalt thou have good success" (Joshua 1:8). For God's people, His word should be the very essence of life, enabling them to say with Job, "I have esteemed the words of his mouth more than my necessary food" (Job 23:12).

c) God's laws were flouted, vv.5-6

i) There was commercial malpractice. "Making the ephah small, and the shekel great, and falsifying the balances by deceit". The Lord had said, through Moses, "Ye shall do no unrighteousness in judgment, in meteyard, in weight, or in measure. Just balances, just weights, a just ephah, and a just hin, shall ye have" (Lev. 19:35-36); "Thou shalt not have in thy bag divers weights, a great and a small. Thou shalt not have in thine house divers measures, a great and a small. But thou shalt have a perfect and a just weight, a perfect and just measure shalt thou have" (Deut. 25:13-15). See also Proverbs 16:11, "A just weight and balance are the LORD'S: all the weights of the bag are his work". But the businessmen had double standards: they carefully observed certain religious requirements, but conveniently overlooked commercial requirements. It has been said that archaeologists working at Tirzah found the remains of shops from the eighth century B.C. containing two sets of weights, one for buying and one for selling (supplied by J. Waldron). The Lord Jesus evicted "those that sold oxen and sheep and doves, and the changers of money" from the temple on two occasions (John 2:13-17, with Matt.21:12-13; Mark 11:15-18; Luke 19:45-46). On the second occasion, he charged the businessmen with turning the temple into "a den of thieves". Nothing had changed in eight hundred years.

ii) There was social malpractice. "That we may buy the poor for silver, and the needy for a pair of shoes". The "poor" and the needy" had become a trading commodity. In the words of J. A. Motyer, 'the poor *(dal)* were every bit a piece of merchandise as the nearest sack of grain'. The business barons were opportunistic - they were in the slave-trade! They trod on people as they mounted the league-table of the wealthy. There was no care - no concern - no sharing - just inhumanity. The words, "that we may buy the poor for silver, and the needy for a pair of shoes" evidently refer to selling people into slavery for 'paltry debts, such as that for a pair of shoes' (J. A. Motyer). The principle, "Bear ye one another's burdens, and so fulfil the law of Christ" (Gal. 6:2), was conspicuously absent. There was no trace of being "kind one to another, tenderhearted" (Eph. 4:32).

3) THE CERTAINTY OF COMING RETRIBUTION, v.7

"The LORD hath sworn by the excellency of Jacob, Surely I will never forget any of their works" (v.7). This is the third time in the book of Amos that the Lord confirms His intentions with an oath: compare 4:2; 6:8. In all three cases He affirms His intention to act in judgment. In the first case, He swears "by his holiness"; in the second, "by himself"; in the third, "by the excellency ('glory', JND) of Jacob", which is probably best understood as reference to the pride of the nation. There are other interpretations. It is suggested that the divinely-taken oath here is as certain and enduring as Israel's pride. On the basis of this interpretation, the words "The LORD hath sworn by the excellency of Jacob", are deeply ironical and at the same time, a terrible indictment. Support for this interpretation may be found in 6:8, "The Lord Jehovah hath sworn by himself, saith Jehovah, the God of hosts, I abhor the *pride* of Jacob, and hate his palaces". The word translated "excellency" (*gaon*) in Amos 6:8; 8:7 is often rendered "pride" in the Old Testament.

It is a chilling vow: "Surely I will never forget any of their works". Unregenerate men and women will prove this to be true on judgment day: "And I saw the dead, small and great, stand before God; and the books were opened: and another book was opened, which is the book of life: and the dead were judged out of those things which were written in the books, according to their works" (Rev. 20:12). Saved people rejoice that it is written, "their sins and their iniquities will I remember no more" (Heb. 8:12). Of the Lord's people it can be said, "God is not unrighteous to forget your work and labour of love, which ye have shewed toward his name, in that ye have ministered to the saints, and do minister" (Heb. 6:10). But even so, believers "must all appear before the judgment seat of Christ; that every one may receive the things done in his body, according to that he hath done, whether it be good or bad" (2 Cor 5:10).

4) THE DESCRIPTION OF COMING RETRIBUTION, vv.8-14
Amos describes the effect of divine retribution in four ways: *(a)* there would be no escape from judgment (v.8); *(b)* there would be no joy in the nation (vv.9-10); *(c)* there would be no word from God (vv.11-13); *(d)* there would be no future for the nation (v.14).

a) There would be no escape from judgment, v.8
Coming judgment is likened to a massive flood, resulting in the total inundation of the land. The Lord would visit His people with irresistible and overflowing judgment: "Shall not the land tremble for this, and every one mourn that dwelleth therein? And it shall rise up wholly as a flood; and it shall be cast out and drowned, as by the flood of Egypt" (v.8). Peter C. Craigie takes this literally and suggests that the verse refers to a still future earthquake whose effects will resemble the Nile in flood. However, it does seem better to take this verse figuratively. The Assyrian invasion of Judah is described in this way: "Behold, the LORD bringeth up upon them the waters

of the river, strong and many, even the king of Assyria...and he shall pass through Judah; he shall overflow and go over, he shall reach even to the neck; and the stretching out of his wings shall fill the breadth of thy land. O Immanuel" (Isaiah 8:7-8).

b) There would be no joy in the nation, vv.9-10

"And it shall come to pass in that day, saith the Lord GOD, that I will cause the sun to go down at noon, and I will darken the earth in the clear day" (v.9). It is not easy to decide whether this is literal or figurative. Both Old and New Testaments certainly refer to darkness as the precursor of imminent judgment. Here are two examples: "And when I shall put thee out (referring to Pharaoh), I will cover the heaven, and make the stars thereof dark; I will cover the sun with a cloud, and the moon shall not give her light. All the bright lights of heaven will I make dark over thee, and set darkness upon thy land, saith the Lord GOD" (Ezek. 32:7-8); "Immediately after the tribulation of those days shall the sun be darkened, and the moon shall not give her light....and then shall appear the sign of the Son of man in heaven" (Matt. 24:29-30).

On the other hand, Jeremiah uses similar language which is evidently figurative: "She that hath borne seven languisheth: she hath given up the ghost; her sun is gone down while it was yet day" (Jer. 15:9). It has been said that 'the figure of the sun going down' at noon was particularly appropriate since Jereboam's reign was the zenith of Israel's prosperity, power, and glory' (supplied by J. Waldron).

Support for the figurative interpretation lies in the way the passage proceeds. Having said, "I will darken the earth in the clear day", the Lord continues: "And I will turn your feasts into mourning, and all your songs into lamentation; and I will bring sackcloth upon all loins, and baldness upon every head; and I will make it as the mourning of an only son, and the end thereof as a bitter day" (v.10). Just as an eclipse of the sun brings immediate darkness, so divine judgment would bring misery upon the nation. The 'melody of their viols' (5:23) would give place to mourning. Darkness would fall on the land. It has been pertinently observed that 'if we really desire the light of God's countenance to shine upon us, then we must walk in the light' (Peter C. Craigie). These people walked in darkness, and darkness fell upon them. Joy comes from obedience: "If ye keep my commandments, ye shall abide in my love, even as I have kept my Father's commandments, and abide in his love. These things have I spoken unto you, that my joy might remain in you, and that your joy might be full" (John 15:10-11).

We cannot leave these verses, which refer to divine judgment upon Israel, without recalling that centuries later divine judgment fell, not on Israel, but upon Israel's Messiah. On that occasion, God caused "the sun to go down at noon", and darkened "the earth in a clear day". According to Luke, "about the sixth hour (noon)…there was darkness over all the earth until the ninth hour. And the sun was darkened" (Luke 23:44-45). It was, again, "as the mourning of an only son, and the end thereof as a bitter day". In the words of the New Testament, "For God so loved the world that he gave his only-begotten Son" (John 3:16). We reverently sing:

> *Well might the sun in darkness hide*
> *And shut his glories in,*
> *When the Incarnate Maker died*
> *For man His creature's sin*

We should also remember that at His return that nation will look upon the very Messiah they rejected, "and they shall mourn for him, as one mourneth for his only son, and shall be in bitterness for him, as one that is in bitterness for his firstborn" (Zech. 12:10).

c) There would be no word from God, vv.11-13
"Behold, the days come, saith the Lord GOD, that I will send a famine in the land, not a famine of bread, nor a thirst for water, but of hearing the words of the LORD: and they shall wander from sea (the Mediterranean Sea) to sea (the Dead Sea), and from the north even to the east, they shall run to and fro to seek the word of the LORD, and shall not find it. In that day shall the fair virgins and young men faint for thirst". Quite clearly, v.13 refers to the thirst for the word of God. See v.11: "I will send a famine in the land, **not** a famine of bread, **nor** a thirst for water, but of **hearing the words of the LORD**". No reference is made to the south: that would involve going to the place where the Lord placed His name! There is a significant progression in vv.11-14: "They shall **wander** (meaning to shake and stagger under affliction)…they shall **run** (in panic: suddenly the word of God becomes valuable)…they shall **fall** (it is all too late)" (vv.12, 14).

The Lord had spoken to the nation, but His word had been rejected (see, for example, 2:11-12; 7:10-13). Now God is silent. Compare the following: "And the word of the Lord was precious (rare) in those days, there was no open vision" (1 Sam. 3:1); "And when Saul enquired of the LORD, the LORD answered him not" (1 Sam. 28:6); "We see not our signs: there is no more any prophet: neither is there among us any that knoweth how long" (Psalm 74:9). What a dreadful situation! As M.F.Unger observes, 'The famine of the word of God was a just retribution for those who had so blatantly turned a deaf ear to the words of the prophets'. Can *we* expect to hear God's voice if we fail to obey His word? The very question carries its own answer.

It should be noted that the younger generation is singled out for particular mention (v.13). The older generation had deprived the younger generation from finding and knowing the truth. What a terrible indictment on the older generation! We must never forget the need for spiritual succession. Read 2 Timothy 2:2.

d) There would be no hope for the nation, v.14
"They that swear by the sin of Samaria, and say, Thy god, O Dan, liveth; and, The manner of Beer-sheba liveth; even they shall fall, and never rise up again". The people who had misled the younger generation, and who had done nothing to help them find joy and satisfaction in worshipping the true God, would face utter ruin.

"The sin of Samaria" (the capital of Israel, and standing for the nation as a whole) was the erection of the golden calves in the land (1 Kings 12:28-30; Hosea 10:5). The word "sin" here (*ashmah*) means 'guilt', although some commentators like to alter the wording of the Hebew text to make it read 'that swear by *Ashimah* of Samaria', which refers to a Canaanite goddess (see 2 Kings 17:30). J. A. Motyer calls this 'a slight and sensible emendation', but the text makes perfectly good sense without trying to alter it! No wonder "the fair virgins and young men faint for thirst" when the people cry, not "The Lord liveth", but "Thy god, O Dan, liveth: and, The manner (the way of doing things) of Beer-sheba liveth". One of the two golden calves erected by Jeroboam was located and worshipped at Dan (see 1 Kings 12:29-30). Interestingly enough, Beer-sheba (see also 5:5) was located in Judah, so some kind of pilgrimage south was involved. As J. A. Motyer observes, 'Religion as such (v.14) can only lead to the eternal loss of falling and never rising. But by contrast those who live by the Word live for ever'.

READ CHAPTER 9:1-15

"The plowman shall overtake the reaper"

We have already noted that Amos Chapters 8 & 9 bring us to the edge of coming captivity, and then take us beyond it, and that the two chapters may be summarised as follows: *(i)* retribution on the land (8:1-14); *(ii)* removal from the land (9:1-10); *(iii)* restoration to the land (9:11-15).

1) RETRIBUTION ON THE LAND, 8:1-14
In studying these verses, we noted the following: *(a)* the sign of coming retribution (vv.1-3); *(b)* the causes of coming retribution (vv.4-6); *(c)* the certainty of coming retribution (v7); *(d)* the description of coming retribution (vv.8-14). This brings us to:

2) REMOVAL FROM THE LAND, 9:1-10
This section of the chapter commences with the last of the five visions given to Amos (see 7:1-3; 7:4-6; 7:8-9; 8:1-3; 9:1), and may be divided as follows: *(a)* the execution of judgment (v.1); *(b)* the inescapability of judgment (vv.2-4); *(c)* the guarantor of judgment (vv.5-6); *(d)* the universality of judgment (vv.7-8); *(e)* the purpose of judgment (vv.9-10).

a) The execution of judgment, v.1
"I saw the Lord standing upon the altar ('by the altar', RV): and he said, Smite the lintel of the door, that the posts may shake: cut them in the head, all of them; and I will slay the last of them with the sword". Isaiah "saw the Lord sitting upon a throne, high and lifted up, and his train filled the temple" (Isaiah 6:1). Like Amos, he was to proclaim divine judgment upon God's people (Isaiah 6:9-12) and, like Amos (see v.9), he was to reveal that a remnant in the nation would be preserved (Isaiah 6:13).

There can be little doubt that in the vision here, the altar seen by Amos was Jeroboam's altar, rather than the altar in the temple at Jerusalem. Jeroboam, the son of Nebat, established this altar at Bethel in order to consolidate his kingdom (Israel in the north, as opposed to Judah in the south) and to ensure that his subjects did not gravitate to Jerusalem to worship the Lord. He therefore established a rival religion, with its own altar, feasts and priesthood, all centred on the golden calves, of which he said, "Behold thy gods, O Israel, which brought thee up out of the land of Egypt". The whole miserable story is found in 1 Kings 12:25-33. Events surrounding Jeroboam's altar are detailed in 1 Kings 13:1-10.

In this connection it is significant to note that "Jeroboam...offered upon the altar ('went up to the altar', margin)...so he offered upon the altar ('went up to the altar', margin)" (1 Kings 12:31-32). More particularly, we are told that Jeroboam "stood by the altar to burn incense" (1 Kings 13:1) and at the very moment that an apostate king stood by a rival altar, "a man of God" came from Judah and "cried against the altar in ('by', JND) the word of the LORD" (1 Kings 13:2). It is not without significance that, centuries later, when another king of the same name, Jeroboam (Amos 1:1; 7:10), was on the throne of Israel, that another "man of God" came from Judah to condemn Israel's false religion. But instead of an apostate king standing by the altar, Amos saw "the Lord (*Adonahy*, the Sovereign Lord) standing on (or, 'standing by') the altar". In the words of J. A. Motyer, 'The counterfeit is replaced by the real, the human by the divine, the king who had come to prop up his dynasty by the King who had come to throw it down'.

The command, "Smite the lintel of the door, that the posts may shake: cut them in the head, all of them", evidently refers to the idol temple in Bethel. See 1 Kings 12:31, "He (Jeroboam) made an house of high places, and made priests of the lowest of the people, which were not of the sons of Levi". It is tempting to say that while blood was placed on the lintels of the houses in Egypt (Exodus 12:22), affording protection from divine judgment, there was no such protection here. But, to the disappointment of the eager expositor (!), the word "lintel" here is quite different to the "lintel" in Exodus 12:22-23. We would call them the 'capitals' or heads of the columns. The "posts" are in fact the 'thresholds'. J. A. Motyer puts it all together like this: 'When the Sovereign calls up His forces, the building receives great shattering blows from above, on the *capitals,* driving them down upon their own *thresholds,* until the whole edifice crumbles on its occupants' *heads.* Many rush away from the downfall, but none escape'. "He that fleeth of them shall not flee away, and he that escapeth of them shall not be delivered". This brings us to:

b) The inescapability of judgment, vv.2-4.

The words, "though they", punctuate the section. There is no spiritual refuge (v.2), no natural refuge (v.3), and no political refuge (v.4). These verses remind us that there will be no refuge for men and women when God summons them to judgment: "And I saw the dead, small and great, stand before God...And the sea gave up the dead which were in it; and death (which receives the bodies of men) and hell (which receives the souls of men) delivered up the dead which were in them: and they were judged every man according to their works" (Rev. 20:12-13)

i) **There is no spiritual refuge**. "Though they dig into hell, thence shall mine hand take them; though they climb up to heaven, thence will I bring them down" (v.2). The graphic language serves to emphasise that there will be no refuge whatsoever for the guilty idolators. By way of contrast, similar language is used to describe the security of the believer: "Whither shall I go from thy Spirit? or whither shall I flee from thy presence? If I ascend up into heaven, thou art there: if I make my bed in hell, behold, thou art there. If I take the wings of the morning, and dwell in the uttermost parts of the sea; even there shall thy hand lead me, and thy right hand shall hold me" (Psalm 139:7-10).

ii) **There is no natural refuge**. "Though they hide themselves in the top of Carmel, I will search and take them out thence; and though they be hid from my sight in the bottom of the sea, thence will I command the serpent, and he shall bite them" (v.3). Neither Mount Carmel, one of the highest elevations in Israel, with its forests and caves, nor, by contrast, the seabed, would afford refuge to the fugitive from divine judgment. 'In the day of their calamity they find that there is no God but One, and that even were there a monstrous deity hidden in the deep it would turn out to be His servant!' (J. A. Motyer). Compare Amos 5:19.

iii) **There is no political refuge**. "Though they go into captivity before their enemies, thence will I command the sword, and it shall slay them: and I will set my eyes upon them for evil, and not for good" (v.4). Moses had predicted this centuries before: "Ye shall be plucked from off the land whither thou goest to possess it. And the LORD shall scatter thee among all people, from the one end of the earth even unto the other...And among those nations thou shalt find no ease, neither shall the sole of thy foot have rest: but the LORD shall give thee there a trembling heart, and failing of eyes, and sorrow of mind. And thy life shall hang in doubt before thee; and thou shalt fear day and night, and thou shalt have none assurance of thy life. In the morning thou shalt say, Would God it were even! And at even thou shalt say, Would God it were morning!" (Deut. 28:63-67).

c) The guarantor of judgment, vv.5-6
He is omnipotent and irresistible: "And the Lord GOD of hosts is he that toucheth the land, and it shall melt, and all that dwell therein shall mourn: and it shall rise up wholly as a flood; and shall be drowned as by the flood of Egypt. It is he that buildeth his stories in the heaven, and hath founded his troop on earth; he that calleth for the waters of the sea, and poureth them out upon the face of the earth: the LORD is his name". The very fact He is "the LORD" guarantees the certainty of coming judgment. He is in absolute control of creation, whether terrestrial or celestial. Whereas the previous reference to "the flood of Egypt" (8: 8) is evidently figurative in that it refers to overflowing judgment, here it is quite literal. The Lord is in command of all creation at any given time. The expression, "his stories ('upper chambers', JND) in the heaven", has been defined as "his celestial palace" (M. F. Unger), and the word "troop" ('vault', JND), meaning an 'arched, vaulted work' (Gesenius), evidently refers to what we call 'the vault of heaven'. Earth and heaven appear to be linked by the vast arch of sky above us.

d) The universality of judgment, vv.7-8
It is important to notice that the Lord is not terminating His covenant with Israel on account of their sinfulness. At first glance it might seem that Israel has lost its unique position and would, henceforth, be regarded simply as another nation without any further distinction. The message of these verses is that there is a very real sense in which Israel is not distinct from any other nation for the simple reason that *all* nations, including Israel, are accountable to God. At the same time, as Amos is about to demonstrate (vv.11-15), Israel is particularly and peculiarly, the people of God.

We must emphasise that the lesson here is that Israel is subject to the decrees and laws of God as much as any other nation. They were not exempted because of their redemption from Egypt. God had directed the affairs of other nations too: "Are ye not as the children of the Ethiopians unto me, O children of Israel? Saith the LORD. Have not I brought up Israel out of the land of Egypt? And the Philistines from Caphtor, and the Syrians from Kir? Behold, the eyes of the Lord GOD are upon the sinful kingdom (that is, upon any 'sinful kingdom'), and I will destroy it from off the face of the earth". Ethiopia is mentioned possibly because it was regarded as remote at the time, yet the Lord had watched over them. Caphtor is usually identified with Crete, although some scholars, including A. W. Streane, favour the coast of the Egyptian Delta. According to C. L. Feinberg, (Jeremiah 47:1-7) sees Philistia as the "remnant of the ancient Aegean civilization headed by Caphtor...Crete was probably the original home of the Philistines before their entrance to Palestine (Deut 2:23)". Kir is unidentified, but it is thought to have been somewhere in Assyria (2 Kings 16:9).

e) *The purpose of judgment, vv.8-9*
While any "sinful kingdom" will be destroyed "from off the face of the earth", and Israel would not be exempted from divine judgment, a remnant would be preserved: "I will *not* utterly destroy the house of Jacob, saith the LORD. For, lo, I will command, and will sift the house of Israel among all nations, like as corn is sifted in a sieve, *yet* shall not the least grain (literally 'pebble', but referring to the kernel) fall upon the earth" (vv.8-9). The word "sift", meaning to 'shake', reminds us that the sieve 'is an instrument of discrimination. It gathers out impurities and leaves intact that which passes the grade' (J. A. Motyer). The fearful judgment about to fall on the nation was designed to remove the chaff; while every "grain" would be preserved, "all the sinners of my people shall die by the sword, which say, the evil shall not overtake us nor prevent us" ('befall us', JND)" (v.10). This is in accordance with Jeremiah 30:11, "For I am with thee, saith the LORD, to save thee: though I make a full end of all nations whither I have scattered thee, yet will I not make a full end of thee: but I will correct thee in measure, and will not leave thee altogether unpunished". Zephaniah describes the result of divine judgment: "I will also leave in the midst of thee an afflicted and poor people, and they shall trust in the name of the LORD. The remnant of Israel shall not do iniquity, nor speak lies, neither shall a deceitful tongue be found in their mouth. Sing, O daughter of Zion; shout, O Israel; be glad and rejoice with all the heart, O daughter of Jerusalem. The LORD hath taken away thy judgments" (Zeph 3:12-15). See also Zechariah 12:9-14.

The object of coming judgment was not, therefore, to extinguish the nation, but to purge the nation in preparation for coming restoration. It should be said that while these verses can be applied to the nation in its entirety (that is, to Judah and Israel), they do have particular reference to Israel, the northern of the two kingdoms. Although the ten tribes were deported by Assyria (2 Kings 17:6), this does not mean that they have become 'lost tribes'. This is clear from Revelation 7 where, with two exceptions (Ephraim and Dan), all the tribes are mentioned. The Lord is thoroughly aware of the location of every one of His people. Every one of His "elect" (Matt. 24:31) will be preserved. Not even "the least grain" will "fall upon the earth". The Lord will "thoroughly purge his floor, and gather the wheat into the garner; but he will burn the chaff with unquenchable fire" (Matt. 3:12).

The expression, "the least grain", reminds us that every believer, however humble and insignificant is precious to God. These verses also remind us that the purpose of discipline is purification and restoration. The New Testament makes this clear in connection with assembly discipline: "For I verily, as absent in body, but present in spirit, have judged already, as though I were present, concerning him that hath so done this deed, in the name of our Lord Jesus Christ, when ye are gathered together, and my spirit, with the power of our Lord Jesus Christ, to deliver such an one unto Satan for the destruction of the flesh, that the spirit may be saved in the day of the Lord Jesus" (1 Cor. 5:3-5).

The 'sifting' of Israel reminds us of the Lord's words, "Simon, Simon, behold, Satan hath desired to have **you** (plural: have you all) that he might sift (you) as wheat". Matthew Henry puts it like this: 'He desired to have them, that he might sift them, that he might show them to be chaff, and not wheat'. The word "sift" comes from *sinion,* meaning 'a sieve'. But, as W. T. P. Woolston points out, 'they **were** wheat! If they had only been chaff, and not really 'wheat', Satan would not have wanted to sift them: it was because they were real that Satan desired to get them in his power'. Although the Lord knew that His disciples would be 'winnowed', He did nothing to stop it, because He knew that the process would remove the chaff. As C. I. Scofield observes: 'Peter was **wheat**, but his self-confidence was **chaff**.'

The preservation of a remnant in Israel ("the least grain") does not mean that there is no hope of future nationhood. The final section of the prophecy describes the glory of Israel after the refining process.

3) RESTORATION TO THE LAND, 9: 11-15
The passage emphasises five aspects of Israel's restoration. They are all guaranteed by the expressions "I will" (vv.11, 14, 15) and "saith the LORD" (vv.12, 13, 15). We should notice that everything is divinely-accomplished. "This is the Lord's doing; it is marvellous in our eyes" (Psalm 118:23).

Using Richard Catchpole's headings, we should notice: *(a)* glory (v.11); *(b)* victory (v.12); *(c)* productivity (v.13); *(d)* liberty (v.14); *(e)* security (v.15).

We must emphasise the literal fulfilment of the passage. It is an absolute nonsense to even attempt to make these promises apply to the church.

a) Glory, v.11
"In that day will I raise up the tabernacle of David that is fallen, and close up the breaches thereof; and I will raise up his ruins, and I will build it as in the days of old". The extended passage (vv.11-12) is quoted by James in the New Testament to emphasise that God always intended the Gentiles to enjoy divine blessing (Acts 15:15-18).

The glory of the kingdom in the days of David and Solomon will not only be restored, it will be exceeded by the glory of Christ's millennial kingdom. The ancient promise will be fulfilled: "Of the increase of his government and peace there shall be no end, upon the throne of David, and upon his kingdom, to order it, and to establish it with judgment and with justice from henceforth even for ever. The zeal of the LORD of hosts will perform this" (Is. 9:7). The New Testament confirms the Old Testament promise: "He shall be great, and shall be called the Son of the Highest; and the Lord God shall give unto him the throne of his father David: and he shall reign over the house of Jacob for ever; and of his kingdom there shall be no end" (Luke 1:32-33). With the division of the kingdom into two parts after the death of Solomon, the "tabernacle (or 'booth') of David" (referring to the dynasty of David) which acted as a shelter over Israel, had suffered major damage. David "reigned over *all* Israel", and the restoration of David's "tabernacle" will therefore involve a united kingdom.

We should be enjoying this 'millennial blessing' **now**. Are **we** subject to divine rule in our lives?

b) Victory, v.12
Restored Israel will exercise authority over all nations: they will "possess the remnant of Edom, and of all the heathen, which are called by my name ('upon who my name is called', JND), saith the LORD that doeth this". Bearing in mind the utter destruction of Edom (Obadiah v.16), the reference to the Edomites by Amos must relate to a small number of survivors. Edom had been the implacable enemy of God's people. Israel's world-wide authority is emphasised by Isaiah: "And it shall come to pass in the last days, that mountain of the Lord's house shall be exalted in the top of the mountains, and shall be exalted above the hills, and *all nations* shall flow into it" (Isaiah 2:2-3).

We should also be enjoying this 'millennial blessing' *now*. Are *we* in control of our implacable enemies, the world, the flesh and the devil?

c) Productivity, v.13

"Behold, the days come, saith the LORD, that the plowman shall overtake the reaper, and the treader of grapes him that soweth seed; and the mountains shall drop sweet wine (new wine), and all the hills shall melt". Compare Isaiah 35:1-2: "The wilderness and the solitary place shall be glad for them; and the desert shall blossom as the rose. It shall blossom abundantly, and rejoice even with joy and singing"; Psalm 72:16, "There shall be an handful of corn in the earth upon the top of the mountains; the fruit thereof shall shake like Lebanon: and they of the city shall flourish like grass of the earth", or 'There shall be abundance of corn (handfuls) in the earth, upon the top of the mountains; the fruit thereof shall shake like Lebanon: and they of the city shall bloom like the herb of the earth' (JND). Barrenness will be abolished. Even the most inhospitable places will be fruitful. A.G.Clarke puts it like this: 'The terraced cornfields stretch right to the hilltops, which are usually rocky and bare - a picture of extraordinary fertility'. This awaits "the manifestation of the sons of God" (Rom 8:19), and until this, "the whole creation groaneth and travaileth in pain together until now".

But then, "the plowman shall over take the reaper" (Amos 9:13). 'The land would become so productive that farmers planting seed for the next harvest would push reapers in the same fields to finish their work so that they could plant the next crop. Normally the Israelites plowed their fields in October and the reaping ended in May, but in the future reaping would still be going on in October because of the huge harvests...The mountains would be so full of fruitful grapevines that they could be described as dripping with sweet wine. All the hills would be dissolved in the sense of flowing down with produce. This verse pictures the reversal of the curse pronounced by God on the earth at the Fall (Gen. 3:17-19)' (supplied by Justin Waldron). See also Jeremiah 31:12. It will then be said, "This land that was desolate is become like the garden of Eden" (Ezek. 36:35).

We should also be enjoying this 'millennial blessing' *now*. Are *we* enjoying "the fruit of the Spirit...love, joy, peace, longsuffering, gentleness, goodness, faith, meekness, temperance" (Gal. 5:22-23)? Can the Lord say of *us*, "From me is thy fruit found" (Hos. 14:8)?

d) Liberty, v.14

"And I will bring again the captivity of my people Israel, and they shall build the waste cities, and inhabit them; and they shall plant vineyards, and drink the wine thereof; they shall also make gardens, and eat the fruit of them". No longer will it be said, "Ye have built houses of stone, **but** ye shall not dwell in them: ye have planted pleasant vineyards **but** ye shall not drink wine of them" (Amos 5:11). See also Ezekiel 36:11, "I will settle you after your old estates, and I will do better unto you than at your beginnings".

We should also be enjoying this 'millennial blessing' **now**. Are **we** enjoying our rich inheritance (Eph. 1:3-14) as people "delivered...from the power of darkness, and...translated into the kingdom of his dear Son" (Col. 1:13)?

e) Security, v.15

"And I will plant them upon their land, and they shall no more be pulled up out of their land which I have given them, saith the LORD thy God". The promise made to Abraham will be fulfilled: "And I will give unto thee, and to thy seed after thee, the land wherein thou art a stranger, all the land of Canaan, for an **everlasting possession**; and I will be their God" (Gen. 17:8). See also Isaiah 60:1, "Thou shalt inherit the land **for ever**, the branch of my planting, the work of my hands, that I may be glorified".

We should also be enjoying this 'millennial blessing' **now**. Are **we** enjoying our rich and "**eternal** inheritance" (Heb. 9:15). We will never be "pulled up" from our enjoyment of all that belongs to us, by divine grace, in Christ, and it will never be taken from us.

On this glad note, Amos concludes his preaching. A disobedient, rebellious and empty people, having been disciplined by God, are brought into blessing. How glad we are to say with David, "He restoreth my soul".

OBADIAH

by
John M Riddle

OBADIAH

INTRODUCTION

Read the whole book
We call Obadiah and his colleagues, 'The Minor Prophets', but this is neither accurate nor complimentary! On the contrary, they were 'Major Men of God!' Their books are only 'minor' in terms of size when compared with those of Isaiah, Jeremiah and Ezekiel. These comparatively small books have been beautifully described as 'the twelve-jewelled crown of the Old Testament.' Taken together, they have been called 'The Book of the Twelve.'

Jeremiah tells us that the true prophet "stood in the counsel of the Lord, and hath perceived and heard his word", 23:18. He also tells us, on eleven occasions, that God rose up early to speak to Israel through the prophets. See, for example, 7:25: "Since the day that your fathers came forth out of the land of Egypt unto this day I have even sent unto you all my servants the prophets, daily rising up and sending them." Obadiah was one of them, and it might be helpful to see his position in relation to the other 'writing prophets.' We must consider *(1)* The period; *(2)* The prophet; *(3)* The prophecy.

1) THE PERIOD
Obadiah evidently belonged to the beginning of the sixth century (i.e. 600-501BC). It would be interesting to commence at the exodus from Egypt, and construct a complete table of the prophets sent by God. It would begin with Moses (Deuteronomy 18:15; 34:10) and Aaron (Exodus 7:1), and include a great number of men (and some women), some named, and some unnamed. The 'writing prophets' alone cover five centuries, viz:

Fifth century (500-401) prophets: Haggai/ Zechariah/ Malachi.

Introduction

Sixth century (600-501) prophets   Jeremiah (part)/ Obadiah /Ezekiel/ Daniel.
Seventh century (700-601) prophets: Nahum/ Habakkuk/ Zephaniah/ Jeremiah
Eighth century (800-701) prophets: Hosea/ Amos/ Micah/ Isaiah.
Ninth century (900-801) prophets: Jonah, and possibly Joel.

Note: the above table is 'rough and ready' in the extreme, but *you* could easily do some 'fine-tuning' and produce a more accurate picture The ninth century (900-801BC) brings us to the era of Elijah and Elisha, which reminds us that there were a vast number of 'non-writing prophets.' You could incorporate these in a new table. For example, the tenth century introduces us to the unnamed prophet who cried against Jeroboam's altar, and the "old prophet in Bethel" (1 Kings 13:11).

This proves that God was not exaggerating when He said, "Since the day that your fathers came forth out of the land of Egypt unto this day, I have even sent unto you all my servants the prophets, *daily* rising up early, and sending them", Jeremiah 7:25. He was never silent. Whilst the oft-quoted words in Acts 14:17 do not refer to the prophets, we can *apply* them in that way, and say that God "left not himself without a witness" as far as the prophetic testimony was concerned. This should encourage us today: through His servants, and sometimes without them, there will be an ongoing testimony to "all the counsel of God" (Acts 20:27), and even when Jerusalem becomes the darkest moral blot on earth, He will give power to His "two witnesses......these two prophets" (Revelation 11:3-12).

E. J. Young (*'Introduction to the Old Testament'*) states that 'the position of the book in the Hebrew canon suggests an early date (ninth rather than sixth century), as does the absence of Aramaic expressions. Moreover, the nations mentioned (e.g. the Philistines) are pre-exilic, not post-exilic, foes.' This view is shared by others who suggest that the prophecy of Obadiah can be placed 'in the reign of Jehoram (circa 852-841BC) when Jerusalem was plundered by the Philistines and Arabians (2 Chronicles 21:16-19), since Edom is referred to by Obadiah as having more than one ally (vv.7 & 11).' (*Unger's Commentary on the Old Testament'*). However, we do notice that Edom is not specifically mentioned in 2 Chronicles 21.

It seems far more likely, however, that the prophecy can be dated with reference to 'the fall of Jerusalem to the Babylonians in 587-586BC, when Edom gleefully participated in the plunder of the city.' (M. C. Unger). While, we are told, 'cogent arguments can be adduced in favour of either view', we do know that the Edomites were present when Jerusalem was sacked by the Babylonians. See Psalm 137:7, "Remember, O Lord, the children of Edom in the day of Jerusalem; who said, Rase it, rase it, even to the foundation thereof." Jeremiah also associates the Edomites with the destruction of Jerusalem. See Lamentations 4:22, "The punishment of thine iniquity is accomplished, O daughter of Zion; he will no more carry thee away into captivity: he will visit thine iniquity, O daughter of Edom; he will discover thy sins." There does seem, therefore, good support for this suggestion. We should notice the correspondence between Obadiah and Jeremiah 49:7-22. See Appendix 1 (page 312).

2) THE PROPHET

Obadiah means 'servant or worshipper of the Lord.' While the name 'occurs about a dozen times in the Old Testament....none of these occurrences can be equated with the author of this prophecy.' (M. C. Unger). Nothing more is known of the prophet. This reminds us that servants of God should be recognised, not for **who** they are, but for **what** they are! See 1 Corinthians 3:5: "Who then is Paul? and who is Apollos? But ministers by whom ye believed, even as the Lord gave to every man." (Note RV here: 'What then is Apollos? And what is Paul? Ministers through whom ye believed; and each as the Lord gave to him').

3) THE PROPHECY

The subject-matter of the prophecy is clear from the outset: "The vision of Obadiah. Thus saith the Lord God concerning **Edom**", v1. 'Obadiah complements the prophecies of Nahum and Habakkuk. While Habakkuk fortells the end of Babylon, and Nahum seals the fate of Assyria, Obadiah sounds the death knell over Israel's long-standing enemy, Edom.' (J. M. Sinclair, writing in the *Believer's Magazine*).

The Edomites were, of course, the descendents of Esau. Esau means 'hairy', and although he was red at birth (Genesis 25:25), the name 'Edom', meaning 'red', occurs first with reference to the "red pottage." See Genesis 25:30. He got his name from his supper! The Edomites were the implacable enemies of Israel, and 'although Esau and Jacob had been partially reconciled, Esau's hatred had been transmitted to his posterity. We should

Introduction

beware of bequeathing bitterness to the next generation.' (J.Hay, *'Is Obadiah Relevant?'*, *Believer's Magazine* article).

After the death of his father Isaac, Esau and his family emigrated from Canaan and settled in Mount Seir. "Thus dwelt Esau in Mount Seir: Esau is Edom." Genesis 36:8. The area, was previously occupied by the Horites (Genesis 14:6), a tribe descended from Seir, and whose name means literally, 'rock dwellers.' The area itself extended southwards from the Dead Sea to the Gulf of Aquaba. It is a remarkably mountainous district with lofty peaks and deep glens, but also with very productive plains. Reference is made to this in the course of the prophecy. See v3, "Thou that dwellest in the cleft of the rock, whose habitation is high."

It was the mountainous terrain of this country that gave the Edomites the security in which they boasted. Identical references in two Psalms, confirm the strategic position of Petra, their capital city: "Who will bring me into the strong city? Who will lead me into Edom?" Psalm 60:9 and 108:10. The Hebrew word for 'rock', as in v3, is *'sela'*: its Greek equivalent is *'petra.'* In this connection, note 2 Kings 14:7; "He slew of Edom in the valley of salt ten thousand, and took **Selah** by war." Petra was rediscovered by the western world in 1812 through a young Swiss, John Lewis Burchhardt, disguised as a sheikh. He described it as 'a rose-red city, half as old as time.' See Appendix 2 (see page 313).

J. Sidlow Baxter *(Explore the Book)* calls Obadiah, 'The prophet of poetic justice.' He takes his title from vv15-16, "As thou hast done, it shall be done unto thee: thy reward shall return upon thine own head. For as ye have drunk upon my holy mountain, so shall all the heathen drink continually." It is customary to divide the book into two major sections. See, for example, J. Sidlow Baxter: *(i)* The destruction of Edom, vv1-16; *(ii)* The salvation of Israel, vv17-21. It does seem, however, that vv15-16, whilst referring to the past, introduce future events. Bearing this in mind, we suggest the following: *(1)* the Destruction of Edom, vv1-14: this deals with past events; *(2)* the Deliverance of Israel, vv15-21: This deals with future events.

Appendix 1

Obadiah

"The vision of Obadiah. Thus saith the Lord God concerning Edom; We have heard a rumour from the Lord, and an ambassador is sent among the heathen, Arise ye, and let us rise up against her in battle. Behold I have made thee small among the heathen. Thou art greatly despised. The pride of thine heart hath deceived thee,

Jeremiah

"I have heard a rumour from the Lord, and an ambassador is sent unto the heathen, saying, Gather ye together, and come against her, and rise up to the battle. For, lo, I will make thee small among the heathen, and despised among men. Thy terribleness hath deceived thee, and the the pride of thine heart, O thou that dwellest in the

Obadiah

thou that dwellest in the clefts of the rock, whose habitation is high; that saith in his heart, Who bring me down to the ground? Though thou exalt thyself as the eagle, and though thou set thy nest among the stars, thence will I bring thee down, saith the Lord." vv1-4.

Jeremiah

clefts of the rock, that holdest the height of the hill: though thou shouldest make thy nest as high as the eagle, I will bring thee down from thence, saith the Lord." 49:14-16.

"If thieves came to thee, if robbers by night, (how art thou cut off!) would they not have stolen till they had enough? If the grape-gatherers came to thee, would they not leave some grapes?" v5.

"If grapegatherers come to thee, would they not leave some gleaning grapes? If thieves by night, they will destroy till they have enough." 49:9.

Appendix 2

After the Babylonian conquest, Edom's capital, Petra, was occupied by the Nabathaeans, an Arabian tribe. It seems likely that the 'rose-red city, half as old as time', discovered by John Lewis Burchhardt, was their work, and therefore of a later date than Obadiah's time.

Petra, now in Jordan, is a great tourist attraction. A large part of the city, lying in a valley reached by a narrow ravine, was carved, not built, out of sandstone. Revolutionary building methods were employed in creating the facades to their buildings hewn out of the rock. They started at the top, so that the weight of unhewn stone always rested on the ground.

From being merchants and carriers, the Nabathaeans became middle-men, buying cheaply and selling expensively. Petra lay halfway on Arabia-Syrian and Arabia-Palestine trade routes. Their chief interest was money-making, and commerce was encouraged by a unique form of taxation. They rewarded a man who increased his income, and fined anyone who allowed it to drop! (Don't tell the Chancellor of the Exchequer!).

READ VERSES 1-14

"How art thou cut off"

In our introduction, we suggested that the book can be divided as follows: *(1)* the Destruction of Edom, v1-14: this deals with past events; *(2)* the Deliverance of Israel, v15-21: This deals with future events. The link between past and future events lies in v15-16, where judgment on Edom is a picture of judgment on "all the heathen."

1) THE DESTRUCTION OF EDOM, V1-14
This section of the prophecy can be divided as follows: *(A)* The pride of Edom, v1-4; *(B)* The destruction of Edom, v5-9; *(C)* The treachery of Edom, v10-14.

A) The pride of Edom, v1-4
The prophecy opens with preparations to invade Edom. Do notice reference to the vision from God, and to the word from God. The former could be misinterpreted without the latter. "The vision of Obadiah. Thus saith the Lord God concerning Edom. We have heard a rumour (JND, 'report': 'tidings') from the Lord, and an ambassador is sent among the heathen, Arise ye, and let us rise up against her in battle." The parallel verse (Jeremiah 49:14) occurs in a passage which describes the conquests of the "king of Babylon": see v28 & v30. The invader is described as an eagle (v22), and this points to the same power. See Habakkuk 1:8, Daniel 7:4. The king of Babylon was assembling his army. But the "Most High ruleth in the kingdom of men" (Daniel 4:17), and the Chaldean invasion was under His control. The Lord God *(Adonai Jehovah)* now speaks: "Behold, *I* have made thee small among the heathen: thou art greatly despised." The reason follows:

"The **pride** of thine heart hath deceived thee, thou that dwellest in the clefts of the rock, whose habitation is high; that saith in his heart, Who shall bring me down to the ground? Though thou **exalt thyself** as the eagle (compare Isaiah 40:31 where "they that wait upon the Lord.....shall mount up with wings as eagles"), and though thou set thy nest among the stars, ***thence will I bring thee down,*** saith the Lord." v3-4. See also v12. The prophecy therefore condemns pride. Spiritual pride is disastrous. The first of six things which the Lord hates is "a proud look", Prov. 6:16-19. Pride manifests itself in a variety of ways:

a) Pride in achievement. We have only to remember **Nebuchadnezzar:** "Is not this great Babylon that I have built for the house of ***my*** kingdom, by the might of ***my*** power and for the honour of ***my*** majesty?", Daniel 4:30. Or ***Uzziah:*** "when he was strong, his heart was lifted up to his destruction", 2 Chronicles 26:16.

b) Pride in ambition. We have only to remember divine judgment on ***"Lucifer,*** son of the morning", Isaiah 14:12-15. Compare 1 Timothy 3:6. Solomon reminds us that "a man's pride shall bring him low", Proverbs 29:23.

c) Pride in ability. See 1 Corinthians 4:7, "What hast thou that thou didst not receive? Now if thou didst receive it, why doest thou glory as if thou hadst not received it?" See also Romans 12:3, "For this I say, through the grace given unto me, to every man that is among you, not to think more highly of himself than he ought to think."

d) Pride in security. The Edomites were proud of their mountain fastness. Compare James 4:13-16, "But now ye rejoice in your boastings: all such rejoicing is evil." See also Revelation 3:17, "Because thou sayest, I am rich, and increased with goods, and have need of nothing...." We must not forget the danger of pride in service, pride of knowledge, and pride of orthodoxy. Perhaps even the proud boast by some assemblies: 'I am not as other assemblies are!'

We must also remember such injunctions as: "Let nothing be done through strife or vainglory; but in ***lowliness of mind*** let each esteem other better than themselves", Philippians 2:3. "Yea, all of you be subject one to another, and be clothed with ***humility:*** for God resisteth the proud, and giveth grace to the humble. Humble yourselves therefore under the mighty hand of God, that He may exalt you in due time", 1 Peter 5:5-6. "He hath shewed thee, O man, what is good; and what doth the Lord require of thee, but to do justly, and to love mercy, and to ***walk humbly*** with thy God", Micah 6:8.

B) The destruction of Edom, v5-9

i) Edom despoiled, v5-6. "If thieves came to thee, if robbers by night (how art thou cut off!) would they not have stolen till they have enough? If grapegatherers came to thee, would they not leave some grapes?", v5. Both robbers and reapers would have left something, but Edom would be completely cut off. There would be nothing left. 'How is Esau searched! His hidden things sought out!', JND.

ii) Edom deceived, v7. The judgment on Edom would be implemented by the nations with whom Edom was allied. See v7: "All the men of thy confederacy, have brought thee (JND, 'pushed thee') even to the border ('driven thee out – even to the border'); the men that were at peace with thee have **deceived** thee, and prevailed against thee; they that eat thy bread have laid a wound under thee." The people on whom Edom counted for support would turn against them, just as Edom had turned against Judah. But behind these nations lay the controlling power of God. Hence:

iii) Edom destroyed, v7-8. "There is none understanding in him. Shall *I* not in that day, saith the Lord, even **destroy** the wise men out of Edom, and understanding out of the mount of Esau?" Wise men and women are essential in national life, and they are essential in assembly life. We should pray for the provision and preservation of spiritual leaders and spiritual leadership.

iv) Edom dismayed, v9. "And thy mighty men, O Teman, shall be **dismayed**, to the end that every one of the mount of Esau may be cut off by slaughter." With the demise of the wise men and the mighty men, the entire nation ("every one of the mount of Esau") was vulnerable. J. M. Sinclair (*Believer's Magazine* article) describes the fulfilment of this prophecy: 'Historically, we may note that just five years after the fall of Jerusalem, the supposedly unassailable fortress of Edom was over-run by the very same Babylonian forces. In 312 BC, Antigonus, a general of Alexander the Great, crushed Edom and despoiled Petra. In 2 BC, the Maccabees almost wiped out the Edomites, and the small remnant perished in the AD 70 slaughter at the hand of the Romans.'

C) The treachery of Edom, v10-14

Edom was destroyed because of the way in which they treated their brother nation when Jerusalem was attacked by the Chaldeans. Their burning hatred and bitter animosity over the years, culminated in the atrocities committed

Chapter 1

at the destruction of Jerusalem. Israel was expressly forbidden to act towards Edom in this way: "Thou shalt not abhor an Edomite; for he is **thy brother:** thou shalt not abhor an Egyptian; because thou wast a stranger in his land." Deuteronomy 23:7. This confirms Deuteronomy 2:4-5: "Ye are to pass through the coast of **your brethren** the children of Esau....Meddle not with them; for I will not give you their land, no, not so much as a foot breadth, because I have given mount Seir unto Edom for a possession."

Edom's hatred had early beginnings. Whilst reference is made to Edom in Exodus 15:15, Deuteronomy 2:4-5 and 23:7, the first historical reference after Genesis 36, is in Numbers 20, where Moses requested permission from the king of Edom to pass through his territory: "And Moses sent messengers from Kadesh unto the king of Edom, Thus saith **thy brother** Israel....Let us pass, I pray thee, through thy country: we will not pass through the fields, or through the vineyards, neither will we drink of the water of the wells: we will go by the king's highway, we will not turn to the right hand nor to the left, until we have passed thy borders." v14-17. He received a curt reply: "And Edom said unto him, Thou shalt not pass by me lest I come out against thee with the sword." A second request was met by more than words: "And Edom came out against him with much people, and with a strong hand." v18-21. Note that the river at Petra is called the Wadi-Musa, the 'river of Moses.'

The same animosity persisted down the centuries until the smouldering fire burst into flame at the destruction of Jerusalem. During the intervening period, Israel gained the ascendancy over Edom. Saul "fought against all his enemies on every side", including Edom. See 1 Samuel 14:47. Their animosity therefore persisted until his reign. Significantly, it was Doeg the Edomite who slew Ahimelech and eighty-four other priests, and virtually annihilated the population of Nob. See 1 Samuel 21-22. David totally subjugated Edom (see 1 Kings 11:15-16, 2 Samuel 8:14, and 1 Chronicles 18:11-13). Jehoshaphat, Jehoram and Amaziah all defeated the Edomites (2 Chronicles 20, 21 & 22). But Jehoram failed to quell the Edomite rebellion, and Amaziah worshipped their gods!

"Thy violence against thy brother" is now described. Note that **a summary** is given in v11: "In the day that thou stoodest on the other side, in the day that the strangers carried away captive his forces, and foreigners entered into his gates, and cast lots upon Jerusalem, even thou wast one of them." The summary is expanded in v12-14, where we notice:

(i) Their passive hatred of Israel. "In the day that thou stoodest on the other side." This is enlarged in v12. *(ii) Their active hatred of Israel.* "In the day that the strangers carried away captive his forces, and foreigners entered into his gates, and cast lots upon Jerusalem, even thou wast as one of them." This is enlarged in v13-14.

i) Their passive hatred of Israel

"In the day that thou stoodest on the other side", v11A. They stood aloof from them. See RV margin. As J. Hay observes 'to ignore the need of a brother is to place a question mark over our profession (James 2:15-17, 1 John 3:17).' Their passive hatred is described in the following way:

a) "But **thou shouldst not** have looked on the day of thy brother in the day that he became a stranger", v12. Compare 2 Timothy 1:15, "All they which are in Asia be turned away from me", and 2 Timothy 4:10, "Demas hath forsaken me...." J. M. Sinclair writes: 'We can see that when possible we should be willing to help our brothers and sisters. In fact, refusing help is here termed by God as "thy violence against thy brother", v10.' See 1 John 3:17. Have we followed the priest and the Levite, by passing by "on the other side?" We can rest assured that God is still displeased if we allow things to injure our brethren, when we could have assisted them. Note Deuteronomy 22:1-4, "Thou shalt not see **thy brother's** ox or his sheep go astray." Compare Abraham: "And when Abram heard that **his brother** was taken captive, he armed his trained servants....and pursued them unto Dan", Genesis 14:14-16.

b) "Neither **shouldest thou** have rejoiced over the children of Judah in the day of their distress", v12. There is no lack of searching comment here. J. M. Sinclair: 'But it is not only the fact that help was refused, but also that Edom rejoiced in the calamity that overcame Israel. When our brother suffers, it is our responsibility to "weep with them that weep", Romans 12:15.' J. B. Hewitt, 'How much are we affected by the weakness and defeat of our brethren? Have you rejoiced in the calamities that have befallen others?' M. C. Unger; 'She was not merely withholding aid from a relative in distress, but thoroughly enjoying seeing that kinsman sink in ignominious defeat.' We must remember Proverbs 17:5, "He that is glad at calamities shall not be unpunished."

iii) "Neither **shouldest thou** have spoken proudly in the day of distress", v12. This was far from the spirit of Galatians 6:1, "Brethren, if a man be overtaken in a fault, ye which are spiritual restore such an one in the spirit of ***meekness***...."

ii) Their active hatred of Israel
"In the day that the strangers carried away captive his forces, and foreigners entered into his gates, and cast lots upon Jerusalem, even thou wast as one of them", v11B. Israel's brother nation actually sided with the enemy. Edom took the side of the world against God's people. Centuries later, Judas "stood....with them" (John 18: 5), and Peter "stood with them" (John 18:18). Their active hatred is described in the following way:

a) "Thou ***shouldest not*** have entered into the gate of my people in the day of their calamity", v13. That is, they added to their afflictions. See Philippians 1:14-16, "Some indeed preach Christ even of envy and strife.... supposing to add affliction to my bonds." These were Christians who were jealous of Paul, and endeavoured to undermine his influence.

b) "Thou ***shouldest not*** have looked on their affliction in the day of their calamity, nor have laid hands on their substance in the day of their calamity", v13. They made capital out of their afflictions. J. M. Sinclair: 'Having stood back and watched as Israel was taken into captivity, and then having rejoiced in his brother's downfall, Edom now further aggravates the position in that he now enters the city and ravages them. So we can learn that we should never take advantage of the misfortunes of our brethren.' J. Hay: 'To benefit by exploiting the underprivileged or disadvantaged, is to follow the steps of Jacob who took advantage of his father's blindness; Ziba who capitalised on Mephibosheth's disability, and the Pharisees who devoured widows' houses. Such behaviour is shameless. A brother in difficulties must be treated well.'

c) "Neither ***shouldest thou*** have stood in the crossway, to cut off those of his that did escape, v14. The Edomites resisted and impeded those that were escaping. They were intent on the complete destruction of God's people. J. B. Hewitt: 'How many saints have we cut off by scandal?' Some people welcome every opportunity to destroy the character and reputation of others. Compare 2 Timothy 2:24-26: "And the servant of the Lord must not strive; but be gentle unto all men, apt to teach, patient, in meekness instructing those that oppose themselves; if God peradventure will given them repentance to the acknowledging of the truth; And that they may recover themselves out of the snare of the devil, who are taken captive by him at his will."

d) "Neither ***shouldest thou*** delivered up those of his that did remain in the day of his distress." J. M. Sinclair: ' The final and most significant of the specified sins of Edom, was the resisting of Israel's escape, and the deliverance of the refugees into the hand of the invader.' We can do exactly the same by maligning God's people before the world. See 1 Corinthians 6:6-8, "Brother goeth to law with brother, and that before unbelievers."

This leads us to another event of rather startling interest. The Greek form of "Edom" is 'Idumea.' It is in actual fact translated 'Idumea' four times in the Old Testament in our Authorised Version (Isaiah 34:5-6, Ezekiel 35:15, 36:5), although, strictly speaking, it should appear as 'Edom.' In the New Testament, it occurs once - in Mark 3: 8. It is therefore significant that Herod, before whom the Lord Jesus appeared, after His appearance before Pilate, was of Edomite blood. And so was his forebear who endeavoured to kill the infant Christ at Bethlehem. Now compare Edom in Obadiah with Herod in Luke 23:

Edom	***Herod***
"Rejoiced over the children of Judah" and "spoke proudly in the day of distress", v12.	"And when Herod saw Jesus, he was ***exceeding glad***" and "with his men of war set him at nought, and mocked him" Luke 23:8,11.
"Entered into the gate of My people in the day of their calamity" and "looked on their affliction in the day of their calamity", v13	It is significantly stated of Herod the Edomite in the day of Christ's affliction: "himself also was ***at Jerusalem*** at that time", Luke 23:7.
"Delivered up those of his that did remain in the day of his distress", v14	***"Sent him*** again to Pilate", Luke 23:11

Obadiah informs us that the Edomites made themselves one with the Gentile oppressors of God's people, v11. Herod and Pilate, the Edomite and the Roman, were made friends together in their treatment of Christ. See Luke 23:12.

Addendum

During the course of discussion, Justin Waldron pointed out the elements of a Gospel message in these verses.

i) "An ambassador is sent", v1. See 2 Corinthians 5:20, "Now then we are ambassadors for Christ."

ii) "A rumour (a 'report', or 'tidings')", v1. We have tidings for men and women. According to Gesenius, the word can mean either good or bad tidings. See 2 Corinthians 2:16.

iii) "The pride of thine heart hath deceived thee", v3." Men and women are proud. Too proud to accept the Gospel. But "he hath scattered the proud in the imagination of their hearts", Luke 1:51.

iv) "If thieves came to thee, if robbers by night.....", v5. Edom would lose everything they treasured. Just like the rich man in Luke 12:16-21.

v) "The men that were at peace with thee have deceived thee", v7. See Titus 3:3, "We ourselves also were sometimes foolish, disobedient, deceived...."

vi) "Shall I not.....destroy the wise men out of Edom", v9. See 1 Corinthians 1:19-25, "I will destroy the wisdom of the wise......"

vii) "Thou shalt be cut off for ever", v10. This speaks for itself. See Proverbs 29:1 etc.

READ VERSES 15-21

"The kingdom shall be the Lord's"

As we have noticed, this short prophecy can be divided as follows: *(1)* The Destruction of Edom, v1-14: this deals with past events; *(2)* The Deliverance of Israel, v15-21: this deals with future events. The link between past and future events lies in v15-16, where judgment on Edom is a picture of judgment on "all the heathen."

1) THE DESTRUCTION OF EDOM, v1-14
In our previous study, we noticed: *(A)* The pride of Edom, v1-4; *(B)* The destruction of Edom, v5-9; *(C)* The treachery of Edom, v10-14. This brings us to:

2) THE DELIVERANCE OF ISRAEL, v15-21
This section can be divided as follows: *(A)* Retribution on the enemies of God, v15-16. *(B)* Restoration of the people of God, v17-21.

A) Retribution on the enemies of God, v15-16
These verses link the past with the future. They clearly predict judgment that has already taken place on Edom, and they also refer to judgment that still lies ahead for the enemies of God's people, including people belonging to the same region. The expression, "the day of the Lord", points to the future. See 1 Thessalonians 5:1-3, 2 Peter 3:10 etc. The reference to future events is confirmed by v17-21. While the events described in these verses have not yet taken place, their connection with the previous verses is clear: "For as ye (Edom) have drunk upon my holy mountain, so shall all the heathen drink continually, yea, they shall drink, and they shall swallow down, and they shall be as though they had not been. *But* on mount Zion shall be deliverance....." There was no deliverance for Israel when Jerusalem was sacked, and the Edomites cried "Rase it, rase it, even to the foundation thereof", Psalm 137:7. But there will be deliverance in the future when the nations of the world converge on Jerusalem. See Zechariah 14:1-3. God

will judge the nations of the world in the same way that he destroyed the Edomites for their hatred of God's people (v5-9). What happened to Edom in the past foreshadows future events. See Isaiah 34, and 63:1-6.

It is worth pointing out that on several occasions, the Old Testament links past and future events without reference to the intervening period. See, for example, Isaiah 61:1-2: "The Spirit of the Lord is upon me; because the Lord hath anointed me to preach good tidings unto the meek.....to proclaim the acceptable year of the Lord, and the day of vengeance of our God." When the Lord Jesus read this passage in Nazareth (Luke 4:16-20), he stopped at "the acceptable year of the Lord", closed the book, and said, "This day is this scripture fulfilled in your ears." The "day of vengeance of our God" has not yet commenced. At the moment, the book remains closed. It is still "the acceptable year of the Lord" or, to use other language, "the day of salvation", 2 Corinthians 6:2. But the "day of vengeance of our God" will come. It will commence when the Lord Jesus opens the book at the very place he closed it two thousand years ago. See Revelation 6:1. It is also worth pointing out that Obadiah emphasises, with all the prophets, that although Israel has been faced with extinction on numerous occasions, God has promised them a glorious national future.

There are at least three important points to notice in these verses *(i)* the period involved; *(ii)* the people involved; *(iii)* the principle involved.

i) The period involved
"For the **day of the Lord** is near upon all the heathen." It is important to distinguish between the various "days" mentioned in the New Testament. There are four. *(a) 'Man's day.'* See 1 Corinthians 4:3, where "man's judgment" (AV) is better translated 'man's day.' We live, at the moment, in 'man's day.' *(b) "The day of Jesus Christ",* elsewhere called "the day of Christ" (Philippians 1:10, 2:16), "the day of our Lord Jesus Christ" (1 Corinthians 1: 8), "the day of the Lord Jesus" (1 Corinthians 5:5, 2 Corinthians 1:14), and "that day" (2 Timothy 4:8). These passages all refer to the Lord's coming, and to His review and reward of our work for Him. This will take place in heaven. *(c) "The day of the Lord."* Unlike "the day of Christ", this refers to events on earth, and includes divine judgment on wicked men, together with the millennial reign of the Lord Jesus. See 1 Thessalonians 5:2, and 2 Thessalonians 2:2, where it is very important to notice the RV/JND translation: 'that ye be not soon shaken in mind.....as that the day of the Lord is present. The Old Testament prophecies abound with references

to "the day of the Lord." *(d) "The day of God."* This expression occurs in 2 Peter 3:12, and refers to the eternal state.

It has been nicely said that the purpose of the "day of the Lord" is to arrive at 'a sunny morning.' Zephaniah describes it as "a day of wrath, a day of trouble and distress, a day of wasteness and desolation, a day of darkness and gloominess, a day of clouds and thick darkness" (1:15), but it prepares the way for the glories of the millennial kingdom, when "the earth shall be filled with the knowledge of the glory of the Lord, as the waters cover the sea", Habakkuk 2:14. While the expression usually occurs in connection with the future, there are occasions when it is used in connection with past events, particularly when those events foreshadow the future. Zephaniah 1:14-18 is a case in point.

(ii) The people involved
"For the day of the Lord is near upon **all the heathen.**" The reason for God's wrath upon the heathen follows: "As thou hast done, it shall be done unto thee: thy reward shall return upon thine own head, For as ye have drunk upon my holy mountain, so shall all the heathen drink continually, yea, they shall drink, and they shall swallow down, and they shall be as though they had not been." The scope of the prophecy now widens. What would happen to Edom, would happen to the nations. Edom had "drunk upon my holy mountain." They had "rejoiced over the children of Judah in the day of their destruction", v12. The words, "as ye have drunk upon my holy mountain", do not refer to the wrath of God upon them, but to the way in which they celebrated the downfall of God's people. This would be perpetuated by "all the heathen" in succeeding centuries. Time and time again, Jerusalem has been conquered by Gentile powers. The greatest of all invasions will take place at the end-time. See Zechariah 14:2, Revelation 16:13-14. The Lord Jesus taught that "Jerusalem shall be trodden down of the Gentiles, until the times of the Gentiles be fulfilled", Luke 21:24. But just as God recompensed the Edomites for their hatred of God's people ("thy reward shall return upon thine own head"), so He will recompense "all the heathen" in the same way ("and they shall be as though they had not been").

We must remember that "He that keepeth Israel shall neither slumber nor sleep", Psalm 121:4. God says of Israel, "He that toucheth you, toucheth the apple of his eye", Zechariah 2:8. The nation that deals treacherously and cruelly with God's people will reap terrible consequences. The judgment of the living nations underlines the point. Read Matthew 25:31-46.

iii) The principle involved
"For the day of the Lord is near upon all the heathen; **as thou hast done, it shall be done unto thee: thy reward shall return upon thine own head.** " The principle of Galatians 6:7 is clear, "Be not deceived, God is not mocked, for whatsoever a man soweth, that shall he also reap." See James 2:13, "He shall have judgment without mercy, that hath shewed no mercy."

J. Sidlow Baxter *(Explore the Book)* puts it like this under the heading 'Poetic Justice!' 'See how this key truth is amplified by the context. Edom had indulged in treachery against Judah (v11-12); therefore Edom should perish through the treachery of the confederates (v7). Edom had seized the chance to rob Judah (v13); therefore Edom should be robbed till his hidden things, or treasures, were searched out (v5-6). Edom had lifted the sword and shown violence against Judah (v10); therefore Edom should perish by slaughter (v9). Edom had sought the utter destruction of Judah (v12-14); therefore Edom should be utterly destroyed (v10, 18). Edom had even sought to hand over and dispossess the remnant of the invaded Jerusalem (v14); therefore, in the end, the remnant of Jacob should possess the land of Edom (v19)). Yes, poetic justice!'

B) Restoration of the people of God, v17-21
Very clearly, the atmosphere of the prophecy now changes. It is no longer Edom in relation to the humiliation of Judah and Jerusalem (v11-12), but Edom in relation to the glory of God's people. The Edomites had drunk on God's "holy mountain" (v16). But the very place which had witnessed the defeat and captivity of God's people would witness their deliverance (v17), and become the centre of divine administration (v21). The emphasis on "mount Zion" reminds us of the covenant with David. See 2 Samuel 7. The early references connect Zion with him. (Omit Deuteronomy 4:48, which refers to a different mountain). See 2 Samuel 5:7, "David took the stronghold of Zion" (there is a parallel passage in 1 Chronicles 11:5); 1 Kings 8:1, "The city of David, which is Zion" (see also 2 Chronicles 5:2). The Lord Jesus will fulfil the covenant with David: "Yet have I set my king upon my holy hill of Zion", Psalm 2:6. God's covenant with David involves the place (Psalm 2:6), the throne (Isaiah 9:7, Luke 1:32) and the nation (Luke 1:33). God will "place salvation in Zion for Israel my glory", Isaiah 46:13.

There are at least four principal things to notice in this section. *(A)* Israel's purity, v17; *(B)* Israel's power, v18; *(C)* Israel's possessions, v19-20; *(D)* Israel's Potentate, v21.

A) Israel's purity, v17

"But upon mount Zion shall be deliverance, and there shall be holiness; and the house of Jacob shall possess their possessions." God's people will enjoy liberty, purity, and recovery.

i) Liberty. "But upon mount Zion shall be ***deliverance***." (JND margin has, literally, 'escape' or 'escaped ones'). The deliverance in question will take place when it seems that Israel has reached its last hour. See Zechariah 14:1-5. Compare Joel 2:32, "And it shall come to pass, that whosoever shall call on the name of the Lord shall be delivered: for in mount Zion and in Jerusalem shall be deliverance, as the Lord hath said, and in the remnant whom the Lord shall call." This verse should be read in conjunction with Joel 3:1-2, which make it clear that Joel is describing the same events as Zechariah.

Like Paul, we can say, "And the Lord shall deliver me from every evil work, and will preserve me unto his heavenly kingdom", 2 Timothy 4:18.

ii) Purity. "And there shall be ***holiness***." The Edomites had indulged in drunken revelry on God's "holy mountain" (v16), and at the end-time, the Gentiles will possess Jerusalem: "The holy city shall they tread under foot forty and two months", Revelation 11:2. Jerusalem is called "the holy city" in Matthew 27:53. The expressions, "holy mountain" and "holy city", describe God's intentions for the city, but in the meantime it has actually become the very reverse. See Revelation 11:8, "The great city, which spiritually is called Sodom and Egypt, where also our Lord was crucified." But God will purge "the blood of Jerusalem from the midst thereof by the spirit of judgment, and by the spirit of burning", with the result that "he that is left in Zion, and he that remaineth in Jerusalem, shall be called holy, even every one that is written among the living in Jerusalem", (Isaiah 4:3-4). Compare Zechariah 14:20-21, "And in that day there shall be upon the bells of the horses, HOLINESS UNTO THE LORD; and the pots in the Lord's house shall be like the bowls before the altar. Yea, every pot in Jerusalem shall be holiness unto the Lord of hosts." No Edomite, or any enemy, will celebrate there: it will then be God's "holy hill of Zion."

We must not forget the command, "But as he which hath called you is holy, so be ye holy in all manner of conversation; because it is written, Be ye holy; for I am holy", 1 Peter 1:15-16.

iii) Recovery. "And the house of Jacob shall possess their possessions." Genesis 15:18 will be fulfilled: "Unto thy seed have I given this land, from the river of Egypt unto the great river, the river Euphrates." This evidently refers to the northern reaches of the Euphrates, and so to territory occupied now by Syria, rather than to the lower reaches of the river and to territory occupied by Iraq. This is expanded in v19-20.

Are we 'possessing our possessions?' God has blessed us with all spiritual blessings in heavenly places in Christ" (Ephesians 1:3), and the chapter continues by describing those blessings: "chosen in him", "predestinated..... unto the adoption of children", "accepted in the beloved", "in whom we have redemption through his blood." What possessions! We are rich beyond imagination! But how much are we enjoying them?

B) Israel's power, v18
Edom will not then deliver up "those of his that did remain in the day of his distress." On the contrary, "the house of Jacob shall be a fire, and the house of Joseph a flame, and the house of Edom stubble, and they shall kindle in them, and devour them; and there shall not be any remaining of the house of Esau; for the Lord hath spoken it." Compare Malachi 4:1: "For, behold, the day cometh, that shall burn as an oven; and all the proud, yea, and all that do wickedly, shall be stubble: and the day that cometh shall burn them up, saith the Lord of hosts, that it shall leave them neither root (no possibility of regrowth) nor branch (no trace of past growth)." This raises two interesting subjects:

i)   The names given to God's people. "The house of **Jacob** shall be a fire, and the house of **Joseph** a flame." God's people are described as "the house of Jacob", as opposed to 'the house of Israel', to emphasise God's grace. It has been beautifully said that the name 'Jacob' emphasises the depths to which the grace of God will go to reach a man, and the name 'Israel' emphasises the height to which the grace of God will lift that same man! (J. G. Bellett). When Israel's Messiah returns ("they shall look on me whom they have pierced), the Lord will "pour upon the house of David, and upon the inhabitants of Jerusalem, the spirit of grace and of supplications", Zechariah 12:10. Compare Malachi 3:6, "For I am the Lord, I change not: therefore ye sons of Jacob are not consumed." The reference to "the house of Joseph", referring to his two sons born in Egypt, Ephraim and Manasseh, emphasises the complete unity of the nation. 'Joseph' stands for the northern tribes. See Ezekiel 37:15-19 etc. The division between Israel in the north and Judah in the south will no longer exist. The name 'Joseph' also reminds us of God's love for His people. See Genesis 37:3

ii) The name given to the enemy. It is still "the house of Esau" and the "mount of Esau!" History records the destruction of Edom in accordance with v1-9, but the latter part of the prophecy evidently points to a revival of the Edomite power. Notice Malachi 1:2-5 in this connection. At present, the "mount of Esau" lies in the southern part of Jordan, and this cannot be without significance.

Other prophecies anticipate the utter destruction of Edom at the end-time. Psalm 83 describes a giant confederacy of nations amongst which Edom is mentioned. Isaiah 34:5-6, which describe the final battle between God and Gentile nations, refers to Idumea (Greek for Edom) as one area of conflict. Isaiah 63 describes the divine conquest of Edom: "Who is this that cometh from Edom, with dyed garments from Bozrah? this that is glorious in his apparel, travelling in the greatness of his strength? I that speak in righteousness, mighty to save. Wherefore art thou red in thine apparel, and thy garments like him that treadeth in the winefat? I have trodden the winepress alone; and of the people there was none with me: for I will tread them in mine anger, and trample them in my fury; and their blood shall be sprinkled upon my garments, and I will stain all my raiment, For the day of vengeance is in mine heart, and the year of my redeemed is come", v1-4. Possibly, this will be the area to which the besieging armies will flee at the return to the mount of Olives of "the King of kings and Lord of lords."

When the millennial kingdom is established, Judah and Ephraim (the complete nation) will "lay their hand upon Edom and Moab, and the children of Ammon shall obey them", Isaiah 11:14. The three nations mentioned in this passage, viz Edom, Moab and Ammon, are also mentioned together in Daniel 11:41 as escaping the onslaught of the "king of the north": "but these shall escape out of his hand, even Edom, and Moab, and the chief of the children of Ammon". The conquest of these nations is evidently reserved for Israel itself, against whom they had been so unremitting in their opposition and hatred.

C) Israel's Possessions, v19-20

Once their enemies "carried away captive his forces, and foreigners entered into his gates, and cast lots upon Jerusalem" (v11), but now "the house of Jacob shall possess their possessions", v17. This is now amplified. The expression, "shall possess", occurs five times in these two verses. In some cases, it is more than repossession: they will possess what they never possessed before! God's people strike out in all four directions:

i) ***To the south.*** "And they of the south shall possess the mount of Esau." "The south" is the Negeb, the southern part of Judah. So Israel will possess what they were denied in Numbers 20:14-21. The prophecy of Balaam will be fulfilled: "I shall see him, but not now: I shall behold him, but not nigh: there shall come a Star out of Jacob, and a Sceptre shall rise out of Israel, and shall smite the corners of Moab, and destroy all the children of Sheth. And Edom shall be a possession, Seir also shall be a possession for his enemies; and Israel shall do valiantly", Numbers 24:17-18. See also Amos 9:11-12: "In that day will I raise up the tabernacle of David that is fallen, and close up the breaches thereof; and I will raise up his ruins, and I will build it as in the days of old: that they may possess the remnant of Edom, and of all the heathen, which are called by my name, saith the Lord that doeth this." There is a further reference to the south at the end of v20.

ii) ***To the west.*** "And they of the plain the Philistines." The "plain" refers to the 'Shephelah', the foothills sloping down from the central highland ridge to the maritime plain. The Philistine territory includes the 'Gaza strip!' The "fields of Ephraim, and the fields of Samaria" lie in the northern part of the land, and are at present Palestinian territory. There will be no question about ownership and occupation of the West Bank then!

iii) ***To the east.*** "And Benjamin shall possess Gilead." As M. C. Unger observes, 'even the tiny tribe of Benjamin will expand across the Jordan River and repossess Gilead.' The territory in question is at present part of Jordan! Compare Zechariah 10:10.

iv) ***To the north.*** "And the captivity of this host of the children of Israel shall possess that of the Canaanites, even unto Zarephath." Zarephath (or Sarepta, Luke 4:26), the present day Sarafand, lies on the Mediterranean coast between Tyre and Sidon in what is now Lebanon! See Zechariah 10:10 again. The Middle East question will be completely solved then! M. C. Unger explains "the captivity" as 'the exiles, the repatriated Israelites of the Kingdom age.'

Other exiles, from Jerusalem, will be repatriated from Sepharad (unidentified, although some suggest that it refers to a place in Media, to the north of Israel), and "possess the cities of the south." Once again, the Negeb, southern Judah. Note that the 'Sephardi' Jews come from the Mediterranean area: Southern Europe, North Africa etc.

D) Israel's Potentate, v21
In that day, all will recognise that "the kingdom shall be the Lord's." Mount Zion will be the centre of deliverance and rule.

"And saviours shall come up on mount Zion to judge the mount of Esau." At the sack of Jerusalem, men came from Edom to wreak vengeance on mount Zion! But in the future, Edom will be administered from Jerusalem! In fact, Jerusalem will be the administrative centre of the world: "For out of Zion shall go forth the law, and the word of the Lord from Jerusalem", Isaiah 2:1-5. At this time, Jerusalem will be "the city of the great King." See Psalm 48: "Great is the Lord, and greatly to be praised in the city of our God, in the mountain of his holiness. Beautiful for situation, the joy of the whole earth, is mount Zion, on the sides of the north, the city of the great King", v1-2. The Lord Jesus quoted this passage in Matthew 5:35.

Then, "all the ends of the world shall remember and turn to the Lord; and all kindreds of the nations shall worship before thee. For the kingdom is the Lord's; and he is the governor among the nations", Psalm 22:27-28. "The just Lord" will be "in the midst thereof", Zephaniah 3:5. "The name of the city from that day shall be, The Lord is there (Jehovah Shammah), Ezekiel 48:35. The Lord Jesus will "sit upon the throne of David, and upon his kingdom, to order it, and to establish it with judgement and with justice from henceforth even for ever", Isaiah 9:7. "The kingdom shall be the Lord's!" It will "never be destroyed: and the kingdom shall not be left to other people", Daniel 2:44.

"Let the whole earth be filled with his glory. Amen and Amen", Psalm 72:19.

Companion volumes in the same series
by John M Riddle:

Joshua, Judges, Ruth
ISBN 9781910513439

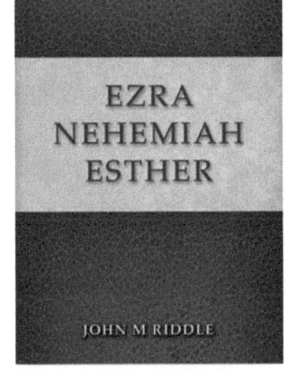

Ezra, Neh., Esther
ISBN 9781910513095

1 Samuel
ISBN 9781907731716

2 Samuel
ISBN 9781907731921

Luke
ISBN 9781909803541

Acts
ISBN 9781907731457

Phil., Col., 1&2 Thess.
ISBN 9781910513224

1&2 Tim., Titus, Philemon
ISBN 9781910513224

Available from:
www.ritchiechristianmedia.co.uk